Populating No Man's Land

Revisiting Communism: Collectivist Economic and Political Thought in Historical Perspective

Series Editor: János Mátyás Kovács

The series will cover the evolution of economic ideas under communism in Eastern Europe (including the Soviet Union) and China. These ideas will be presented in the context of the global history of collectivist economic thought. The core of the series will include a number of country monographs, comparative analyses and a multiple-volume anthology of studies that have not been published in English yet.

Populating No Man's Land

Economic Concepts of Ownership under Communism

Edited by
János Mátyás Kovács

LEXINGTON BOOKS
Lanham • Boulder • New York • London

Published by Lexington Books
An imprint of The Rowman & Littlefield Publishing Group, Inc.
4501 Forbes Boulevard, Suite 200, Lanham, Maryland 20706
www.rowman.com

Unit A, Whitacre Mews, 26-34 Stannary Street, London SE11 4AB

British Library Cataloguing in Publication Information Available

Library of Congress Cataloging-in-Publication Data

Names: Kovács, János Mátyás, editor.
Title: Populating no man's land : economic concepts of ownership under communism / edited by János Mátyás Kovács.
Description: Lanham : Lexington Books, [2018] | Series: Revisiting communism: collectivist economic and political thought in historical perspective | Includes bibliographical references and index.
Identifiers: LCCN 2018024744 (print) | LCCN 2018029179 (ebook) | ISBN 9781498586344 (Electronic) | ISBN 9781498539210 (cloth : alk. paper)
Subjects: LCSH: Property and socialism. | Communism.
Classification: LCC HX550.P7 (ebook) | LCC HX550.P7 P68 2018 (print) | DDC 335.43—dc23
LC record available at https://lccn.loc.gov/2018024744

Contents

Acknowledgments

We wish to express our gratitude to the Institute for Human Sciences, Vienna, for hosting the *Between Bukharin and Balcerowicz* program. The members of the program's scientific Advisory Board were also extremely helpful. Thanks are due especially to Christina Poessel and Christian Rogler for organizing the research activities and Ninja Bumann for working on the manuscript of the volume. Last but not least, we are very grateful to Isabella Weber for the valuable advice given to the author of the Chinese chapter and Thomas Richardson Bass for editing the volume in English.

Introduction

Why Communism? Why Ownership?

János Mátyás Kovács

The history books of modern economic thought are disturbingly incomplete. They are missing a potentially vast chapter covering the evolution of collectivist economic ideas. Western types of collectivist thought such as Ricardian socialism, the concept of capitalist war economy, theories of corporatism, or some statist doctrines of *Soziale Marktwirtschaft* have not prompted intellectual historians to suggest much in the way of refined schemes of classification (Marxism being an exception). The largest gap within this unwritten chapter has emerged due to a widespread neglect of the varieties of collectivism under communism.

With the unfolding of the recent global financial crisis, collectivist/interventionist ideas reemerged across the world—ranging from concepts of a sharing economy, basic income, community financing, workers' cooperatives, and special taxes on the rich, through doctrines of the *developmental* and *entrepreneurial* state, to the claim of nationalizing utilities or Occupying Wall Street. Meanwhile, even the heterodox schools of economics in the West remained dominated by the *end of history* mood of 1989. It seems as if the revolutions in Eastern Europe resulted in the final victory lap of private ownership and the market, and thus the century-long debate on the rationality of "economic calculation in a socialist *Gemeinwesen*" (Ludwig von Mises) could be terminated. Undoubtedly, with the help of new institutional, evolutionary, and behavioral schools among others, neoclassical economics has developed a more balanced and nuanced view of ownership and the market process during the past few decades than what was suggested by classical Austrian thinkers. Nevertheless, the end of communism[1] in Eastern Europe has not ceased to serve as a trump proving the superiority of capitalism. During the past decades, even the communist party-state in China has allowed private property to control a large segment of the economy and nurture markets, suggesting to many that this kind of ownership is indispensable (therefore, invincible). Accordingly, it cannot be a relevant research problem in economic theory for the foreseeable future.

At the same time, state interventionism, even *dirigisme*, is on the rise in Eastern Europe, while Chinese governments have not yielded as much of their power as their counterparts did in the former Soviet Bloc in the early 1990s. In a number of ex-communist countries from Hungary to Russia, that is, in alleged strongholds of neoliberalism, a huge part of property is still in the hands of members of the ex-communist *nomenklatura* while other forms of private ownership that emerged after 1989/91 are losing ground once again. Large banks, utility companies, and pension funds are being renationalized, private firms are being subjected to discretionary regulation by the government, and new state-owned firms are being established. Foreign investors suffer discrimination, price controls have been reintroduced, and income redistribution by the state is increasing. Where business and politics seemed separate, and where this separation seemed to be safeguarded by the rule of law, they became intertwined again in informal ways. Both state capture and its opposite, when government conquers business life and accumulates assets, are fundamental features of this old-new political economy. In some countries society is ruled by a quasi-monoparty. Cronyism, kleptocracy, feudal privileges, and the like are all clear signs of both surviving and emerging regimes of organized corruption, reminding observers of the *South* rather than the *West*.

In the West, private property rights are currently being challenged from below by leading experts, rising social movements, and nascent parties on the *new new-left* like Syriza in Greece and Podemos in Spain, with the aim of renewing capitalism and democracy on the basis of *horizontal* (civic, grassroots) collectivism. This challenge is growing and has ceased to be the privilege of the Greens. It also has found its way into the programs of other established parties like the Labour Party in the United Kingdom or the Democratic Party in the United States. Here, some of the collectivist projects (like the nationalization of railways) are meant to be implemented under civic control and the rule of law. *New collectivism* has a different philosophy and mode of operation on the other side of the former Iron Curtain. A number of top leaders of authoritarian/populist conviction have worked hard, almost since the collapse of the *ancien régime*, to retain or revive state ownership (combined with private gains for the mighty) and to craft a mixed economy burdened with a bloated public sector and operating under strong government control on behalf of an illiberal state. Collectivism is exercised from above *vertically* along hierarchical/bureaucratic lines—a temptation for the extreme right as well.[2] The apologists of these new statist regimes find it convenient that, due to a deep lacuna in economic history-writing, their opponents cannot just reach for a number of books on the shelf, which would evidence the dangerous disadvantages of similar attempts at hybridization in the reform-communist past.

FILLING THE SHELF

An important reason for launching the series *Revisiting Communism: Collectivist Economic Thought in Historical Perspective* was exactly to produce such books. Illiberal regimes of today think similarly to their predecessors when approaching an imaginary middle from the opposite side. Communist reformers[3] softened state ownership whereas the current rulers have decided to sap the strength of private ownership. Both presume that such a middle-of-the-road position is not only feasible but also optimal.

Our research group starts the series with this comparative volume on ownership, perhaps the most important issue of political economy[4] under and after communism.

> The productive forces of our country, especially in industry, were social in character, the form of ownership, on the other hand, was private, capitalistic. Relying on the economic law that the relations of production *must necessarily conform* with the character of the productive forces, the Soviet government socialized the means of production, made them the property of the whole people, and thereby abolished the exploiting system and created socialist forms of economy. Had it not been for this law, and had the Soviet government not relied upon it, it could not have accomplished its mission. (Joseph Stalin 1951)

> Privatization of the state-owned economy is not yet on the agenda. We cannot do it immediately; my colleagues would not agree to it. But we must put all forms of ownership on an equal footing immediately and let different types of ownership compete with the state firms. (Václav Klaus 1990)

As these two quotations suggest, we will present a wide spectrum of ideas that range from radical nationalization (and provisional toleration of small-scale private property) through cooperative, communal, and managerial ownership as well as workers' self-management. We continue all the way down to the blueprints of—first informal or simulated, then real but half-hearted—privatization. Exactly this half-heartedness will help explain why statist patterns of collectivism are being accepted so widely in the former communist world today. Importantly, these patterns did not have to reemerge because they never completely vanished after 1989. Here, our volume goes against the grain, challenging a widely held view of a massive neoliberal breakthrough in economic thought during the late 1980s—even if the rhetoric of some luminaries of the postcommunist transformation borrowed libertarian catchwords.

It is exactly the tremendous inertia of state-collectivism that may justify the *commemorative* character of this volume and its *never again* message. The lengthy experimentation full of trials and errors which economists had to pursue in order to get out of the dead-end street of pervasive nationalization and other forms of collectivization demonstrates the risks of vertical collectivism. Under certain circumstances (such as the monopoly of a party-state, a communist world power, and a ruling collectivist worldview), it can crowd out both horizontal collectivism and individualism in economic thought, paralyzing even the dissenters' imagination. This is a serious warning about the *stickiness* of collectivist doctrines especially when their horizontal variants have not been tested *en gros* on the societal level. Such a test would not be free of risk. As the history of communism proves, one can start as a grassroots collectivist and move to hierarchical collectivism without much ado.[5]

A CONTRIBUTION TO INSTITUTIONAL ANALYSIS

Our study of ownership concepts[6] under communism is not rooted in the mere ambition to warn the reader about the dangers of a collectivist revival. Also, we do not want to fill a gap in the history of economic thought just because it is there. Our research group is convinced that—although the ownership theories to be presented in this volume frequently did not reach the scientific level required by contemporary economics in the West—one can identify a fair number of original ideas of social property and its mixes with individual ownership, the value of which cannot be confined to their *exotic beauty*. The Conclusion will display eight attempts at such kinds of invention. Referring to them, we promise to present a few *hidden treasures* of economic scholarship, reintroduce unjustly forgotten authors as well as reveal the internal dynamics of local research communities and their transnational linkages which otherwise would remain imperceptible for outsiders. However, even many of the not-quite-original ideas were unique in terms of their ferocity and size of real-world experimentation.

To take the example of the concepts of state, cooperative, and communal ownership, many early Western prototypes were reinterpreted (distorted) and put into practice during the communist period. In addition, the experiments were carried out simultaneously in a great number of countries and for many decades. It is of equal importance that the critique of these forms of ownership,[7] which resulted from the repeated tests performed in the gigantic laboratory of communism, produced a wide range of scholarly arguments of empirical relevance. If translated into the formal language of modern economics, these arguments may be able (a) to enrich the standard literature of government failure with specific types (e.g., extreme versions of fuzzy/ blurred property rights, principal-agent relationships, rent seeking, incomplete contracts, etc.) in new institutional economics; and seen from a broader perspective, (b) to support the Mises-Hayek thesis of the impossibility of rational calculation under collectivist rule excluding private ownership. (It is perhaps the scholarly critique of the theory of workers' self-management that earned the greatest recognition in both fields.[8]) However, even if the arguments remain in their original verbal/historical form, they provide new insights in the *old institutional* analysis of property relations that was initiated by Marxists, members of the German Historical School, American institutionalists from Thorstein Veblen to John Galbraith, and Ordo-liberals. Finally, since some excellent Western scholars achieved much of the empirical results in studying ownership practices under communism (as discussed subsequently), revisiting the evolution of ownership concepts could rehabilitate them by challenging the stigma of Kremlinology.

Although it may seem absurd to take sides in the grand debate about the comparative virtues/vices of economic individualism and collectivism without evaluating the *progress reports* of the communist laboratory, this is exactly what has been happening in the profession since 1989. Neither did economic historians analyze the experiments in a systematic fashion nor did historians of economic thought waste too much time with the conceptual background, a subject that primarily intrigued our research group. What could illustrate this more lucidly than the discontinuation of the Socialist Calculation Debate in the mainstream of economic science? The collapse of the Soviet empire served as final proof of the impossibility thesis—an approach Friedrich von Hayek, who witnessed the end of communism in Eastern Europe, did *not* take. In this way, an undoubtedly strong piece of practical evidence, the simultaneous implosion of communist regimes, is substituted for a detailed investigation of the failures of a durable collectivist experiment, by both economic and intellectual history.[9]

This allowed the skeptics much room for maneuver in refuting the thesis as well as looking for old-new collectivist solutions again. Arguments such as "the collapse had political rather than economic reasons," "it was due to the lack of markets rather than that of private property," "capitalism cannot also do without public ownership," and "economic calculation by private owners may also be irrational," started mushrooming at the margins of standard economic knowledge and triggered new projects located somewhere between the concepts of market socialism and the social market economy.[10]

During the past quarter of a century, collectivist ideas of ownership under communism and their scientific critique have seldom attracted careful scrutiny, neither in the respective national histories of economic thought nor as a subject of transnational comparison. Yet, as archival materials rapidly erode and key eyewitnesses pass away, this is the last occasion when a conceptual reconstruction of economic ideas under communism can be accomplished with both empirical precision and intellectual empathy.

GOING BEYOND THE STATE OF THE ART

Until now, a reader interested in the fate of ownership regimes under communism and their intellectual history could only find a small number of insightful studies in economic history, sociology, political science, and law discussing the evolution of certain really existing institutions of communist economies including ownership. Moreover, the development of economic ideas is not the focus of these works.

The literature portraying the evolution of ownership concepts in the economic thought of the individual communist countries will be presented in the national chapters of our volume. In that literature one looks for thematic monographs in vain, and will find at best a few articles dealing with theories of ownership. However, usually these lack a comprehensive research agenda. As regards the few comparative works such as Kornai (1992), Berend (1996, 2009), Bruszt and Stark (1998), Roland (2000), Janos (2000), and Aslund (2002), they do not focus on ownership per se, and when they do bother to discuss property relations, they examine institutions and policies rather than ideas, and/or cover only a few countries and periods in depth. Even a concise history of Eastern European or Chinese economic thought in the 20th century, which might contain a brief chapter on ownership theories, has not been written yet. Moreover, to our knowledge, no edited volume has been published (either in English or in other languages) that would rest on a series of coordinated country studies on the evolution of economic concepts of ownership. In this field even ad hoc conference volumes are missing. Memoirs that would include the author's ideas on relevant property issues are also rare (see Kornai 2008).

The proliferation of comparative research projects on postcommunist privatization in the 1990s did not really help fill this gap because their participants also were interested in practices rather than ideas, and used the communist period only as a point of departure to explain the postcommunist transformation (see, for example, Major (1993); Frydman and Rapaczinski (1994); John Earle et al. (1994); Ira Lieberman et al. (1997)).

Works such as these replaced promising research programs developing in the West from the late 1950s. Understandably, the pioneers of these programs wanted to comprehend the institutions of ownership by means of neoclassical models (e.g., Benjamin Ward, Evsey Domar, and Jaroslav Vaněk) or industrial or sectoral case studies (e.g., Joseph Berliner, David Granick, and

Gregory Grossman) instead of methodically tracing the evolution of local concepts. The case studies were complemented by other *old-institutionalist* inquiries and a growing number of *new-institutionalist* ones (cf. Murrell 1991). The former were primarily cultivated by scholars active in the field of Comparative Economic Systems (CES) such as Morris Bornstein, William Duffy, Paul Gregory, Helmut Leipold, John Michael Montias, Egon Neuberger, Alec Nove, Frederic Pryor, Robert Stuart, Hans-Jürgen Wagener, and Peter Wiles, many of whom studied ownership theories and applied a transnational frame of analysis. The latter offered more precise instruments of institutional explanation of property relations but were less attentive to ideas of ownership, and usually relied on incomparable case studies (see the works of Maxim Boycko, Bengt Holmström, Peter Murrell, Mancur Olson, Svetozar Pejovich, Andrei Shleifer, Robert Vishny, etc.). Thus, despite the fact that CES was challenged by New Comparative Economics (Djankov et al. 2003), anyone interested in ownership thought has had to be content with the results of the former. As time passed, the systems theorists increasingly focused on technical details of governance (decision-making, information, motivation, coordination, etc.)[11] rather than on the conceptual features of property regimes, and refrained from dynamic comparison. They built quite a few static (cross-sectional) typologies that overemphasized national specifics, and after a while these became boringly repetitive.

Of course, issues of ownership also intrigued economic sociologists and social anthropologists (such as Michael Burawoy, Elizabeth Dunn, Chris Hann, Caroline Humphrey, Martha Lampland, Alena Ledeneva, Kálmán Rupp, David Stark, Iván Szelényi, Katherine Verdery, Janine Wedel, and Suava Zbierski-Salameh) who launched valuable research projects on property structures, particularly in the informal economy and the countryside. Industrial sociology also started flourishing in some communist countries (e.g., Tardos 1983; Wasilewski 1990). However, they examined popular rather than scholarly ideas of ownership, and their results were rarely subjected to international comparison. Yet, as will be pointed out in the Conclusion, their supply of exciting new research perspectives and metaphors speeded up the radicalization of reform economists. True, the bulk of empirically grounded reference, for example, to feudal (oligarchical, clan-based, etc.) or communal rules of ownership and their blends came too late to contribute to a profound economic *cum* legal analysis of the really existing property regimes, especially of what could be called *nomenklatura ownership* prior to 1989.

Legal researchers such as George Armstrong, William Butler, Ferdinand Feldbrugge, John Hazard, Olimpiad Ioffe, Murray Raff, Norbert Reich, and William Simons also followed closely the evolution of property law in communist countries, and the interest of many of them grew with the advance of postcommunist privatization. Nevertheless, with a few exceptions such as Damsa (2016), Heller (1998), and Mattei (2000) the ideational and comparative aspects of regulating ownership have been overshadowed by technical case and country studies of law-making. In these studies, however, some basic ideas appeared which reflected the ways in which economists were approaching the notion of ownership in the communist era, oscillating between preferences for formal or informal rules, disentangling mixed property rights, or picking and choosing from their bundle.

As for indigenous economic research on concepts of ownership in Eastern Europe and China, leading reform economists like Aleksander Bajt, Wlodzimierz Brus, Branko Horvat, János Kornai, Kazimierz Łaski, Tibor Liska, Ota Šik, Márton Tardos, Xue Muqiao, and Wu Jinglian published thought-provoking conceptual works on communist property relations from the early 1960s. The country chapters of this volume will enumerate many of these. As mentioned, the arrival of new institutional economics was delayed in Eastern Europe, but its property-rights school had some followers in the region by the late 1980s (see Kovács 2012).

However, attempts at a potential synthesis of these kinds of research perspectives were swept away by the 1989 revolutions. The first projects that looked beyond the *oeuvre* of leading reformers and sought to rehabilitate less famous but equally talented experts (including those working on ownership theories) as well as writing a comparative history of economic ideas under communism have remained without followers during the past decades (cf. Kovács and Tardos (1992); Wagener (1998); Kaase and Sparschuh (2002)).

Some of those who resumed working on the intellectual history of communism are inclined to portray the evolution of economic ideas in the context of an international consensus among (conspiracy by) neoliberal theorists (see Bockman 2011; Damsa 2016). For a diametrically opposite approach, see Grosfeld (1992) and the case studies on the reception of new institutional economics in Eastern Europe in Kovács and Zentai (2012). See also Mihályi (2005), Avramov (2007), and Aligica and Evans (2009).

All in all, if economic concepts of ownership were studied at all, then the authors tended to presume that

- by the mid-1950s, the Marxist-Leninist hybrid of *social ownership*, a unique species in ownership theory, was incorporated in the Stalinist canon of communist political economy based on (a) the duality of state and cooperative property (postulating the internal harmony of the former and its superiority over the latter), (b) the harmful nature of private property (a toxic relic of capitalism), and (c) the negligible role played by communal ownership, self-management, and by what was called *personal property*;
- for many decades, this canon, elevated onto the level of national constitutions, managed to crowd out the concept of private ownership from

economic theory as well as other concepts of social ownership grounded in local traditions (with some exceptions such as China and Yugoslavia);

- if one nonetheless insisted on constructing a typology of ownership projects around the ideal type of social property, then they could be best compared with the help of their national real types such as the Yugoslav theory of workers' self-management, the idea of managerial ownership in Hungary, or the model of Chinese communal property;
- these concepts notwithstanding, it was the Soviet pair of nationalization and collectivization that counted as the only major innovation in ownership theory under communism; its opposite, privatization, and the intermediary doctrines between them were essentially a result of imitation, that is, production of low-quality copies of the Western originals instead of local invention;
- both nationalization/collectivization and privatization won a sweeping victory in the economic research community in most communist countries in the 1950s and 1980s, respectively;
- the evolution of ownership concepts was a steady move away from the initial doctrine of social ownership to attain a wide acceptance of the program of privatization under late communism; during this journey, the ways in which economists thought about ownership grew more and more sophisticated.

In other words, it was tacitly supposed that, in relating the above narrative, one could safely ignore that:

- the Stalinist canon was (a) not innovative inasmuch as, by postulating the duality of state and cooperative ownership, it prolonged the old socialist/communist dilemma of vertical versus horizontal collectivism; (b) unstable because it contained *poisonous* material—cooperative and personal property—that encouraged the theorists to think about the non-statist ingredients of these ownership regimes, and ultimately, to touch upon the taboo of the prohibition of private ownership; and (c) incomplete because it proved unable to respond to three recurrent challenges in the sacred territory of the state economy, which were posed by powerful claims of managerial ownership, workers' self-management, and communal property, respectively; these challenges provoked some introspection into the behavior of the state economy, and made the thesis of internal harmony questionable;
- beneath the surface of an alleged Soviet hegemony in political economy, a large variety of stimulating economic ideas were to be found, which strove to identify some of the *real* subjects of social property, and which provided original solutions in ownership theory in terms of both social and individual property and their combinations;

- many of these solutions were home-grown, stemming from local tradition and invention rather than the emulation of Western patterns; ironically, emulation often resulted from an East-East exchange of ideas, in which the share of mandatory Soviet supply of ownership projects was diminishing; furthermore, until the conservative turn of the 1970s, economists in the West kept sending a great many collectivist signals to their colleagues behind the Iron Curtain;
- methodological nationalism may prove to be a proper device in defining the real types of ownership projects (e.g., Yugoslav-style self-management) but it puts the evolutionary variants of that particular type in the shade (the *Yugoslav style* was different in the 1950s and the 1980s), or other possible real types in the same country (e.g., the concept of private agriculture in Yugoslavia); moreover, it disregards the national varieties of the same real type (like, for example, the Hungarian or Polish versions of self-management, or their combination transformed by Soviet economists in the *perestroika* period), which resulted from a multilateral communication between economists in the communist era;
- ownership concepts exhibited evolutionary patterns, different from a clear, unilinear path leading from nationalization to privatization, which were messy and uneven in both time and space, including in-built obstacles to development, forgotten and recurrent ideas, as well as long phases of setbacks and advances, deceleration and acceleration;
- ownership theories evolved as much along the lines of political radicalization as along those of scientific refinement; ownership was poorly examined by economists in legal terms; they paid at most lip-service to property-rights theory in new institutional economics, and also their analysis of the relationship between property and basic sociological and political categories such as power, class, and interests was rudimentary;
- it was difficult to unearth the anatomy of the party-state by reading what economists wrote about ownership; the Trotsky-Djilas hypothesis of the *new class* was long available but its main pillar, *nomenklatura* ownership, lacked both empirical foundation and theoretical elaboration (even the term was not in general use) until the collapse of communism, or even later.

IN SEARCH OF PRIVATE OWNERS?: A KEY ASSUMPTION

The above reservations reflect the working hypotheses with which our research group embarked upon its comparative inquiry. Here, they are formulated in a sharp opposition to the state of the art to make the goals of our study appear clear. Hopefully, the individual chapters and the Conclusion will justify most of the major assumptions. Their key—and probably most surprising—constituent, however, deserves special attention before the reader, without being informed about the purpose of its title, starts immersing in the volume. A few words about normative ambiguities are due, particularly concerning private ownership, the main enemy demonized by communist political economy. Interestingly enough, uncertainty was transparent in theorizing all kinds of ownership from the very outset of communist rule. Although initially, with the exception of the first years of New Economic Policy (NEP) in the Soviet 1920s, a radical drive for nationalization dominated official economic discourse in the whole communist bloc following both 1917 and 1945, social property was not meant to become exclusive in the short and medium term, and "social" was not synonymous with "state-owned." Many economists interpreted nationalization as a natural continuation of governmental regulations in war economies and/or as socialization in its original Marxian sense. Statist-centralist preferences, no matter how strong they were, competed with those of cooperative and communal ownership as well as self-management which could not be eradicated entirely in most communist countries, or actually emerged there. Moreover, some years after the communist takeover in Eastern Europe, a series of crucial adjustments took place in ownership theory, making it even more inconsistent, fragmentary, and even self-contradictory. The adjustments, rooted in the dysfunctional behavior of "social owners," resulted in experimentation (*bricolage*) based on tradition, emulation, and invention. Nevertheless, the changes did not necessarily offer private owners more freedom.

Frequently, only the emphasis on state property was shifted on to other regimes of social ownership. The idea of private property was like a river that had been forced underground by nationalization and collectivization, but from time to time, it floated to the surface in a large variety of forms: full and partial, formal and informal, quasi and real. Ironically, as radical as the beginning of the story of ownership concepts had been, by the end it became tame and half-hearted. At the twilight of the system, social ownership was not replaced by private ownership in economic theory with the same passion as at the dawn of communism when private ownership was usurped by the state.

This volume's working title had been "From Radical Nationalization to Moderate Privatization." Yet, however important it would be to stress the cautious nature of the Eastern European privatization projects prior to 1989, and to offset the image of a neoliberal breakthrough, such a working title would wrongly suggest an incessant and intransigent will of the economic profession to make private property legitimate again. The phrase "Populating No Man's Land" seems a better solution because it refers to a desperate search for flesh-and-blood owners (or representatives of owners) who could efficiently cultivate that alleged public territory created by nationalization for everybody (hence, nobody).[12] The number of economists who wanted to see genuine private owners as *new settlers* was insignificant. The simulation of private ownership, that is, the quest for identifying quasi-private owners,[13] was all the more popular. Slowly but steadily, it became obvious that nobody's property actually meant somebody's property: it was the communist ruling elite that—under the pretext of representing everybody—had already populated a large part of the no man's land, expropriating (or preying on) it informally. Hence, re-populating would be a more accurate phrase to use. However, demanding the reestablishment of non-simulated private ownership seemed too great a leap forward to most economists for a long time.

Leaving behind the Stalinist canon that celebrated social property controlled by a rather faceless party-state, the advocates of ownership change wanted to set the stage for an army of colorful and relatively independent economic actors who try and err, succeed and fail. By suggesting various property regimes, they never lost their faith in collectivism completely, and even near the end of communism strove to elaborate Grand Designs of *capitalism without capitalists*. Many of them hoped that the new—non-private or quasi-private—owners fabricated in their *Hexenküche* would be able to dump not only social property but also informal private ownership emerging in the niches of the planned economy.

After the frenzy for nationalization ebbed in the 1950s, more and more economists started working out ways of populating the no man's land of social ownership with a well-defined group of business-minded (rational) actors who are interested in using the assets at their disposal (*usus*) more responsibly as well as drawing income from them (*usus fructus*). In the end, some of the proposals included limited rights to buy and sell the assets, but not bequeath or inherit them (*abusus*). Governance seemed to the economic profession a cardinal issue but full ownership less so. Personifying the social owner, and establishing its relative independence from central authorities were the crux of reforming the Stalinist canon of ownership—a gigantic experiment in social engineering, in which the re-creation of a proprietary class of private individuals featured not even as a secondary goal. If it nonetheless seldom did, private property was either conceived as some kind of workers' (citizens') shareholding, as a means of *nomenklatura* buyout, or as individual ownership with severe limitations concerning size, asset specificity, citizenship of the owner, and the like almost until communism took its last breath, and often even thereafter. In addition to simulation, *pluralization*, that is, ensuring a *peaceful coexistence* of different regimes of ownership and, ultimately, putting them on an equal footing (cf. Klaus's motto), were a much more popular claim among economists than privatization as such. True, at the time, it was unimaginable in Eastern Europe that communist ruling elites could accept large-scale private ownership and still remain capable of sustaining a communist dictatorship—today a platitude in the wake of historic changes in China.

Was moderation with regard to private ownership due to self-censorship combined with ignorance and a lack of fantasy or due to a never-ending trust in the socialization of ownership? Even years after 1989, one could not detect but a handful of leading economists in Eastern Europe who stood against the half-collectivist consensus and advocated unambiguously non-collectivist procedures of privatization (*ad absurdum*, selling any state-owned asset to anybody on the free market). This stance points the way in which the above question can be answered. (More on this in the Conclusion.) No doubt about it, the economic profession tipped over during the 1990s. However, looking back from the 2010s, and knowing the current skepticism regarding liberalism in the ex-communist countries, one may suppose that when the communist and the postcommunist periods are taken together, the general acceptance of large private property by the economic profession has been the exception while moderation has been the rule.

METHODOLOGY: SHOOTING SPARROWS WITH A CANNON?

Researchers intending to cut a path through virtually unexplored territory had best be conservative when choosing their techniques of inquiry. The authors of this volume subscribed to this rule of thumb. In challenging the state of the art with new working hypotheses, we decided to combine well-established methodologies in writing the history of economic thought under communism. They range from Kuhn's concept of scientific revolutions and the theory of Lakatosian research programs to the discursive approach of the Cambridge School of the history of ideas, Koselleck's *Begriffsgeschichte* or the *histoire des mentalités* of the Annales School, and we also borrow from micro-history and *histoire croisée* (entangled history). This—hopefully healthy—eclecticism did not originate in an *anything-goes* attitude to writing intellectual history but in a desire to make our research methods fit for studying our somewhat peculiar field. To put it bluntly, we had to reckon with the fact that, for a long time, economic ideas on ownership were developed through speeches held at party congresses rather than scholarly conversations in faculty clubs.

If science is forced to evolve under severe ideological and political constraints, such as the monopoly of a particular worldview, cultural isolation, or censorship, then the externalist techniques of history-writing may be more helpful than, say, looking for the *hard cores* and *protective belts* of scientific research programs, presuming, in the spirit of Imre Lakatos, that in the first place, inner academic choices and rational drivers determine the evolution of economic ideas. Forcing an internalist explanation would mean shooting sparrows with a cannon (Kovács 2013). Discursive methods, however, may prove very fruitful because political regimes with totalitarian or authoritarian intentions tend to replace critical reflection with word magic and coded language of indoctrination. In our case, good examples are the use of "state property," "people's property," "socialist property," and "social property" as synonymous terms in official rhetoric as well as hiding de facto state ownership behind the term of cooperative ownership. At the same time, it would be futile to experiment with a *marketplace of ideas* model to comprehend the diffusion of economic knowledge. Supposing even a semi-free competition among ownership concepts would be a grave exaggeration, with the exception of the last few years of communism in certain countries. Neither the glorification of social ownership in the Soviet Bloc nor the partial decomposition of the Stalinist canon followed the logic of market choice in scientific production. Focusing on the long-term inertia of mentality, as defined by Annales scholars, however, helps the historian understand why it was so hard for economists of collectivist persuasion to accept private ownership even when the *Zeitgeist* turned to liberalism/conservatism in the West during the 1970s. And, on the contrary, the idea of paradigm change (scientific revolution) may be essential in explaining the sudden acceptance even of radically liberal projects of privatization in some of the ex-communist countries during the early 1990s. Finally, we thought that entangled history could help discover the hidden relationships between scholars in different countries in an empire, the intellectual life of which was supposed to be governed from Moscow.

Assembling the constituents of these methodologies, it was not easy to cope with their frictions, but one thing was clear: the emerging blend of research techniques would make us immune to the temptation of both celebrating, in a Whiggish manner, that economists in the communist era finally managed to reach an ideal (liberal) consensus in ownership theory, and reproaching them, with a presentist arrogance, of having been too slow in revising their *collectivist fixations* and taking over, say, cutting-edge concepts of property rights from the West.

To avoid fabricating a methodological patchwork in a capricious fashion, a volume like ours needs a solid background. The book the reader holds in his/her hand is the first result of a long-term research program launched by the editor in the Vienna Institute for Human Sciences (IWM) in 2014.[14] The program's title, *Between Bukharin and Balcerowicz. A Comparative History of Economic Thought under Communism*, indicates the symbolic boundaries of our research. By the October Revolution, the young Bolshevik thinker Nikolai Bukharin had turned his back on his professor, Eugen Böhm-Bawerk in Vienna, and started writing a book on the *Economic Theory of the Leisure*

Class, which challenged the marginalist paradigm as a whole and marked the beginning of what proved to be a long detour from the history of Western economic thought. The end of the digression can be represented by the young Solidarity advisor Leszek Balcerowicz's turn to neoclassical economics and free-market ideas in the second half of the 1980s.

However, locking in our research efforts between the 1917 and 1989 revolutions would arguably result in oversimplification by excluding both the antecedents and the repercussions of scientific change. Simply put, Bukharin might have been more tolerant toward *hedonistic individualism* in the theories of marginal utility if he had not stood under the influence of collectivist doctrines represented by German and Russian social democracy and the model of the war economy during the First World War. Similarly, Balcerowicz would perhaps be less devoted to laissez-faire if he had not had to face the tenacity of certain collectivist ideas during the agony of communism and after.

Our research program covers almost all ex-communist countries of Eastern Europe (in its traditional Cold War sense, including the Soviet Union) and—unlike sporadic comparative ventures in this field—does not ignore China;[15] it concentrates on the transformation of economic ideas but does not tear them out of their contexts in economic, political, and social/cultural history (thereby combining *internalist* and *externalist* methods of intellectual history-writing); and examines how East-West dialogue affected the development of economic thought under communism but does not overlook East-East communication.

We focus on the ideas not only of those economists who lived and worked in the selected countries but also of their émigré and foreign colleagues who studied similar issues. Besides the *high culture* of economic thought, including eminent scholars, their schools, and scientific discoveries, our program also examines the *mass culture* of economic knowledge (e.g., university textbooks, documents of the communist party, articles in economic newspapers, and so on). In this way, we may be able to explore, to twist Quentin Skinner's phrase, the "importance of small texts" as the context of the few *great texts* emerging in the communist era. For similar reasons, ample room is devoted to key problems in the sociology of knowledge, ranging from an institutional history of leading research centers and university departments, through the advisory and political activities of economists, all the way down to the political control of economic research and education, and the rules of censorship. The research methods go beyond a *close reading* of scientific texts to include archival research, in-depth interviews, case studies, and the like.

We apply five main research perspectives (chronological, thematic, qualitative, sociological, and methodological) in writing the history of economic thought under communism. Following an overview of the consecutive stages of the evolution of ideas, the researchers turn their gaze upon a selection of essential themes characteristic of economic research programs in the communist period. Then they cover the life work of a few (certainly fewer than Schumpeter's ten) great economists in each country, and examine the underlying sociological/political conditions of changes in economic ideas. In the end, the monographs tackle some fundamental methodological issues (e.g., origins and diffusion patterns of economic knowledge under communism, the relationship between local traditions, emulation, and original discoveries, etc.) as well as asking the Big Question: how do the scientific costs and benefits of the historical detour initiated by scholars like Bukharin relate to each other?

For the nine ex-communist countries under scrutiny here, prominent local economists and their research teams[16] are preparing sizeable national monographs that will be subjected to a detailed comparative analysis. A thematic volume like this is an indispensable intermediary product in preparation for both. Here, by selecting a crucial field of political economy, ownership, the authors can experiment with the other four research perspectives and the techniques of comparison. Our volume consists of three parts. Following the Introduction, nine country chapters observe the logic of the *Between Bukharin and Balcerowicz* program in order to ensure a considerable degree of comparability without straitjacketing the authors (and annoying the readers with repetitions). The Conclusion offers a comparison of the ownership concepts both across countries and along the research perspectives, experimenting with evolutionary types and highlighting the difficulties caused by the failure to define *nomenklatura* ownership.

NOTES

1. One of the most difficult linguistic tasks was for us to decide whether we would designate the system/era/countries to be studied as *socialist* (relying on local and early international discourse) or *communist* (relying on much of the relevant literature). Our decision remained two-sided even after phrases like "state socialism," "real socialism," "really existing socialism," and "Soviet-type society" had been excluded. We chose *communism* despite the fact that, according to its representatives, it was yet to come, and retained *socialism* only when we wanted to refer to how the local actors of the time used the word (e.g., *socialist ownership relations*).

2. In this volume we apply a broad definition of economic collectivism, including all kinds of doctrines that emphasize the priority of society/community/nation, and idealize group (and criticize individual) ownership. (Party-)state intervention, central planning, in-kind distribution, militarization, and so on—that is, essential constituents of real-world collectivism under communism almost until its collapse—are not necessarily considered to be part of the definition. The question of what is to be meant by group ownership has no clear answer in the literature. In principle, certain forms of

structured ownership or *co-ownership* such as a corporation or a partnership of three private owners also could be regarded as group ownership. For the property rights of the members of cooperatives, communes, and self-managed firms, that is, of dominant institutions of group ownership, see the Conclusion.

The terms of "public," "common," "collective," and "communal" property, that is, customary concepts describing capitalist societies, have also multiple interpretations in current sources all over the world (cf. communalism versus communitarianism). Also, due to the fact that—as unfortunate as it may be—economists normally did not indulge in legal argumentation in the communist era, the reader will seldom encounter in the country chapters regular categories of property law (such as *usus*, *usus fructus*, and *abusus*) or fine distinctions between ownership and possession, different forms of exclusion/inclusion, and so on.

In our case, it seems helpful to depart from the concept of social ownership, as defined in official communist discourse, and focus on four types: state, cooperative, and communal property as well as workers' self-management. Then, individual (personal and private) ownership is to be examined, together with their numerous combinations with these types of social property. This is just a first approximation. For further details, see the table of ownership terms in the Conclusion.

For the sake of simplicity, the authors apply the words "ownership" and "property" interchangeably unless we expressly want to refer to property as the object of ownership. For the risks of conflating the two notions, see Mattei (2000).

3. This volume focuses on the academic background of communist reformers (reform communists), that is, on the research programs of the so-called reform economists (reform-minded economists, market reformers, market socialists). Their research communities included, besides economic (legal, sociological, etc.) theorists and historians, also a few policymakers, company managers, and journalists. Cf. Kovács (1992).

4. Our notion of ownership follows the textbook definition offered by new institutional economics that describes ownership as a bundle of property rights (and duties) over physical and intellectual objects of property, pertaining to its acquisition, use, disposal, control, income, transfer, liquidation, loss, and so on, as well as to the exclusion of other owners and the enforcement of all these rights (see Demsetz 1967; Furubotn and Richter 1998). Similar taxonomies were suggested by authors such as Wesley Hohfeld, Tony Honoré, and Jeremy Waldron. The well-known triad of possession, use, and disposition also could have been applied. But for students of communist property regimes, the Achilles heel of which is the *abusus* of capital the "*usus (ius utendi)—usus fructus (ius fruendi)—abusus (ius abutendi)*" typology of Roman law seems the most convenient.

5. For similar "traps of collectivism," see the Conclusion.

6. Hereafter, the terms "concepts," "theories," "ideas," "projects," "doctrines," and "designs" of ownership/property will be applied as synonyms.

7. The terms "forms," "institutions," "types," or "regimes" of ownership/property will be used interchangeably in the volume.

8. Of course, it would be too much to say that, for example, the new-institutionalist theory of property rights was invented in Eastern Europe but—as will be shown below—the ongoing debate on the Yugoslav system of self-management did

contribute to the theory at its early stages of evolution, and the experience of stormy institutional changes in and after 1989 led to its consolidation. The latter opened the eyes (unfortunately, too little, too late) of leading Western scholars such as Ronald Coase, Douglass North, and Oliver Williamson to the problems of ownership in a communist economy and for its institutional legacy (Franičević 2012; Kovács 2012).

9. In cherishing the memory of economic theorists who took part in the Socialist Calculation Debate, Peter Boettke's series on *Socialism and the Market* (2000) deserves the greatest appreciation. Historians of economic thought owe special thanks to Tadeusz Kowalik and Jerzy Osiatyński for publishing the works of Oskar Lange and Michal Kałecki, respectively. After the first anthologies edited by Nicholas Spulber (1964) and Alec Nove and Mario Nuti (1972) had been published, no similar works appeared in English. Edited volumes came out from time to time that included a few contemporary articles (e.g., Jones and Moskoff 1991), and some prominent authors were rediscovered (e.g., Barnett 2011; Toporowski 2013). As for the postcommunist period, the supply of English-language works coming from the ex-communist countries is understandably much larger, and there is less need for anthologies. An important example for a well-edited collection is provided by Hare et al. (1997).

10. See "Discussion on Socialist Market Economy" (1989), Nuti (1992), Bardhan, and Roemer (1993), Roosevelt and Belkin (1994), Roemer and Wright (1996), and Bockman (2011). See also the sharp debate of Pranab Bardhan and John Roemer (1992; 1994) with Andrei Shleifer and Robert Vishny (1994) in the *Journal of Economic Perspectives*. The latter authors answer Roemer's question "Can there be socialism after communism?" with a resolute "no." For a somewhat hesitant answer, see Stiglitz (1994).

11. See, for example, Neuberger and Duffy (1976). János Kornai (2000, 2016) returned to the comparison of communist and capitalist systems to stress the importance of ownership among the comparative variables.

12. Interestingly, the metaphor of no man's land, expressing an old truism about the communist economy from the Soviet 1920s onward, today reminds the observer of the parable of the *tragedy of the commons*, though it has never been modeled as profoundly as that. Yet, as suggested by Elinor Ostrom (1990) in her theory of common-pool resources, the latter could have offered at least a partial solution in the framework of horizontal collectivism to economists who wanted to insist on projects of social ownership that could avoid free riding and the overuse of resources. For the inadequacy of the parable to describe what was really happening in no man's land, see Heller (1998). Probably, the fundamental difference was that, while in principle the owners of the commons have equal access and power, social ownership was exercised, in the last analysis, by the *nomenklatura*, and the majority of society had to be pleased if they were allowed by the ruling elite to informally expropriate (steal) a tiny part of *people's property*. Of course, *within nomenklatura* ownership the overuse of public resources due to the competition between various groups of elites was a frequent phenomenon.

13. In looking for an appropriate adjective, "quasi-private" appeared to be a good compromise between "pseudo-private" and "surrogate."

14. For more information on the research objectives and techniques as well as the participants of the program, see http://triple-b-project.net/.

15. We conducted research on nine countries (Bulgaria, China, Czechoslovakia, German Democratic Republic, Hungary, Poland, Romania, Soviet Union, and Yugoslavia). The non-inclusion of other communist states from Albania to Vietnam was not due to any scientific preference but to the lack of research funds and academic links.

16. The team leaders are Oleg Ananyin, Roumen Avramov, Shitao Fan, Julius Horvath, János Mátyás Kovács, Jože Mencinger, Bogdan Murgescu, Maciej Tymiński, and Hans-Jürgen Wagener. They are assisted by the scientific advisory board of the program. Its members are Peter Boettke, Vojmir Franičević, Jerzy Osiatyński, Pekka Sutela, and Chenggang Xu.

BIBLIOGRAPHY

Aligica, Paul Dragos, and Anthony Evans. 2009. *The Neoliberal Revolution in Eastern Europe: Economic Ideas in the Transition from Communism.* London: Edward Elgar Publishing.

Aslund, Anders. 2002. *Building Capitalism.* Cambridge: Cambridge University Press.

Avramov, Roumen. 2007. *Komunalniat kapitalizam: Iz balgarskoto stopansko minalo* [Communal capitalism: Reflections on the Bulgarian economic past]. Volumes I–III. Sofia: Fondatzia balgarska nauka i kultura, Centre for Liberal Strategies.

Balcerowicz, Leszek, Aleksander Bajt, Włodzimierz Brus, Karel Dyba, András Hegedüs, Branko Horvat, Gennadii Lisichkin, László Szamuely, and Márton Tardos. 1989. "Discussion on Socialist Market Economy." *Acta Oeconomica* 40: 207–412.

Bardhan, Pranab, and John Roemer. 1992. "Market Socialism: A Case for Rejuvenation." *Journal of Economic Perspectives*, Summer 6 no. 3: 101–16.

———, eds. 1993. *Market Socialism: The Current Debate.* New York: Oxford University Press.

———. 1994. "On the Workability of Market Socialism." *Journal of Economic Perspectives*, Spring 8, no. 2: 177–81.

Barnett, Vincent. 2011. *E.E. Slutsky as Economist and Mathematician: Crossing the Limits of Knowledge.* London: Routledge.

Berend, Iván T. 1996. *Central and Eastern Europe 1944–1993: Detour from the Periphery to the Periphery.* Cambridge: Cambridge University Press.

———. 2009. *From the Soviet Bloc to the European Union. The Economic and Social Transformation of Central and Eastern Europe since 1973.* Cambridge: Cambridge University Press.

Bockman, Johanna. 2011. *Markets in the Name of Socialism. The Left-Wing Origins of Neoliberalism.* Berkeley: Stanford University Press.

Boettke, Peter, ed. 2000. *Socialism and the Market.* Vol. I–IX. London: Routledge.

Brus, Włodzimierz, and Kazimierz Łaski. 1989. *From Marx to the Market.* Oxford: Oxford University Press.

Bruszt, László, and David Stark. 1998. *Postsocialist Pathways*. Cambridge: Cambridge University Press.

Damsa, Liviu. 2016. *The Transformation of Property Regimes and Transitional Justice in Central Eastern Europe*. Berlin: Springer-Verlag.

Demsetz, Harold. 1967. "Toward a Theory of Property Rights." *The American Economic Review* 57, no. 2: 347–59.

Djankov, Simeon et al. 2003. "The New Comparative Economics." *Journal of Comparative Economics* 31, no. 4: 595–619.

Earle, John et al., eds. 1994. *Small Privatization.* Budapest: Central European University Press.

Franičević, Vojmir. 2012. "Soft Institutionalism. The Reception of New Institutional Economics in Croatia." In *Capitalism from Outside? Economic Cultures in Eastern Europe after 1989*, edited by János Mátyás Kovács and Violetta Zentai, 241–62. Budapest—New York: CEU Press.

Furubotn, Eirik, and Rudolf Richter, eds. 1998. *Institutions and Economic Theory. The Contribution of the New Institutional Economics.* Ann Arbor: The University of Michigan Press.

Grosfeld, Irena. 1992. "Reform Economics and Western Economic Theory: Unexploited Opportunities." In *Reform and Transformation. Eastern European Economics on the Threshold of Change*, edited by János Mátyás Kovács and Márton Tardos, 62–79. London: Routledge.

Hare, Paul et al., eds. 1997. *The Transition to the Market Economy: Critical Perspectives on the World Economy.* London: Routledge.

Heller, Michael. 1998. "The Tragedy of the Anticommons: Property in the Transition from Marx to Markets." *Harvard Law Review* 111, no. 3: 621–88.

Janos, Andrew C. 2000. *East Central Europe in the Modern World.* Berkeley: Stanford University Press.

Jones, Anthony, and William Moskoff, eds. 1991. *The Great Market Debate.* Armonk, NY: Sharpe.

Kaase, Max, Vera Sparschuh, and Agnieszka Wenninger, eds. 2002. *Three Social Science Disciplines in Central and Eastern Europe: Handbook on Economics, Political Science and Sociology (1989–2001).* Berlin–Budapest: GESIS—Collegium Budapest.

Klaus, Václav. 1990. "No Third Way Out: Creating a Capitalist Czechoslovakia." *Reason Magazine*, June. Available online, accessed April 24, 2017: https://reason.com/archives/1990/06/01/no-third-way-out.

Kornai, János. 1992. *The Socialist System.* Oxford: Oxford University Press.

———. 2000. "The System Paradigm." In *Paradigms of Social Change*, edited by Waltraud Schekle et al., 111–33. Frankfurt/New York: Campus Verlag.

———. 2006. *By Force of Thought: Irregular Memoirs of an Intellectual Journey.* Cambridge, MA: Massachusetts Institute of Technology Press.

———. 2016. "The System Paradigm Revisited." *Acta Oeconomica* 66, no. 4: 547–96.

Kovács, János Mátyás. 1992. "Compassionate Doubts about Reform Economics (Science, Ideology, Politics)." In *Reform and Transformation. Eastern European Economics on the Threshold of Change*, edited by J.M. Kovács and Márton Tardos, 299–333. London: Routledge.

———. 2012. "Beyond Basic Instinct? On the Reception of New Institutional Economics in Eastern Europe." In *Capitalism from Outside? Economic Cultures in Eastern Europe after 1989*, edited by J.M. Kovács and Violetta Zentai, 281–310. Budapest—New York: CEU Press.

———. 2013. "Ágyúval verébre? A kelet-európai közgazdasági eszmék történetéről (1917—1989)" I, II [Shooting sparrows with a cannon? On the history of Eastern European economic thought]. *2000*, 25 no. 5: 25–32, no. 6: 22–30.

Kovács, János Mátyás, and Márton Tardos, eds. 1992. *Reform and Transformation. Eastern European Economics on the Threshold of Change*. London: Routledge.

Kovács, János Mátyás, and Violetta Zentai, eds. 2012. *Capitalism from Outside? Economic Cultures in Eastern Europe after 1989*. Budapest: Central European University Press.

Lieberman, Ira et al., eds. 1997. *Between State and Market. Mass Privatization in Transition Economies*. World Bank Report no. 17078. Washington, DC, The World Bank.

Major, Iván. 1993. *Privatization in Eastern Europe: A Critical Approach*. London: Edward Elgar Publishing.

Mattei, Ugo. 2000. *Basic Principles of Property Law*. Westport: Greenwood Press.

Mihályi, Péter. 2005. *A privatizáció szellemi előkészítése* [Intellectual preparations for privatization]. Budapest: APVRt.

Murrell, Peter. 1991. "Can Neoclassical Economics Underpin the Reform of Centrally Planned Economies?" *Journal of Economic Perspectives* 5, no. 4: 59–76.

Neuberger, Egon, and William Duffy. 1976. *Comparative Economic Systems: A Decision-Making Approach*. Boston: Allyn and Bacon.

Nove, Alec, and Mario Nuti, eds. 1972. *Penguin Readings on Socialist Economics*. Baltimore, Harmondsworth.

Nuti, Mario. 1992. "Market Socialism: The Model That Might Have Been but Never Was." In *Market Socialism or the Restoration of Capitalism?* edited by Anders Aslund, 17–31. Cambridge: Cambridge University Press.

Ostrom, Elinor. 1990. *Governing the Commons. The Evolution of Institutions for Collective Action*. Cambridge: Cambridge University Press.

Rapaczynski, Andrzej, and Roman Frydman, eds. 1994. *Privatization in Eastern Europe: Is the State Withering Away?* Budapest: Central European University Press.

Roemer, John, and Erik Olin Wright. 1996. *Equal Shares: Making Market Socialism Work*. London—New York: Verso.

Roland, Gerard. 2000. *Transition and Economics*. Cambridge: MIT Press.

Roosevelt, Frank, and David Belkin, eds. 1994. *Why Market Socialism? Voices from Dissent*. Armonk, NY: M E Sharpe.

Rupp, Kálmán. 1983. *Entrepreneurs in Red: Structure and Organizational Innovation in the Centrally Planned Economy*. Albany: SUNY Press.

Shleifer, Andrei, and Robert Vishny. 1994. "The Politics of Market Socialism." *Journal of Economic Perspectives*, Spring 8, no. 2: 165–76.

Spulber, Nicholas, ed. 1964. *Foundations of Soviet Strategy for Economic Growth.* Bloomington: Indiana UP.

Stalin, Joseph. 1951. *Economic Problems of Socialism in the USSR.* Available online, accessed April 24, 2017: https://www.marxists.org/reference/archive/stalin/works/1951/economic-problems/index.htm.

Stiglitz, Joseph. 1994. *Whither Socialism?* Cambridge: MIT Press.

Tardos, Márton, ed. 1980. *Vállalati magatartás, vállalati környezet* [Enterprise behavior, enterprise environment]. Budapest: Közgazdasági és Jogi Könyvkiadó. (1983. Hungarian Enterprise Behavior, *Eastern European Economics* 21, no 3–4.)

Toporowski, Jan. 2013. *Michal Kałecki: An Intellectual Biography. Rendezvous in Cambridge, 1899–1939.* New York: Palgrave Macmillan.

Wagener, Hans-Jürgen, ed. 1998. *Economic Thought in Communist and Post-Communist Europe.* London: Routledge.

Wasilewski, Jacek. 1990. "The Patterns of Bureaucratic Elite Recruitment in Poland in the 1970s and 1980s." *Soviet Studies* 42, no. 4: 743–57.

Chapter 1

From Nationalization to Nowhere

Ownership in Bulgarian Economic Thought, 1944–1989

Roumen Avramov

TURNING POINT?

Right after the Second World War, a far-reaching restructuring of ownership relations was not first on the immediate political agenda, but its idea had already permeated Bulgarian society in different ways. The first half of the 1940s saw the culmination of an increasingly intrusive state involvement in economic affairs since the onset of the Depression. As early as 1933, the Financial Committee of the League of Nations concluded that "the Bulgarian government *de facto* follows a policy of 'planned economy' aiming at stricter regulations of output, trade, prices and even credit" (League of Nations 1933, 13). Relying almost entirely on discretionary decisions, or through its leading role in the consolidation of the ailing banking sector and the publicly controlled major national banks, the government had established a clear-cut interventionist model. Meanwhile, with the authoritarian coup of May 1934, the social vision preached by the ruling elites became, in line with *l'air du temps*, openly anti-liberal. Thus postwar events furthered an inertial drift, in the ambiance of which any *statist* model seemed politically palatable and intellectually legitimate. Its feasibility was reinforced by reconstruction, which unavoidably required coordinated governmental initiatives. Usually considered as a harsh break, the new regime actually drew heavily from strong prewar local traditions and from its global stance. The general feeling of a crumbled liberal estate blurred the political differences between the 1930s and the 1940s: in the mid-1940s vast segments of society were prepared to accept (or at least to be less surprised by) the planned economy; the public mood and the economic structure on the eve of the communist takeover were pregnant (or infected) with collectivist solutions.

This readiness had intellectual roots, too. The educational landscape in economic sciences was dominated by the German Historical School and narrative versions of the subjective theory of value. The academic establishment taught courses on political economy (Danailov 1906, 1934; Tzankov 1931; Mishaikov 1933) inspired by Wilhelm Roscher and Gustav Schmoller, and explicitly distanced itself from William Jevons, Léon Walras, or Alfred Marshall. Although the neoclassical and the marginalist approach were duly presented, they were devoid of their formal and mathematical apparatus and considered alien to domestic realities. Instead, great attention was devoted to *economic systems*, that is, to holistic views about the socioeconomic order ranging from *individualistic* to *socialist* models. As a rule, those comparisons produced both eclectic syntheses and compromising promotions of a *third way*. But in the 1930s the center of gravity shifted toward explicitly statist solutions, *dirigiste* economic management, and *harmonious coordination* between private and public principles. The growing ideological influence of the Third Reich accentuated the drive. The legal system was not an obstacle. Well integrated in academia, with eminent scholars apparently committed to its basic values and principles, civil law proved to be flexible enough to adopt—when necessary—the appropriate rules for expropriation. An example of a "lawful" attack against property rights was the spoliation of the Jews through a series of anti-Semitic laws enacted and implemented between 1941and 1944.

Actually, decisive changes were forthcoming, and it is not by chance that their inherent course was identified by the most articulate Bulgarian economist at the time. Having graduated from the (American) Robert College in Istanbul and from the London School of Economics in 1934, Assen Christophoroff originated from a very different background than the academic monks of Sofia University. He was the solitary exponent of the Anglo-Saxon tradition, declaring himself a pupil of J. M. Keynes and L. von Mises, and an adept of the Cambridge and Vienna schools. Back in Sofia, he joined the Statistical Institute for Economic Research (SIER) at Sofia University—a center of excellence with a modern positivist program for the study of the Bulgarian economy and thus an enclave in the local scholarly milieu.[1] In 1943 Christophoroff published a monograph on the war economy where he lucidly indicated that one of the most important consequences of "wartime capitalistic socialism" would be the appeal "of the seemingly limitless possibilities of the central political authority to regulate, re-channel, and restructure the economic activities, existing institutions, and the very outlines of the economic and political systems" (Christophoroff 1943, 360).

Despite the lofty positions of the communists in the government who emerged from the September 1944 coup, they had to share power with *bourgeois* parties, with more moderate elements, and with members of the military-political club *Zveno*.[2] The eviction of non-communist factions and a total ban on the opposition were performed during the next three years. In this interlude Christophoroff espoused a typically reformist position, while teaching political economy and publishing subtle analyses on postwar stabilization issues. In early 1945 he candidly formulated his views on the prospective economic order, reflecting the dominant expectations of the liberal intelligentsia and other groups of society. Those circles cherished the illusion that a kind of mixed economy could be established with a friendly, complementary functioning of different sectors. Christophoroff associated the ideology of the new government with the program proposed in 1937 by A. C. Pigou, who had formulated a draft for a relatively bold transformation of capitalism (progressive income tax, inheritance tax, generous social expenses, control over the industry, nationalization of some sectors, investment planning). The crucial question was at what point did the reformed system become a *non-capitalist* economy. Christophoroff's answer was that Pigou does not transgress the "main trait of individualism—free prices as regulators of the production and consumption" (Christophoroff 1945).

The new economy was imagined by him as a coexistence of a substantial segment pertaining to the state, another (also sizable) segment owned by the cooperatives and the (no-less-important) private sector. Christophoroff was not naïve and knew that this idyllic distribution—doomed to reappear in the terminal years of the communist regime during the 1980s—was an ideal construct. On the one hand, even before 1944 he acknowledged that without perfect information it is impossible to assess empirically the superiority (in terms of rationality and effectiveness) of one or another economic/political system.[3] On the other hand, he was aware that at the end of the day the configuration of a property's stakes is not an exercise in comparative rationality but the outcome of social forces. In 1947, Christophoroff reminded that "the lack of individual security, coupled with the existing inequality of opportunities imparts considerable charm to every proposal for the reform of the economic system" (Christophoroff 1947, 224). By rejecting economic liberalism, the *ordinary citizen* is ready to embrace in turn state interventionism, even more *dirigisme*, and ultimately collectivism (i.e., socialism/communism) that buries "the last remains of economic individualism and of capitalism" (Christophoroff 1947, 224).

The fulfillment of the prophecy was a question of months. In September 1947 the Paris Peace Treaty with Bulgaria entered into force and, hands free, the Communist Party took complete control. In October 1947 Christophoroff was fired from the university;[4] on December 24 the industrial companies and the financial sector were nationalized. It is worth mentioning that the motives for the law did not contain ideological slogans or class hatred but just technocratic concerns like the rationalization of the banking system, money circulation, or the preservation of bank secrecy.

THE ROYAL PATH

After 1947, *almost all* of the leftovers of private property (*chastna sobstvenost*),[5] together with *all* non-communist doctrines on ownership, were eliminated. The attitudes on the matter were carefully instigated and/or closely monitored by the ideological apparatus. Truly independent sources of ideas were nonexistent. Even the most outspoken economists from academia were coopted in working groups and commissions at different levels and thus involved in the political skirmishes. Controversies took place *ex ante* (the official line's logic could not be questioned publicly) or concerned the gaps between rhetoric and implementation. Following several rounds of compromises and political sanctions, the ideas always coagulated into party decisions. *Theory was engraved into statistics and into the approved policies*: the figures summarize the evolution of the ownership structure, a mirror image of the prevailing conceptual views. Without surprise, collectivistic forms exerted total dominance in communist Bulgaria. From 57 percent of national income in 1959, the share of state property reached 87 percent in 1989. It was virtually exclusive in industry (87 percent of output in 1948 and 93 percent in 1974), in other major *productive* sectors (except agriculture where cooperative forms were important), and in finance.

The canonical doctrine on socialist ownership (*sotzialisticheska sobstvenost*)[6] crystallized in the early 1950s as a literal replica of the twists in Soviet dogma. Until the mid-1960s, teaching political economy was entirely based on Soviet textbooks. Successive editions of the famous tract by Konstantin Ostrovitianov from 1954 and its following editions (four till 1963) were translated and remained the official reference. Only at the end of the 1950s were some shy pretentions for singularity formulated. They cautiously suggested emphasizing certain particularities of the Bulgarian transition to communism and to surmount the simple copying of the Muscovite curriculum but vehemently denied any intention to propose a *Bulgarian* political economy. The first autochthonous *official course* was launched in 1966 (Dobrev 1966). Although during the following 20 years reviews of the syllabi were recurrent, the revisions were of limited importance and did not challenge the traditional collection of dogmas.

Among them, ownership occupied a central place as the foundation of the whole construct. The Bulgarian idiosyncrasies boiled down to the proudly presented but residual importance of the cooperative sector. The leading position of state property (*darjavna sobstvenost*), however, was never questioned. A claim (in the mid-1960s) to eliminate the chapters on ownership from textbooks on the grounds that Marx's *Capital* does not contain them was promptly discarded. The editorial rule for the manuals was to conceal professional controversies and to present a polished version that ultimately followed a strict party line. Thus, during the economic reforms of the 1960s, this subject was presented parsimoniously, fully compliant with the official wording and steering clear of polemics. In turn, from the early 1970s on, the *centralist-statist* view regained control. Finally, the last version adjusted the old rhetoric to the *market line*. Actually, the building blocks and stylistic codes remained untouched, and until 1989 entire segments (in particular, on ownership) migrated from text to text. In Bulgaria, unlike in some other communist countries, the effort to produce a textbook of political economy was never perceived as a catalytic experience aiming at challenging the intellectual status quo or as an opportunity to convey nonconformist messages. Rather the contrary: since the 1960s the publishing of manuals proliferated as an inoffensive and lucrative business trailing behind the official canon and eluding any risk of confrontation.

Ownership studies promptly developed into a specific field of the academic political economy's small world. Papers, monographs, conferences, and discussions among the faculty were continuously dedicated to the topic. The issue ranked high in the ideological sector, too, and deserved the consideration of the party apparatchiks. This exuberant theorizing and erratic political concerns produced recurring controversies and publications.

Endless discussions were generated by playing with the nuances of the terms *owner*, *manager*, *usus*, *usus fructus,* and *abusus.* Those notions composed a universal language able to express alternative positions in a tolerated perimeter. Roman law's triad was employed as a convenient frame for debating the quadrature of the circle: how to reconcile state ownership with the *law of value* and the obvious need of pecuniary exchange of commodities; the futile balance between centralism and autonomy of the enterprises; profits, wages, and the primary incomes' repartition biases; and how to appease both the plan and the market. The same set of constructs was permutated for the argumentation of everything—from contradictory hypotheses to hollow eclecticism. Personal preferences, particular accents, or the adopted chain of reasoning could lead either to *pro-market* positions or to orthodox views. The setting, for instance, could be occasionally employed (in 1968) for a hardly disguised advocacy of Yugoslav self-management (*samoupravlenie*), presented as a model where the ultimate owner (*the people through the state*) rents its assets to the enterprises without undermining the socialist character of the economy (Belev 1968). Another, particularly speculative derivative in this rearrangement of concepts was deliberation over whether ownership constitutes a *distinct* or a *central* component, or the very *totality* of the *relations of production.* Those discussions among political economists had little practical incidences. To declare that the enterprise is the manager/user of the state asset was irrelevant if the regulations in the hands of the planning institutions prevented the management or use of the factors of production.

Major swings between the reformist and conservative stance always provoked more or less comprehensive reappraisals of the approach to *management* but not to the existence of collectivist ownership. After a retreat from the reform experiments of the 1960s, direct top-down management dominated the scene. Despite the obstinate presence of monetary transactions, during the 1970s centralistic solutions were promoted on the grounds of technocratic and efficiency arguments in favor of greater state-owned organizational units. The shift included both agriculture and industry, where *branch associations* were transformed (at the expense of enterprises) into the ultimate subjects of financial autonomy. The next step (from the early 1980s) moved the pendulum in the opposite direction. The party coined a new slogan ("The state is the owner; the workers' collectivities are the managers") and the academic debate was reactivated. New tones appeared with a stress on individuals, collectives, and managers' interests. It was observed, in particular, that the latter's *natural* risk-avoiding mindset set them in opposition to the proposed more decentralized schemes (Miloshevski 1985, 13). The period coincided with a growing attention to the establishment of small enterprises which (in response to global trend) was seen as the next magic answer to socialist shortages.

The mainstream assumed that the two forms of existing property (state and cooperative) had a socialist character since they excluded exploitation. Of the two species, state property, however, was considered superior and more mature, better corresponding to the alleged trend of *socialization, cooperation, and specialization of productive forces*. Cooperatives differed from state-owned entities in their genetic link to private property, in specific organizational principles, or in the compensation system allowing lesser guarantees for remuneration and certain income differentiation. The received wisdom was that progress would erase linearly the initial differences, cooperatives were doomed to disappear, and the two forms would harmoniously merge into a single *communist ownership*.

As a matter of fact, the process proved to be lengthy and contradictory. It took almost 30 years to impose—by administrative means—a plain state profile on agricultural cooperatives. They were gradually integrated in the planning process, which meant aligning their institutional management and revenue distribution to the corresponding standards in state enterprises. At the turn of the 1970s the compulsory inclusion of the peasants' cooperatives into *agro-industrial complexes* (APK) gave birth to large-scale state-owned businesses. For a few years cooperatives preserved their juridical and financial autonomy inside those entities, but soon (1975) they were reduced to mere APK branches. Yet, the cooperative sector kept its institutional existence as a privileged and attractive sinecure, a political ally and administrative support closely watched by the party.

Regardless of these developments, it was obvious that the outcome was not to be the dream of communist property, and in the early 1970s ideologues adjourned *sine die* its official promulgation. In an ironic historical revenge, in the twilight of the regime, cooperatives were completely rehabilitated and were promised true rejuvenation. The predetermined elimination of the *inferior* by the *superior* form was forgotten. One of the most active former apologists of the "merger theory" did not hesitate to proclaim that the cooperative arrangement of production should become a universal form in the socialist economy and that "our entire society will turn into a cooperative organization" (Aroyo 1989, 32). The party's platform of 1987 embarked on a vocal promotion of multiplicity in the types of property, while rejecting alienated, *anonymous* ownership. Only fair competition between the different forms was to exist in the new world.

The specific approach and stylistics of the discussions on ownership in communist Europe secluded them from the global mainstream. In Bulgaria, the leading intellectual influence came, of course, from Soviet academia. There was no nuance there that did not produce an echo in the country. To take part in those controversies was safe and the corresponding disputes outlined the boundaries of *free* critical thinking. Curiosity about other socialist states was occasional and the tone of the comments closely matched the party's official political attitude vis-à-vis the corresponding partner. It is telling in this respect that the first draft (August 1963) of Bulgaria's economic reforms was produced via copying and pasting the Yugoslav self-managerial model by a group of economists sent to Belgrade with this assignment during the bilateral rapprochement (Petrov 2016, 5). Eventually, successive versions took a different shape. They veered from the original due to considerations of domestic politics, the 1964 changeover in Moscow, and—for the termination of the reforms—the effects of the Prague Spring.

The West seemed an improbable source of inspiration in this field. The Iron Curtain, however, was not completely opaque. It was harmless, for example, to integrate the usual slang on ownership into some fashionable terminology borrowed and adapted from *universalistic* theories. The transfer was anything but rigorous and rested on poorly understood or misinterpreted sources. It was in this way, for instance, that the issue was adorned with cybernetic or systems management concepts without touching on basic Marxist constraints.[7] It happened, too, that—in tune the well-known story of Molière's prose-speaking Mr. Jourdain—the discussions hit problems debated in the West without realizing the implicit convergence. The recurring topics of how to manage socialist property, to motivate managers, or to coordinate the interests of the stakeholders were actually part and parcel of agency theory; the most fervent defender of central planning, Evgeni Mateev, wrote about ownership as an institution, ignoring the existence of new institutional economics.

In reality, chaotic fragments of *bourgeois thinking* served both sides. The *centralist* camp could support its claims by referring to technological trends of complexity and concentration or by pointing out examples of indicative and corporate governance planning. J. K. Galbraith's work and the concept of technostructure were particularly appreciated. In his recently published memoirs Georgi Petrov (a champion of the reforms of the 1960s) confesses to the shock and revelation he experienced in 1970–1971 during a three-month fellowship in France. After a definitive dropping of the reformist project, he found inspiration in the statist French economy. This model seemed to confirm the compatibility of market relations with a heavily regulated price system, and hence was read as an invigorating proof of the feasibility of *regulated market socialism*. This second breath of optimism prolonged his illusion that the market can coexist with *sacrosanct* socialist ownership—a view Petrov shared until 1989 (Petrov 2016, 83, 88, 90). He admits in his memoir that he only started to read Milton Friedman and to compile a textbook on corporate finance (the matter he was teaching for decades) based on American authors in the 1990s.

ON THE MARGINS

State property reigned unconditionally but even the communist world was imperfect and for different reasons the party (and political economy) had to abide the presence of impure forms. Despite its official consecration as *socialist property*, cooperative ownership (*kooperativna sobstvenost*) was the most ambiguous sector on the margins. The heir of an old tradition, it experienced remarkable development since the early 20th century. Its economic weight in pre-communist Bulgaria was impressive, an important financial and institutional infrastructure was built around it, and its dense web had permeated the whole social texture. The cooperative establishment was an extremely influential lobby benefiting from the consensual support of the political elites.

The prewar charm of the cooperative idea and its eventual consistency with the party's ideological line constituted a precious asset for the communist regime. The economic rationale behind it was the perception of cooperativism as an adequate form for a society characterized by chronic capital shortages; as a modernization of the poor seemingly within reach. The requirement for limited initial resources was attractive, and even more so when there was a possibility to obtain access to credit against the unlimited collective liability of its members. This model (of German and Austrian origin) spread the illusion of a kind of *capitalism without capital*; cooperatives became the preferred alternative to shareholding; a union of persons was more appealing and less demanding than an alliance of capitalists. Such choices entailed implicit costs in terms of economic behavior and culture. They predetermined the narrow scope of the ventures, undermined market rationality, corrupted credit flows, amalgamated incompatible activities, avoided the liquidation of nonviable entities, and thus generated recurrent bailouts, permanent transfers of losses, and budget subsidies. In addition, the dense network was an ideal milieu for political brokerage whose segments were captured by different political parties, including the communists.

More importantly for the current discussion, cooperative views developed into an elaborate anti-capitalist ideology. As the economic analyst and businessman Stoyan Bochev put it critically in 1928, "While cooperatives are used everywhere [outside Bulgaria] as correctives of capitalism, here they are utilized as an antipode, an exit and an antithesis of the capitalistic stage in the economic evolution [...]. [We] desire to obtain the wealth provided by the bourgeois capitalistic order but without capitalism." Bochev complained that capitalism is alien to the "national psychology" and "people are fascinated by collectivistic and statist theories" (Bochev 1928, 514). Two decades later this circumventing strategy was perfectly fit to be recycled for the propaganda of the new regime.[8]

The cooperative movement constituted a natural platform for different antiliberal currents in Bulgarian society. Its ideologues stigmatized profit-seeking (they favored the increase of personal incomes) and presented this form as a messianic instrument for social harmony. Cooperatives were entrusted to cultivate among their members collectivism, and egalitarianism—to fight greed, speculation, and other capitalist sins. They saw to mold *a new archetype* possessing ascetic integrity, embedding and spreading the virtues of communal life. Those normative qualities had to foster a sense of moral exclusivity and superiority. The target—as in communism—was nothing less than to change human nature.

Aggressive indoctrination and proselytism promoted its values (for instance, "brotherly collaboration and mutual aid") and its behavioral patterns that were going to become part of the new order's ideology. Loyalty to the cooperative was as important (and its break as severely despised) as future loyalty to the party. Cooperativism produced reams of optimistic reports and agitprop materials. This distinct economic subculture reached the status of a *state ideology* with all the corresponding implications: the intent to introduce compulsory membership; cooptation and selection of applicants; deep suspicion toward *subversive* acts and thoughts, with the corresponding sanctions; widespread reporting on private and social life. Finally, the preeminence of social over individual goals allowed for the sustaining of the idea that "property loses its absolute meaning" (Kepov 1931, xxv).

After 1944 such a legacy was more than welcome. The myth of the pre-communist movement was prized and advertised, even if cooperative ownership was being profoundly transformed into a form without content. In fact, the new cooperatives were *productive*, that is, members contributed their land and other capital assets, while before the war that type of contribution was relatively rare (the majority being credit, consumer, and trade establishments). It was precisely this forceful surrendering of land and assets that provoked the strongest opposition during the 1950s and extended the process over more than a decade.

The main inconvenience of cooperative ownership for the regime was the private property rights of the members. They were never legally abolished and the most pressing political and ideological aim was to eradicate any residual *economic* bond with the initial personal capital stake. Nationalization of large estates was carried out with the 1946 agrarian reform. Until 1957, the rest of the land was almost completely collectivized while the members preserved their deeds. This arrangement conserved the *formal* ownership claims: plots were inherited (which proved essential in the post-1989 restitution), albeit the right of disposal was strictly limited. Selling, exchanging, or gifting inside the cooperative was allowed in principle, but if the owner decided to leave the organization he received outside parcels of much lower quality in exchange. In practice, agricultural land lost its status of economic asset, the market vanished and the capitalization of private property was gradually suppressed. In 1953 the cooperatives' national congress decided to renounce the rent paid to the proprietors for the use of their land.[9] The productive capital underwritten to the cooperatives by their members was physically irrecoverable or compensable only at penalizing terms. All this meant an economic (not legal) nationalization. Additionally, *spontaneous* donations to the state of land incorporated in the cooperatives were widespread. The establishment of the APK further diluted the tenuous link to the original land property: the members of the former cooperatives had to offer their land to the state and their capital was transferred to the new entity. Not unexpectedly, a regaining of interest toward the political and economic potential of the cooperative idea at the end of the 1980s occurred again in the old, prewar tradition: as a palliative and prudently distant rapprochement to private (not at all to capitalist) property.

The second polluted area which was politically/theoretically tolerated was the private *use* of land. Neither the cooperative nor the APK had ever subsisted alone. They were surrounded by a dense array of *household plots* granted to their members/personnel but also to other solicitors (workers or employees in the cities). Nearly all citizens in the country were entitled to receive such limited parcels. They created areas of intense private farming where productivity exceeded by far than in the state/cooperative sector. The substantial surplus over personal consumption was sold. Tenants could not acquire the plots and the relations with the state/cooperative enterprises (distribution of the land, labor inputs, remunerations, social security allocations, planning, and purchase of the output) were officially regulated. But designed as an accepted complement to the evident vacuum left by the shortages of the *socialist sector*, the plots were actually exploited as private ventures.[10] By the mid-1980s a great deal of the tenants actually devoted most of their time to this activity, and many hired people in violation of the presumption that the parcels were strictly personal. During the terminal years of the regime new forms of private usage and leasing of the land were introduced. They extended market practices without redesigning the official legal ownership structure.

Finally, the only long-term asset allowed to be owned by households was dwellings. Bulgaria had an extremely high proportion (over 90 percent) of privately owned homes, but the handling of this personal property was severely restricted. Although they could be inherited, the acquisition (in fact, distribution) of homes was centralized, and their free selling was not allowed (municipalities were obligatory intermediaries and prices were fixed). Leasing was regulated, but it constituted an expanding private service, encouraged by the state in order to promote tourism. In 1973 stricter quantitative restrictions were imposed with respect to the amount of living space owned.

At the same time, the legal protection of home ownership was real. This was in part a sequel to the petit-bourgeois pre-communist urban social structure. The new regime realized the strong corrupting potential (for individuals and for entire social strata, especially the *nomenklatura* and intelligentsia) of the controlled repartition of private homes in the cities. Of course, the authorities kept at their disposal a number of confiscation tools. With political and social "motives," they used them on a large scale during the immediate post-1944 years. Later on, specific categories of the population were recurrently affected. Direct or indirect spoliations of homes were organized against political émigrés or against Bulgarian Turks who were forced to leave the country in three successive waves. In all those cases property rights were trampled.

THROUGH THE LOOKING GLASS

By definition, communism rules out any *private business*. In reality, this norm was infringed upon on a daily basis, but the political economy of socialism was unequipped to conceptualize the phenomenon. During the entire lifespan of the regime, economists furtively glanced through the looking glass without ever understanding Alice's alternative world.

In strictly legal terms, private economic activities in Bulgaria, as in the other communist countries, were not completely forbidden and agriculture was not their sole field. The 1947 Constitution nominally allowed private property and businesses, whereas the 1971 Constitution omitted them and reduced ownership to its three *socialist* components—state, collective (cooperative property; and that of public organizations), and personal (*lichna sobstvenost*). The doctrine, however, considered the remnant of the private sector as a realm of the condemned and a source of deviant behavior. Its scope was seen as a necessary evil and an indicator of communist society's immaturity. Actually, during the first two decades of the regime, private property was submitted to ruthless and systematic crowding. After the *transition period* mildly pragmatic positions were adopted, without withdrawing from the basic ideological tenets. Modest openings occurred in parallel with the economic reforms of the mid-1960s, and mid-1980s, while the most radical steps were made in 1988–1989.

The *New System for Planning and Economic Management* (1963–1968), which constituted the first major attempt to modify the functioning of the communist economy, did not address ownership. Minor concessions were made to microscale private activities. Georgi Petrov, the most enthusiastic supporter of the reform, conveyed his messages by observing the Marxist syllogisms and advocated the utmost *autonomy* of the enterprises; their right to govern the distribution of the earned revenues; (not exclusively) free contractual prices; and uniform and stable taxes and financial regulators. He assumed that the supply response to those managerial innovations would be immediate but they remained packed in the frame of state property which remained unchallenged.

Although Petrov was an active member of the working groups drafting the reforms,[11] their course never uncompromisingly followed his recommendations.[12] In retrospect, he honestly admits the limits of his approach to ownership and the fact that playing the reformist game meant being instrumentalized in the power struggles of the party's factions. He recognizes, too, that in spite of the apparently extremist tone of his proposals they did not transcend the threshold (Petrov 2016, 90, 126–27). It was not a question of (self-)censorship but of intellectual horizon. Private property was simply inconceivable against a background of Marxist indoctrination, within a conceptual and educational context that shaped the scholarly community, and within a closed cognitive milieu and political setting.

Academic political economy did not tackle the private sector directly. It is revealing that its first and only thorough review (in a detailed comparative perspective with other socialist countries) was published merely in 1985 (Popov 1985). The author, Nikola Popov, was a well-positioned scholar sticking entirely to the professional mindset.[13] His study transparently disclosed the limits of what could be said about this topic in the academic community. The title itself enunciated the verdict that the private dimension is doomed to fade out in a socialist economy and Popov reconfirmed the fundamental incompatibility between them; he preferred to write about *private economic activities* instead of the private sector. His attitude was defensive and not proactive; the text was compensatory, devised to *justify* the existence of a phenomenon, not to extend its field. Hints that (with good intention) could be interpreted as benevolent are the acknowledgment of private activities' necessity (even by gently accepting that part of them were illegal). He predicted, for example, that their existence would last well into the "mature socialist economy" due to unavoidable chaotic elements introduced by *subjective* management errors and by elusive knowledge about *objective* economic trends, and criticized past *premature* rushes to eliminate any private activity. Unlike the centralists who took for granted the elimination of all recurrent shortages by the planned system, Popov appealed to overcome minor shortages legally by means of private activities. But his attitude was in no way a radical (not to mention, privatization) agenda. It was just a palliative proposal combining, for example, a positive opinion on joint ventures with the West with warnings against making too favorable steps in favor of the private sector in politically *unreliable* socialist countries.

Lawyers, criminologists, the police, and the judiciary were much better prepared to verbalize this reality in a sober and commonsensical way. Operating hand in hand with life's dark side, they were unconstrained by doctrinal normative prescriptions and had direct contact with events perceived as economic crimes. A review of Popov's monograph by Nikolai Vachev, professor of law, was particularly telling. He expressed undeniably more down-to-earth positions—not completely cut-off from pre-communist rule of law—than the reviewed.

The reviewer presented a great variety of open or covert private activities and drew a far more realistic economic sketch. He could skip the (mandatory for political economists) sophisticated reasoning by asserting that shortages are simply the outcome of ignoring the law of supply and demand. From another perspective, the review highlighted how the accretion of legislation actually had built an almost comprehensive legal regime, which regulated (thus legitimized) a great number of small-scale individual and/or private endeavors (Vachev 1986, 30). The rules recognized the right of private possession and the use of *small means of production* with an explicit ban of capitalist (*exploitation*) ownership, excluded the hiring of workers and allowed family employment, and introduced differentiated instructions in several sectors. Alongside the *personal plots* in agriculture, specific guidelines overseen by different administrative bodies were introduced for retail trade, services, tourism, or handicrafts. The condescending conclusion was suggestive about the epistemological potential of economic thought in this field. "It seems," wrote the reviewer, "that the challenge to accept the private activities concerns mainly the theoreticians. In front of their slowly reacting view private activities are developing robustly without waiting for the 'scientific rationalization' of the phenomenon" (Vachev 1986, 34).

This approach touched a murky zone. On the one hand, it included the institutionalized interface between state property and other (collectivistic or individual) forms of ownership such as individual plots. On the other, it comprised some legal private activities, essentially renting out of private homes. It also included the area consisting of a vast and ever-present *grey economy* where formal property rights were a fiction and the self-made *socialist entrepreneur* was born. No wonder that the qualitative and quantitative traces of this sphere were absent from the academic literature and official research programs. Ideology simply could not cope with the existence of the underground economy in a supposedly planned system. Factual evidence about those activities was dispersed in confidential reports of the police, in the files of the courts, or in the spreadsheets of the monobank where indirect data were extant as residues, errors, or omissions in the never-balanced accounts of the money flows (Avramov 2009).[14]

Finally, East-West economic contacts gradually expanded Bulgaria's experience with private property. Joint forms proliferated from the early 1980s, but with a careful split between the investors: any true merger between the state and foreign capital was avoided. If such ventures generated a literature dealing with legal and economic technicalities, the studies rarely discussed conceptual problems related to ownership. Those encounters in foreign companies present in the country, as well as in Bulgarian firms abroad, provided possibilities for learning-by-doing in a market context, with capitalist partners. It is questionable, however, whether the participants acquired authentic experience as private owners to the extent that they were simple employees in name, with the security of the state as shareholder.

During the regime's last years, private property was treated more frequently in academic scholarship. The party spurred this impulse, seeking palliative instruments to remain in power. But the whole process was plagued with inconsistencies, notional misunderstandings, and pervasive confusion between ownership and management issues.

It could have been expected that bolder proposals for privatization would come from the emerging radical approach to the country's most pressing economic problems shaped by a compact and clearly identified group of economists.[15] Their diagnosis and its policy implications were not a program draft but an *informal alternative reform project,* the originality of which was twofold: while the reforms of the 1960s were a pure product of the party's machine, this project was generated by an autonomous research endeavor; they overtly applied neoclassical instruments in a general equilibrium setting without trying to twist or truncate their messages.

Many of these economists avoided ownership as they considered the topic the most speculative emanation of official political economy. In another escapist posture, the group skipped the usual discussions of *economic mechanisms*. Ventsislav Antonov pointed out that each new version of the regulations had simply redesigned and reproduced the old system with a concomitant rise in its entropy. Consecutive reform blueprints were acceptable for the regime because they preserved direct planning and continued to subordinate to it all behavioral rules. The group started by problematizing in a dis/equilibrium perspective the policy objectives of the regime, mainly its ideologically motivated *growth fetishism*. Although property rights were missing from this initial agenda, its evolution introduced them implicitly. By the end of the 1980s, attention shifted to inflation and monetary stabilization, that is, to critical problems underlying the growth/structural outlook. Antonov clearly indicated that from this point of view *structural changes* signify a readjustment of relative prices, including those of capital and labor (Antonov 1989; 1990). Thus, the proximate aim was to monetize the economy, which could only happen through price liberalization. The unveiling of the disequilibria in monetary terms was forcibly a *synchronic* operation including the commodity, credit, and foreign exchange markets, interest rates, the government budget, and incomes. But it also presumed granting radical autonomy to enterprises.

The last step remained undiscussed before 1990 and ignored the role of such forces as political instincts of self-preservation, vested institutional interests, or social structure. The 1960s and the 1980s met at this point, as both relied on economic automatisms and disregarded the imperative of ownership transformation. The two major reformist agendas in communist Bulgaria had quite different intellectual settings but converged in their benign neglect of the need for dismantling socialist ownership. Understandably, a massive turn toward private property was unimaginable in the climate of the first period. Even if it was conceivable by the late 1980s, the accent was put on growth, monetary, and stabilization questions. Very soon this blindness and the explosive potential embedded in the coming property changeover had to be realized.

A likely alternative window to private ownership in academia was the study of capitalist economies. In the few papers dedicated to property, however, subversive messages were missing. Postwar nationalization in the West were routinely denounced as measures in favor of the capitalists; popular shareholding and the *managerial revolution* were regularly dismissed; analyses of the grey economy by Sovietologists were rejected, although they allowed for a timid acknowledgment of some state ownership; and privatization during the Thatcher/Reagan era did not attract much attention. It was only in 1988–1989 that property patterns in developed countries emerged as relevant in some utilitarian sense. The official conversion to *socialist shareholding* fostered an interest in different aspects of Western reality. Knowledge about the capitalist economy had already lost part of its ideological connotation. Instead, it had acquired direct applicability and the previous strict divide between communism and capitalism was being slowly replenished. But, as a whole, the profession was unprepared to offer concrete solutions and financial details commissioned from the top: outside the chorus of amateur and ignorant voices, common sense, and informed opinions were scarce.

The decisive impetus came from the official reform agenda. In 1987 the party launched the most ambitious reshuffling of macro-management. In a last effort to inject efficient incentives into the ailing system, the regime proceeded to conduct a vast rearrangement of the organizational structure of the economy. The first step was the pompous "transfer of the state property to the collectivities of workers [i.e., to the enterprises] for its management (*stopanisvane*)." Decided in July 1987, it was sealed by a solemn declaration of the Parliament in the autumn of the same year. The core of this move was the proclaimed shift to full territorial/entrepreneurial self-government/management (*samoupravlenie*) and autonomy, accompanied by a series of deregulatory measures. Their inconsistency, coupled with the lack of credibility and enthusiasm on the part of the *collectivities*, led to a second round decided in December 1988.[16] The freedom of establishing *firms* was presented as a newly found panacea that would at last eliminate the superfluous intermediate management levels of the economy.

The master file of the party's policy was Decree (*Oukaz*) 56 enacted in January 1989. The document was an ersatz corporate law, legitimating on paper all forms of property/companies (including foreign). Some space was left for private initiatives and *individual labor activities*, shareholding was introduced, and personal pecuniary interests/motivation suddenly became respectable. At the same time, severe constraints preventing the functioning of a genuine market economy were patent everywhere in the legal compendium. *Labor shares* could be issued exclusively to the company's employees and up to a limited amount (one percent of the firm's capital); they (as all the shares were to be owned by citizens) were only nominative. Strongly biased principles were applied to the interactions with the state. The proclaimed self-management was subordinated to the plan, to government procurement, to centralized remuneration rules, and to regulations obeying arbitrary *strategic* socioeconomic development goals (material, financial, and Forex balances; macroeconomic structural changes; the international division of labor and socialist integration). Prices were supposed to be contractual but remained fixed or limited for *very important products for the living standard*. No real foreign exchange market was foreseen. Despite the seemingly liberal regime for foreign investments, numerous licensing procedures were needed, repatriation of profits in foreign exchange was actually restricted, and real estate property was incomplete (excluding land).

An energetic campaign for the establishment of shareholding companies was set in motion. For months the government was occupied with decisions approving corporate by-laws, appointing members of the managing boards, and registering cross-transfers of capitals between state enterprises. By June 1989, 390 state owned, 132 communal, 36 cooperative, eight owned by public organizations, and 2,812 *citizen's* firms were registered. But that was in no way a threat to the leading role of state property. Guaranteed blocking quotas were introduced for its stake (lower in retail trade, services, and agriculture), individuals' firms were not allowed to acquire shares from the stock of state firms, and restitution of agricultural land was not even mentioned.

By now it is widely accepted that those steps laid the foundation for the subsequent post-communist expansion of private economic activity, of the first private entities, and of insiders' corrosion/privatization of state property. It is commonly agreed that the numerous leakages opened by these measures (their antecedents in the grey economy could be found much earlier) served an eventual generalized siphoning off of assets and that they molded the proto-models of the symbiosis/collusion between state and private sector during the muddy years of 1990–1996.

Politically speaking, this was not more than a rhetorical change, its credibility was very low, and public skepticism about the good faith of the party-state, which continued to keep all the command tools, was extremely high. According to a well-established tradition, *public* scholarly debate followed suit *after* the political decisions. The proceedings of a series of conferences dedicated to different aspects of property were published *in extenso*. The eternal academic protagonists in the *ownership discussion* adjusted their tone without altering the instruments or the concepts employed. The stylistic change, however, had some effects and the verbal critique from *the market side* (most often quite superficial) was mildly censored, even rewarded. Georgi Petrov, for instance, had no difficulties to voice his objections against the inconsistent way economic reforms were implemented after 1987 and (in their more radical wording) from January 1989. The blame literally was recycled from his criticism from the 1960s. But he also could formulate a full-fledged self-management program.[17] More unusually, Hristo Vladov evoked for the first time the *socialist calculation debate*. Surprisingly, he adopted a positive mood, accepting that Ludwig von Mises was right to question the feasibility of state ownership and bureaucratic management. He stated that the Lange-Taylor ideas to imitate the market were unviable, and that was proven by the failure of optimal planning in the 1960s (Vladov 1989, 41–42). Ventseslav Dimitrov boldly defined the ritual transfer of property to workers as an agitprop gesture failing to touch the core problem, that is, the right to sell the assets (Dimitrov 1989, 18–20). Based on his acquaintance with the financial structure of capitalist economies, Dimitrov pointed out the incoherence of the party's official model where shares were conceived not as authentic ownership titles but only as documents transferring limited managerial rights. He outlined a series of obligatory reforms of the financial sector (establishment of full-fledged commercial banks and of a stock exchange; dismantling of the monobank) that were not really envisaged by the authorities (Most of those measures were introduced after 1990.). But even from this point of view he discussed only two concrete schemes: the establishment of holdings for the state-owned firms and the technicalities of the "labor shares" (unrestricted dividends, possible options for debt-equity swaps, etc.).

Uncensored debate about property rights was definitely over when it approached the ultimate taboo: selling or acquiring state-owned assets to or by individuals. To trespass this barrier meant to challenge the monopoly of power and (for the ideologues) to enter capitalism. Consciously or not, this step was never made in Bulgaria. If leaving some breadth to private activity was still bearable under certain circumstances, its active extension at the expense of the state through *privatization* was unpronounced until the fall of Todor Zhivkov's regime in November 1989.

The concept was ideologically unpalatable and lacked any theoretical support whatsoever. One example among the many symptoms of this situation was the never-ending discussion whether the *absolute* rent from land was completely eliminated. The problem fed a myriad of papers searching meticulously for any hidden vestige of capitalization of private property by the cooperatives' members, and trying to split it from the more acceptable *differential* rent. In another form, the subject reappeared during the 1980s when many orthodox economists were obsessed with the dynamic development of individual activities in the rural sector or elsewhere. Considered as a dangerous deviation from the *socialist principle of income distribution according to labor's contribution*, the phenomenon was defined as private profiteering from state assets (not far from reality) and an intolerable source of income differentiation.

The practice, the conceptual design, and the archival evidence attest that the official rhetoric after 1987 had no substance. Without entering the overdebated issue about the existence/absence of a premeditated master plan for post-communist domination, let's offer two expressive quotations. At the climax of the campaign for the incorporation of autonomous, state-owned joint-stock companies during the summer of 1989, the Politburo member overlooking the security sector (a former interior minister) instructed the Ministry of Interior's staff that

> the open economy supposes an even greater and substantial role of State security in those processes [...]. Our main problem is the rapid elaboration of a new approach for the 'inter-penetration' of State Security with the newly created firms. We have literally 'to melt' and 'to sink' in those structures without dismantling our organizational links, informational systems, and interaction under different forms of cover [...]. We have [...] to earn a new place for our staff in the economic system, to assure its tangible presence and its influence, in the desired direction, on the economic development of our country in the modern world. (Ministry of Interior 1989, 101–02, 115)

At the same time, the party's leader Zhivkov was quoted as saying that the management of the firms could engage *aged comrades working in other fields if they stay on the right party positions*. There is no need to search in those statements for any grand vision about private ownership and/or capitalism. They simply indicate a definite reluctance to abandon the communists' grip over the economy. The *nominated* actors actually played key roles in the nascent version of Bulgarian capitalism and in the transformation of the political into economic power.

Let us remark here that Decree 56 did not even mention private property explicitly. Instead, the employed terms were *citizens' ownership* (*firmi na grajdani*) or (partial) workers' shareholding (*trudovi akzii*). On the other side, the most active supporters of a redesign of property rights found real difficulty in imagining how all this was going to happen and, in particular, how the financial flows between institutional sectors would assure privatization of the overwhelming state-held assets. According to the most optimistic expectations, the financial capacity did not allow for the transformation of more than five to six percent of the capital into private shareholders' equity and the tangible perspective was restricted to small transactions or the appearance of a greenfield private sector.

In 1989 neither Bulgarian society nor the economic profession were ready to understand the ownership profile of a capitalist economy, and hence the very essence of capitalism. Privatization was still a missing item from the agenda; the future resembled—like in 1944–1946—an idyllic mosaic of a mixed economy, but this time with a vague structure and under the enlightened aegis of the state. The transformations that ensued were, however, so profound that they filled the intellectual void surrounding property rights with unexpected celerity and brought to the fore their essential practical dimensions.

EPITAPH

With its multiple ramifications (wealth, power, management), ownership is a crucial issue underlying the decision-making hierarchies at the micro and macro levels in all socioeconomic systems. This does not exclude its dissimilar handling by different schools of thought.

At first glance, ownership does not seem essential for the marginalist/neoclassical paradigm, to the extent that from its perspective, factors' marginal prices reflect the competition in separate (labor and capital) markets interwoven by the laws of general equilibrium. Nevertheless, economic theory managed to reconcile the terms in a more elaborate context. The (neo-)institutionalist approach, for instance, reintroduced property rights by considering them as key guarantor for the fluidity of markets, while within the Socialist Calculation Debate Mises and Hayek extensively discussed the effects of suppressing private property.

In Marxist political economy, in turn, the notion acquired overarching functions and the status of an ontological category. This is one of the consequences of the Hegelian, normative and teleological nature of the construct, which diverts this discipline—and even more so, the political economy of socialism—from the hypothesis testing and falsification approach in social sciences. In the limpid and schematic redistributive logic of Marxism, the core issue is about who has the *right* to appropriate/alienate the surplus value, conceived as a *detachable part* of the product (or of its value) and allocated according to the outcomes of class struggle.[18] Correspondingly, state property grew into an all-embracing tangible reality imposing its inexorable imprint on economic life. It also became an ideological *deus ex machina* that nurtured and legitimized both political power and whatever experiments with the economy it devised.

In the Orwellian communist world with its vernacular based on intentional *quid-pro-quos* and corruption of the words' semantics, property was one of the pivotal tropes. It served as a vehicle of the ambiguous communication used to formulate alternative views in the vocabulary of an imposed meta-language. After all, this situation is not unknown. It reminds us, for example, of the medieval universal religious codes for the transfer of (new) ideas. In any event, in frames where the power-knowledge dichotomy is ever-present, the *context* seems often more important than the *content*. In particular, a divergent message about ownership expressed in its correct wording primarily was perceived as a political event (actually, it was).

But this does not preclude the question about *intrinsic quality* and the Bulgarian case is a perfect illustration. Meaningless language produces meaningless knowledge, subtracts rigor, and thus treating the ownership debates as deliberate verbal detours intending to communicate meaningful content is wrong. Discourse shapes thinking; in this instance the adopted tongue generated an epistemological void and handicapped generations of economists. Communist *property studies* never escaped their consummate dogmatic, ideological, and political quintessence, which was either irrelevant to or damaging for real problems. This scholarship built a scholastic domain *par excellence*, a niche for professional ideologues and the most conservative academics. A side-effect of the overproduction of such texts was further isolation from economics developed outside the communist commonwealth.

This literature led to nowhere. Nothing from those writings was able to survive beyond the term of the regime and now they have the significance of dead languages and extinct species.

NOTES

1. Largely autonomous from Sofia University and partially funded by the Bulgarian National Bank, the SIER was established in 1935 by the Russian émigré Oskar Anderson who had arrived in Bulgaria in 1921. A leading statistician, fellow of the Econometric Society, Anderson obtained the support of the Rockefeller Foundation for the founding of SIER. The Institute cooperated closely with a number of leading research institutions (among them Ragnar Frisch's institute) and worked on League of Nations' projects. Anderson left Bulgaria for the University of Kiel in 1942 and in 1947 took a position in the University of Munich. While at SIER, A. Christophoroff authored a masterly performed study on the Bulgarian business cycle (1939).

2. Prime Minister Kimon Georgiev (until November 1946) was the founder of *Zveno*. He was a key figure in the organization of the 1944 takeover after having masterminded the overthrow of constitutional governments in 1923 and 1934.

3. Nevertheless, under the postwar circumstances, he evaluated quite positively the fact that the Bulgarian National Bank was state owned—a profile that was an exception at the time.

4. He moved to a mountain home where he spent most of his time until his death in 1970. In 1951–1952 Christophoroff was interned in a camp upon political allegations. Afterward he dedicated himself to writing and published brilliant ironic fiction and translations from English (namely, Jerome K. Jerome and James Joyce).

5. The joint ventures with state-owned stakes were nationalized in February 1949. The state bought in cash, at nominal price, the shares of the cooperative partners; ten percent of those of the private partners were acquired in cash, while bonds were issued for the remaining 90 percent. The cooperative banks were closed in 1951.

6. The term "social ownership" was not used in Bulgaria.

7. In 1968 Ivan Nikolov published a book presenting the usual categories of the Marxist political economy (including ownership) as information flows and models (Nikolov 1968). General systems theory was the broad setting of Evgeni Mateev, the main opponent to the reforms in the 1960s. Two decades later he produced a voluminous monograph defending his former centralistic positions in those terms (Mateev 1987).

8. Those aspects are discussed in detail in Avramov (2007).

9. Correspondingly, the share of this component declined from 40 percent of peasants' income initially to less than 0.1 percent by the end of the 1950s.

10. Private renting of land for the important sector of tobacco growing was the rule.

11. The group of reformers included Georgi Petrov (b. 1929), Grisha Filipov (1919–1994), David Davidov (1925–1993), and Emil Hristov (1924–2009). Except Petrov, who until 1989 (and beyond) did not leave his academic position, the others occupied key positions after the first reforms: Filipov was prime minister in 1981–1986, Davidov served as minister in different occasions, and Hristov as adviser to the party leader Todor Zhivkov. In those capacities they implemented fairly centralistic economic policies.

12. In 1969 G. Petrov published a bitter account of the reforms' outcomes (Petrov 1969). Despite the precautionary wording and the ideological restraints, the book gives a clear idea about the gap between the initial design and the incomplete final version.

13. At that moment he was the head of the Chair of Political Economy at Sofia University. Although in 1988 Popov clashed with the official hierarchy and was even temporary excluded from the Party, he never departed from the profession's conventional approach. His half-hearted sympathy with private property was confirmed by his post-1989 passionate support of the Chinese political model.

14. Sociological surveys carried out for academic projects or for the sake of the Party's information network contained relevant bits of evidence about private activities. Due to the professional barriers, economists did not take part in their processing and conceptualizing the results.

15. The leading figure was Ventsislav Antonov. All the members of this small community took executive responsibilities after 1989, Ivan Kostov being prime minister in 1997–2002. I have discussed at length the intellectual pattern and trajectory of the group in Avramov (2007), vol. III, and Avramov (2008).

16. This line was accompanied by declarations of intent to implement a package of decentralizing economic measures and by completely incredible promises to democratize the existing political structure through self-government/management at all levels.

17. This happened a couple of months after the eviction of Zhivkov, at the round table talks between the Communist Party and the nascent political opposition.

18. The epistemological incompatibility between the two paradigms is patent in Marx's complete blindness to nascent marginalism. In his published writings and manuscripts there is no single mention of the pioneering theories of Jevons, Menger, and Walras whose founding texts had appeared a decade or more before Marx's death.

BIBLIOGRAPHY

Antonov, Ventsislav. 1989. "Neravnovesie i ikonomicheski rastej: vazdeistvie na strukturnite neravnovesia varhy tempa na rastej" [Disequilibrium and growth: Effects of the structural disequilibria on the rate of growth]. *Ikonomicheska missal* 2: 72–86.

———. 1990. "Teoretichni osnovi na inflatziata pri sotzializma" [Theoretical foundations of inflation under socialism]. *Ikonomika*, June (Supplement): 16–28.

Aroyo, Jacques. 1989. "Diskusia po problemite na sotzialisticheskata sobstvenost, Noemvri 1988" [Presentation at the discussion on the problems of socialist ownership, November 1988]. *Ikonomicheska missal* 5: 31–35.

Avramov, Roumen. 2007. *Komunalniat kapitalizam: Iz balgarskoto stopansko minalo* [Communal Capitalism: Reflections on the Bulgarian economic past]. Volumes I–III. Sofia: Fondatzia balgarska nauka I kultura, Centre for Liberal Strategies.

———. 2008. *Pari I De/Stabilizatsia v Balgaria, 1948–1989* [Money and de/stabilization in Bulgaria, 1948–1989]. Sofia: Ciela.

———, ed. 2009. *Balgarska narodna banka: Sbornik Dokumenti* [Bulgarian National Bank: Selected documents]. Volume V. Parts 1–4 (1948–1990). Sofia: Bulgarian National Bank.

Belev, Nedelcho. 1968. "Obshtonarodnata sotzialisticheska sobstvenost i samostoiatelnostta na darjavnite predpriatia." [Socialist ownership and the autonomy of state enterprises]. *Ikonomicheska missal* 6: 83–98.

Bochev, Stoyan. 1928. "Balgaria i tchuzhdite kapitali" [Bulgaria and the foreign capitals]. *Spisanie na balgarskoto ikonomichesko drujestvo* 9: 505–15.

Christophoroff, Assen. 1939. *Razvitie na koniunkturnia tzikal v Balgaria 1934—1939* [The business cycle in Bulgaria 1934–1939]. Sofia: SIER.

———. 1943. *Uvod v politicheskata ikonomia na voennoto stopanstvo* [Introduction to the political economy of the war economy]. Sofia: The author's publication.

———. 1945. "Evolutziata na liberalizma" [The Evolution of Liberalism]. *Brazda* January 15: 13–14.

———. 1947. *Lekzii po teoreticheska politicheska ikonomia* [Lectures of theoretical political economy]. Part II. Sofia: State School for Financial and Administrative Sciences.

Danailov, Georgi. 1934 [1906]. *Osnovni nachala na politicheskata ikonomia* [Principles of political economy]. Plovdiv: Hristo G. Danov.

Dimitrov, Ventseslav. 1989. "Diskusia po problemite na sotzialisticheskata sobstvenost, Noemvri 1988" [Presentation at the discussion on the problems of socialist ownership, November 1988]. *Ikonomicheska missal* 7: 18–21.

Dobrev, Krastiu, ed. 1966. *Politicheska ikonomia: Uchebnik* [Political economy: Textbook]. Sofia: Bulgarian Communist Party Publishing House.

Kepov, Ivan. 1931. "Stopnansko i kulturno sastoianie na nasheto selo" [Economic and cultural situation of our countryside]. In *Balgarskoto selo: Yubileen sbornik* [The Bulgarian village: Jubilee collection]. Sofia: Priaporetz. iii–xxx.

League of Nations. Financial Committee. 49th Session. 1933. Report of the Council on Bulgaria. Geneva, April 24–May 5.

Mateev, Evgeni. 1987. *Struktura I upravlenie na ikonomicheskata sistema* [Structure and management of the economic system]. Sofia: Nauka i izkustvo.

Miloshevski, Angel. 1985. "Povishavane roliata na stokovo–parichnite otnoshenia pri sotzializma" [Enhancing the role of pecuniary commodity relations under socialism]. *Ikonomicheska missal* 7: 3–14.

Ministry of the Interior. 1989. Minutes from the meeting of the staff with the Member of Politburo Dimitar Stoyanov. Archives, Fund 1, Inventory 12, File 903. 10 July.

Mishaikov, Dimitar. 1933. *Osnovni nachala na politicheskata ikonomia* [Principles of Political Economy]. Sofia: Nov jivot.

Nikolov, Ivan. 1968. *Kibernetika I ikonomika* [Cybernetics and economy]. Sofia: Nauka i izkustvo.

Petrov, Georgi. 1969. *Stokovi otnoshenia I tzenoobrazuvane pri sotzializma* [Commodity relations and pricing under socialism]. Sofia: Nauka i Izkustvo.

———. 2016. *Lajlivite reformi v Balgaria* [The fake reforms in Bulgaria]. Sofia: The author's publication.

Popov, Nikola. 1985. *Sachtnost, formi i nasoki na izjiviavane na tchastnata stopanska deinost pri sotzializma* [Character, forms, and trends in the vanishing of the private economic activities under socialism]. Sofia: Nauka i izkustvo.

Tzankov, Alexandar. 1931. *Politicheska ikonomia* [Political Economy]. Sofia: Knipegraph.

Vachev, Nikolai. 1986. "Chastnostopanskata deinost v usloviata na sotzialisma" [Private economic activity under socialism]. *Ikonomicheska missal* 9: 26–35.

Vladov, Hristo. 1989. "Diskusia po problemite na sotzialisticheskata sobstvenost, Noemvri 1988" [Presentation at the discussion on the problems of socialist ownership, November 1988]. *Ikonomicheska missal* 5: 41–44.

Chapter 2

From Control of the *Commanding Heights* to Control of the Whole Economy and Back

Chinese Ownership Theories Since 1949

Fan Shitao

This chapter tells the story of China's struggle to define ownership relations since the founding of New China in 1949.[1] Because the question of ownership cannot be understood in isolation from the broader ideological confrontations over the role of the economy during China's revolution and then during its reformist project, we embed the story of ownership in the relevant political, intellectual, and economic histories. We do so in a basically chronological format to provide non-China specialists with a sense of the dynamic unfolding of China's search for a new form of political economy. It is important to note that in no way was China's path a "*one-way street.* As we show, both in the past and in the present, China has undergone major shifts in its ownership structures, leaving open the question of whether China should move toward greater privatization or whether the present structure, despite its creative amalgamation of ownership, might be a stable configuration. It is impossible to pay due respect to all the individual contributors who dedicated their lives to solving the question of ownership under Chinese socialism. Some of them became famous; others have more or less disappeared from the present stage and are in danger of being forgotten by history.[2] All that we can do here is to provide a flavor of their debates and present a starting point for further research. We have paid particular attention to Xue Muqiao, a revolutionary veteran, economist, and economic official, who, since the 1930s, greatly contributed to the debates on the Chinese political economy during various stages and later became an important voice in China's search for a reform strategy under Deng Xiaoping. His story serves as an important anchor for our analysis. At the same time, we provide an account of the influence and thinking of several other economists who became important at specific moments, but we do not claim to comprehensively capture the contributions of the great number of Chinese intellectuals who engaged in the various rounds of ideological and theoretical struggles over ownership.

This chapter is divided into four chronological parts. The first section, on the years from 1949 to 1956, summarizes ideas about ownership at the time of the revolution and during the early years of the *ownership coexistence* that followed the principle of *growing into the plan*.[3] The second section, covering the period from 1956 to 1978, describes the first two major rounds of debates over an appropriate economic model, which not only departed from the Stalinist model but also reflected China's specific historical conditions. In the course of these two debates the articulated ownership theories set the tone for the later reform period. The third section, on the period from1978 to 1997, tells the story of China's major reform debates that introduced creative, pragmatic thinking about new forms of public ownership and set the stage for Chinese concepts of ownership to the present. The fourth section, on the years since 1997, provides an outlook on more recent proposals and policies regarding ownership reform. It remains brief since the major theoretical innovations occurred during the earlier periods.

GROWING INTO THE PLAN: FROM STATE CONTROL OF THE *COMMANDING HEIGHTS* TO UNIVERSAL PUBLIC OWNERSHIP (1949–1956)

In 1940, Mao Zedong, the leader of the rapidly expanding Chinese Communist Party (CCP), articulated the theory of *New Democracy* that called for a gradual transition to socialism based on cooperation among the various social classes (Mao [1940] 1975, 339–84). Similar to Lenin's vision, in economic terms this meant state ownership of big banks, big industry, and big commerce. The state economic sector was to play a leading role in the transition to socialism. Yet capitalist ownership was not to be abolished; rather, it was to be integrated into the socialist economy under the leadership of the proletariat (Yu 2005). With regard to land reform, Mao called for "confiscat[ing] the landlords' land and allocating it to the landless peasant" (Mao [1940] 1975, 2.353). This position contradicted the then Stalinist orthodoxy. In order to increase productivity, the redistribution of land and land reform allowed for a degree of inequality (Karl 2010, 61). In essence, the transitional economy envisioned a mixed-ownership system.

After the success of the revolution in 1949 and in the face of the challenges to rebuild the national economy, establishment of *New Democracy* in the

People's Republic of China became the core of the Common Program of the Chinese People's Consultative Conference, which functioned as a provisional constitution. The program stressed a policy of general cooperation between public and private entities, between capital and labor, between cities and the countryside, and between China and foreign countries. In this spirit, five ownership types were to complement one another in the development of the Chinese economy: the state-managed sector (*guoying jingji*), the cooperative sector (*hezuoshe jingji*), the individual ownership sector or the individual sector (*geti jingji*)[4] of peasants and craftsmen (*shougongyezhe*), the private capitalist sector (*siren zibenzhuyi jingji*),[5] and the state-capitalist sector (*guojia zibenzhuyi jingji*)[6] (National Committee of the Chinese People's Consultative Conference [1949] 1991, 1–13).

Yet relations among these different ownership sectors were not meant to be relations among equals. The state-managed sector was to occupy a leading position. All so-called economic *life lines*, or *arteries* (*mingmai*), were to be under the direct management of the state. The concept of economic *life lines* originated from Mao Zedong's interpretation of Lenin's *commanding heights* (Mao [1947] 1975, 155–76). Just as cutting the arteries will kill a person, controlling the economic *life lines* was a question of life and death for the socialist economy. Therefore, the state-managed economic *life lines* constituted the core of the socialist economy. The functioning of such *life-line* industries, commerce, and banks directly affected the livelihood of the people. Hence, the state-managed sector provided the main material basis for the development of the productive powers of the state and acted as the leading economic force in the entire society. At the same time, all state-owned resources and enterprises were to be under the ownership of all the people.

Aside from the emphasis on the development of the state-managed sector, policies toward the other sectors were differentiated based on the nature of their ownership. The cooperative sector, as part of a *semi-socialist economy*, was to enjoy preferential treatment and government support. The activities of the private capitalist sector were to be limited to serving the livelihood of the people, but at the same time the people's government was to encourage enthusiasm for such businesses and to support their development. In addition, private capital was encouraged to develop state-capitalist forms of management and cooperation, such as the formation of joint ventures. Finally, land reform was a necessary condition for the development of the productive forces and industrialization. In those areas where land reform had already been implemented, the land rights of the peasants were to be protected. In those areas where land reform had yet to be implemented, collectivization was to be introduced (Mao [1947] 1975, 167–69).

The evolution of China's ownership policies from 1949 to 1952 represented a dynamic unfolding of the New Democracy program. During the first years of the People's Republic, the main emphasis was on developing the state-managed sector. Meanwhile, the private sector and the various other ownership types were also growing, but at a much slower pace. The later reform period in the 1980s has been referred to as *growing out of the plan* (Byrd 1988, 12; Naughton 1995). We might understand this early period as *growing into the plan*, or transitioning to an economy in which public ownership was dominant.

The main task of the CCP was not to nationalize industries, banks, and commerce but rather to bring these enterprises under the control of the new government. Sun Yat-sen (1922) had already promoted the nationalization of key enterprises in his "Three Principles of the People" (*sanminzhuyi).*[7] On the eve of the communist revolution, under the Kuomintang government production of many of the key inputs was undertaken by state-owned enterprises (SOEs). At the same time, the communist-led areas had established a number of public enterprises and banks. The People's Bank of China was based on the merger of those banks managing the money supply in the various areas under the communist government, while the state-run trading agencies of the People's Republic mainly grew out of the trading companies in the communist areas (Xue 1996, 175–99). By the end of 1949, the communist government controlled most of China's modern railway and transport undertakings, banks, foreign trade, and large-scale industrial output (Xue et al. [1958] 2011, 19).

In addition to directly strengthening the state-managed sector, the dominance of the public sector was achieved through taxation, the registration of businesses, and credit and labor policies that favored the state-managed, cooperative, and state-capitalist sectors rather than their private counterparts. For example, although the communist government supported unionization and collective-bargaining efforts by workers and peasants in the private sector, there was an emphasis on aligning the interests of workers, the state, and enterprises in the state-managed sector (Dong 1996, 160). As a result of the combined effects of these policies, the public sector gained greatly in relation to the private sector during the course of the 1949–52 period.[8]

Beginning in 1952 the CCP moved away from its policy of coexistence, competition, and cooperation among the different ownership types under the New Democracy program. Tensions between the state and the capitalists intensified in 1951 when, as a consequence of market shortages during the Korean War, private producers gained increased bargaining power. The Central Committee then initiated the *five-anti campaign*[9] to empower workers to criticize and oppose their employers. As a result of this campaign, owners of private capitalist businesses lost control over management, personnel, and finance (Xu 1959, 288–89).

In this context, in 1953 Mao Zedong formally proposed the so-called general line for the transition period. In the general line, the party's task for the transitional period was "basically to accomplish the country's industrialization and the socialist transformation of agriculture, handicrafts, and capitalist industry and commerce over a fairly long period of time." The essence of the party's general line for the transition period was now "to make the socialist ownership of the means of production the sole economic foundation of state and society," and socialist ownership was to include both cooperative and state ownership (Mao [1953] 1977, 102). This codified the CCP's departure from a policy of ownership coexistence toward universal public ownership (*gongyouzhi*).[10] In the same year, national planning began with the launch of the First Five-Year Plan. Lacking any viable alternative and under the influence of Soviet advisers, China sought to follow a centralized Stalinist economic model while emphasizing the need for national and regional self-sufficiency (Karl 2010, 85).

Even before this shift, the coexistence paradigm of the early years had been subject to a crucial exception: the landlord class, which had dominated the agrarian sector in China for millennia, was to be destroyed during the land reform movement launched in 1950. By 1952 the revolutionary redistribution of land had been completed in the entire country (Karl 2010, 80–81). Unequal land ownership, exploitative rents, clan powers, and elements of bureaucratic-financial capital in the countryside had been eliminated. Yet, even though the peasants supported individual land ownership and *petty bourgeois* individual producers were still tolerated in the *Common Program*, the transition to socialism was thought to require collectivization. In theory, collectivization would increase productivity due to the increased returns realized under large-scale production. This promised both to enable an improvement in the livelihood of the peasants as well as to create an agricultural surplus that was required for industrialization. From the perspective of the individual peasants, it meant that they were required to join agricultural production cooperatives and relinquish their land, livestock, seeds, and other means of production. In a similar way, craftsmen were encouraged to join handicraft cooperatives.

In the meantime, several previously private enterprises had to become joint ventures managed entirely by the state. However, the previous owners—if they had not fled the country with the Kuomintang—could still retain shares in these enterprises. Their returns were regulated by a unified system, which provided a fixed annual interest of 5 percent. The symbolic peak of the socialist transformation took place at a celebration held on Tiananmen Square in January 1956 that included the participation of more than 200,000 people. With Mao Zedong and other leaders in attendance, mayor of Beijing Peng Zhen announced: "Our capital has entered a socialist society" (Lin 2009, 219). This was regarded as the *decisive victory* of the socialist transformation.

The establishment of universal public ownership meant that ownership coexistence had come to a close. China basically had established a Soviet type of political economy. The private economy was no longer legitimate and the individual sector was strictly limited. Centralized mandatory state planning expanded from the state-owned sector to the entire economy and became the primary means of nationwide resource allocation. Instead of being perceived as an end in itself, public ownership would play an important economic role. Public ownership was to liberate the productive forces and was believed to be a necessary step on the path toward socialism. As Mao put it in a speech to the Supreme State Conference:

> The socialist revolution aims at liberating the productive forces. The changeover from individual to socialist collective ownership in agriculture and handicrafts and from capitalist to socialist ownership in private industry and commerce is bound to bring about a tremendous liberation of the productive forces. Thus, the social conditions are being created for a tremendous expansion of industrial and agricultural production. (Mao 1956b)

UNIVERSAL PUBLIC OWNERSHIP, SOCIALISM, AND THE STRUGGLE OVER THE RELATIONSHIP BETWEEN THE FORCES AND RELATIONS OF PRODUCTION (1956–1978)

During the initial post-liberation years, the Soviet Union increasingly served as "China's primary model of socialist economic development" (Ling 1988, 542). Yet, as Lin (1981, 3) points out, this moment of Stalinist economic policies and organization was very brief. Between 1956 and 1957, *summing up experiences* and *learning from past mistakes* was on the top of the agenda of the planners, policymakers, and economists (Ibid., 8). The sectoral disproportions, material bottlenecks, and lack of coordination in execution of the First Five-Year Plan were to be avoided during the next Five-Year Plan that was being drafted at the time. Stalin's death and the news of Khrushchev's *secret speech* created a brief atmosphere of political openness. In this context, Chinese debates gave rise to reform theories, many of which still influence Chinese ownership discourse today.

In March 1956 the Chinese Central Committee received the text of Khrushchev's speech. At a meeting to discuss the speech, Mao summarized Stalin's contribution in the same way as Chinese reformers would later evaluate Mao's own contributions: "Seventy percent were correct and of primary importance, thirty percent were false and of secondary importance" (Shen 2009, 22–27). Mao found that Khrushchev's criticism of Stalin provided an opportunity for China to define its own way of building socialism instead of copying the Soviet model. His comments in "On the Ten Major

Relationships" (Mao [1956a] 1977, 22–27) and his "Reading Notes on the Soviet Text *Political Economy*" were surprising to many observers at the time. According to Mao, Stalin had failed to capture the complex relationship between a planned economy and the bureaucratic state (Karl 2010, 93).

In September 1956 the CCP held its Eighth Party Congress. One of the major conclusions of the congress was that China had already established a new kind of production relations. Therefore, the basic contradiction was no longer between classes but between China's advanced socialist system and its backward forces of production (Party Documents Research Office of the CCP Central Committee 2011, 1.536–538). The primary task of the CCP would now be to promote the development of China's forces of production. But this conclusion resulted in a conflict between Chairman Mao and his party. The drafters of the congress documents drew on an article by Lenin, "Backward Europe and Advanced Asia" ([1913] 1977). Initially they succeeded in persuading Mao. But two weeks later Mao questioned the primary task of developing the forces of production, and about one year later he voiced his clear objections. In "On the Ten Major Relationships" Mao ([1956a] 1077) put forward an idea which later became important in reform thinking—that the goal of production relations is to "motivate local, enterprise, and worker enthusiasm."[11] But with the gradual escalation of the CCP's criticism of what Boris Kidrič, president of the Yugoslav Economic Council, in 1957 called the "whittling down of the state" in Yugoslavia, the concept of the autonomy of enterprises began to be criticized and in fact it was deleted from the CCP reform program. By 1957, "individualism," a derogatory term of individual rights and interests in official ideology, was defined as the ideology of *anti-party and anti-socialist rightists*. Then, to *mobilize enthusiasm* by individual *material stimulation* was clearly in conflict with the mainstream ideology (Mao [1960] 1998, 924–25).

Chen Yun, one of China's most important economic officials, was at the time a vice premier of the State Council. In his report to the Eighth Party Congress, entitled "New Questions after the Basic Establishment of Socialism," Chen announced the following vision: The state sector and the collective sector operate the main part of Chinese industry and commerce, complemented by a regulated amount of individual enterprises. Planned production constitutes the main part of industrial and agricultural production, complemented by independent production for the market within permitted limits and under the guidance of the state plan. In the integrated socialist market, the state controls the major part, complemented by the free market allowed to operate within defined limits under the guidance of the state (Chen [1956] 1995, 1–13). Chen Yun's basic outline of the position of different ownership forms within the Chinese economy was supported by the Eighth Party Congress documents. Individual enterprises and country markets were allowed to exist throughout the pre-1978 period. However, their scale and scope varied greatly with the changing political winds. In particular, during the years of the Cultural Revolution (broadly defined from 1966 to 1976) the extent of their activities was strictly limited. It was only after the rise to power of Deng Xiaoping and Chen Yun in the late 1970s that Chen's articulated vision became the core of China's economic policy.[12]

Debates over the organization of China's socialist economy during the first post-revolution decade were not only carried out among the highest political levels but also among many economists. An interesting and widely overlooked instance is the Planning System Discussion Group, established by the State Planning Commission in 1956–57, which included some 10 senior economists and officials. For a period, the group was headed by the economist Xue Muqiao, who at the time was deputy director of the State Planning Commission and director of the State Statistical Bureau. This group held dozens of internal seminars during which fierce arguments took place between two opposing views. Some members of the group held that China's planning system was not reaching far enough and that the number of commodities under the plan should be expanded.[13] Others believed that the central planning authorities only understood production conditions of a very small share of commodities that were produced under the plan. Therefore, the scope of the central plan should be reduced and specialized departments and localities should be granted authority to make their own plans. Xue Muqiao belonged to the latter group, whose opinions were supported by Premier Zhou Enlai and two vice premiers. The final report of the group drafted by Xue (1957) and entitled "Proposal on the Current Planning System" put forward detailed suggestions about a fundamental reform of the planning system based on the principles of a *big plan and small freedoms* and *unified leadership, divided management*. The report suggested that mandatory planning be partially replaced by indicative planning and *guidance planning* as well as by the existence of a market for non-basic goods, which would not be subject to state planning. Some 20 years later, these methods of planning in Xue's report had an important influence on the debates over enterprise reform under Deng Xiaoping's leadership (Fan and Xue 2017).

In parallel with these debates regarding reforming, or improving, the industrial planning system, reorganization and experimentation of agricultural production also was discussed widely. After the implementation of collectivization in 1956, Deng Zihui, a leading agricultural official, suggested at an April 1956 work meeting that in order to improve agricultural production "it is imperative to contract labor and output." He argued that it would be "impossible to have advanced agricultural production cooperatives [*gaoji nongye shengchan hezuoshe*] without contracting work and output to lower levels" (Deng [1956] 1996, 412–20). The official newspaper, the

People's Daily, subsequently reported that agricultural "production teams and individual members of production cooperatives should enter into output and work-assignment contracts" (He 1956), and many provinces did in fact begin trial contracts for work and output. For example, in Zhejiang Province, Li Yunhe, vice party secretary of Yongjia County, with the support of his superiors began fixing farm output quotas for each household, which were imitated rapidly by surrounding counties.

Yet in 1957 the so-called two-road debate over whether work and output contracting was socialist or capitalist erupted. Mao, who sought to improve conditions in the countryside by relying on the revolutionary consciousness of the masses rather than on individual economic incentives, criticized contracting as capitalism. The trials in Yongjia County were condemned as taking the capitalist road, reversing collectivization, and hampering class struggle. Li Yunhe was labeled a *rightist* and expelled from the party as part of the Anti-Rightist Campaign that was launched in the same year (Li [1997] 2000, 258–78). Other trials in Sichuan, Anhui, Guangdong, and elsewhere were abandoned in a similar manner.[14]

The moment of openness created by China's desire to break away from the Stalinist development model came to a temporary halt from 1958 to 1961 with the Great Leap Forward and the rapid spread of the people's commune (*renmin gongshe*) system. In 1958 Mao noted that the system of public ownership established in 1956 was still *underdeveloped socialism*. In the spirit of placing priority on advancing production relations, Mao believed that China should first move "from collective ownership [*jiti suoyouzhi*] to pure socialist ownership by the whole people [*quanmin suoyouzhi*]," and then to "universal communist public ownership" (Mao [1960] 1998, 737, 800). Since collective ownership mainly existed in the rural areas, the transition from collective ownership to socialist ownership by the whole people would primarily take place in the rural areas and it would progress "from ownership by the production teams to ownership by the people's communes [*gongshe suoyou*], and finally to ownership by the whole people" (Ibid., 737). In this context, the people's communes were the central focus for building socialism and for making the transition to communism. They were to be the basic unit of a communist society. Mao believed that, depending on local conditions, it would take between three to more than six years to move from the collectives to the communes (Du et al. 2002, 519–20). However, the actual dynamic far outpaced Mao's expectations. After Mao formally proclaimed on August 9, 1958, that "People's communes are good," there was a rapid increase in the number of people's communes. On September 10, the Central Committee resolution "On the Establishment of the People's Communes in the Rural Areas" was announced, and by October, the nation's 740,000 agricultural cooperatives had all become communes (Ibid., 525). Such unprecedented speed reveals that the spread of the communes was a mass movement that occurred in reaction to the call by Mao rather than as a result of a centrally planned process to embark on socialist agricultural production.

The people's communes were to be "large in size and collective in nature [*yida ergong*]" (Mao [1960] 1998, 868). Several advanced production cooperatives would be merged to form a commune (Du et al. 2002, 526). Because the production tools formerly under the collective ownership of the cooperatives were merged into people's communes, the scale of public ownership in the rural areas increased dramatically. At the same time, a large number of laborers were mobilized under the guidance of the communes.

Beyond these changes in the organization of agricultural production and commerce, another important difference between the people's communes and the advanced cooperatives was that the communes brought every aspect of the people's lives into the public sphere, including schooling, military service, public dining in canteens, health care, kindergartens, and so forth, based on the principle that all members of the communes were to be treated according to uniform standards.

With the launch of the Great Leap Forward (1958–60), Mao announced that the communes should break through any economic constraints. The result was fierce competition among the communes to come up with ever-more unfeasible production plans. Calls by the central planning authorities to keep the plans within realistic bounds were met with harsh criticism from Mao (Fang and Jin 2001, 529). The outcome of Mao's promotion of the enthusiasm of the masses was catastrophic. Between 1959 and 1961 famine spread throughout the country and tens of millions of rural commune members died from starvation.[15] The material constraints to revolutionize production relations were demonstrated most brutally. Struggling for their lives, about 30 percent of the rural population engaged in production outside of the commune, such as working individually or in households, in order to increase their food supply (Du 2005, 88–95).

To resolve the severe food crisis, in the summer of 1962 most of the *supreme leaders* of the CCP voiced support for fixing farm output quotas for each household (*baochan daohu*). It was at this time that Deng Xiaoping expressed his famous slogan, which later would become a proverbial motto for his reforms: "It does not matter whether a cat is yellow or black, it is a good cat as long as it catches mice" (MacFarquhar and Schoenhals 2006, 69). Deng supported experimenting with a household responsibility system. Yet Mao soon expressed strong opposition to the idea of contracting. He said that China had to focus on class struggle as the key link instead of reverting to reliance on individual economic incentives (Party Documents Research Office of the CCP Central Committee 2011, 2.1258). The lesson that Mao drew from the Great Famine was to end further promotion of the ownership transition as well as to decrease the scale of the people's communes. Instead, the *three-level ownership* (*sanji suoyou*) of the commune system (production team, brigade, and commune) was to be stabilized. In 1961 Mao agreed to reduce the basic accounting unit from the brigade to the production team and to allow commune members to decide for themselves whether they wanted to maintain communal canteens (Party History Research Center 2011, 578).

In order to strengthen the people's confidence in the communes, Mao and Premier Zhou Enlai established a model commune—the Dazhai Commune in Xiyang County of Shanxi Province. A new national slogan called for "Learning agriculture from Dazhai," which served as the basic program for Chinese agricultural development from 1964 to 1978. Chen Yonggui, the party secretary of the Dazhai commune in 1964, would in 1975 become a vice premier of the State Council in charge of agriculture.

The shock caused by the famine prompted Chinese economists in the early 1960s to revive the 1956–58 debates. One of the leading voices at the time was Sun Yefang. Sun had been trained in Moscow in the 1920s. Serving as acting director of the Institute of Economics under the Chinese Academy of Sciences, he put forward proposals to reform the management system, emphasizing that the key issue was the "rights and responsibilities of enterprises as independent accounting units" as well as their "relationship with the state" (Sun [1961] 1998, 2.231). Other problems, such as the relationship between the central bureaucracy and the local-level bureaucracies, or between specialized departments and regions, were secondary to the problem of managerial control of enterprises, and they could easily be resolved once the question of enterprise management was settled. He further pointed out that ownership rights and operation rights should be differentiated. Sun advocated two types of ownership rights with regard to the means of production of enterprises under ownership of the whole people: first, the right to possess, use, and dispose of the means of production and, second, proprietary rights over such means of production. The state authorities should only have the second right, whereas the enterprises should be assigned the first right by the state authorities. However, in 1964 Mao criticized the Institute of Economics under Sun's leadership. This was followed by a series of criticisms organized by the Central Propaganda Department. Sun was denounced as an "enterprise-autonomy revisionist" (Chen 1984, 71). Two years later, at the beginning of the Cultural Revolution, he was targeted as a "bourgeois reactionary authority" and the official CCP journal *Hongqi* attacked his reform ideas as "counter-revolutionary programs undermining the socialist economic system and restoring capitalism." Soon thereafter, hundreds of articles (if not more) using an even sharper tone criticized Sun. In 1968, Sun was imprisoned for seven years (Garms 1980, 9).

Ironically, the sharp criticism launched against Sun brought him great fame because his reform ideas were disseminated throughout the country as negative examples. Subsequently, his distinction between management and proprietary rights exerted a fundamental influence on enterprise reform during the Deng Xiaoping era. Furthermore, even though Sun Yefang was under great pressure, he became all the more confident about his views. While in prison, he did not have access to pen or paper, but in his mind he continually revised and developed his ideas for a political economy textbook (Chen 1984, 91–93). Unfortunately, this book was completed posthumously. When Tito died in 1980, Sun wrote an article "deeply mourning the great Marxist Comrade Tito," the founder of "enterprise self-autonomy" that opposes the centralized management system of the Soviet Union and enlarges the authority of the enterprises (Sun [1980] 1998).[16]

The year 1966 marked another important turning point in China's history of ownership. In August teenage middle-school *Red Guards* launched a nationwide *Red* movement to eliminate the so-called four olds—old thinking, old culture, old customs, and old habits (Riskin 1987, 186). They entered the houses of people who were suspected of cultivating the *four olds*, attacked and criticized them, and confiscated their property. In the face of such great threats, households throughout the country destroyed much of their personal property, including letters, books, photographs, and so forth.[17] Another major change in China's ownership relations followed the August 1966 *order* by the Red Guards that all privately owned houses should be given to the state. Private homeowners were to hand over their ownership certificates, for which they would receive a receipt (Hua 2012, C01). In November 1967, the central government issued a document entitled "Reply to the Record of Nationalization of Urban Land," which required that "private homesteads with houses built in urban areas" must be nationalized (Ibid.). Despite the fundamental break with the political orientation of the Cultural Revolution in the course of the reform and opening, land remained nationalized. In 1982, when the Chinese constitution was revised, Article 10 stipulated that "the land of the city belongs to the state." Thereafter, there were no private property rights over land either in the cities or in the countryside. Even today, housing ownership in cities is limited to 70 years of user rights.

In order to make their case against those who were found to be counterrevolutionary elements, the Red Guards printed pamphlets with Mao's speeches attacking economic officials, intellectuals, and economists. These pamphlets were circulated throughout the country. The pamphlets, including excerpts from Sun Yefang, Xue Muqiao, and other economists, were intended to prove that their thoughts were "anti-party, anti-socialist, and anti-Mao Zedong" (*Shanghai jingji yanjiusuo geming zaofandui and Neikan fanxiubing* 1967). As an unintended outcome, such excerpts attacked by pamphlets became the first references for the new economic policies of the reform era.

By 1969 China's ownership patterns had stabilized, even if maintained through political pressure. The only major change to occur in the later years of the Cultural Revolution was the revival of commune and brigade enterprises (*shedui qiye*). As early as 1958, when Mao promoted the people's commune movement, he had envisaged the communes as organizations that integrate workers, peasants, traders, soldiers, and intellectuals. Part of this approach maintained that the communes should own and operate their own enterprises. However, due to the failure of the Great Leap Forward, the vast majority of rural industrial enterprises were closed down. In 1966, Mao issued his "May 7th Directive" (Mao 1966, 53–56), in which he called for the reestablishment of industrial enterprises in the communes and the brigades. Because of the chaos during the early period of the Cultural Revolution, there was no momentum in this direction until 1970 when social order was restored. By 1974, 78 percent of all communes and 60 percent of all brigades were operating their own enterprises. In 1975, Mao requested that Deng Xiaoping, who by then had returned to the center of power as a vice premier, issue two letters and a report on commune and brigade enterprises for the National Work Conference on Rural Issues. Subsequently, the commune and brigade enterprises continued to be consolidated and developed (Xue [1978a] 2011, 59–65). These commune and brigade enterprises, which developed extremely rapidly, provided an important institutional base during the early years of Deng Xiaoping's reforms.

GROWING OUT OF THE PLAN: BACK TO OWNERSHIP COEXISTENCE (1979–97)

"Had Chairman Mao died in 1956, there would have been no doubt that he was a great leader of the Chinese people [...]. Had he died in 1966, his meritorious achievements would have been somewhat tarnished but still very good. Since he actually died in 1976, there is nothing we can do about it," said Chen Yun at the Central Party Work Conference in November–December 1978 (Lardy and Lieberthal 1983, xi). The Chinese reform era began in December 1978 with the Third Plenum of the Eleventh Central Committee of the CCP. Chen Yun's statement, issued some two years after Mao's death, captures the spirit of this turning point in Chinese history. A reevaluation of China's postrevolutionary history and a redefinition of the relationship between historical progress and the economy were at the core of the shift in debate. Mao had hoped to break away from *economism* and to achieve socialism by revolutionizing production relations through continuous class struggle. This relationship was reversed by those who set the stage for the reform and opening-up program, first and foremost the veteran revolutionaries Deng Xiaoping and Chen Yun, as well as senior economists such as

Xue Muqiao. In their view, China was a backward country. In order to make historical progress and achieve socialism at a higher stage of development, China first had to build the necessary material foundation.[18] Hence, whatever helped to develop the forces of production would also serve China's socialist path. It was in this context that universal public ownership was determined not to have fulfilled the CCP's promise to bring about a "tremendous liberation of the productive forces" (Mao 1956b). At the same time, universal public ownership, as an element in the revolutionary relations of production, was no longer seen as an end in itself or as a necessary condition for Chinese socialism. The issue of ownership, together with that of plan versus market,[19] began to be treated from a functionalist perspective.

The fundamental shift in China's conception of ownership during the reform period represented a return to the coexistence of various forms of ownership under the dominance of public ownership, an idea initially devised by Xue Muqiao. Beginning in 1978 Xue repeatedly had criticized Mao Zedong's "large in size and collective in nature" concept of ownership—without explicitly referring to Mao by name (e.g., Xue [1979b] 2011). At an important CCP Central Committee meeting held in September 1980, as the representative of the State Council's Office of Economic Reform, Xue delivered a report on a market-oriented economic reform program. He formally proposed the following: "At the current stage of China's socialist economy, China's economic system should be a commodity economy with the dominance of public ownership of the means of production and ownership coexistence" (Xue [1980a] 2011). In Xue's view, having only two kinds of ownership (collective and state) was insufficient to serve China's development. Instead, a multilevel ownership structure, ranging from a state-run sector to individual economic activities, was necessary (Xue [1980b] 2011).

Such an ownership structure with a dominant public sector complemented by diverse ownership forms was institutionalized in China between 1979 and 1996, and in some ways it still persists today. The program was gradually implemented rather than being implemented all at once. During this period, the public economic sector was given priority and it remained dominant in terms of both scale and scope. In particular, key industries, commerce, and banking remained under public ownership. At the same time, however, non-state sectors were gradually allowed to emerge and to expand. During the first period of the reform era, growth of the non-state sector served as an important engine of China's rapid economic growth.

In terms of the basic ownership structure, the reform period is very similar to the years of the New Democracy (1949–56). In fact, the New Democracy program played an implicit role in the formation of the reform concept of the socialist "coexistence of diverse forms of ownership." Shortly before Xue Muqiao had proposed the concept of ownership coexistence, he had noted: "If we had continued the program of New Democracy, things would have been better."[20]

But there is a fundamental difference between the ownership systems during these two periods. The directions of the two processes of growth, which were used to change the ownership structure, were totally opposite. The earlier period (1949–56) was one of *growing into the plan*, whereby public ownership was to become increasingly dominant and eventually universal. During the latter period (1979–96), the reverse was the case. The non-public sector was gradually introduced into the economy, and its scope and scale were allowed to expand. Yet, despite this crucial difference, the similarity of a gradualist strategy as well as of ownership coexistence under dominance of the public sector remained.

FROM ALLOWING PERSONAL ENTREPRENEURSHIP TO LEGALIZING PRIVATE ENTERPRISES

China's tolerance of a certain degree of private enterprises began with permitting individual entrepreneurship. In 1978 and 1979 a wave of educated youth who had been sent to the countryside during the *Cultural Revolution* began to return to the cities. In this context, the urban economy faced a serious employment crisis (Bonnin 2013). The state sector was unable to absorb all of the unemployed returnees. Xue Muqiao noted that the root cause of the employment crisis was the *blind pursuit of ultra-pure public ownership.* He therefore favored the implementation of a *three-door* employment policy (encompassing the doors of SOEs, collective enterprises, and personal entrepreneurship) (Xue 1978a).

CCP leaders supported his suggestions. In August 1980, a central meeting of the National Work Conference on Employment decided to "encourage and foster the development of the individual sector in cities and towns" (*Renmin ribao* 1980). The 1982 Constitution of the People's Republic expanded the scope of development of the individual sector by stating: "Within the framework of the law, individual enterprises of urban and rural laborers are a complement to the socialist public economy." Legal approval for personal entrepreneurship not only played an important role in resolving the unemployment problems but also opened the door for the introduction of private business.

The success of the individual sector soon created a desire to hire workers. It was highly controversial whether this would reintroduce exploitation, which would undermine the socialist nature of the Chinese economy. Official documents in 1980 still clearly stated: "Hiring workers is not allowed" (Several issues, 1981). But in 1981, works by Lin Zili, an eminent scholar of Marx's writings, cited Marx's statement in *Das Kapital* that as long as the number of employees does not exceed seven persons an enterprise is not classified as capitalist. The State Council used this finding to justify a new regulation in 1981 that allowed businesses to hire up to five *apprentices* and invite up to two assistants (Guowuyuan guanyu 1981).

In practice, this limit was quickly surpassed. Some enterprises hired even more than 100 employees. But despite fierce debates about whether such an expansion of private wage laborers would imply a return to capitalism, the Chinese leadership under the guidance of Deng Xiaoping adopted a *wait-and-see* strategy and encouraged the expansion of private enterprises to employ workers.[21] In early 1983 the CCP Central Committee noted: "Large-scale employers or private enterprises should not be encouraged or publicized. But we should not rush to ban them."[22]

The idea of China being at a *low*, or *primary*, stage of socialism due to its backward productive forces provided a solution to the theoretical challenge of reconciling private employment and ownership with socialism. As early as 1959, Xue Muqiao had suggested at an internal session the idea of a low stage of socialism (*shehuizhuyi diji jieduan*) (Xue 1996, 262), and in 1978 he revived this concept in a report to the Central Party School (Xue [1978b] 2011; Fan and Xue 2017). Independently of Xue, during the 1979 Theory Conference Su Shaozhi and Feng Lanrui also introduced the idea of a low stage of socialism to the Chinese reform discourse, using the term "undeveloped socialism" (*bufada shehuizhuyi*) (Fewsmith 1994, 69–70). Thereafter they published an article further explaining this idea (Su and Feng 1979, 14–19). But it was regarded as providing a basis for questioning the socialist nature of the country. However, when propaganda officials found an article in which Deng Xiaoping had stated that "our present society is still not at the first stage of the Communist society envisioned by Marx," the harsh criticism of Su Shaozhi and Feng Lanrui that had been planned was canceled (Yu 2008, 1–7). Shortly thereafter, at the end of 1979, Xue Muqiao's *Economic Problems of Socialism in China*,[23] which articulated the same thinking, successfully passed the review of the Central Propaganda Department[24] and was published. The book sold almost 10 million copies and popularized the concept of the *low stage of socialism* (Tao and Zhang 2006, 57–59). The concept of the *primary stage of socialism* (*shehuizhuyi chuji jieduan*) was eventually written into an important central document by Yu Guangyuan, a senior economist and friend of Su Shaozhi and Feng Lanrui. In 1982, Yu also included the phrase in a report to the general secretary of the CCP: "China's socialism is still in the primary stage of development; the material civilization is not developed" (Yu 2008, 1–7). Five years later, on March 21, 1987, the group drafting the report for the Thirteenth Party Congress submitted a letter to Deng Xiaoping. The letter read:

> We are in the primary stage of socialism, we can only progress gradually, and we may not anxiously seek the purest form of socialism. We must allow for a long-term coexistence of multiple forms of ownership under the dominance of public ownership. (Zhao [1987] 2016, 4.47–48)

With Deng Xiaoping's support, the notion of the primary stage of socialism was formally included in the political report given by Premier Zhao Ziyang at the Thirteenth Party Congress in October 1987. Thereafter, the 1988 revision of the Chinese constitution legalized the existence of private enterprises. However, it should be noted that even though this legal change formally allowed private enterprises to grow beyond the public sector, there was to be no privatization of existing enterprises or any weakening of the public sector.

It is interesting to note that after Deng Xiaoping's death in 1997, CCP general secretary Jiang Zemin further discussed the duration of the primary stage of socialism in his report to the Fifteenth National Congress of the CCP. He stated that the primary stage would "need at least one hundred years." He continued: "As for the consolidation and development of the socialist system, it will require a much longer time, requiring generations, ten generations, and even dozens of generations working tirelessly" (Jiang 1997, 16). From Confucius to the present, it has only been several dozen generations.

FROM COMMUNES TO THE HOUSEHOLD CONTRACTING SYSTEM

The breaking up of rural communes and the introduction of a household contracting system were the most consequential reforms of China's ownership structure in 1980s, changing the livelihood of vast parts of China's population as well as the working of the Chinese economy. In this process, local initiatives, central policies, extensive empirical research, and fundamental theoretical debates interacted in complex and historically unique ways. The main issue of debate was the accounting unit for agricultural production: it was decentralized from the production teams, then to the groups, and finally to the households, effectively resulting in decollectivization.

After Mao's death in 1976, there were tensions within the CCP regarding the future direction of the commune system, harkening back to the debates in earlier years (see Section 3).

In the winter of 1977, an important decision on the fate of the communes was proposed when the Central Committee issued Document No. 49, which envisaged a change in the basic accounting unit from the production team to the larger unit of the brigade, and suggested that this should be tried out immediately in 10 percent of the communes (Wu 1993, 291). This policy met with resistance in some places, whereas it was welcomed in others. Wan Li, the governor of Anhui Province, implicitly opposed such an ownership upgrading, which had originated with Mao's views during the Great Leap Forward and the policy of "Learning from Dazhai." Wan emphasized that the autonomy of the production teams should be respected and grassroots efforts to fix output quotas for each group of peasants within the production teams should be supported (Wan [1978] 1995, 103–5). He permitted trial experimentation which led to immediate increases in agricultural output, thus encouraging further experimentation. Despite strong disagreement within the party, at the Third Plenary Session of the Eleventh Central Committee in 1978 the central leadership decided to permit experiments fixing farm output quotas for production groups. The fixing of household quotas remained illegal, but Wan Li still quietly advocated it in Anhui Province, and scattered experiments with this form of contracting spread throughout the country.

Additionally, economists took action. Wu Jinglian, Sun Yefang's colleague, was designated by Yu Guangyuan in 1975 to write a book entitled *The Dazhai Experience and Marxist Political Economy*. But Wu found that there was a huge difference between Dazhai's reality and the official propaganda. As a result, Wu was politely expelled from Shanxi Province. After a period, the vice premier who had been promoted from Dazhai asked Wu to complete the book. This time, Wu used a delaying strategy to avoid writing the book. Furthermore, at an important meeting in the spring of 1979 he bravely made a systematic criticism of the erroneous facts and policies in the official Dazhai propaganda (Wu 1979). This was aimed at reducing the pressures to upgrade ownership based on the "Learning from Dazhai" campaign.

In the summer of 1979, Lu Xueyi, a researcher at the newly established Chinese Academy of Social Sciences (CASS), visited over 100 cadres and farmers in Anhui Province and then presented his findings in a report entitled "The Problem of Fixing Farm Output Quotas for Households Should Be Restudied." He showed that assigning production responsibility to households resulted in a substantial increase in grain output. Lu bluntly challenged Mao's 1962 criticism of fixing household quotas and argued that there should be only one standard to measure the impact of policies, that is, whether they promote the development of production. If assigning household quotas enhances output, it would serve socialism and not capitalism (Lu [1979] 2005, 10–16). His report was distributed among a small circle of leaders and it played an important role in legitimizing the fixing of household output quotas (Wu 2013, 362).

In early 1980 two strong proponents of the agricultural reforms were promoted. Wan Li became vice premier in charge of rural issues, and Hu Yaobang became general secretary of the party. Shortly after, Deng supported trials of household quotas in two speeches. Subsequently, the newly appointed premier, Zhao Ziyang, wrote a letter to the Central Committee advocating the trial of assigning household quotas. Employing Mao's rhetoric of mass politics, Zhao argued that the masses should decide for themselves whether to carry out such trials. At a September 1980 meeting for the first secretaries of all provinces, the agrarian question was fiercely debated. The minutes of the meeting concluded that in remote and impoverished areas "where the masses have lost faith in the collective," household contracting "is permitted and is nothing to be afraid of." This opened the door for a nationwide rollout of the system (Wu and Ma 2016, 86).

Research dedicated to resolving China's agrarian question by implementing trials of household quota contracting emerged in the early 1980s. Chinese undergraduate and graduate students as well as young researchers who had returned to Beijing after stints in the countryside during the Cultural Revolution gathered in the lecture halls and dorm rooms of Beijing's universities to discuss how to improve the livelihood of the peasants. On their own initiative, they began publishing reports in the summer of 1980 and co-conducted empirical investigations in pioneering Anhui Province in 1981 (Fewsmith 1994, 34–36), attracting the attention of high-level policy advisers. In particular, Deng Liqun, at the time deputy director of CASS and later an important propaganda official, and Du Runsheng, at the time director of the State Agricultural Commission, arranged financial and institutional support to enable these young researchers to officially establish the Rural Development Research Group, which became one of China's agricultural policy think-tanks during the early reform era (Fewsmith 1994, 40–41; Naughton 2002, 626). Wang Gengjin, a former senior official in charge of Chinese agricultural planning and now a vice director of the Agricultural Economics Institute in CASS, was designated as the director of the group; Yang Xun, a middle-aged associate professor at Beijing University, and Chen Yizi, a young colleague of Wang Gengjin were vice directors. Such alliances between communist veterans and young reformers are characteristic of some of the most influential economic research activities during the 1980s. In late 1981 the Rural Development Research Group was asked to prepare briefing materials on household contracting for the Central Work Meeting on Rural Issues. In late 1981 these briefings were used as background materials for the drafting of central government Document No. 1, which states that fixing household output quotas shall be permitted to establish a "multi-form collective agricultural responsibility system" (1982, 1–6; Liu 2010, 421–22).

An important input for the next Document No. 1 came from Lin Zili's theoretical work and surveys of the household contracting trials. Lin Zili (1983) proposed "all-around household contracting" (*baogan daohu*), which permitted responsibility for both output and work distribution to remain with the household. Theoretically, he showed that ownership and management rights could be separated and that household contracting combined centralization of ownership with decentralization of management. In early 1983 Document No. 1, of which Lin Zili was a main drafter, was officially passed. Then what had been regarded as capitalist restoration only a few years earlier became central CCP policy by 1983 and was praised as a major innovation in Marxist theory of agricultural cooperation (Wu 2010, 36–40). This put an end to the related debates that had gone on for more than 20 years.

Although the household contracting reform was carried out on the basis of renting out collective land, it was still quite vigorous in nature. Within two years, tens of millions of family farms had emerged all over the country. On this basis, in 1984 the CCP officially abolished the people's commune system. Some cooperatives remained, but they were no longer the basic form of organizing agricultural production. Since then, the household all-around contracting system has been part of the mainstream in China's reform discourse and it is celebrated as one of the major successes in China's transformation.

The crucial achievement of the all-around household contracting system was its success in combining public ownership with individualized economic incentives, as reconfirmed and expanded in 1998. Many of those who advocated the contracting of land in the 1980s are today strong opponents of further land reform, and they are lobbying against turning land contracts into permanent use rights. Others, for example, economist Wu Jinglian, hold the minority position that permanent use rights of agricultural land are needed (Wu and Ma 2016, 90).

THE EMERGENCE OF TOWNSHIP AND VILLAGE ENTERPRISES WITH DIVERSE OWNERSHIP PATTERNS

According to Deng, "in the rural reform our greatest success—and it is one we by no means had anticipated—has been the emergence of a large number of TVEs. These small enterprises engage in the most diverse endeavors, including both manufacturing and trade. The Central Committee takes no credit for this. Their annual output value has been increasing by more than 20 percent a year for the last several years" (Deng [1987a] 1994, 238).

With the spread of the household contracting system in rural areas, commune and brigade enterprises boomed. They were renamed township and village enterprises (TVEs) in 1984. Deng Xiaoping praised their success without claiming credit, even though he was the one who had supported their rise in 1975.[25] The explosive growth of the TVEs after implementation of the household contracting system was unanticipated even by its strongest proponents.[26] While, due to the low scale of production and backward technology, TVEs were by no means the main driver of China's industrial revolution in the 1980s, TVEs were nonetheless an important factor in contributing to China's overall growth (Nolan and Wang 2004, 131).

The ownership structure of the TVEs is complex and diverse. According to the definition of TVEs in a 1984 Central Committee document, TVEs are cooperative enterprises established by communes (townships) and brigades (villages). They operate either directly by cooperatives, jointly by some members, by individual enterprises, or by some other forms (State Commission for Restructuring 1990, 142–43). In order to classify the diverse TVE ownership forms, Chinese literature labels them based on the names of the places where the different types are dominant. For example the Wenzhou Model (*Wenzhou moshi*) is known for its predominantly private household industry (Dong 1988, 245–79; Nolan and Dong 1989); the Pearl River Delta Model (*Zhujiang sanjiaozhou moshi*) refers to Guangdong's large number of joint ventures with Hong Kong or Macao firms or fully foreign-owned enterprises in processing or manufacturing industries (Vogel 1990); the Sunan Model (*Sunan moshi*) refers to TVEs that remained under collective ownership and were established by townships or villages that distributed their after-tax profits. Xue Muqiao holds that the Sunan Model is a form of public ownership in the hands of an administrative level lower than the provincial, municipal, or county level (Xue [1987] 2011, 12.169). The Sunan Model was the most influential model in China until 1997. Despite this diversity in the ownership structures of the TVEs, the overall situation can be summarized as follows: "A large share of the assets is owned by the whole of each local community, of which the TVE workers are a small minority, even in the most advanced areas" (Nolan and Wang 2004, 132). Due to this dominant ownership structure, local bureaucrats in fact make key economic decisions for the TVEs and they have "strong incentives to employ well-paid, dynamic, profit-seeking managers who make money for the whole community" (Ibid., 132).

STATE-OWNED ENTERPRISES AND EXPERIMENTS TO SEPARATE OWNERSHIP AND MANAGEMENT

Although TVE growth in output and their innovative ownership structures have been impressive, the most crucial question of ownership restructuring focuses on SOEs in charge of all key industries, banks, and commerce. Chinese veteran reformers were fully aware that changing the organization of the *commanding heights* would be most consequential for the whole economy. They rejected the idea of change in one *big bang* as a form of utopianism in the same manner as Mao's Cultural Revolution (Nolan and Wang 2004).

On Mao's birthday in 1976 the official version of "On the Ten Major Relationships" (Mao [1956a] 1977) was published for the first time. This was followed by an upsurge of study and debate. In Xue Muqiao's view, this new interest was related to proposals for "reform of the planning and management system" that were included in Mao's work, such as the proposal to expand the powers of local authorities and for enterprises to mobilize their own initiatives (Xue [1978c] 2011, 257).

In October 1978, Zhao Ziyang (then party secretary of Sichuan Province) launched an experimental program in six factories of Sichuan Province to expand their operational autonomy and to allow them to retain a portion of their profits (*fangquan rangli*). This successful pilot marked a significant first step toward enabling SOEs to become more independent economic entities. The State Council released its first set of policy documents on state-owned enterprise reform in July of 1979, most notably the "Several Provisions on Expanding the Autonomy of State-owned Industrial Enterprises," and it expanded enterprise autonomy (*qiye zizhuquan*) reforms nationwide in 1980.

Ma Hong, an important reform economist of the older generation, thought "reform of the economic management system should begin from expanding enterprise autonomy" (Ma Hong [1979] 1986, 251–52). Jiang Yiwei (1980), a respected veteran revolutionary and Ma Hong's close colleague, believed that the systemic reform should focus on the "theory of an enterprise-based economy" (Ma Hong [1979] 1986, 48). In 1984, the Central Committee adopted the "Decision on Reform of the Economic System," which formally declared the reform of SOEs as the focus of urban economic reform efforts.

One of the core insights that guided China's SOE reforms in the 1980s was that ownership and management can be separated. Initiatives starting from the pilot programs of expanding enterprise autonomy in 1979 to the enterprise contract system reforms in 1981–83 and in 1987–88 focused on expanding the powers of enterprise managers in various ways. In 1988, the National People's Congress adopted the Law of Industrial Enterprises Owned by the Whole People. It states: "The property of the enterprise shall be owned by the whole people, and shall be operated and managed by the enterprise with the authorization of the state in line with the principle of the separation of ownership and managerial authority." Many Chinese economists and government leaders argued that this was the most essential part of enterprise reform. Managers of SOEs very much welcomed this idea, although some were less enthusiastic about implementing accounting procedures that would reveal or call attention to enterprise losses or mismanagement.

The separation of ownership and managerial authority refers to the works by Sun Yefang and Lin Zili that we discussed earlier. But there were also major contributions by younger Chinese economists. Tian Yuan (1990, 145–49), for example, argued that Oskar Lange's proposal for simulating a market under public ownership remained incomplete because it overlooks that not only prices but also a simulation of capital are required for the coordination of investment. Hence, Tian Yuan supported the proposal that China's SOEs could be transformed into public joint-stock companies, whereby the state would remain the owner while management authority would be assigned on a competitive basis.

There was harsh criticism of China's approach to enterprise reform, both within China and abroad. Wu Jinglian and Qian Yingyi, in "On Corporatization," argued that the direction of state-owned enterprise reform should be the establishment of a corporate governance structure (Wu and Qian 1993). Soon thereafter, the concept of insider control (*neiburen kongzhi*), as proposed by Masahiko Aoki (1994), had a significant impact on rethinking the idea of enterprise autonomy. The establishment of a corporate governance structure became a central topic in discussions on the reform of SOEs after 1993. However, the vast majority of enterprises maintained sole public proprietorship or introduced only a small amount of equity even when they underwent the process of corporatization. Instead of placing priority on the interests of minority shareholders, the state still retained effective control over enterprises.

OUTLOOK: SOCIALISM AT THE *COMMANDING HEIGHTS* (1997–PRESENT)

As China progressed with its reform policies in the 1990s, intense debates emerged over the dominant position of public ownership and SOEs in China's national economy. Reformers used Lenin's concept of the *commanding heights* to argue that public ownership would not have to control the major part of each enterprise and every industry for the national economy to remain socialist. Instead, the crucial point was that public ownership would retain control over some key sectors of the economy. As we have seen, the CCP has been in control of the *commanding heights* ever since it seized power in 1949. Yet, until 1997 the state had expanded its control far beyond the key economic sectors. Hence, the call for only controlling the *commanding heights* amounted to a call for a massive reduction of the state sector.

In the course of the marketization policies of the 1990s following the concept of *socialist market economy*, the private sector was growing rapidly and putting increasing pressure on the state-owned sector. The share of the state-owned sector in GDP declined from 47.7 percent in 1990 to 42.1 percent in 1995 (Wu and Fan 2014). In this context, the imperative of *doing a good job with SOEs* was placed at the top of the government's agenda.

The decision of the Third Plenary Session of the Fourteenth Central Committee in November 1993 to adopt a new interpretation of public ownership opened the door for a wide range of proposals. The decision held that "nation-wide public ownership should be the mainstay in the national economy but it may vary in different places and trades." The session further adopted a decision to change the ownership structure of small enterprises. It states that "as for the small state-owned enterprises, the management of some can be contracted out or leased; others can be shifted to a partnership system in the form of stock sharing, or sold to collectives or individuals" (Wu and Ma 2016, 151–52). In 1995, Jiang Zemin and Vice Premier Wu Bangguo changed the principle of "doing a good job with SOEs" to "doing a good job with the whole state-owned sector, grasping the big and letting the small go" (Li 1995, 7–15). This new policy, which would result in public ownership no longer being the main form in terms of GDP, met with severe criticism from officials and scholars alike. Between early 1995 and 1997, critics successively distributed four long typescript articles, which are commonly referred to as the "Ten-Thousand-Chinese-Character Manifestos" (*wanyanshu*). They sharply criticized this new trend in ownership policy and appealed for a strengthening of national support for public ownership of the economy and for limiting the rapid development of the private economy. Among the Ten-Thousand-Chinese-Character Manifestos, the third manifesto, entitled "Several Theories and Policy Problems Concerning Retaining a Dominant Position for Public Ownership,"[27] was the only one signed with a pen name; the others all remained anonymous. This third article was distributed at the 1997 National People's Congress meeting and at the meeting of the Chinese People's Political Consultative Conference. It argued that socialism regards ownership by the whole people (namely state ownership) as an advanced form of public ownership that must be pursued. This includes first that the state-owned economy, the system of many large, medium, and small independent-accounting industrial enterprises as well as the *economic life lines* of the country should remain unified and complete. Second, the state-owned economy should dominate the collective sector. Third, the non-public sector of the economy should be in a supplementary position in relation to the public sector.[28]

In early 1997, the Development Research Center under the State Council set up a research group, under the leadership of Wu Jinglian, to study the *strategic reorganization of the state-owned economy*. The task of this group was to issue a *sharp response* to the Ten-Thousand-Chinese-Word Manifestos. On the one hand, Wu Jinglian (1997, 1.183–91) aimed to present the aims of socialism as being independent of public ownership. In his view, the essence of socialism is to pursue social justice and common prosperity, which cannot be achieved by a particular share of the state-owned economy.[29] On the other hand, the group suggested that China should "shrink the state-owned economy" and encourage non-state-owned sectors (Wu et al. 1997).

The Fifteenth Congress of the CCP did not accept all the suggestions of the research group but it absorbed some specific proposals. The congress report stated that for important industries and key fields, which make up the *life lines* of the national economy, the state-owned economy shall remain in a dominant position. In other fields, asset reorganizations and structural adjustments could be carried out to strengthen key points and to improve the overall quality of state-owned property. At the Fourth Plenary Session of the Fifteenth Central Committee in 1999, a decision on SOE reform was passed. The decision specified that the "important industries and key fields related to the life lines of the national economy" were those industries related to national security, industries that constitute a natural monopoly, industries providing public goods, high and new technology industries, and key enterprises in all important sectors.

The restriction of SOE activity to the *commanding heights* represented a major change from the 1978–97 period. Between 1997 and 2002 the Chinese economy underwent what some describe as large-scale privatization that was unprecedented in China's socialist history (Naughton 2007; Zeng 2013). But in Chinese literature, the word "privatization" is generally not used. Instead, terms such as the "strategic reorganization of the state-owned economy" or the "restructuring of enterprises" (*guoqi gaizhi*), or at least a fundamental change in the ownership structure, are called for. A nationwide investigation by the State Statistical Bureau in 1998 revealed that out of more than 87,000 SOEs that had been investigated, 25 percent were taking restructuring measures and another 25 percent were intending to take such measures. In 2002, a nationwide investigation by the State Economic and Trade Commission found that 86 percent of the SOEs had accomplished restructuring by the end of 2001 (Yao 2008, 152). During the same period, large numbers of township enterprises based on the collective *Sunan Model* transitioned to the private-ownership *Wenzhou Model*.

However, the privatization deals that were carried out between 1998 and 2002 were generally not consistent with the suggestions of Wu's research group that they should be open, transparent, and based on rule of law. Indeed, the process was characterized by corruption due to insider-controlled transactions that were beneficial to those who previously had held crucial state positions. For example, even a study generally sympathetic to privatization still warned: "Privatization will benefit everyone, but the privileged classes are likely to find ways of further enriching themselves" (Qu Hongbin 2002, as quoted in Nolan 2004, 17).

In 2006, the "Guidelines on State Capital Adjustment and SOE Reorganization," circulated by the General Office of the State Council, marked a strengthening, or at least stabilization, of the position of the SOEs. The guidelines pointed out that the SOEs shall maintain *absolute control* in seven industries, including military industries, power grids, and power generation, oil and petrochemical sectors, telecommunications, coal, civil aviation, and shipping. In the backbone enterprises of nine industries, such as equipment engineering, automobile manufacturing, electronic and information technology, construction, iron and steel, metallurgy, chemical products, survey and design, and science and technology, "relatively strong control by the state" should be maintained (Wu 2011, 2.663–667). In fact, a renewed expansion of state-owned monopolies could be observed in the following years (Eaton 2015).

The relationship between SOEs and the state authorities continues to be based on the principle of the separation of management and property that gained prominence in the 1980s. The supervision departments for state-owned property establish principles for the management of human affairs, for the management of enterprise affairs, and for management of the capital of the large SOEs under direct state management. In turn, SOEs are allowed greater autonomy over their day-to-day operation. Nevertheless, important linkages between the state and these SOEs still exist. The senior managers of these enterprises are appointed by the State-owned Asset Supervision and Administration Commission or by the Organization Department of the Central Committee. This institutional structure is also maintained for those large SOEs that underwent corporatization and for the listed subsidiary companies on the stock market.

In recent years, there has been a tendency to enlarge the scope of the SOEs through government-directed mergers and overseas expansions and to strengthen party-state control. Examples of this include ongoing anti-corruption campaign, of which an important focus is the state-owned economy, and efforts to strengthen the role of party committees in company governance. The current challenge due to the decreasing growth rate has put the question of the role and structure of SOEs and the state-owned economy back on the top of the political agenda. It remains to be seen what will occur during the next chapter in the history of China's complex ownership policies.

CONCLUSION

China's history of ownership relations since the communist revolution is complex, nonlinear, and must be understood in the context of China's struggle to find its own socialist path as well as its own quest for development. Therefore, this chapter places the intellectual history of ownership in its historical background, and uses the concepts of *ownership coexistence*, *universal public ownership*, and *back to ownership coexistence* to describe the main trends in ownership thinking since 1949. It also introduces the debates about the economy's *commanding heights* to reflect the strategic reorganization of the state-owned economy between 1997 and the beginning of the 21st century.

After 1989, the CCP experienced two difficult years, but thereafter it began massive market-oriented reforms that far exceeded the reforms in the 1980s. However, political reforms remained stalled, and to this day China still retains many important characteristics of a party-state, and the CCP in power is still a Leninist party. Chenggang Xu (2011) employs the term "decentralized authoritarianism" and Wu Jinglian (2012) uses the phrase "semi-command, semi-market economy" to describe China's current situation.

This situation represents the basic background to the intellectual development of Chinese ownership thought. Because ownership is critical to the socialist vision, to which the CCP adheres as a guiding ideology, discussions about ownership remain closely related to the orthodox ideology and political power. Therefore, intellectual innovation in China regarding ownership is still subjected to enormous pressure and resistance similar to what economists such as Sun Yefang, Xue Muqiao, Yu Guangyuan, and Wu Jinglian had faced earlier.

At the beginning of the reform and opening, when Włodzimierz Brus first visited China, he told his Chinese counterparts that one of the prerequisites for successful economic reforms is free and unrestrained discussions on the theoretical and practical problems of the reforms (Wu 1985). Until now, such discussions remain a matter of great importance in China. Because discussions of ownership are tied to CCP propaganda, economists often try to disguise some forms of private property as public ownership, just like the private township enterprises pretended to wear *red hats*. For the short term, this is politically feasible, but in the long run it will limit the extent of discussions on ownership reform. The limited space for discussions about the process of state-owned economic reorganization also raises additional concerns about corruption.

With the exception of Xue Muqiao's book *Economic Problems of Socialism in China*, this chapter does not cite any other political economy textbooks. Following the Korean War, as part of China's educational reforms the study of all non-Marxist social sciences was terminated. With the help of Soviet experts, the study of economics was reorganized according to the Soviet model. In 1955, the Propaganda Department of the CCP assigned Xue Muqiao, Yu Guangyuan, and Sun Yefang to write political economy textbooks, but none of them had completed this task before the beginning of the Cultural Revolution. Therefore, leaders such as Mao Zedong and Liu Shaoqi had only read Soviet textbooks on political economy. In contrast, during the Deng Xiaoping era many new political and economic teaching materials were published. However, Xue Muqiao's comments on political economy textbooks were the following: "In the past, Soviet and Chinese economic books all dealt with policy rather than theory because there was no systematic investigation of the objective laws of socialist economic operation" (Xue [1990] 2011, 38). Indeed, teaching political economy generally changed in tandem with changes in the party's economic policies.

China's ownership theories have also been linked to those in the rest of the world. During the Maoist era, the greatest international source of inspiration for China was Lenin and Stalin. However, Yugoslavia had an important influence on China's expansion of corporate autonomy, although it is not easy to identify how much of this influence was due to the complex Sino-Yugoslav relationship. For example, it is difficult to judge whether Mao Zedong's "On the Ten Major Relationships" was directly influenced by Yugoslavia. When the Cultural Revolution entered its later stages in the 1970s and the Chinese people began to question current policies, their readings were naturally derived from the works of Marx and Engels. Some of Marx's famous works, including *Das Kapital* and *Critique of the Gotha Programme*, were important starting points for Chinese thoughts on ownership reform, such as the debates on the individual economy or the *primary stage of socialism.*

Beginning in 1979, Eastern European reformers were invited to join in these debates. Two of the first such reformers to visit China were Włodzimierz Brus and Ota Šik. Later, at two major conferences organized by the World Bank—in 1982 at Moganshan and in 1985 on the Bashan Boat—renowned Eastern European and international economists, including János Kornai, Aleksander Bajt, James Tobin, and Alexander Cairncross, provided their insights (Gewirtz 2017; Kornai 2006; Lim 2008). In addition to these visits, numerous translations of foreign works became available and Chinese delegations were sent all over the world to learn from experiences abroad. In the late 1980s, works about ownership by János Kornai and other foreign scholars began to be popular in China. Almost every Chinese economist was familiar with *the economics of shortage*, *soft-budget constraint*, and other concepts imported from abroad (Gewirtz 2017). In the 1990s, Wu Jinglian and Qian Yingyi's article "On Corporatization" marked the beginning of an attempt by economists to combine corporate governance with reform of China's SOEs. Today, we can observe an increasing number of Chinese economists trained at leading American economics departments joining the debates over ownership reform. In addition, overseas economists, such as Nobel Memorial Prize winners Ronald Coase, Oliver Hart, and Eric Maskin have also pondered Chinese ownership issues (Coase and Wang 2012; Hart 2017; Maskin, Qian and Xu 2000).

NOTES

1. I have benefited greatly from valuable comments and suggestions from Xu Chenggang, Isabella Weber, Nancy Hearst, Julian Gewirtz, and Wendy Leutert. All statements of facts, opinion, or analysis are those of the author.

2. Lin (1981) remains the best English-language summary of the Chinese debates on economic theory from 1949 to 1980. Fang (2004; 2013) provides the

most important records on economic policy debates from 1977 to 1989. Liu (2010), Wang (1991), Yu (1996), Zhang (1994), and Zhang (2009) include introductions to writings by various Chinese economists. English-language accounts remain limited. The following books provide a helpful starting point for the reform period: Fewsmith (1994), Hsu (1991), Naughton (1995, 2007), and Wu (2005). Karl (2017) fills a gap by investigating *the economic*, both as a concept and in practice, during the 20th century. Gewirtz (2017) tells the little-known story of how Chinese intellectuals and leaders sought help from foreign economists to reform the economy.

3. Isabella M. Weber (2017) devised the concept of *growing into the plan* to capture the essence of the Chinese transformation to the planning system. See also Naughton (1995).

4. Individual ownership refers to small farms or enterprises. Such small-scale producers were believed to involve only a negligible degree of exploitation because the number of employed workers was insignificant.

5. Different from *individual economy*, *private capitalism* in Chinese discourse of the time implied *exploitation* due to the large number of workers employed.

6. State capitalism in China referred to capitalists supervised by the state through contracts or joint ventures.

7. The three principles are nationalism (*minzuzhuyi*), democracy (*minquanzuyi*), and the people's livelihood (*minshengzhuyi*).

8. For example, according to estimates by Liu Shaoqi ([1952] 1992, 367–68), the public sector accounted for 67.3 percent and the private sector accounted for 32.7 percent of China's gross industrial product (excluding handicrafts) during the first half of 1952, as compared to 43.8 percent and 56.2 percent respectively in 1949.

9. The *five-antis* included "bribery, tax evasion, theft of state property, cheating on government contracts, and stealing of economic information" (Xue 1981, 28).

10. In China the term of social ownership was never used in official documents including Chinese constitutions, it was only applied in Chinese translations of Marxist writings. Since the beginning of the Deng Xiaoping era, some scholars tried to replace the popular term of *public ownership* in Chinese literature by social ownership with little success. Though there is no obvious difference between *public ownership* and *social ownership* in essence, most Chinese intellectuals prefer to use *public ownership* probably because *public* was a popular and positive word in ancient China. In this chapter *public ownership* is used interchangeably with *social ownership* except direct citations.

11. The 1978 Third Plenary Session of the Eleventh Central Committee of the CCP is often regarded as the beginning of the *reform and opening period* or the *Deng Xiaoping era* (Vogel 2011).

12. The 1981 "Government Work Report" of the Fourth Session of the Fifth National People's Congress pointed out: "Comrade Chen Yun's opinions are still of practical significance for the current reform" (Zhao [1981] 2016, 1.362).

13. In contrast to the Soviet Union where about 3,000 commodities were produced under the plan, in China only about 300 commodities were planned.

14. In the autumn of 1958, shortly after China began to establish the people's communes, small-scale trials of fixing farm output quotas for each household appeared in Gansu, Henan, Hunan, Guizhou, and elsewhere. But by the second half of 1959 such trials were prohibited.

15. Most specialists estimate that there were between 18 million and 32 million victims of the Great Famine (Cao 2005; Yang 2009).

16. After Sun's death in 1983, his friends and colleagues set up the Sun Yefang Foundation to commemorate his brave spirit of exploration to *uphold truth* despite great pressures. Today, the Sun Yefang Economic Science Prize is one of China's most influential awards given to economists.

17. In August and September, 33,695 households were attacked in Beijing and 84,222 households were attacked in Shanghai (MacFarquhar and Schoenhals 2006, 117).

18. An important context behind this shift to a more orthodox understanding of historical materialism was the revival of Marxist scholarship during the early years of reform, as described by Meisner (1985).

19. The transition toward accepting a greater role for the market was first codified in 1980 by defining China's target reform model as a "commodity economy with the dominance of public ownership of the means of production and ownerships coexistence," which had been suggested by Xue Muqiao. After some twists and turns, in 1984 the Third Plenum of the Twelfth Central Committee of the CCP basically accepted this target model. In 1992 China's target reform model was redefined as a *socialist market economy*, whereby the market economy was to be the basic mechanism for resource allocations. This was by no means a linear process; rather it involved fundamental political and theoretical struggles among Chinese intellectuals and politicians, focusing on the role and possible ways of reorganizing China's ownership system. At the same time, practical experiments often preceded or inspired the theoretical breakthroughs.

20. This quote was reported by Li Jun, Xue Muqiao's son-in-law. Xue said this to Li in the spring of 1980 when Xue was chairing the Chinese economic reform program. It has been verified in numerous discussions by the author with Li Jun and Xue Xiaohe, Xue Muqiao's daughter.

21. Deng Xiaoping summarized the Chinese strategy as follows: "For example, right now people are talking about the problem of privately hired labor. I have said to many comrades that it is not worth showing that we are taking action on this question and that we can wait two years. [...] In general, it is only small enterprises and peasant households working under the contracted responsibility system. Compared with the more than one hundred million workers, the number of privately hired workers is very small. [...] It would be easy to take action against the practice of hiring labor, but if we did that then people might think we were changing our policy again. [...] But we have to consider when and how to do it. By taking action I mean attacking some restrictions to the practice [...]. [W]e must not unthinkingly cause uncertainty or confusion. It is important for us to encourage people to use their heads and find ways to develop our economy in a pioneering spirit. We should not dampen their initiative; that would not be good for us" (Deng [1987b] 1994, 216–17).

22. In January 1983, in its second Central Document No. 1, entitled "Some Questions Concerning Current Rural Economic Policy," the Central Committee pointed out: "If rural individual industrial and commercial households and farming experts ask for helpers or need apprentices, they can refer to the 'State Council on Urban

Non-agricultural Individual Economic Policy Requirements' for implementation. If they need more employees or helpers than mentioned in the provisions of the above report, we should not advocate it, provide open publicity, or rush to ban it. Rather, we should make the best use of the situation to develop different forms of a cooperative economy" (Xinhua News Service, April 10, 1983).

23. This Chinese title was clearly inspired by Stalin's *Economic Problems of Socialism in the U.S.S.R.* (1952), but it became jumbled by the official translation (Xue 1981). In fact, although the book was based on an orthodox Marxist-Leninist framework, at that time in China it contained many original thoughts.

24. The reviewing agency designated by the Central Propaganda Department was the Institute of Economics of the Academy of Social Sciences, which then asked Wu Jinglian to write the official report on the book. When checking Xue Muqiao's family files, the author found the report.

25. One wonders why Deng did not take credit. One possible explanation is that he was not a chief advocate of the TVE policy in 1975. In any case, however fascinating, this is only a peripheral question.

26. In 1980, when the fixing of output quotas on a household basis was officially allowed, there were 11.4 million commune and brigade enterprises in China, with some 30 million employees; in 1985 there were 12 million township enterprises, with 70 million employees; finally, in 1990 there were 18.5 million township enterprises, with 93 million employees (Wu 2010, 101).

27. Duan Ruofei, the chief editor of *Dangdai sichao* [Contemporary Ideological Trends], chaired a meeting to revise the original version of this article. But Duan was reluctant to tell Fan Shitao the name of the author nor did he approve of the title "Ten-Thousand-Chinese-Word Manifesto" (Fan Shitao 2014).

28. This article was never published. An earlier version appeared as a special commentator's article in *Dangdai sichao* [Contemporary Ideological Trends], no. 4 (1996).

29. Wu Jinglian submitted the suggestion to *re-define socialism* to General Secretary Jiang Zemin and Prime Minister Zhu Rongji. In light of the political sensitivity of the issue, he signed his own name to the document rather than using the name of the research group.

BIBLIOGRAPHY

Aoki, Masahiko. 1994. "Controlling Insider Control: Issues of Corporate Governance in Transition Economies," EDI Working Papers: Studies and Training Design Division, No. 94–43. Washington, DC: World Bank. Available online, accessed April 24, 2017: http://documents.worldbank.org/curated/en/162441468331751207/Controlling-insider-control-issues-of-corporate-governance-in-transition-economies.

Bonnin, Michel. 2013. *The Lost Generation: The Rustication of China's Educated Youth (1968–1980)*. Translated by Krystyna Horko. Hong Kong: The Chinese University Press.

Byrd, William. 1988. "The Impact of the Two-Tier Plan/Market System in Chinese Industry." In *Chinese Economic Reform: How Far, How Fast?* edited by Bruce Reynolds, 5–18. Boston: Academic Press.

Cao, Shuji. 2005. "1959–1961nian Zhongguo de renkou siwang jiqi chengyin" [Deaths of the population in 1959–1961 and the causes]. *Zhongguo renkou kexue* 1: 16–30.

Central Document No. 1. 1982. "Zhonggong zhongyang zhuanfa 'Quanguo nongcun gongzuo huiyi jiyao'" [Summary of the National Rural Work Conference transmitted by the CCP Central Committee]. In *Zhongguo nongye nianjian 1982* [China Agricultural Yearbook 1982], 1–6. Beijing: Nongye chubanshe.

Chen, Xiuliang. 1984. *Sun Yefang geming shengya liushinian* [Sixty years of Sun Yefang's revolutionary career]. Shanghai: Zhishi chubanshe.

Chen, Yun. 1995 [1956]. "Shehuizhuyi gaizao jiben wancheng yihou de xin wenti" [New problems after the Socialist transformation]. In *Selected Works of Chen Yun,* 3: 1–13. Beijing: Renmin chubanshe.

Coase, Ronald, and Ning Wang. 2012. *How China Became Capitalist.* New York: Palgrave Macmillan.

Dangdai sichao teyue pinglunyuan [Special Commentator]. 1996. "Guanyu jianchi shehuizhuyi gongyouzhi zhuti diwei de ruogan lilun he zhengce wenti" [Several theoretical and policy questions on the dominant position of Socialist public ownership]. *Dangdai sichao* [Contemporary Ideological Trends], no. 4 (translated in Foreign Broadcast Information Service, FBIS-CHI-97-096, May 1997).

Deng, Xiaoping. 1994 [1987a]. "Gaige de buzi yao jiakuai" [We shall speed up reform]. In *Deng Xiaoping xuanji 1982–1992* [Selected works of Deng Xiaoping 1982–1992]. Beijing: Renmin chubanshe.

———. 1994 [1987b]. "Speech at a Meeting with Members of the Committee for Drafting the Basic Law of the Hong Kong Special Administrative Region," April 16. In *Selected Works of Deng Xiaoping, 1982–1992*. Beijing: Foreign Languages Press.

Deng, Zihui. 1996 [1956]. "Gonggu xianyou she, wending xinde shengchan guanxi" [Stabilizing the new relations of production in the present cooperatives]. In *Deng Zihui wenji* [Collected works of Deng Zihui], 440–49. Beijing: Renmin chubanshe.

Dong, Fureng. 1988. "Wenzhou nongcun shangpin jingji fazhan daolu wenti" [Issues on the development of the commodity economy in the Wenzhou countryside]. In *Jingji fazhan zhanlüe yanjiu* [Research on the Strategy of Economic Development], 245–79. Beijing: Jingji kexue chubanshe.

Dong, Zhikai, ed. 1996. *1949–1952nian Zhongguo jingji fenxi* [Chinese Economic Analyses, 1949–1952]. Beijing: Zhongguo shehui kexue chubanshe.

Du, Runsheng. 2005. *Du Runsheng zishu: Zhongguo nongcun tizhi biange zhongda juece jishi* [Du Runsheng's statement: A significant decision on China's rural system reform]. Beijing: Renmin chubanshe.

Du, Runsheng et al. 2002. *Dangdai Zhongguo de nongye hezuo* [The agricultural cooperative system in contemporary China]. Beijing: Dangdai Zhongguo chubanshe.

Eaton, Sarah. 2015. *The Advance of the State in Contemporary China: State-Market Relations in the Reform Era.* Cambridge: Cambridge University Press.

Fan, Shitao. 2014. "An Interview with Duan Ruofei," September 25, unpublished manuscript.

Fan, Shitao, and Xue Xiaohe. 2017. *Xue Muqiao nianpu* [Xue Muqiao chronology]. Beijing: Zhongxin chubanshe.

Fang, Weizhong, ed. 2004. *Zai fenglang zhong qianjin: Zhongguo fazhan yu gaige biannian jishi (1977–1989)* [Forward in the Storm: A Chronicle of Chinese Development and Reform (1977–1989)]. Beijing: unpublished manuscript.

———. 2013. *Shisannian jishi* [A chronicle of thirteen years]. Beijing: Zhongguo jihua chubanshe.

Fang, Weizhong, and Jin Chongji, eds. 2001. *Li Fuchun zhuan* [Biography of Li Fuchun]. Beijing: Zhongyang wenxian chubanshe.

Fewsmith, Joseph. 1994. *Dilemmas of Reform in China: Political Conflict and Economic Debate.* Armonk, NY: M.E. Sharpe.

Garms, Eckard. 1980. "Vorwort." In *Wirtschaftsreform in China—Chinesische Beiträge zur Theoriediskussion von Sun Yefang u.a.*, edited by E. Garms, translated by A. Mixius and E. Garms, 7–30. Hamburg: Mitteilungen des Instituts für Asienkunde.

Gewirtz, Julian. 2017. *Unlikely Partners: Chinese Reformers, Western Economists, and the Making of Global China.* Cambridge, MA: Harvard University Press.

1981. "Guowuyuan guanyu chengzhen feinongye geti jingji ruogan zhengcexing guiding" [Policy provisions of the State Council on the urban non-agricultural individual economy]. In *Fazhan chengzhen geti jingji* [The development of the urban individual economy], 9. Beijing: Gongshang chubanshe.

Hart, Oliver. 2017. "Hetong lilun he zhongguo xiayibu gaige" [Contract theory and the next step of China's reform]. *Zhongguo gaige* [China's Reform], no. 1.

He, Cheng. 1956. "Shengchanzu he sheyuan dou yinggai 'baogong baochan'" [Production groups and members of cooperatives should all "contract work and output"]. *Renmin ribao* [People's Daily], April 29, 2.

Hsu, Robert. 1991. *Economic Theories in China, 1979–1988.* Cambridge: Cambridge University Press.

Hua, Xinmin. 2012 "Wode fangzi, shuide tudi? Zhongguo chengshi tudi suoyouquan de shuli he zhuiwen" [My house, whose land? A case study of urban land ownership in China]. *Dongfang zaobao* [Oriental Morning Post], December 27, C01.

Jiang, Yiwei. 1980. "The Theory of an Enterprise-Based Economy." *Social Sciences in China* 1, no. 1: 48–71.

Jiang, Zemin. 1997. "Gaoju Deng Xiaoping lilun weida qizhi, ba jianshe you Zhongguo tese shehuizhuyi shiye quanmian tuixiang ershiyi shiji" [Holding high the banner of Deng Xiaoping theory: Building the cause of socialism with Chinese characteristics to the twenty-first century]. In *Zhongguo gongchandang shiwuci quanguo daibiao dahui wenjian huibian* [Collection of documents on the Fifteenth Congress of the Chinese Communist Party]. Beijing: Renmin chubanshe.

Karl, Rebecca. 2010. *Mao Zedong and China in the Twentieth-Century World.* Durham, NC: Duke University Press.

———. 2017. *The Magic of Concepts: History and the Economic in Twentieth-Century China.* Durham, NC: Duke University Press.

Kornai, János. 1990. *The Road to a Free Economy: Shifting from a Socialist System: The Example of Hungary*. New York: W. W. Norton.

———. 2006. *By Force of Thought: Irregular Memoirs of an Intellectual Journey*. Cambridge: The MIT Press.

Lardy, Nicholas R., and Kenneth Lieberthal, eds. 1983. *Ch'en Yun's Strategy for China's Development: A Non-Maoist Alternative*. Armonk, NY: M.E. Sharpe.

Lenin, V. I. 1977 [1913]. "Backward Europe and Advanced Asia." In *Lenin Collected Works*, 19: 99–100. Moscow: Progress Publishers.

Li, Peng. 1995. "Guanyu zhiding guomin jingji he shehui fazhan jiuwu jihua he 2010nian yuanjing mubiao jianyi de shuoming" [A note on the formulation of the Ninth Five-Year Plan for National Economic and Social Development and the 2010 Vision]. *Qiushi* [Seeking Truth] 11: 7–15.

Li, Yunhe. 2000 [1997]. "Nongcun gaige de zuichu tansuo: Yi Zhejiang Yongjia baochan daohu an shimo" [An initial exploration of the rural reforms: On the case of the household-based contracting system in Yongjia]. In *Li Yunhe lunwenji* [Collected Papers of Li Yunhe], 258–78. Beijing: Zhongyang wenxian chubanshe.

Lim, Edwin. 2008. "Zhongguo gaige kaifang guochengzhong de duiwai sixiang kaifang" [The Opening of Thinking to the Outside World in the Process of China's Reform and Opening]. In *Zhongguo jingji: Wushi ren kan sanshinian* [China's Economy: Fifty People on Thirty Years: Reflections and Analysis], edited by Wu Jinglian et al. Beijing: Zhongguo jingji chubanshe.

Lin, Cyril. 1981. "The Reinstatement of Economics in China Today." *The China Quarterly* 83: 1–48.

Lin, Yunhui. 2009. *Xiang shehuizhuyi guodu: Zhongguo jingji yu shehui de zhuanxing* [Transition to Socialism: China's economic and social transformation]. Hong Kong: Chinese University of Hong Kong.□

Lin, Zili. 1983. *Lun lianchan chengbaozhi: Jianlun ju you Zhongguo tese de shehuishuyi nongye fazhan daolu* [On the output-related household contract system: And the path of socialist agricultural development with Chinese characteristics]. Shanghai: Shanghai renmin chubanshe.

Ling, Huanmin. 1988. "Intellectual Responses to China's Economic Reform." *Asian Survey* 28, no. 5: 541–54.

Liu, Hong. 2010. *Bashi niandai: Zhongguo jingji xueren de guangrong yu mengxiang* [The 1980s: The glory and dreams of China's economists]. Guilin: Guangxi shifan daxue chubanshe.

Liu, Shaoqi. 1992 [1952]. "Guanyu Zhongguo zenyang cong xianzai zhubu guodu dao shehuizhuyi qu de wenti" [On China's gradual transition to socialism]. In *Jianguo yilai zhongyao wenxian xuanbian* [Selected important documents since the founding of the state], edited by Chinese Communist Party Literature Research Center, 3.367–371. Beijing: Zhongyang wenxian chubanshe.

Lu, Xueyi. 2005 [1979]. "Baochan daohu wenti yingdang chongxin yanjiu" [The problem of fixing farm output quotas for each household should be restudied]. In *Lu Xueyi wenji* [Collected works of Lu Xueyi], 10–16. Shanghai: Shanghai cishu chubanshe.

Ma, Hong. 1986 [1979]. "Gaige jingji guanli tizhi yu kuoda qiye zizhuquan" [Reforming the system of economic management and enlarging enterprise autonomy]. In *Ma Hong xuanji* [Selected works of Ma Hong], 251–69. Taiyuan: Shanxi renmin chubanshe.

MacFarquhar, Roderick, and Michael Schoenhals. 2006. *Mao's Last Revolution.* Cambridge, MA: Belknap Press of Harvard University Press.

Mao, Tse-Tung. 1975 [1940]. "On New Democracy." In *Selected Works of Mao Tse-Tung*, 2.339–384. Peking: Foreign Languages Press.

———. 1975 [1947]. "The Present Situation and Our Tasks." In *Selected Works of Mao Tse-Tung,* 4.155–176. Peking: Foreign Languages Press.

———. 1977 [1953]. "The Party's General Line for the Transition Period." In *Selected Works of Mao Tse-Tung*, 5.102. Peking: Foreign Languages Press.

Mao, Zedong. 1977 [1956a]. "Lun shi da guanxi" [On the Ten Major Relationships]. In *Selected Works of Mao Zedong*, 5.267–288. Peking: Foreign Languages Press.

———. 1956b. "Speech at the Supreme State Conference." Available online, accessed April 24, 2017: https://www.marxists.org/reference/archive/mao/works/red-book/ch03.htm.

———. 1998 [1960]. *Mao Zedong du shehuizhuyi zhengzhijingjixue pizhu he tanhua* [Reading notes on the Soviet text *Political Economy*]. Beijing: People's Republic of China History Association.

———. 1966. "Dui zonghouqinbu guanyu jinyibu gaohao budui nongfuye shengchan baogao de piyu" [Comment on the General Logistics Department's report on further improving production of the army's agricultural and sideline industry]. In *Jianguo yilai Mao Zedong wengao*□ [Mao Zedong's manuscripts since the founding of the state], 12.53–56. Beijing: Zhongyang wenxian chubanshe.

Maskin, Eric, Yingyi Qian, and Chenggang Xu. 2000. "Incentives, Information, and Organizational Form." *The Review of Economic Studies* 67, no. 2: 359–78.

Meisner, Maurice. 1985. "The Chinese Rediscovery of Karl Marx: Some Reflections on Post-Maoist Chinese Marxism." *Critical Asian Studies* 17, no. 3: 2–16.

National Committee of the Chinese People's Political Consultative Conference. 1991 [1949]. "Zhongguo renmin zhengzhi xieshang huiyi gongtong gangling" [Common Program of the Chinese People's Political Consultative Conference]. In *Jianguo yilai zhongyao wenxian xuanbian* [Selected important documents since the founding of the state], edited by Chinese Communist Party Literature Research Center, 1:1–13. Beijing: Zhongyang wenxian chubanshe.

Naughton, Barry. 1995. *Growing Out of the Plan: Chinese Economic Reform, 1978–1993.* Cambridge: Cambridge University Press.

———. 2007. *The Chinese Economy: Transitions and Growth.* Cambridge, MA: The MIT Press.

———, ed. 2013. *Wu Jinglian: Voice of Reform in China.* Cambridge, MA: The MIT Press.

Nolan, Peter. 2004. *China at the Crossroads.* Cambridge: Polity Press.

Nolan, Peter, and Dong Fureng, eds. 1989. *Market Forces in China: Competition and Small Business: The Wenzhou Debate.* London: Zed Books.

Nolan, Peter, and Xiaoqiang Wang. 2004. "Beyond Privatization: Institutional Innovation and Growth in China's Large State-Owned Enterprises." In *Transforming China: Globalization, Transition and Development*, edited by Peter Nolan, 131–84. London: Anthem Press.

Party Documents Research Office of the CCP Central Committee. 2011. *Mao Zedong zhuan* [Biography of Mao Zedong]. Beijing: Zhongyang wenxian chubanshe.

Party History Research Center. 2011. *Zhongguo gongchandang lishi, di er juan* [History of the Chinese Communist Party, Volume II]. Beijing: Zhongguo dangshi chubanshe.

Riskin, Carl. 1987. *China's Political Economy: The Quest for Development since 1949*. Oxford: Oxford University Press.

Renmin ribao. 1980. "Fangkuan zhengce shidang fazhan chengzhen feinongye geti gongshangye" [Relaxing the policy to develop urban non-agricultural individual businesses], August 21, 2.

"Several Issues About Further Strengthening and Improving the Agricultural Production Responsibility System." In *China Agricultural Yearbook 1981*, 409–11. Beijing: Nongye chubanshe, 1981.

Shanghai jingji yanjiusuo geming zaofandui and Neikan fanxiubing [Revolutionary Rebel Team from the Economics Institute of the Shanghai Academy of Social Sciences and Anti-revisionist Soldiers of the Internal Journal]. 1967. *Xue Muqiao, Sun Yefang shi Liu Shaoqi zai jingji zhanxian shang fubi zibenzhuyi de ganjiang* [Xue Muqiao and Sun Yefang are on the economic front of Liu Shaoqi's restoration of capitalism]. Shanghai: Shanghai jingji yanjiusuo geming zaofandui and Neikan fanxiubing.

Shen, Zhihua. 2009. "Heluxiaofu mimi baogao de chutai ji Zhongguo de fanying" [Khrushchev's secret speech and China's response]. *Bainianchao* [Hundred year tide], 8: 22–27.

State Commission for Restructuring, ed. 1990. *Shiyijie sanzhong quanhui yilai jingji tizhi gaige zhongyao wenjian huibian* [Major documents since the Third Plenum]. Beijing: Gaige chubanshe.

Su, Shaozhi, and Feng Lanrui. 1979. "Wuchan jieji qude zhengchuan hou de shehui fazhan jieduan wenti" [Problems of the stages of socialist development after the proletariat seizes power]. *Jingji yanjiu* [Economic Research], 5: 14–19.

Sun, Yat-sen. 1922. *International Development of China*. New York: Knickerbocker Press.

Sun, Yefang. 1998 [1961]. "Guanyu quanmin suoyouzhi jingji neibu de caijing tizhi wenti" [The financial and economic system issue within the ownership by the whole people]. In *Sun Yefang quanji* [Complete works of Sun Yefang], 2.229–242. Taiyuan: Shanxi jingji chubanshe.

———. 1998 [1980]. "Shenqie daonian weida de Makesizhuyizhe Tietuo tongzhi" [Deeply mourning the great Marxist Comrade Tito]. In *Sun Yefang quanji* [Complete works of Sun Yefang)], 2.253–255. Taiyuan: Shanxi jingji chubanshe.

Tao, Ying, and Zhang Huan. 2006. "Yiben yinshu jin yiqianwan ce de jingji zhuzuo" [An economics book sold nearly ten million copies]. *Chuban shiliao* [Publication of historical materials], 2: 57–59.

Tian, Yuan. 1990. "Prices." In *The Chinese Economy and its Future,* edited by Peter Nolan and Dong Fureng, 139–50. Cambridge: Polity Press.

Vogel, Ezra F. 1990. *One Step Ahead in China: Guangdong under Reform.* Cambridge, MA: Harvard University Press.

———. 2011. *Deng Xiaoping and the Transformation of China.* Cambridge, MA: Belknap Press of Harvard University Press.

Wan, Li. 1995 [1978]. "Zongzhong shengchandui de ziyou quan" [Respect the autonomy of the production teams]. In *Wan Li wenxuan* [Selected works of Wan Li], 103–5. Beijing: Renmin chubanshe.

Wang, Jue, ed. 1991. *Zhongguo shehuizhuyi zhengzhi jingjixue sishinian, 1949–1989* [Forty years of China's socialist political economy, 1949–1989]. Beijing: Zhongguo jingji chubanshe.

Weber, Isabella M. 2017. *Economic Thinking Behind China's Growth Miracle: The Case of Price Reform.* PhD Dissertation, University of Cambridge.

Wu, Jinglian. 1979. "Guanyu xuanchuan Dazhai de jige wenti" [Several questions about propagating Dazhai]. *Lilun gongzuo wuxuhui jianbao* [Theoretical work conference briefing], 220: 1–10.

———. 1985. "Cong Xiongyali de jingyan kan woguo dangqian de gaige" [Viewing our country's present reform from the perspective of the Hungarian experience]. *Jingji shehui tizhi bijiao* [Comparative Economic and Social System], no. 3.

———. 2005. *Understanding and Interpreting Chinese Economic Reform.* Mason, OH: Thomson Higher Education.

———. 2010. *Dangdai Zhongguo jingji gaige jiaocheng* [Textbook on Chinese economic reform]. Shanghai: Shanghai yuandong chubanshe.

———. 2012. "Economics and China's Economic Rise." In *The Chinese Economy: A New Transition*, edited by Masahiko Aoki and Wu Jinglian, 13–31. New York: Palgrave Macmillan.

———. 2013 [1997]. "Guanyu shehuizhuyi de zai dingyi wenti" [On the problem of a redefinition of socialism]. In *Wu Jinglian wenji* [Collected works of Wu Jinglian], 1.183–191. Beijing: Zhongyang bianyi chubanshe.

———. 2013 [2011]. "Guoyou jingji de buju tiaozheng he guoyou qiye de gaige buneng tingbu" [Adjustment of the layout of the state-owned economy and reform of state-owned enterprises cannot stop]. In *Wu Jinglian wenji* [Collected works of Wu Jinglian], 2.663–667. Beijing: Zhongyang bianyi chubanshe.

———. 2014 [2013]. "Xueshu yongqi yu shehui dandang" [Tribute to Lu Xueyi: Academic courage and social responsibility]. In *Zhimian dazhuan shidai* [Confronting a great transformation period], 360–64. Beijing: Shenghuo, dushu, xinzhi, sanlian shudian.

Wu, Jinglian et al. 1997. "Shixian guoyou jingji de zhanlüe xingzu: Guoyou qiye gaige de yizhong silu" [Realizing the strategic reorganization of the State-owned Economy Team: One thought on the reform of state-owned enterprises]. *Guanli shijie* [Management World], 5: 1–12.

Wu, Jinglian, and Fan Shitao. 2014. "China's Economic Reform: Processes, Issues and Prospects." In *Routledge Handbook of the Chinese Economy,* edited by Gregory C. Chow and Dwight H. Perkins, 55–75. London: Routledge.

Wu, Jinglian, and Ma Guochuan. 2016. *Whither China: Restarting the Reform Agenda*. Translated by Xiaofeng Hua and Nancy Hearst. Oxford: Oxford University Press.

Wu, Jinglian, and Qian Yingyi. 1993. "Lun gongsihua" [On corporatization]. *Jingji ribao* [Economic Daily], August 24.

Wu, Si. 1993. *Chen Yonggui chenfu Zhongnanhai: Gaizao Zhongguo de shiyan* [Chen Yonggui's ups and downs in Zhongnanhai: Trials for transforming China]. Guangzhou: Huacheng chubanshe.

Wu, Xiang. 2010. "Jingji xuejia Lin Zili" [The economist Lin Zili]. *Yanhuang chunqiu* [Annals of the Yellow Emperor], 12: 36–40.

Xu, Chenggang. 2011. "The Fundamental Institutions of China's Reforms and Development." *Journal of Economic Literature* 49, 4: 1076–1151.

Xu, Dixin. 1959. *Zhongguo guodu shiqi guomin jingji de fenxi* [Analysis of China's National Economic Transition]. Beijing: Kexue chubanshe.

Xue, Muqiao. 1957. "Dui xianxing jihua guanli zhidu de yijian" [Proposal on the current planning system]. In *Xue Muqiao wenji* [Collected works of Xue Muqiao], 4.249–259. Beijing: Zhongguo jinrong chubanshe.

———. 1978a. "Noted Economist on Employment." *Beijing Revie*w 33 (August 17), 13–15.

———. 1981. *China's Socialist Economy*. Beijing: Foreign Languages Press.

———. 1996. *Xue Muqiao huiyilu* [Memoirs of Xue Muqiao]. Tianjin: Tianjin renmin chubanshe.

———. 2011 [1978a]. "Guanyu shedui qiye wenti" [On the issue of commune and brigade enterprises]. In *Xue Muqiao wenji* [Collected works of Xue Muqiao], 7.59–65. Beijing: Zhongguo jinrong chubanshe.

———. 2011 [1978b]. "Guanyu 1958–1966nian guomin jingji jianshe de qingkuang he jingyan" [On the situation and experience of national economic construction in 1958–1966]. In *Xue Muqiao wenji* [Collected works of Xue Muqiao], 7.66–78. Beijing: Zhongguo jinrong chubanshe.

———. 2011 [1978c]. "Guanyu jihua guanli zhidu de yixie yijian" [Some observations on the planning management system]. In *Xue Muqiao wenji* [Collected works of Xue Muqiao], 7.254–259. Beijing: Zhongguo jinrong chubanshe.

———. 2011 [1979b]. *Zhongguo shehuizhuyi jingji wenti yanjiu* [Economic problems of socialism in China]. In *Xue Muqiao wenji* [Collected works of Xue Muqiao], 191–251. Beijing: Zhongguo jinrong chubanshe.

———. 2011 [1980a]. "Dui guanyu jingji tizhi gaige de chubu yijian de shuoming" [Illumination on the preliminary proposal on economic reform]. In *Xue Muqiao wenji* [Collected works of Xue Muqiao], 8.128–132. Beijing: Zhongguo jinrong chubanshe.

———. 2011 [1980b]. "Zailun jingji jiegou he jingji guanli tizhi gaige" [More on the economic structure and the reform of the management system]. In *Xue Muqiao wenji* [Collected Works of Xue Muqiao], 8.212–221. Beijing: Zhongguo jinrong chubanshe.

———. 2011 [1987]. "Woguo shengchan ziliao suoyouzhi de yanbian" [The evolution of the ownership of production in our country]. In *Xue Muqiao wenji* [Collected works of Xue Muqiao], 12.164–186. Beijing: Zhongguo jinrong chubanshe.

———. 2011 [1990]. "Gei Yang Huanjin de sanfengxin" [Three letters to Yang Huanjin]. In *Xue Muqiao wenji* [Collected works of Xue Muqiao], 14.35–45. Beijing: Zhongguo jinrong chubanshe.

———. 2011. *Xue Muqiao wenji* [Collected works of Xue Muqiao]. Beijing: Zhongguo jinrong chubanshe.

Xue, Muqiao et al. 2011 [1958]. "Zhongguo guodu shiqi de jingji" [China's economy during the transition period]. In *Xue Muqiao wenji* [Collected works of Xue Muqiao]. Beijing: Zhongguo jinrong chubanshe.

Yang, Jisheng. 2009. *Mubei: Zhongguo liushi niandai dajihuang jishi* [Tombstone: The story of China's Great Famine in the 1960s]. Hong Kong: Tiandi tushu youxian gongsi.

Yao, Yang. 2008. *Zuowei zhidu chuanxin guocheng de jingji gaige* [Economic reform as a process of institutional innovation]. Shanghai: Gezhi chubanshe.

Yu, Guangyuan, ed. 1996. *Zhongguo lilun jingji xueshi, 1949–1989* [Chinese economic theories, 1949–1989]. Zhengzhou: Henan renmin chubanshe.

———. 2005. *Xinminzhuzhuyi shehui lun de lishi mingyun* [The historical fate of the theory of a new democracy society]. Wuhan: Changjiang wenyi chubanshe.

———. 2008. "Cong 'jieduan fengbo' dao 'shehuizhuyi chuji jieduan'" [From the "stage of the storm" to the "primary stage of socialism"]. *Yanhuang chunqiu* [Annals of the Yellow Emperor], 8: 1–7.

Zeng, Jin. 2013. *State-led Privatization in China: The Politics of Economic Reform.* London: Routledge.

Zhang, Wenmin. 1994. *Zhongguo zhengzhi jingjixue shi dagang, 1899–1992* [Outline of the history of China's political economy, 1899–1992]. Beijing: Zhongyang dangxiao chubanshe.

Zhang, Zhuoyuan, ed. 2009. *Zhongguo jingjixue liushinian, 1949–2009* [Sixty years of economics in China, 1949–2009]. Beijing: Zhongguo shehui kexue chubanshe.

Zhao, Ziyang. 2016 [1981]. "Dangqian de jingji xingshi he jinhou jingji jianshe de fangzhen" [The current economic situation and the future direction of economic construction]. In *Zhao Ziyang wenji, 1980–1989* [Collected works of Zhao Ziyang, 1980–1989], 1.339–373. Hong Kong: Xianggang zhongwen daxue chubanshe.

———. 2016 [1987]. "Guanyu caoni shisanda baogao dagang de shexiang gei Deng Xiaoping tongzhi de xin" [Letter to Comrade Deng Xiaoping on drafting the outline of the Thirteenth Congress Report]. In *Zhao Ziyang wenji, 1980–1989* [Collected works of Zhao Ziyang, 1980–1989], 4.47–48. Hong Kong: Xianggang zhongwen daxue chubanshe.

Chapter 3

From Nationalization to Privatization

Understanding the Concept of Ownership in Czechoslovakia, 1948–1990[1]

Julius Horvath and Vítězslav Sommer

The scholarly literature discussing the issue of ownership under socialism in Czechoslovakia is concerned primarily with the changes in the ownership structure under regimes of nationalization after 1945, collectivization after 1948, and privatization after 1989. As a consequence, the historiography of ownership relations is focused almost exclusively on the political history of nationalization, collectivization, and privatization, while the theoretical and intellectual dimensions of this topic tend to be omitted.

Reform-minded communist scholars published the first accounts of ownership change under communism as early as in the 1960s. These influential promoters of the "Czechoslovak road to socialism" were seriously concerned with the period between 1945 and 1953, when state socialism was established and when far-reaching changes to the ownership structure were carried out. Their research interest resulted in the publication of several works dealing with the economic foundations of economic governance in Stalinism and beyond. In this context, it is worth highlighting the extraordinarily important works written in the 1960s by historian Karel Kaplan, in which the process of nationalization was analyzed critically for the first time after 1945 (see Kaplan 1968, 1969; Jech 1968). A similar perspective was employed also by reform-minded communist historiography of the collectivization of agriculture.[2] In short, a specific genre of "reform historiography" aimed to analyze the most recent history of Czechoslovakia and, simultaneously, to construct the historical legitimacy of the political project of reform communists.[3] From the perspective of economic-reform debates, this literature about nationalization and collectivization was highly relevant and politically engaged as well. After 1989, the issues of nationalization and collectivization were primarily discussed in the context of research on policymaking under socialism (see, for example, Kaplan 2012; Kuklík 2010). However, the collectivization of agriculture was usually conceptualized more as a repressive policy measure than as a specific domain of economic governance.[4]

The issues of workers' participation and self-management (*samospráva*) were closely connected with the debates about economic reform and forms of ownership under communist dictatorship. In the 1960s, these controversial topics were integrated into the polemics about democratization of the socialist political system. Workers' participation thus was discussed primarily as an important component of power relations in the sphere of industrial production. It was analyzed primarily in sociological studies and was further elaborated in the context of radical reformist political thought (see Kovanda 2014; Slejška 1968).[5] In the 1980s, this topic was further conceptualized in *perestroika*-style economic-reform debates (Pullmann 2011). However, it was not reflected by historians after 1989 in its entirety and remained at the margins of research on the history of working class and management in socialist Czechoslovakia (see Heumos 2006; Kaplan 2007).

The lack of research on this issue contrasts with the fact that the character of socialist ownership deeply influenced the character of the economy and the state. The Czechoslovak model of ownership never got close to Yugoslav self-management. It was a Soviet-inspired *etatist* (statist) model throughout the socialist period. According to the prevailing ideology of the Czechoslovak Communist Party, the interests of party, workers, and managers were to coincide. Allegedly, the representatives of communist power consulted trade unions and involved them in the decision-making bodies. But that typically made the workers' representatives simply an additional member of the decision-making bodies, with no voice of their own.

In Czechoslovakia during the socialist period the traditional socialist dogma of the superiority of state ownership (*státní vlastnictví*) prevailed. State and collective ownership (*kolektivní vlastnictví*) was seen as a mythical concept which made socialism different from the capitalist system and which determined the nature of socialist economic relations. Socialist doctrine declared that state and collective ownership guaranteed the working of the new laws of economy. Capitalism was seen as anarchy, while state property guaranteed that the laws of socialism (for example, planned and proportional development) could be implemented. As a result of this orthodox approach, in 1989 the Czechoslovak economy functioned with an extraordinarily high percentage of state ownership even by the standards of socialist countries.[6]

This chapter consists of two main sections. First, we discuss the concept of ownership as it was understood during the socialist period. Second, we present the discussions that preceded the early projects of privatization.

OWNERSHIP UNDER THE SOCIALIST REGIME

General Observations on the Character of Ownership

In the 20th century, Czechoslovak society experienced different forms of asset redistribution. Both nationalization and privatization were—for a short period of time—popular with masses, even if both meant a transfer of political power from one type of elite to another.[7]

After its foundation in 1918, Czechoslovakia experienced various politically motivated changes in private ownership. Society first faced the confiscation of some of the property of the *nouveaux riches*, who made their fortune during the war years. Transformations in land ownership were also initiated with the intention to weaken the political and economic power of German and Hungarian aristocracy. At the end of the 1930s and in the early 1940s, the property of owners of Jewish descent was confiscated. After 1939 in Slovakia, ownership by Czech nationals was restrained and in some cases property was confiscated. After the Second World War the new Czechoslovak government confiscated the property of German and Hungarian owners and of those who had collaborated with the Germans. Also the property of Germans who were expelled from Czechoslovakia was confiscated. Between 1946 and early 1948 an additional round of nationalization took place.

Thus, when the communists took power in February 1948, it was no surprise for the general public that the government continued with this unfortunate practice. Following the 1950s, after a large-scale nationalization of industry and small businesses and collectivization of agriculture, there were no significant changes in ownership structure for the rest of the socialist period. However, after the breakup of the communist regime the next phase was again characterized by far-reaching changes in ownership: by de-nationalization, that is, privatization, of assets.

Initially, the Czechoslovak Communist Party envisaged a place for small private-property owners, especially in services. However, slowly after taking total power, there were conscious actions to weaken and gradually to eliminate the remnants of private ownership. The Czechoslovak Constitution of 1948 contained provisions protecting small and medium-size enterprises and farms of 50 hectares or less. However, these provisions were ignored during nationalization and collectivization.

The new socialist Constitution of 1960 recognized only two types of property: state and cooperative. However, gradually the importance of cooperative (*družstevní vlastnictví*) decreased.[8] The Constitution omitted private property from its typology of ownership but Article 9 mentions the possibility of having small private enterprises not exploiting the labor of others.[9]

Communist economists viewed nationalization as a matter of principle, a precondition for the successful road toward communism, and also as a matter of expediency, that is, they believed that state ownership meant higher economic efficiency.[10] Without nationalization the communists could not have achieved a complete control of society.[11]

One of the basic characteristics of private property rights is that non-owners of the property are excluded from its use. In socialism there was no clear legal owner of property (means of production) and surely it was not an individual. Theoretically the owners of the property under socialism were the people, that is, society as a whole was the proprietor. However, in reality the real owners were representatives of the government and of the party's organs, whether federal, national, or local. But among these entities the division of the functions of ownership was never fully separated.

One component of property rights is the right to control the residual income stemming from ownership. However, in socialism residual incomes were not well defined, and more importantly, whatever the residual income meant it had to flow into a central state coffer. Another component is the right to sell or rent the property to individuals or enterprises. It seems that even communist officials could not exercise these rights. This created an interesting conundrum in which the owner could keep the property for too long a time, potentially forever.[12]

Astute observers of socialist reality like János Kornai and Lubomír Mlčoch[13] noticed that behind the impersonal state (government, party) one finds clearly identifiable power groups formed in the actual context of individual enterprises. These officials had the right to manage and control property. We lack case studies analyzing how in particular Czechoslovak enterprises the rights of control of property were exercised. Kornai (1992) argues that bureaucracy exercised its control over property unevenly, that is, the relative influence of different bodies in the government and the party structure was not predetermined for a certain type of control, and it rather changed together with the political process.

Again, property rights of individuals over assets consist of the right to consume the asset, to obtain income from the asset, and to alienate the asset (Barzel 1989). However, all three ways of handling property imply transaction costs. Transaction costs would be zero only if property rights would be complete, which does not hold even under private ownership and clearly not under vague socialist property rights. The incompleteness of property rights meant that an owner (citizen, state, government, or party) did not have more knowledge about the assets than those who used them every day (managers, engineers, and other employees).[14]

DISCUSSIONS ON OWNERSHIP BETWEEN 1948 AND 1989

Since the establishment of the communist regime in 1948, ownership became one of the cornerstones of new economic and social order. The structure of ownership was substantially transformed, which affected the everyday life of the population and was reflected also in the spheres of social theory and expert knowledge. There were two main and occasionally competing perspectives for the analysis of ownership: economic and legal.[15]

During the first two decades of socialism the legal structure of ownership relations was constructed and embedded in various legal acts.[16] According to Czechoslovak law, there were three fundamental forms of ownership: social ownership (*společenské vlastnictví*), personal ownership (*osobní vlastnictví*), and private ownership (*soukromé vlastnictví*) (Holub-Bičovský 1985; Knapp 1952). For the functioning of the economy the most important was the dominance of social ownership composed of state ownership, which was recognized as the backbone of ownership structure and the most important ownership form in socialism, and collective ownership (mostly, cooperative ownership).[17] Personal ownership was characterized as an individual consumer's appropriation of certain parts of social products (Colotka 1956, 8; Holub-Bičovský 1985, 12). It was the outcome of socialist redistribution, which was organized by the state, and it was a form of ownership specific to socialism (Colotka 1956, 25; Zdobinský 1957, 41). An important constituent of personal ownership were flats and family houses, although it was difficult to define its position in socialist ownership relations.[18] Private property was recognized as an anachronistic form of ownership incompatible with socialism. According to legal pundits at the time, it still existed but slowly was disappearing as a remnant of the capitalist past (Knapp 1952, 224–25). Private ownership was not regarded as personal ownership, for example, land or real estate, if used for profit making. However, the possession of private ownership was significantly restricted and controlled by the authorities and this negative attitude of the socialist state toward private ownership was embedded in legislation (Holub-Bičovský 1985, 95–96, 103–04).

Although this structure of ownership remained intact until 1989, scholars and experts recognized it as historically situated and definitely not carved in stone. According to them, these ownership relations were an expression of a particular stage in the historical development from socialism to communism and, moreover, it also reflected changes in the functioning of the socialist economy. After the 1970s, for example, collective ownership in agricultural cooperatives was described as an ownership form that was practically eliminated by the growing industrialization of agricultural production. Although it was formally characterized as a collective ownership of individual producers, it was in fact managed as if it were a part of social property in the possession of the state (Vydra 1981, 137–38).

Czechoslovak economic thinking started to reflect on the subject of ownership more thoroughly from the late 1950s. A controversy was initiated in 1959 by the article "Ownership and Economic Relations" written by Čestmír Kožušník (1959) and published in the party journal *Nová mysl.*[19] Kožušník mentioned the Marxist notion of *legal fiction*, arguing that ownership—if characterized exclusively in legal terms as a relationship between man and his/her property—was not a real ownership. According to Kožušník, ownership emerged in the interaction between people, in the process of economic relations, and was independent of law. The economic form of ownership was thus a "social form of appropriation by individuals," a "social form of production," that is, an "economic relation among people in the process of production" (Ibid., 696). The reality of ownership was not based on the ownership legislature but on the *modes of production* and *relations of production.*[20] It was not possible, according to Kožušník, to *explain the economy by law* and to ignore the centrality of economic relations for the constitution of ownership. It meant that a mere legal change of ownership, for example, in the form of nationalization, was not a guarantee of efficiency and did not produce economic relations (Richterková 2013, 20).

The publication of Kožušník's article provoked a debate about the dynamic between economic relations and ownership relations. For the purposes of this discussion a public meeting of the Department of Political Economy at the Higher School of Economics in Prague was organized in March 1960.[21] Kožušník's article was criticized publicly, mainly by political economist Miroslav Křížek who argued, by referring to Stalin's writing about ownership, that the article was misleading and methodologically flawed. Kožušník simplified the whole topic, according to Křížek, because he discussed ownership exclusively as an economic category.[22] Moreover, Kožušník allegedly missed the important point that the ownership of the means of production was a foundation of the overall relations of production. The contributions of economists to this controversy moved in different directions, thus no consensus was reached. As a consequence, the ownership debate continued in the following years (see *Z diskusních příspěvků* 1962; Hába 1962; Málek 1964). Ota Šik in his book *Economy, Interests, Politics* (1962) gave a quite extensive coverage of the topic, providing a relatively positive evaluation of Kožušník's views. The establishment of socialist economic relations was portrayed by Šik as a basic precondition for the development of new, socialist legal norms of ownership. In short, the existence of socialist ownership was, according to him, determined by the development of socialist labor, redistribution, and mode of production (Šik 1964, 242–88).

The ownership controversy in the late 1950s and early 1960s was a rather abstract exercise in Marxist political economy and did not reflect the everyday practice of the Czechoslovak economy. However, in the course of the 1960s economists involved in the debate about economic reform introduced a quite different approach to the issue of ownership. Although the attempts to theorize ownership from an abstract perspective were still present in the literature, the shift toward a more policy-oriented research agenda was more than evident.[23] The most important topic of economic reform debates was the role of the market in the economy and the establishment of a system of economic governance based on the interaction between planning and the market.[24] In the context of economic reform the issue of ownership was discussed primarily from the angle of a possible change in the position of enterprises. The aim of reform economists was to elaborate a new concept of enterprise as a relatively autonomous unit (see, for example, Suchan 1968; Levčík and Kosta 1968). This also challenged the prevailing theory of ownership and the existing ownership structure.

In his article about "social ownership in the market system," Bohumil Komenda (1969) discussed the influence of the changing position of enterprises on the conceptualization of ownership. This contribution was quite a harsh critique of state ownership. Komenda argued that universally applied and centrally organized state ownership caused society to be unable to influence the economy, which was in fact governed by a small and uncontrollable group of *apparatchiks*. This system of economic governance caused the economy to develop extensively but without any significant *final effect*. According to Komenda, state ownership was a "specific type of social ownership alien to its own purpose" and was actually transformed in a group ownership of central apparatus officials (Ibid., 874). The aim of the reform thus was to replace state ownership with enterprise ownership, that is, not to abandon social ownership but to change its form, and to establish a complex system of rules preventing the reemergence of strictly centralized economic governance as well as making the shift from social to group ownership impossible.

The question about how to organize the economic independence of the firm became a contested issue in the second half of the 1960s. As was evident at the Enterprise Symposium organized in December 1968 by the Club of Young Economists, although there was a general agreement among reformers that a more relaxed relationship between central authorities and enterprises was inevitable, the introduction of some kind of self-management remained a controversial issue (Mlčoch 1969).[25] At this conference the relationship between ownership and the *inner structure of the firm* was discussed by Václav Klaus who became a leading policymaker after 1989. Klaus claimed that the only way that economists could fully satisfy "humanist socialist ideals" was to "design a proposal for an efficiently functioning and rationally behaving firm" (Ibid., 279). However, this also entailed a choice among ownership forms because self-management was, according to Klaus, based on group ownership whereas the managerial system was embedded in state ownership. Klaus thus suggested to subordinate the ownership arrangement to economic rationality.

To reform economists it seemed inevitable to rethink the existing ownership structure. However, there was a general consensus that possible shifts in the ownership relations had to respect the fact that private ownership of the means of production was an unacceptable alternative and, as was highlighted by Komenda, the primacy of social ownership also was worth maintaining. The reformers of the 1960s did not consider substantial re-privatization as an achievable policy, neither in industry nor in agriculture (Kosta 2005, 31–32). Among the issues on the table one found permission for private persons and their families to own business units providing small-scale services.[26] There were also discussions on the extent of control over the party bureaucracy, in both the large and medium-sized companies, along with recommendations to weaken the power of bureaucracy over socialist ownership. A move from the party-state to workers' collectives was understood as a progressive step.

In the second half of the 1960s, Ota Šik supported the introduction of workers' councils. However, he was not in favor of giving the councils substantial powers as was the case in Yugoslavia. The role of workers' councils was to be limited to the choice of upper-level enterprise management, to the approval of profit distribution, and of the general course of developing the enterprise.

In the reform year of 1968, some changes occurred to the autonomy of socialist firms. A new law allowed the foundation of workers' councils and also slightly increased the autonomy of enterprises. They were to be governed by managers as well as by the members of the council.[27] The law recognized public (*veřejný*) and state (*státní*) enterprises. Public enterprises would stay in collective ownership (almost 90 percent of all firms). In these enterprises the elected councils would imitate the role of owners.[28] Finally, the new regulations also recognized enterprises founded by other public enterprises. Kýn (1970, 304) writes that in Czechoslovakia in January 1969 councils were elected in more than 100 companies, out of around 2,000.[29] The workers' councils were in operation from late spring of 1968 till almost the end of 1969, when the last workers' council at Škoda Plzeň dissolved itself. Kosta (2005, 38) mentions that there was a clear political pressure from the Soviet side to close these councils.

After the crush of the 1968 reform—in the so-called normalization period[30]—the question of ownership again became a taboo. Ideas like market socialism, independence of enterprises, or workers' participation were condemned as revisionist concepts and the instruments of counterrevolution.

In the early 1970s, Czechoslovak economic literature dismissed the reform economics of the previous decade in the name of central planning and a return to a rigid, ideological political economy.[31]

Hence, the issue of ownership was discussed from a theoretical perspective and, simultaneously, as part of the critique of reform economics (see Hába, Bavlnka, and Kameníček 1976; Hába and Křížek 1976; Hába and Koláček 1972; Nikolič 1972). Most importantly, the idea of enterprise ownership was criticized as the core of revisionist discourse. As claimed by Pavel Dušan Nikolič, the concept of enterprise ownership was an outcome of the "lack of understanding" and "distorting" of the "universally valid principles of Marxist political economy" (Hába, Bavlnka, and Kameníček 1976, 214–15).[32] This harsh critique portrayed the reformist view as a reduction of the complex Marxist theory of ownership to a search for the legal subject of ownership in socialist firms. Zdeněk Hába and Miroslav Křížek even elaborated the genealogy of this revisionist theory of ownership, originating in the late 1950s with Kožušník's article and culminating in the Prague Spring economic reform based on market socialism and the idea of enterprise independence (Hába and Křížek 1976, 241–59). After 1968, there were no more significant attempts to open and rethink the question of ownership in a more straightforward way until the middle of the 1980s in the field of economic research.[33]

During the normalization period the existing ownership structure was frozen, and any implicit attempt to change it was considered anti-socialist. In the second half of the 1980s, pragmatic communist politicians, under the influence of *perestroika*, launched a discussion about the future of socialist ownership. These writings reviewed below, however, were presented in such a manner that could not be connected to the reform ideas of the 1960s and thus labeled revisionist.

Initially, Gorbachev's reforms were not welcomed by the more conservative Czechoslovak leadership. However, later the tone of official publications began to change as it seemed that Gorbachev's reforms would survive and might influence the character of socialist property relationships. In these times, one observes the emergence of articles that question the leveling of incomes and discuss the importance of wealth stratification. The argument would run as follows: higher efficiency in the workplace should be honored by society, not only by moral but also by material recognition. In addition, discussion emerged about the role of the enterprise and profit in socialism. Such discussions typically appeared in the journal *Politická ekonomie*.

According to Babin (1987, 79), the nationalization of private property did not create real ownership since that would require that owners of socialist property would have "the spirit of an owner." The author also noted that developing this spirit would require a long and complex process in the future.[34] In 1987 Zdeněk Hába (1987)—one of the intellectual gurus of the normalization process—criticized the prevailing concepts of the political economy of ownership and proposed that the state should rent its property in exchange for a share in the profit of individual or family economic activities.[35] Hába opposed the views from 1968 that favored workers owning firms. Klusoň (1988) expected an increase in the share of private property in the economy, while he argued that the predominance of state and cooperative ownership should remain. Interestingly, he also conjectured the possibility of a limited ownership of shares of enterprises by individuals. He argued that if citizens were involved in share ownership then that would have a positive impact on consumer behavior. Štěpánek (1989) compared Soviet and Czechoslovak laws on state companies. He criticized the Czechoslovak legal arrangements because they left the socialist enterprises in an *abstract ownership of nobody* in contrast to Soviet law in which the socialist enterprise was *a free association of free producers*. He also wrote that nationalization should not necessarily mean total state ownership, and that a socialist economy also can work on other foundations than state ownership. Lukas (1989) criticized the voting process for new directors in certain firms. He suggested that some state enterprises should be transformed into joint-stock companies and sold to non-state owners.

Politická ekonomie also published papers and translations from various Soviet and Eastern European economists. For example, Rudnickij (1988) wrote about the Soviet experience of improving the motivation for individual and family economic activity. He seemed to support strengthening the role of private property in the economy if it does not lead to exploitation. He proposed that the socialist enterprise should be considered as a subject of ownership and not only a state-managed instrument of production of the state. Kulikov (1989) criticized the dogmatic approach toward state property and argued that *perestroika* should re-build ownership relations. Social ownership was, according to him, a false concept, as society was not a subject of the law, but a sum of different subjects. He also stressed that changes in ownership should not weaken the idea of state control of the economy. Pajestka (1989) presented the reform process in Poland and wrote that Polish society was in the process of de-mythologizing the question of ownership. He emphasized that people should be interested in the development of capital, and that the question of ownership makes sense only when owners effectively exercise their ownership rights. The author believed that few would care about the purity of the ownership concept if higher effectivity could be achieved.

This short review points to the fact that, even in the official publications, ownership again began to be a topic to discuss by the end of the 1980s.[36] In the next section we will present unofficial discussions that had a much larger impact on shaping the opinions about ownership after the breakup of socialism. Our interest will be in the discussions of economists around

Václav Klaus, Tomáš Ježek, and others who became important proponents of privatization in the early 1990s. (For example, Ježek served as the head of the Czech privatization agency between 1992 and 1994.) We will label this group of economists as liberals or neoliberals.

INTELLECTUAL MILIEU OF ECONOMISTS IN PRAGUE IN THE 1980s

Toward the end of the 1980s, (neo)liberal economists avoided the direct discussion of the question of ownership.[37] They understood that ownership changes required a substantial political shift in Czechoslovakia. Ironically, economists who openly discussed the issue of ownership were closer to the party-state and understood changes in ownership structures as changes in the policy of the communist party. However, people like Klaus and Ježek were clearly outside the power structures and knew that significant change in ownership happens only if the political system changes. They also understood the personal risks of discussing the issue of ownership publicly without any political backing.

They were inspired by the theory of property rights, especially the earlier work of Armen Alchian, Harold Demsetz, Svetozar Pejovich, and Richard Posner. Some of their important writings were known and studied in Prague already in the early 1980s. In addition, the works of Friedrich Hayek, Milton Friedman, George Stigler, and Ronald Coase were also discussed in the intellectual milieu of Prague in the 1980s. Concerning ownership, the vision was that private property and control of enterprises were, at least to a large extent, equivalent, and ownership was clearly dominant to governance.

Most participants of the unofficial discussions about privatization believed that what mattered was a fundamental change in ownership: to replace state property with private property *en bloc*. As in Czechoslovakia no real private sector existed at all, privatization was seen as a central aspect of building a market economy. In other words, privatization was the transformation. Only later was it realized that other factors are also needed for the proper workings of a private property system. Czechoslovak reality showed that assigning property rights to a person who shows no care for the property actually might lead to new types of inefficiency. In other words, in the 1980s, Czech liberals were of the opinion that ownership of means of production represented the largest difference between capitalist and socialist systems. It was believed that assigning clear property rights automatically makes for efficient economic behavior.

The failures of socialism were understood to a large extent as stemming from the elimination of private property rights. For example, public space was often neglected as it was perceived as belonging to no one, a space to which no property rights were assigned. The (neo)liberals believed that the most important difference between socialist and capitalist enterprise was in the enterprise's objectives: the latter focused exclusively on profit with an attention to costs and customers, while the socialist firm—which potentially could be interested in profits, too—followed the objectives of the owners, thus economic decisions became politicized. Inefficiencies arose because they were not a central concern of the owner. That weak corporate governance can lead to inferior performance, even under private ownership,[38] was not clearly foreseen.

It seems that Czechoslovak (neo)liberals took the textbook competitive model as a good representation of the actual economy. They seemed to operate within the hypothetical framework of stylized western economics. However, these views were challenged, already at the time, by theories like the principle-agent model, rent-seeking models, and asymmetric information that emphasized the transaction costs inherent in property rights changes and put an emphasis on both governance and ownership.

Original views concerning socialist ownership were presented in the works of Lubomír Mlčoch. His manuscripts written in the first half of the 1980s were published only later.[39] Mlčoch argued that in socialism managers, together with party officials, exercised some property rights over goods that were in shortage, sometimes in return for favors from other groups of managers. Mlčoch (2000, 11) wrote that central planning methods were cooperative games. Officially, planning was vertical; in reality, the lower-level actors of the planning process aimed at securing the largest share from society's resources. Official planning was an important smokescreen that allowed them to hide their rent- and wealth-seeking behavior. Planning was an important ritual that maintained the social structure of socialist society.

According to Mlčoch, during the communist period the informal authority over socialist property was in the hands of top managers, leading communist functionaries, and additional members from different power circles. In his opinion, this was an embryotic form of property rights. To some extent, these informal property rights were transformed into formal legal rights in the first years of the Czechoslovak transformation. In Mlčoch's view, a coalition of managers, local and national party *apparatchiks*, and government bureaucrats dominated corporate governance in most companies before 1989. But in the end the managers of socialist firms had the most important word. Mlčoch referred to this situation as an upside-down pyramid or reverse pyramid, in contradiction of the typical textbook view of the command hierarchy. A weak monitoring of managers by the party-state as formal owners upended the socialist system, filling the managerial posts with real power. For Mlčoch the socialist enterprise manager, not the state planner, was the crucial figure.[40]

He claimed (Mlčoch 2000b, 11) that at the horizontal company level seller-customer (i.e., supply-demand) relations prevailed. This meant that one could observe market relations in a socialist economy, even if in a distorted form. Property rights were not defined in strict legal terms as in the capitalist economy; however, the entitlements were real. Managers, the local party elite, and the representatives of branch ministries received entitlements due to their social status. "Generally, these entitlements were less easily divisible and transferable, even though trading of these entitlements did indeed occur using a form of barter."[41]

COMPETITION OF IDEAS ON OWNERSHIP AND EARLY PROJECTS OF PRIVATIZATION

The new elite in economic scholarship emerging after the Velvet Revolution consisted of two prominent groups of experts around Valtr Komárek and Václav Klaus respectively.[42] Initially, Komárek was more popular and closer to Václav Havel. In the spring of 1990, however, Havel endorsed Klaus's economic program, and the Czechoslovak government accepted the Finance Ministry's harmonogram of privatization, which was prepared by Klaus and his team.[43]

Before the revolution there was a belief that the socialist ownership structure should be changed step by step, that is, privatization should be gradual.[44] Nevertheless, privatization was immediately put on the agenda by (neo)liberals represented by Václav Klaus and Tomáš Ježek. It was an advantage for them that former dissidents had almost no interest in economic matters. They considered economics a technical field that should remain in the hands of specialists.[45] Furthermore, the managers of state companies did not speak with a clear voice, and were—in most cases—members of the former establishment and thus lacked political credibility.[46]

In 1989/1990, a number of privatization proposals were formulated. František Vlasák organized a group of economists under the auspices of the Czechoslovak government.[47] This group—which was close in spirit to Valtr Komárek—took a less radical approach, suggesting that the state should improve the performance of firms: it should invest capital into enterprises, and once they were in better shape they should be sold on the marketplace to private owners, one by one. By default, the state would play an important role in these decisions. This was refuted by Klaus and Ježek, who pointed to the fact that such a procedure would be too slow, and the country would still resemble a socialist state, with the state as a crucial asset owner.[48]

There were also proposals from economists like Ota Šik and Miloš Zeman who supported a version of worker/employee stock ownership.[49] This was criticized heavily by the (neo)liberals because workers were symbols of the old regime, and their property did not seem to be a guarantee of any significant economic progress.

Koncepce (1990) is the basic document of Czechoslovak privatization approved by the government in the spring of 1990. It was prepared by the Federal Ministry of Finance. Moving state property into the hands of citizens was to be a complicated process as domestic subjects did not own sufficient resources to buy state assets, and selling the national property to foreigners seemed politically unacceptable at the time. The document also expected controversy due to restitution claims.[50] *Koncepce* (1990) envisioned that the denationalization of property should proceed in two steps: first, via commercialization,[51] and then via privatization.[52] Already this document stated that a large portion of national property should be offered to the general public for free,[53] as the segment of society that could afford to buy assets must have obtained its savings from questionable sources. The document divided state property into three groups: property not to be privatized, property to be transformed into new state joint-stock companies, and property to be transferred to local ownership and sold at the local level. The Ministry of Privatization was to decide whether a given enterprise from the second or third group would enter the first wave of privatization (typically enterprises which seemed politically easier to privatize), or the second wave (companies with large workforces, like in heavy industry).[54]

Ježek (2007) writes that around 27 percent of the state wealth was not involved in free privatization using coupons (vouchers), but was sold directly for cash to new owners. However, coupon privatization represented the most interesting attempt for a change in ownership.[55] It was to happen fast and on mass base.[56] According to the expectations, once coupon privatization succeeded, it could help build the market for shares of privatized companies, that is, the capital market.

Informally, the early privatization procedures put lots of power in the hands of enterprise managers. Managers, together with their teams, had written the privatization projects that were mostly accepted by the privatization agency.[57] This seems to support the view of Mlčoch as presented earlier. Privatization does not necessarily need to be seen as a complete change in ownership. It "substitutes less formal entitlements for a legal system of property rights and to make existing markets—so far inefficient and inflexible, non-competitive, monopolizing and discriminating—more open, competitive, and efficient" (Mlčoch 2000b, 12).

CONCLUSION

One purpose of this chapter was to acquaint those unfamiliar with the discussions on ownership in communist Czechoslovakia. We surveyed the body of knowledge built up by those contributing to these discussions along several lines, especially chronological, but also based on differences between schools of thought and political ideologies. In Czechoslovak economic thought the authors writing on ownership relations were motivated by a variety of purposes and followed different aims. Clearly, political opinion about the communist regime was one of their guiding principles. They were influenced by the reality of its power, and their art of writing was affected by the possibilities of persecution. Hence, to understand their views, one needs to not only look at the published works of the economists in question, but also to see the context in which these views were formulated. Also, in order to guess what economists really believed, we had to go a little beyond economic theory per se. That was the reason for including a short section on postcommunist privatization. The suddenly emerging high-profile policy positions of some economists in 1989 offered us evidence also about how they had thought about ownership earlier.

We saw discussions on ownership issues in light of economic policy reforms as well as theoretical controversies. In the center of these controversies was the evaluation of the importance of state ownership. If one sees nationalization as the most important characteristic of the communist order, then after its breakup the issue of premier importance is to privatize as fast as possible. But if one considers the issue of governance as more significant, then it is not rapid privatization that matters most but rather the relationship between owners and the managerial class. Consequently, the latter view favors a slower process of privatization and a concentration on governance. Readers may find that this issue is still unsettled.

NOTES

1. We would like to thank Vanda Šerbulová and Václav Rameš for their research help. Vítězslav Sommer's contribution to this chapter was researched and written with the support of the Czech Science Foundation (GAČR) as part of the project GJ15-19437Y entitled "The Road to Technocratic Socialism: Concepts of Governance in Czechoslovakia (1953–1975)."

2. For the reform communist research on socialist theories of agricultural economics, see Václavů (1968). For the early 1960s research on collectivization of agriculture, see Jech (1963).

3. For the history of "reform historiography," see Sommer (2011).

4. For the most prominent account, see Jech (2008).

5. For the perspective of the dissident radical left in the late 1970s, see Uhl (1982).

6. Kornai (1992, 72) presents shares of public sector in communist economies in 1988. In Czechoslovakia this share is 99.3 percent while for example in the German Democratic Republic it was 96.4 percent, in Hungary 92.9 percent, and in Poland 81.2 percent.

7. For the political and legal history of ownership changes in 20th century Czechoslovakia, see Kuklík (2010).

8. Government regulations, laws, and different types of rules were issued without any special regard to cooperative property. Cooperative enterprises persisted but were treated as just another type of state property. Thus, there was a tension between economic concepts that treated both types of property as basically equal and legal concepts that treated them separately.

9. In addition, Article 10 guaranteed the personal ownership of consumer goods.

10. See, for example, Ludvík Frejka (1951). He believed that the confiscation of property was fair as the property, in his opinion, was obtained by exploitation.

11. In the early years of communism, it might have been appealing for pro-regime economists to present their activities as improving the welfare of society, as initially the aims of economic transformation were relatively clear: achieving full employment and the mobilization of resources for growth. However, at the end of the day, the communist system did not generate an internal mechanism that would replace the motive of profit with something else that would increase the common good of the society.

12. Kornai, for example, writes that property rights were concentrating "in the hands of those with the greatest influence on the setting of the plans, state income and expenditure, prices, and wages. But at these levels of decision-making rights, the personal income and wealth of the most influential individuals is unconnected with the income and wealth of the state-owned firms. None of the profits of the state-owned firms passes automatically into the pockets of these members of the bureaucracy." See Kornai (1992, 73).

13. Mlčoch began his academic career in the late 1960s with a booklet on the theory of the firm. After 1968 he was forced to move—as politically unreliable—to a manufacturing company in Prague, where he gained firsthand knowledge of the real functioning of the socialist enterprise.

14. Barzel (1989) conjectures that there is a difference between potential and actual output of an employee, which represents his/her ownership, as it would be prohibitively costly for the owner to know this difference. One can understand socialist property rights similarly, that is, the state was unable to delineate property rights perfectly, and this allowed managers and their teams to obtain private gains from state property during the socialist period.

15. For an introduction to socialist ownership law in Czechoslovakia, see Bělovský (2009).

16. From the perspective of ownership law, the most important legal acts were the 1960 Czechoslovak Constitution (the so-called socialist constitution), the 1964 Civil Code, and the 1964 Economic Code. Contrary to other communist countries, the ownership law was not regulated by a unified legal arrangement in Czechoslovakia. See Čížkovská (1975, 102).

17. State ownership was characterized as a crucial ownership form for the functioning and further development of socialism; see Polák (1985) and Čapek (1961). The attempt to replace the centrality of state ownership with more emphasis on collective ownership, as was done in Yugoslavia, was heavily criticized as a dangerous form of "revisionism." See Čapek (1961, 17–26).

18. A legislative norm regulating the ownership of flats was introduced as late as 1966. The rules of personal ownership of flats and family houses were not precisely defined and raised a controversy among legal experts. See Čížkovská (1975, 121–23) and Luby (1971).

19. For the intellectual biography of Kožušník and his involvement it this debate, see Richterková (2013, 19–20).

20. Kožušník argued that a certain legal form of ownership could cover completely different relationships of production. For example, state ownership could exist in capitalism as well as in socialism, that is, in two entirely different systems of economic relations. Kožušník wrote about the "smoke screen" of legal reasoning.

21. For the summary of this meeting, see KPE (1960, 727–29).

22. Křížek published his critique in the form of an article, see Křížek (1961).

23. For theorizing ownership in political economy, see Oliva (1966) or Bálek (1965). The relationship between "commodity production" and ownership in socialism was conceptualized by Dušan Plachtinský who discussed the highly topical issue of the independent economic ownership of enterprises. See Plachtinský (1966).

24. For the relationship between plan and market in Czechoslovak reform communist economic thought, see Šik (1968).

25. For a critique of self-management and a call for the introduction of a managerial style of enterprise organization, see Vostatek (1969).

26. The socialist services companies were inefficient, cumbersome, and not customer friendly. The reformers of the 1960s favored a decision that would allow—conditioned on the approval of local authorities—private contracts in small-scale services. These included shoe-repair, carpentry, tailoring, barbering, and similar activities.

27. Council members would have a word concerning the distribution of net income of the enterprise but would leave the daily issues to management. Different to the Yugoslav model, the workers' council did not receive stronger competencies than the management.

28. In state enterprises the government nominated the council members.

29. Kýn (1970) mentions that around three-quarters of the council members were engineers, about one-fifth workers, the rest being administrative employees.

30. Machonin (2000, 52) states that normalization period meant stagnation in civilizational and cultural development.

31. For the early critique of reform communist economic thought, see, for example, Truhlář and Reiser (1971); Fremer, Šedivec, and Koláček (1973); or Vejvoda (1971).

32. In this volume Nikolič authored the chapter dedicated to the "critique of revisionist conceptions of ownership" in Czechoslovakia.

33. In the second half of the 1980s, the Marxist theory of ownership was discussed by sociologist Richard Růžička (1987, 1989). This author also attempted to reflect on ownership in socialism as a "spontaneously developing" structure.

34. In support of this statement he quoted from speeches of Yuri Andropov.

35. He favored such proposals also after the breakup of socialism when he was active in the preparation of the economic program of the old-new communist party.

36. In March 1988, a conference on the "Alternatives of Socialist Economic Reforms" was held in Győr, Hungary. At this conference émigré economists and also experts who came from communist countries met. Participants included Alec Nove, Wlodzimierz Brus, Morris Bornstein, economists from Hungary and Poland, and also Czechoslovak nationals like Jiří Kosta, Radoslav Selucký, Jiří Sláma, Václav Klaus, and one of the coauthors of this chapter. At this meeting it was clearly supported that capital markets should be introduced and that the leading role of the party should be revised. Jiří Sláma said that there had been general agreement in Győr that independence for enterprises should lie at the root of the new model. According to Sláma, "The conventional notion of socialist ownership should perhaps be broadened; I believe the rethinking that is going on in this respect in Moscow and Hungary amounts to a small revolution" (Kusin, 1988).

37. In June 1988, Tomáš Ježek presented a paper on the usefulness of the Austrian and Chicago schools of economics in understanding the behavior of the Czechoslovak economy. Similarly, the influence of ideas of monetarists and/or libertarians clearly transpired from the presentations of Václav Klaus.

38. For example, in the context of the asymmetry of information, that is, owners (state or private) do not have the same access to information about corporate assets and performance as the managers. There was a belief that ultimately private ownership works better as it puts more efficient restrictions on the potentially inefficient behavior of corporate managers, for example, through stock market evaluation. Stiglitz (1995) challenged the argument that property rights and generally ownership is of such a crucial importance. He claimed that most large multinational firms are run by managers, and not by owners. Does it matter for the manager whether he/she works for dispersed shareholders or for the state?

39. See, for example, Mlčoch (1990). Versions of this work were circulating in Prague before its official publication.

40. Mlčoch (2000b, 10) writes: "Western comparative economics had given up its own evidence and accepted arguments of the official communist ideology, according to which the state is charged with executing property rights on behalf of the society as a whole. The exaggerated emphasis made by Western economists to direct forms of control that lead vertically from a planning center via hierarchical structures is a characteristic trait of the command economy concept. This interpretation helped to sustain the illusion that the Central Planning Board was an actual proprietor in Real Socialism."

41. Mlčoch (2000b, 13) explains: "Universal property in socialism is best understood in the following way: individual property rights disintegrated into a complicated network of a coalition structure with extremely vague contours. Moreover, some of these rights were not specified at all. On the unclearly demarcated borders of its ill-operationalized property rights, in no man's land, informal and thus irregular ownership relations were expatiating, taking the form of a specific socialist entrepreneurship that was counted as state overhead cost."

42. In the early months of 1990 Klaus and Komárek represented two policy approaches. Klaus was in favor of strong restrictive policies in the monetary and fiscal sphere. Komárek was rather in support of expansionist policies to battle rising

unemployment and decreasing national income. Komárek (1990) was a strong proponent of market economy; however, he was much less in support of fast privatization. He argued that in the Czechoslovak economy a large monopolistic heavy industry prevailed, and wanted first to break its power. In addition, a market price mechanism should be introduced as well as competition by foreign producers. These steps were anticipated to stabilize the Czechoslovak economy; the re-born enterprises should be privatized thereafter.

43. Klaus received strong support from the mass media in favor of radical economic reform. Schwartz (2006) writes that in the late spring of 1990 the population began to favor fast reform as compared to a gradual one.

44. In the research report written in 1989 and published in the early 1990 under the leadership of Josef Zieleniec, economists such as Tomáš Ježek, Roman Česka, Vladimír Rudlovčák, Jiří Jonáš, Karel Kříž, and Josef Kotrba recommended that the state banks temporarily hold the ownership of state enterprises until the time was ripe for privatization.

45. This turned out to be a complete misunderstanding of modern politics. In spring 1991, Klaus created a new political party and later won the national elections.

46. There was also nobody to match the stature of Klaus in the discussion about economic policy.

47. Vlasák was deputy prime minister of the Czech government, while at that time Klaus was Minister of Finance in the Federal Czechoslovak government. The proposal of the group led by Vlasák was called the Proposal of a Transition Strategy to a Market Economy.

48. The (neo)liberal elite had a natural skepticism toward state officials. That was one reason why they at times objected to public sales; such sales would be more time-consuming to prepare and their preparation would require the help of representatives of ministries and other state organizations.

49. After leaving Czechoslovakia in 1968, Ota Šik published a great variety of articles and books, of which the most famous is *The Third Way* (Der Dritte Weg) of 1972. See Schwartz (2006).

50. There were different problems with restitution and there was also a strong political bias against it. It was a legal nightmare to assess in what way and to whom to return property confiscated some 50 years before, which in some cases did not even exist. A number of those who would ask for property restitution were living abroad, and thus were not exposed to oppression.

51. Commercialization meant changing the form of state companies to state joint-stock companies with boards appointed by the Ministry of Finance.

52. After the breakup of socialism, the Czechoslovak economic system remained fully centralized—quite unlike in Hungary and Poland. Enterprises were still legally subordinated to the center, and the government did not need to lobby for the consent of managers in the process of privatization.

53. For Ježek and Klaus the primary reason was ideological, that is, to create a group of new owners. They did not require that owners should already have market skills; the idea was that learning by doing would produce these skills.

54. The sovereign debt of Czechoslovakia was very low in the early 1990s, especially as compared to Hungary, Poland, and Yugoslavia. Thus, there was less pressure for public sales to raise revenue for the budget and debt repayment.

55. Papers on coupon privatization appeared already toward the end of the 1980s. A paper by Lewandowski and Szomburg was already discussed in the summer of 1989 in Prague. Jan Švejnar in a *Plan-Econ* report provided another paper on voucher privatization.

56. An outspoken critique of coupon privatization came from Miroslav Grégr, minister in the Czech government between 1990 and 1992 and founder and chairman of the Czech Industrial Association. He disputed that coupon holders would improve the situation in enterprises; neither would they bring new capital to these enterprises. Grégr favored more extensive involvement of managers in privatization. This was criticized by (neo)liberals, who pointed to the involvement of managers with the previous regime. See Schwartz (2006).

57. The Ministry of Privatization received 11,252 projects for 2,727 enterprises and had couple of months to decide. See Schwartz (2006).

BIBLIOGRAPHY

Alternativní přístupy ke scenáři přechodu k tržní ekonomice [Alternative approaches to the transition to market economy]. Prague: Prognostický ústav ČSAV. 1990.

Babin, Ján. 1987. "Teoreticko-praktické aspekty základního výrobního vztahu v socialismu" [Theoretical-practical aspects of the basic productive relation in socialism]. *Politická ekonomie* 35, no. 1: 79–93.

Bálek, Stanislav. 1965. *Výrobní síly, výrobní vztahy, vlastnictví* [Productive forces, relations of production, ownership]. Prague: Ideologické oddělení ÚV KSČ pro potřeby VUML.

Barzel, Yoram. 1989. *Economic Analysis of Property Rights*. Cambridge: Cambridge University Press.

Bělovský, Petr. 2009. "Občanské právo" [Civil law]. In *Komunistické právo v Československu: kapitoly z dějin bezpráví* [Communist Law in Czechoslovakia: Chapters from the history of injustice], edited by Michal Bobek, Pavel Molek, and Vojtěch Šimíček, 425–62. Brno: Masarykova univerzita, Mezinárodní politologický ústav.

Colotka, Peter. 1956. *Osobné vlastníctvo I* [Personal ownership I]. Bratislava: Vydavateľstvo Slovenskej akadémie vied.

Čapek, Karel. 1961. *Správa národního majetku* [Administration of national property]. Prague: Nakladatelství Československé akademie věd.

Čížkovská, Věra. 1975. *Vlastnická soustava evropských socialistických států* [Ownership systems of European socialist countries]. Prague: Academia.

Frejka, Ludvík. 1951. *O ekonomii kapitalismu a socialismu* [On economics of capitalism and socialism]. Prague: Svoboda.

Fremer, Miloslav, Václav Šedivec, and František Koláček, eds. 1973. *Některé rysy revizionismu v politické ekonomii v druhé polovině 60. let v ČSSR* [Certain aspects of revisionism in the political economy in the second half of the 1960s in Czechoslovakia]. Prague: Svoboda.

Hába, Zdeněk. 1962. "Poznámky k poměru vlastnictví a ekonomických vztahů" [Comments on the relationship between ownership and economic relations]. *Politická ekonomie* 10, no. 5: 444–51.

Hába, Zdeněk, and František Koláček, 1972. "Socialistické společenské vlastnictví [Socialist social ownership]. *Politická ekonomie* 20, no. 8: 693–703.

Hába, Zdeněk, and Miroslav Křížek. 1975. *Socialismus a vlastnictví* [Socialism and ownership]. Prague: Svoboda.

Hába, Zdeněk, Josef Bavlnka, and Jiří Kameníček, eds. 1976. *Otázka socialistického vlastnictví* [The issue of socialist ownership]. Prague: Academia.

Hába, Zdeněk. 1987. "Otázky pro politickou ekonomii socialismu" [Questions for the political economy of socialism]. *Politická ekonomie* 35, no. 8: 785–89.

Heumos, Peter. 2006. *Vyhrňme si rukávy, než se kola zastaví!: dělníci a státní socialismus v Československu 1945–1968* [Roll up our sleeves, before the wheels stop turning!: Workers and state socialism in Czechoslovakia 1945–1968]. Prague: Ústav pro soudobé dějiny AV ČR.

Holub, Milan, and Jaroslav Bičovský. 1985. *Občan a vlastnictví v čs. právním řádu* [Citizen and ownership in the Czechoslovak legal system]. Prague: Panorama.

Jech, Karel. 1963. *Probuzená vesnice: k dějinám revoluce na našem venkově v letech 1945–1948* [A village awakened: On the history of revolution in our countryside in 1945–1948]. Prague: Nakladatelství politické literatury.

———, ed. 1968. *The Czechoslovak Economy 1945–1948: Collected Papers*. Prague: State Pedagogical Publishing House.

———. 2008. *Kolektivizace a vyhánění sedláků z půdy* [Collectivization and expulsion of peasants]. Prague: Vyšehrad.

Ježek, Tomáš. 2007. *Zrození ze zkumavky: Svědectví o české privatizaci 1990–1997* [Birth from the test-tube: Testimony about Czech privatization 1990–1997]. Prague: Publishing House Prostor.

Kaplan, Karel. 1966. *Utváření generální linie výstavby socialismu v Československu (od Února do IX. sjezdu KSČ)* [Making of the general course of socialist construction in Czechoslovakia: From February 1948 to the Ninth Party Congress]. Prague: Academia.

———. 1968. *Znárodnění a socialismus* [Nationalization and socialism]. Prague: Práce.

———. 2000. *Kořeny československé reformy 1968* [The origins of Czechoslovak reform 1968]. Brno: Publishing House Doplněk.

———. 2007. *Proměny české společnosti (1948–1960), Část první* [Transformations of Czech society, first volume]. Prague: Ústav pro soudobé dějiny AV ČR.

———. 2012. *Proměny české společnosti (1948–1960), Část druhá, Venkov* [Transformations of Czech society, second volume, countryside]. Prague: Ústav pro soudobé dějiny AV ČR.

Klusoň, Václav. 1988. "K prognóze vývoje hospodářského mechanismu" [On the prognosis of economic mechanism development]. *Politická ekonomie* 36, no. 11: 1123–38.

Knapp, Viktor. 1952. *Vlastnictví v lidové demokracii. Právní úprava vlastnictví v Československé republice* [Ownership in people's democracy: Legal arrangement of ownership in the Czechoslovak Republic]. Prague: Orbis.

Komenda, Bohumil. 1969. "Společenské vlastnictví v tržním systému" [Social ownership in a market system]. *Nová mysl* 23, no. 7: 871–82.

Koncepce procesu odstátnění a privatizace [Concept of de-nationalization and privatization]. Federální ministerstvo financií [Federal ministry of finance], předkládá [submitted by] Václav Klaus, Petr Pithart, and Milan Čič. 1990.

Kosta, Jiří. 2005. "K historii a koncepci československé ekonomické reformy v letech 1965–1969" [On history and concept of Czechoslovak economic reform in 1965–1969]. *Acta Oeconomica Pragensia* 13, no. 3: 27–47.

Kovanda, Karel. 2014. *Zápas o podnikové rady pracujících 1968–1969* [Struggle for workers' councils 1968–1969]. Prague: Ústav pro soudobé dějiny AV ČR.

Kožušník, Čestmír. 1959. "Vlastnictví a ekonomické vztahy" [Ownership and economic relations]. *Nová mysl* 13, no. 7: 693–708.

KPE. 1960. "Diskuse k otázkám vlastnictví a ekonomických vztahů" [Discussion about the issues of ownership and economic relations]. *Politická ekonomie* 8, no. 8: 727–29.

Křížek, Miroslav. 1961. "O vlastnictví a ekonomických vztazích" [On ownership and economic relations]. *Politická ekonomie* 9, no. 6: 481–93.

Kuklík, Jan. 2010. *Znárodněné Československo: od znárodnění k privatizaci—státní zásahy do vlastnických a dalších majetkových práv v Československu a jinde v Evropě* [Nationalized Czechoslovakia: From nationalization to privatization—State interventions to ownership and other rights in Czechoslovakia and elsewhere in Europe]. Prague: Auditorium.

Kulikov, Vsevolod. 1989. "Společenské vlastnictví a demokratizace ekonomického života" [Social ownership and democratization of economic life]. *Politická ekonomie* 37, no. 3: 249–62.

Kusin, Vladimir. 1988. "Free-Wheeling Reformist Debates in Gyor." Radio Free Europe Report, March 29. Available online, accessed April 24, 2017: http://osaarchivum.org/files/holdings/300/8/3/text_da/37-5-18.shtml.

Kýn, Oldřich. 1970. "The Rise and Fall of Economic Reform in Czechoslovakia." *American Economic Review* 60: 300–306.

Levčík, Bedřich, and Jiří Kosta. 1968. "Koho reprezentuje socialistický podnik?" [Who is represented by socialist enterprise?]. *Politická ekonomie* 16, no. 3: 239–47.

Lewandowski, Janusz, and Jan Szomburg. 1989. "Property Reform as a Basis for Social and Economic Reform." *Communist Economies* 1: 257–68.

Luby, Štefan. 1971. *Vlastníctvo bytov* [Ownership of Flats]. Bratislava: Vydavateľstvo Slovenskej akadémie vied.

Lukas, Jiří. 1989. "K některým aspektům přestavby hospodářského mechanismu" [On certain aspects of rebuilding the economic mechanism]. *Politická ekonomie* 37, no. 12: 1441–52.

Machonin, Pavel. 2000. "Modernization Theory and the Czech Experience." In *Economic and Social Changes in Czech Society after 1989: An Alternative View*, edited by Milan Sojka, Pavel Machonin, and Lubomir Mlčoch, 48–111. Budapest: Open Society Support Foundation.

Málek, Jaroslav. 1964. "K vlastnickým koncepcím" [On the concepts of ownership]. *Politická ekonomie* 12, no. 8: 772–76.

Mlčoch, Lubomír. 1969. "Symposium o podniku" [Symposium on enterprise]. *Politická ekonomie* 17, no. 3: 278–81.

———. 1990. *Chování československé podnikové sféry* [Behavior of Czechoslovak firms]. Praha: EÚ ČSAV Praha.

———. 2000a. *Úvahy o české ekonomické transformaci* [Reflections on Czech economic transformation]. Prague: Vyšehrad.

———. 2000b. "Restructuring of Property Rights: An Institutional View." In *Economic and Social Changes in Czech Society after 1989: An Alternative View*, edited by. Milan Sojka, Pavel Machonin, and Lubomir Mlčoch, 7–47. Budapest: Open Society Support Foundation.

Nikolič, Pavel Dušan. 1972. "Politickoekonomické úvahy o ekonomických zájmech, socialistickém podniku a společenském vlastnictví" [Political-economical reflections on economic interests, socialist enterprise and social ownership], *Politická ekonomie* 20, no. 11: 995–1010.

Oliva, Felix. 1966. "K základním teoretickým otázkám politické ekonomie" [On basic theoretical questions of political economy]. *Ekonomický časopis* 14, no. 7: 652–63.

Pajestka, Józef. 1989. "Některé teoretické aspekty ekonomické reformy v Polsku" [Certain theoretical aspects of economic reform in Poland]. *Politická ekonomie* 37, no. 8: 931–43.

Plachtinský, Dušan. 1966. "Úvahy o socialistickej tovarovej výrobe a vlastníctve" [Reflections on socialist commodity production and ownership]. *Ekonomický časopis* 14, no. 9: 777–96.

Polák, Josef. 1986. *Socialistické vlastnictví, jeho správa, ochrana a kontrola* [Socialist ownership: Administration, protection and control]. Prague: Práce.

Pullmann, Michal. 2011. *Konec experimentu: přestavba a pád komunismu v Československu* [The end of the experiment: *Perestroika* and the fall of communism in Czechoslovakia]. Prague: Scriptorium.

Richterková, Zuzana. 2013. *Přínos Čestmíra Kožušníka českému ekonomickému myšlení (v kontextu diskuze o plánu a trhu)* [The contribution of Čestmír Kožušník to Czech economic thought (in the context of the planning and market debate)]. Prague: Národohospodářský ústav Josefa Hlávky.

Rudnickij, Viktor. 1988. "Možnosti realizace soukromého vlastnictví v SSSR" [Possibilities of the realization of private property in USSR]. *Politická ekonomie* 36, no. 12: 1273–81.

Růžička, Richard. 1987a. "Společenské vlastnictví a problém rozporu" [Social ownership and the problem of contradiction]. *Sociologický časopis* 23, no. 5: 501–15.

———. 1987b. "Společenské vlastnictví, způsob života a zájmy" [Social ownership, way of life, and interests]." *Sociologický časopis* 23, no. 6: 545–61.

———. 1989. "Socialistické vlastnictví: ekonomický, technologický a sociologický zřetel" [Socialist ownership: Economic, technological and sociological perspectives]. *Sociologický časopis* 25, no. 6: 561–77.

Schwartz, Andrew Harrison. 2006. *The Politics of Greed: How Privatization Structured Politics in Central and Eastern Europe*. New York: Rowman and Littlefield Publishers.

Slejška, Dragoslav, ed. 1968. *Člověk v závodě: Výsledky sociologického výzkumu v závodě Prachovické cementárny a vápnice n.p.* [Man in the factory: Outcomes from the research in Prachovice cement and lime plant]. Prague: Sociologický ústav ČSAV.

Sojka, Milan, Pavel Machonin, and Lubomír Mlčoch. 2000. *Economic and Social Changes in Czech Society after 1989: An Alternative View*. Budapest: Research Support Scheme, Open Society Support Foundation.

Sojka, Milan. 2000. "Ten Years of Transformation in the Czech Way: Transformation, Inequality and Integration." In *Economic and Social Changes in Czech Society after 1989: And Alternative View*, edited by Milan Sojka, Pavel Machonin, and Lubomir Mlčoch, 112–13. Budapest: Open Society Support Foundation.

Sommer, Vítězslav. 2011. *Angažované dějepisectví: Stranická historiografie mezi stalinismem a reformním komunismem, 1950–1970* [Engaged historiography: Party historiography between Stalinism and reform communism, 1950–1970]. Prague: Nakladatelství Lidové noviny—FF UK.

Stiglitz, Joseph. 1995. *Whither Socialism?* Boston: MIT Press.

Strategie radikální ekonomické reformy [Strategy of radical economic reform]. Předkláda [submitted by] Vladimír Dlouhý and Václav Klaus, Státní plánovací komise a Federální ministerstvo financí [State planning committee and federal ministry of finance]. 1990.

Suchan, Karel. 1968. "Podnik a centrum" [Enterprise and center]. *Politická ekonomie* 16, no. 2: 101–11.

Šik, Ota. 1953. Zákon plánovitého proporcionálního rozvoje národního hospodářství: Záznam přednášky ze semináře ke statím J. V. Stalina [Law of the proportional development of national economy: Transcript of lecture at the seminar on J. V. Stalin's papers]. Prague: Vysoká škola politická ústředního výboru Komunistické strany Československa, April 25.

———. 1962. *Ekonomika, zájmy, politika: jejich vzájemné vztahy do socialismu* [Economy, interests, politics: Their mutual relations under socialism]. Prague: Nakladatelství politické literatury.

———. 1965. *K problematice socialistických zbožních vztahů* [On the issue of socialist commodity relations]. Prague: Nakladatelství Československé akademie věd.

———. 1968. *Plán a trh za socialismu* [Plan and market under socialism]. Prague: Academia.

Štěpánek, Miloš. 1989. "Zákon o státní podniku ČSSR a SSSR" [National enterprise law in Czechoslovakia and USSR]. *Politická ekonomie* 37, no. 3: 293–301.

Šulc, Zdislav. 1998. *Stručné dějiny ekonomických reforem v Československu (České republice) 1945–1995* [Short history of economic reform in Czechoslovakia (Czech Republic) 1945–1995]. Brno: Doplněk.

———. 2007. *Jak se rodila, kam smerovala, a proč byla potlačena tzv. Šikova reforma* [The Birth, Direction and Reason for Suppressing of the so called Šik Reform]. *Acta Oeconomica Pragensia. Acta Oeconomica Pragensia* 15, no. 7.

Švejnar, Jan. 1989. "A Framework for the Economic Transformation of Czechoslovakia." *PlanEcon Report* 5, no. 52: 1–18.

Truhlář, Oldřich, and Josef Reiser. 1971. *Projevy revizionismu v teorii a hospodářské praxi při prosazování ekonomické reformy v ČSSR* [Revisionism in theory and economic praxis in the promoting of economic reform in Czechoslovakia]. Prague: Horizont.

Uhl, Petr, ed. 1982. *Program společenské samosprávy* [Program of social self-government]. Köln: Index.

Václavů, Antonín. 1968. "O agrární otázce v socialistickém hnutí" [On the agrarian question in the socialist movement]. *Revue dějin socialismu* 1, no. 1: 5–58.

Vejvoda, Jaroslav. 1971. "Příspěvek k analýze vývoje naší ekonomické teorie v šedesátých letech" [Contribution to the analysis of our economic theory development in the 1960s]. *Politická ekonomie* 19, no. 4: 293–304.

Vostatek, Jaroslav. 1969. "Čtyři typy podniku a socialistické odměňování" [Four types of enterprises and socialist remuneration]. *Politická ekonomie* 17, no. 4: 307–21.

Vydra, Vladimír. 1981. *Družstevní a všelidové vlastnictví* [Cooperative and social ownership]. Prague: Academia.

Zdobinský, Stanislav. 1957. *K některým otázkám osobního vlastnictví* [On certain aspects of personal ownership]. Acta Universitatis Carolinae 1957. Prague: Univerzita Karlova v Praze—Státní pedagogické nakladatelství.

"Z diskusních příspěvků k otázce vlastnictví" [From the Contributions to Discussion about Ownership]. *Politická ekonomie* 10 (1962), no. 3: 234–39.

Chapter 4

Ownership under East-German Communism—A One-Way Street

Hans-Jürgen Wagener and Franz Rudolph

Ownership of the means of production is generally seen as a core relationship determining the character of politico-economic systems.[1] Any true communist takes it for granted that social ownership (*gesellschaftliches Eigentum, Volkseigentum*) of these means is a *sine qua non* for socialism or communism. To him private property socialism is simply a contradiction in terms. When we analyze East-German thinking about ownership in this chapter, it should be made clear that it was extremely orthodox over the whole period. The precarious state of the German Democratic Republic (GDR) made the country totally dependent upon the Soviet Union, and orthodoxy stood for allegiance to the Soviet Union. Furthermore, Germany was the birthplace of Marx and Engels. Who else would be more qualified to interpret and to preserve pure doctrine?

The chapter is divided into four sections. Socialist thinking has a long tradition in Germany. Three strands will be highlighted in the first section followed by a brief overview of the period 1945–1990 which saw the rise and decline of the East-German state. The second section concentrates on the theoretical perspective, beginning with the Marxist theory of socialization. The subchapter on the theoretical perspectives, specifically on socialization in Marxist theory, has been written by coauthor Franz Rudolph, giving the reader an insider's view on socialist thinking. The concept of social ownership emerges as a necessary result of historical development. It remains, however, rather vague about the concrete allocation of property rights. The political economy of socialization deals with phenomena at the basis of social relations; according to Marxian doctrine, property rights are a legal and, hence, a superstructure phenomenon.

This becomes even more apparent in section three, the thematic perspective, confronting state, cooperative, and personal property. Although

East-German thinking about ownership exhibits a surprising conformity, there have been critical views. They will be described in section four. Until the dismantling of the Berlin Wall, they fall under *revisionism.* Only the end-game of the GDR triggered a brief discussion about reforms that remained staunchly conservative regarding questions of ownership.

DOMINANT CONCEPTS OF OWNERSHIP PRIOR TO THE COMMUNIST TAKEOVER

Prewar Germany had a rich tradition of ideas and practices of non-capitalist or non-private property relations within the social-democratic and communist movement as well as outside it. Karl Marx and Ferdinand Lassalle (1825–1864), together with most of the later-day radicals and reformists, may have been of similar opinion about the final stage of a socialist society, but they quarreled about the political action needed to put it into practice and about the intermediate stages. This is not the place to trace the manifold currents of socialist thinking. With respect to *really existing socialism* in East Germany, it suffices to distinguish three important strands: syndicalism, the socialist and non-socialist cooperative movement, and economic democracy. The heyday of syndicalism immediately followed the First World War (Bock 1973). Europe was in a revolutionary spirit, but in no country had the communist parties yet occupied the ideological and strategic commanding heights. Numerous radical leftist groups and organizations put forward anarchist, syndicalist, council-democratic, and utopian ideas. What they had in common was a strong opposition against the concentration of property rights in the hands of the state and a hierarchical bureaucratic political structure. Shop-floor democracy and workers' self-management were the basic organizational ideas. More or less spontaneous mass action, and not conspiratory party discipline, was the strategy as, for instance, advocated by Rosa Luxemburg. After the revolution of 1917, Soviet Russia chose a road to socialism that made a conflict inevitable. It was solved, for the Soviet empire once and for all, by Lenin's ([1920] 1964) pamphlet against the radical Left, *"Left-Wing" Communism: An Infantile Disorder*, and the decisions of the Tenth Party Congress of the Bolsheviks in 1920. The Workers' Opposition was defeated, formation of platforms was banned, and party and state were cemented as core organizational elements of socialist society. It was a decision against workers' self-management and for exclusive property rights of the state, even if the same congress introduced the New Economic Policy, with its provisional concessions made to private ownership, as a necessary intermediate stage of socialist development.

The cooperative movement started in the 19th century. It had a socialist and a social-liberal background disputed between Ferdinand Lassalle and Hermann Schulze-Delitzsch (1808–1883). The former saw state-subsidized productive cooperatives as a counterweight to large capitalist firms and as a stepping stone on the path toward full socialism. The latter advocated wholesale and retail cooperatives, credit cooperatives, and the like to support middle-class handicraft and trade, and to make them self-supporting and competitive within the capitalist economy.[2] Membership in a cooperative left individual entrepreneurship unaffected, but implied liability for cooperative activities. The idea was hugely prolific and helped small and middle-class craft, trade, and farming to survive in a capitalist environment. Today, there is still a wide network of cooperatives all over the world that are organized according to the principles of Schulze-Delitzsch and Friedrich Raiffeisen (1818–1888).

Productive cooperatives in agriculture were more of a collectivist character. The Frankfurt (Main) chair of economics and sociology Franz Oppenheimer (1864–1943) considered himself a liberal socialist defending market coordination on the one side and criticizing (monopoly) power-based exploitation on the other (Preiser [1964] 1970). In particular, he saw the monopolization of the non-augmentable production factor of land, which he called *land blockade* (*Bodensperre*), as the cause for social inequities. A land reform was needed which did not imply the abolition of private property in general, but only the abolition of great estates. Cooperative settlement (*Siedlungsgenossenschaft*) would solve the contradiction between small private holdings and the advantage of economies of scale. This collectivist idea was deliberately anti-capitalist and anti-communist (Oppenheimer 1896).

The program of industrial democracy had been inaugurated by the team of Sidney (1859–1947) and Beatrice (1858–1943) Webb (1897). It was taken up by the German trade union movement in the 1920s under the term "economic democracy" (*Wirtschaftsdemokratie*). The ultimate goal, again, was socialism, but the road led through organized capitalism and not the dictatorship of the proletariat, called the *novel enlightened absolutism* of an *enlightened minority of the proletariat* by Fritz Naphtali (1888–1961), the economic theoretician of the movement (Naphtali 1928, 9). Economic democracy combined workers' codetermination within the firm, limiting capitalist despotism with their enhanced influence in the polity, resulting in anti-monopoly and social legislation and a growing segment of public enterprise.[3] In short, private property rights were not to be abolished, but to be constricted. Article 165 of the Weimar Constitution of 1919 had envisaged codetermination that resulted in a weak legal provision (*Betriebsrätegesetz* of 1920) and a system of corporate economic councils that was put into practice only under National Socialism.

POLICY AND OWNERSHIP (1945–1990)

None of these ideas and models was of recognizable influence in the course of Sovietization following the defeat of Nazi Germany. This was regretted when it was all over: "The 'hour 0' led to adopting the Stalinist model of socialism, instead of returning to own civil traditions and really preserving and changing them in a new society" (Ettl, Jünger, and Walter 1990, 166). Soviet ideology and Soviet institutions were the paradigm on which the East-German system was governed. This did not only stem from a conviction about the superiority of the paradigm among the governing elite, but also was considered a political necessity. The GDR existed, more so than any other of the people's democracies in Eastern Europe, by the goodwill and active support of the Soviet Union.

The development of the ownership regimes of East Germany is closely linked to her general history. The period 1945–1971 was the Ulbricht era and the years 1971–1989 were the Honecker period. The two German states were founded in 1949; in 1961 the Berlin Wall was erected, while 1989 saw its fall. Not a year later, the GDR ceased to exist. Using the regime's language, these were the turning points that resulted in four periods (Weber 2012, 136–38):

1945–1949 Antifascist-democratic transformation
1949–1961 Creation of a socialist basis
1961–1971 Building of developed socialism
1971–1989 Organization of the society of developed socialism

The first period saw an immediate transformation of the East-German ownership structure. Land reform (*Bodenreform*) started briskly in September 1945, which encompassed about one-third of total agricultural land, namely large estates and land owned by Nazi dignitaries. Two-thirds of the nationalized stock was redistributed in small parcels to agricultural workers, poor farmers, refugees from lost territories, and also non-agricultural workers.[4] The rest was mainly transferred to state farms. This was not the land reform envisaged by Oppenheimer, but followed the Soviet template where the first legal act of the Bolshevik government in 1917 had been the Decree on Land, nationalizing all land and redistributing it for perpetual use.

In the first years, there was an ambivalent attitude toward ownership relations in the countryside. It might be asked why collectivization, the obvious aim of Soviet-type socialization, was not introduced right away. Winning the support of the peasantry by distributing private property rights, as 1917 in the Soviet case, was likely much less urgent than the foreign policy aim to only partially distance East Germany from the West. Stalin and his immediate successors wanted to keep open the option of a peace treaty and German reunification—at the price of neutrality and retreat of all, in particular American, occupying forces as was achieved in Austria by the end of 1955. Walter Ulbricht (1893–1973) must have foreseen this as a deadly threat to the existence of the GDR and his power, and pressed for the resolute introduction of socialism that he was allowed to propagate in 1952.[5] This was the beginning of the collectivization campaign.

In the meantime large- and medium-scale industry had been nationalized as well. Initially, the Soviet occupying force dismantled large factories. But soon they realized that using them in situ would be more productive. So, a large part was transferred into Soviet ownership in the form of Soviet joint-stock companies (*Sowjetische Aktiengesellschaften, SAG*)[6] (Steiner 2004, 28–32). The rest became so-called people's enterprises (*Volkseigene Betriebe, VEB*).

The period 1953–1961 was characterized by internal political conflicts that resulted in the stabilization of Ulbricht's power and his Stalinist course. After the Twentieth Party Congress of the Communist Party of the Soviet Union (CPSU), criticism of the Stalinist model of planning became widespread throughout the whole Eastern Bloc and there was a loose consensus about the minimal requirements to get rid of the shortcomings. The consensus can be summarized as follows (Brus 1986, 53):

- Devolution of decision-making to lower entities (enterprises or groups of them),
- Radical curtailment of detailed plan indicators and their replacement by financial indicators (profitability),
- Motivation of the work force by incentives linked to economic results.

This did not imply a change in social ownership but a change in the structure of property rights. At the same time, forced collectivization came under attack not only from peasants but also from GDR agricultural science. The independent family farm, and hence small-scale private property (*Privateigentum*), was seen as productive form of organization for an extended period of transition to socialism. Unlike Poland, for instance, where Władysław Gomułka (1905–1982) had called collectivization to a halt, in the GDR representatives of such views like Fritz Behrens, Arne Benary, Gunter Kohlmey, and Kurt Vieweg were stigmatized as *revisionists*, removed from their academic positions, and even put on trial.

The decade 1961–1971 can be called the reform period. In 1963 the "New Economic System of Planning and Management" (*Neues Ökonomisches System der Planung und Leitung*) was inaugurated. It suggested Ulbricht's idea that socialism, as a transition to communism, is a stage of social development of its own of extended duration and with its own economic system.

Many topics of the *revisionists* were resumed, but not the *revisionists* themselves. A central problem to the reform, however, was the unresolved tension between centralized state property rights and the achievement of decentralized decision-making. It can be found in the textbook *Politische Ökonomie des Sozialismus und ihre Anwendung in der DDR* (1969). The book, prefaced by Ulbricht himself, had been compiled by a large group of economists and political practitioners headed by the party's chief economic official Günter Mittag (1926–1994). But when the textbook finally was published in 1969, the reform was practically dead and Ulbricht's era almost at an end. With him the book disappeared from the shelves: "It also was forbidden to quote the book; it simply did not exist" (Krömke in Pirker et al. 1995, 42).

The Honecker era (1971–1989) saw a return to centralized state planning, enhanced by an even more centralized industrial organization in the form of combines (*Kombinate*), large conglomerates of horizontally and vertically integrated firms. It started with the nationalization of the remaining sector of small-scale private and semi-private enterprises in 1972, some 11,000 firms (Espenhayn 1990, 1090). State and cooperative property rights became the exclusive forms of socialist ownership relations. None of these was put into question till the very end.

SOCIALIZATION

The Marxist Position

Progressive socialization (*Vergesellschaftung*) of labor and production and the concomitant change into a new quality are among the central categories of Marxist political economy. The increasingly social character of labor is the decisive foundation for "the proof that socialism will inevitably replace capitalism" (Richter 1984, 145).

Progressive socialization can be described as a permanent dialectical process of increasing division, specialization, and differentiation of labor on the one hand, and mutual dependence, interrelation, cooperation, and concentration on the other. Its historical evolution manifests itself not simply in a permanent quantitative accumulation, but also results in qualitatively new stages. Such is the case with the capitalist mode of production. Here, the cooperative character of the labor process, the collective utilization of means of production, becomes a "technical necessity dictated by the very nature of the instrument of labour" (Marx [1867] 1976, 508). The planned direct cooperation of producers within the capitalist factory is contrasted by the indirect spontaneous intermediation of productive interrelations within society as a whole. This is the "fundamental contradiction of capitalism," the solution to which "is possible only by way of socialist revolution" (Richter 1984, 110).

Under communism, this contradiction is eliminated. Total labor has an immediate social character.

The scholarly discussion of the process of socialization thus was inseparably linked to fundamental questions of Marxist theory. This included the development of:

- the dialectic between productive forces and production relations,
- the ownership of the means of production,
- the fundamental contradiction of capitalism,
- the economic foundations of socialist revolution,
- the social organization of production (division of labor, cooperation, concentration, combination, centralization).

The socialization of production is a general historical trend with universal properties independent of its concrete historical formation. It chiefly consists of a permanent process of division and centralization of labor and is characterized by growing trends in:

- the number of stages a product has to pass before completion or consumption,
- the variety of production, that is, the differentiation of instruments and objects of production, products, technologies, branches, and so on,
- the interdependence of activities, stages of production, production units, branches, and so on,
- the number of activities included in this interdependence (for example, science).

The correct placing of the process of socialization in the dialectic of productive forces and production relations was decisive for determining its nature. In particular, it had to do with identifying the specific quality of this process in different social formations. If the socialization of production is a general historical law materializing in any social formation, the nature of socialization can be characterized only by indicating the general and the specific. This pertains all the more to the socialist process of socialization, since it does not proceed spontaneously, but has to be deliberately designed. Many phenomena and categories linked to the capitalist process applied thus only within this specific historical context. Three major facts about capitalist production, according to Marx ([1894] 1981, 375) are:

- The concentration of the means of production in a few hands, which means that they cease to appear as the property of the immediate producers and are transformed into social powers of production—even if these are the private property of capitalists. The latter are trustees of bourgeois society, though they pocket all the fruits of this trusteeship.

- The organization of labor itself as social labor: through cooperation, division of labor, and the association of labor with natural science. On both these counts the capitalist mode of production abolishes private property and private labor, even if in antithetical forms.
- Establishment of the world market.

"[T]he same processes—division of labor, organization of production, and management of labor—enter with their productive functions the system of productive forces, while their socio-economic forms are instances of the respective production relations" (Institut 1976, 166). Progressive socialization is the basic argument explaining the transition from capitalism to socialism. The increasingly social character of production more and more encounters the limits of private property capitalism. Progress of productive forces requires a change from indirect to direct social labor, from private to social ownership, from an anarchically functioning to a socially planned and managed economy. "The centralization of the means of production and the socialization of labour reach a point at which they become incompatible with their capitalist integument. This integument is burst asunder. The knell of capitalist private property sounds. The expropriators are expropriated" (Marx ([1867] 1976, 929).

Hence, the solution of the contradiction can only consist of the abolition of private property. East-German political economy discerned between formal and real socialization, that is, between socialization of the means of production and of production itself. While the nationalization of the means of production changes property relations, the production process remains unchanged for the moment. Real socialization of socialist production will be accomplished only during an extended historical process, which implies: "Agriculture, mining, manufacture, in one word, all branches of production, will gradually be organised in the most adequate manner. National centralization of the means of production will become the national basis of a society composed of associations of free and equal producers, carrying on the social business on a common and rational plan" (Marx 1872).

The change of property relations turns out to be instrumental for changing indirect into direct social labor: "From the moment when society enters into possession of the means of production and uses them in direct association for production, the labour of each individual, however varied its specifically useful character may be, is immediately and directly social labour" (Engels [1894] n.d., 345).

Seen from today, these statements necessitate the testing of at least the following two hypotheses, namely that the increasingly social character of labor

- is incompatible with an economic system in which the producers communicate with each other only via an exchange of commodities,
- requires direct social labor, that is, an economy which is managed on the level of society as a whole.

The course of history has shown that the *fundamental contradiction of capitalism* is not antagonistic. Since the time of Marx and Lenin, the intensity of socialization of production has increased enormously without being impeded fundamentally by capitalist development, which still is regulated autonomously. The socialist system, on the other side, based on social ownership and direct social labor, did not succeed in ensuring a higher development of productive forces and outpacing capitalism.

The fundamental contradiction of capitalism postulated by Marxist political economy may be described as a contradiction between the social division of labor and the division of labor within the factory. The transition to a socialist system suspends this contradiction: a total division of labor becomes the object of deliberate planning and management. This does not imply that under socialism all differences between social and factory division of labor have been eliminated. It is crucial, however, that both forms have a qualitatively new relationship.

Understanding this new quality is an important precondition for planning the process of socialist socialization. It had an immediate impact upon solving practical tasks like improving the social organization of production. At the same time, the dialectic of a social and factory division of labor was linked to a number of similar relations. This concerns the relationship among plan and market (commodity-money relations), direct and indirect socialization, social and collective interests, socialization and individualization, the whole of the economy and its separation into relatively independent units, and so on.

GEMEINSCHAFT AND *GESELLSCHAFT*

Marx's view of the ever-increasing socialization of labor and production, basically derived from Adam Smith, has proved a very powerful prediction. The number of products and services has proliferated exponentially since his days. Labor has been specialized and diversified. Research and development is indispensable for modern production. Supply chains of firms have become longer and longer. Interdependence has been extended across the globe, as he correctly foresaw.

There is no doubt that the concentration of production in huge, even multinational enterprises characterizes modern economies. Yet neither competition nor the sector of small and medium enterprises (SMEs) have disappeared. The latter still offers the bulk of employment and has a significant contribution to innovation. Socialist political economy talked large of state-monopoly capitalism and overlooked the real developments. Even if Lenin's vision of communism ("the whole of society will have become a single office and a single factory, with equality of labour and pay" (Lenin [1918] 1964, 479) was not implemented, the abolition of the entire SME sector and the concentration of the total economy in a few combines did not enhance innovation, productivity growth, or international competitiveness as expected.

The "fundamental contradiction of capitalism" has gained system-determining importance. It hypothesizes an impossibility theorem: the coexistence of the factory and the social division of labor and their respective coordination mechanisms, that is, central planning and management and the market. As a matter of fact, it is a bold statement without theoretical foundation. The issue itself has puzzled mainstream economics for a long time and was tackled adequately by Nobel-laureate Ronald Coase ([1937] 1988, 55): the demarcation between the firm and the market is determined by the costs of organizing a transaction within a firm and of *organizing* it by the price mechanism. Communist political economy has no theory of the firm and the market and one would look in vain in East-German textbooks for Coase's transaction costs.

It is undisputable that any far-reaching socialization of production and labor needs cooperation from the side of the state. The economic result of formally independent capitalist firms is strongly influenced by governance quality and the institutional setting within which they operate. The modern state, as industrial state, social state, welfare state, education and health state, for instance, no longer corresponds with Lenin's ([1918] 1964) description of the capitalist state. Nevertheless, Lenin's concept of state-monopoly capitalism triggered a broad literature on the topic in the GDR (for instance, Gündel 1967) that also swept over to West Germany.

Remarkably, political economy and sociology in the GDR did not take up or discuss Ferdinand Tönnies's (1855–1936) concepts of *Gemeinschaft* (community) and *Gesellschaft* (society), nor their elaboration by Max Weber (1864–1920). Tönnies distinguished between the social systems of communism and socialism, as the subtitle of the first edition makes clear (*Abhandlung des Communismus und des Socialismus als empirischer Culturformen,* Tönnies [1887] 1979). His philosophical-sociological approach owes a lot to Marx (and in many respects is only a weak extraction of Marxian economics). The important point, however, is that he puts the individual and its emancipation center stage. Historically, *Gemeinschaft* is the *prius*. It manifests in a patriarchal household embedded in a local community. Typical features are social ownership and consumption, the production of use values, the forming of a communal will, and communal guidance where necessary. It sounds trivial to assert that Marx and later Marxist political economists saw communism as a paradigmatic case of *Gemeinschaft*: "For an example of labour in common, i.e. directly associated labour, we [...] have one nearer to hand in the patriarchal rural industry of a peasant family" (Marx [1867] 1976, 171).

Gesellschaft, by contrast, consists of independent self-interested individuals who communicate via market exchange. Its extent is principally unlimited, globalization being its final stage. National states and national borders are alien in this context, whereas *Gemeinschaft* exists only in relation to a concrete association, be it the household, the firm, or the state. *Gesellschaft* needs separated, not necessarily private, property rights. The socialist materialization of *Gesellschaft*, which is not worked out but favored by Tönnies, must be a variety of market socialism. Thus, *Gesellschaft* is the outcome of the historical processes of the emancipation of the individual and progressive socialization, a truly dialectical development.

There lies a communist dilemma that becomes apparent if we have recourse to Max Weber's definition of communalization (*Vergemeinschaftung*) and socialization (*Vergesellschaftung*) (Weber [1921] 2014, 29–31). Weber accepts Tönnies's concepts, trying only to generalize them. He means by communalization a social relation based upon subjectively sensed togetherness. He analyzed the household as the basic element of such relations (Weber [1921–1922] 2009). The socialist community evidently falls under this rubrum. Socialization means, according to Weber, a social relation based on a rationally motivated balance or coordination of individual interests that will take place in contracts between autonomous parties and market exchange. It is the outcome of the progressive rationalization of the world.

Rationalization is also the meaning of the Marxist concept of socialization which communist theory tries to embed in a communal setting—and not in the anonymous market. One should not be misled by Weber calling market society, in the unfinished parts of his magnum opus, *market community* (*Marktgemeinschaft*). He is adamant about its nature: "Where the market is left to its inherent laws, it will only be regarding the business object, no person, no fraternal and piety obligations, none of the primordial human relations supported by personal communities" (Weber [1921–1922] 2009, 55). Real world social relations are composed of both ideal types, *Gemeinschaft* and *Gesellschaft*, with rationalizing *Gesellschaft* expanding progressively. The communist dilemma consists of an attempt to combine globalizing rationalization with communal social relations or of an assertion of an *objective* historical law to such effect.

OWNERSHIP, PROPERTY RIGHTS, AND PRODUCTION RELATIONS

Ownership (*Eigentum*) is one of the most complex categories of socialist political economy. As a legal concept it defines the command of material and immaterial goods. As a socio-economic concept it describes the entirety of social relations and processes in the production process (*Ökonomisches Lexikon* 1978–1980, Vol. A–G, 493–94). Here, it is almost synonymous with the concept of production relations. This idea can be traced back to Marx ([1847] 1972, 165): "To define bourgeois ownership means nothing else than describing all social relations of bourgeois production."

Western concepts of legal ownership and economic property rights address other socio-economic facts. Theoretical treatments of production relations and property rights lead in totally different directions. Nevertheless, the concept of property rights may be helpful when analyzing concrete socialist production relations or various forms of ownership under communism. On the whole, it may be true that all social relations of bourgeois (or socialist) production imply private (or social) ownership of the means of production. Yet production relations consist of a great number of elements, the most important being (*Politische Ökonomie* 1969, 216–17):

- The relations of producer and owner of means of production in connection with the character of labor,
- Social classes and social groups and their interactions,
- Relations due to the division and organization of labor,
- Governance and coordination of separate production processes,
- The exchange of labor and products between producers,
- Forms of distribution and material stimulation.

It seems as if the system of production relations widely conforms to the economic system, the analysis of which is the subject of economics (including also its sociological aspects) as Marx did in *Capital*. However, it is a peculiarity of Marxism-Leninism to treat the system of production relations preferentially as a topic of philosophy (Pokrytan 1973; Friedrich 1981) and political economy. No doubt, the elements of production relations are influenced, if not determined, by ownership relations. The other, material (*stoffliche*), side of the production process (production functions, input-output relations, scale economies, etc.), however, lies outside the domain of production relations and, hence, the scope of political economy (Friedrich 1981, 52–53). They may be considered subject matter of economics proper, which is represented mainly in particular sections of the field (for instance, growth theory, price theory) or in mathematical or quantitative economics.

The compartmentalization of economics goes even further: next to the material and social, the institutional (legal) aspect also is treated separately. The whole question of ownership and production relations is embedded in the historical theory of socialization of production.

East-German political economy has postulated a "fundamental production relation of socialism" (*Ökonomisches Lexikon* 1978–1980, Vol. H–P, 801) that defines the specific character of the economic system. There is no consensus, however, whether ownership can be regarded as "the fundamental economic condition of production relations" (Friedrich 1981, 55).

Regarding ownership as a particular independent element would finally lead to analyzing ownership as legal relation. It would lead to the analysis of what belongs to whom, who disposes of what, who is using what, and so on, that is, to the identification of certain relations between subject and object. Such are, as known, no economic, but legal relations. It is impossible to identify the economic content of ownership beyond and independent of the analysis of the totality of production relations (Pokrytan 1973, 21–22).

However, in order that production relations do not remain an empty shell, we will in the end have to know "what belongs to whom, who disposes of what, who is using what, etc." It is hard to see how the one can be separated from the other: legal institutions of ownership regulate economic decision-making, information flows, and motivation structures within the production process. They are by no means purely subject-object relations, but an institutional framework of social relations.

While ownership as a legal right is the result of a conscious act of legislation, a volitional act, production relations are not, but the result of *objective* historical processes, as historical materialism teaches. If we stick to historical materialism, legal rights are a phenomenon of the superstructure that ought to correlate with the economic basis. At the economic basis it is the ever-more complex development of productive forces that calls for production relations with predominant social ownership, that is, conscious central planning and guidance of the production process. Legal social ownership rights are a necessary correlate. The complex development of productive forces is universal in principle. Under capitalism private ownership gets less and less direct due to concentration, and the state adopts more and more governance tasks, thus transforming competitive private ownership capitalism into state-monopoly capitalism. But evidently there is a limit to such adaptation to the development of productive forces. In the end, capitalism is unable to cope with scientific-technical progress and socialism will surpass it. Such was the doctrine; its empirical content is not at stake here.

Historically, in the transition from capitalism to communism, ownership has played a crucial role: only the expropriation of private property has created social ownership in the legal sense. This, too, is a volitional act, and a revolutionary one, which may pave the way to social ownership in the economic sense, but does not create it automatically. In the Russia of 1917 this was certainly not the case. For Marx and the materialist hierarchy of basis and superstructure, there is a logical precedence of economic relations: "Are economic relations regulated by legal conceptions, or do not, on the contrary, legal relations arise out of economic ones?" (Marx [1875] 1970).

The historical process of introducing social ownership under communism has, however, reversed Marx's logical sequence. It was the result of political power, not the result of economic evolution. The dynamics of ownership, according to Marx, are governed by both: the revolutionary act annihilating the old power and ownership relations and, within the established system, the evolutionary process adapting production relations to changes in productive forces. To give an example of the latter, the separation of ownership and management, typical of modern capitalism, originated not from legal regulations, but from economic advantage—from developments within production relations, namely the splitting of ownership titles, and developments of productive forces or the professionalization of managerial skills. Legal regulations, not touching the original ownership right, were adjusted later (cf. corporate law).

East-German political economy of capitalism had difficulties to grasp such institutional developments within modern capitalism. As a textbook subject it concentrated on Marx's analysis of capitalism, which was the capitalism of the 1850s, and on Lenin's analysis of monopoly capital and imperialism, which was the capitalism of some 50 years later, fusing both to state-monopoly capitalism. The conclusions Marx and Lenin drew from their analyses seemed to come true in the great crisis of the 1930s. Capitalism, however, showed a surprising resilience and it would have been necessary to analyze the institutional changes to that effect. While the textbooks remained unimpressed, East-German business economists took notice of modern management methods that reflected changed economic relations.

STATE PROPERTY

After the revisionism debate of the late 1950s (see below), the idea of socialist ownership (*sozialistisches Eigentum*) was uniform and orthodox in the GDR. "As societal socialist ownership it cannot exist otherwise than in the form of state ownership. [...] The socialist state is the legal and economic subject of people's property" (Luft 1982, 826).[7] This seems to contradict the characteristic trait of socialist production relations to create identity of workers and owners: "All workers are equal owners" (Ibid., 824) or "Under socialism the worker is social owner of the means of production and producer of material goods in one person" (*Politische Ökonomie* 1969, 217). The Marxist-Leninist tenet of identity and harmony of interests under socialism obviously dissolves the contradiction: "Individual, state, and society were considered in our theory as principally non-contradictory unity" (Koziolek 1996, 142). No questions, please.

It would be wrong, however, to conclude that the socialist worker should take direct control of his means of production. "People's property can by no means be divided between state and firm" (Luft 1982, 826). The orthodox thesis of the indivisibility of people's property serves as a cornerstone of centralism and legitimizes any state intervention in the production process. Helmut Koziolek (1996, 139) sees in it one of the main causes of the limited effect of the reforms and their smooth liquidation in 1971. If all property rights are concentrated in the hands of the state, respectively its bureaucracy, workers as social owners without individual property rights need a particular conscience to perform with appropriate effort and not to shirk. "What belongs to all requires the industrious labor of each" (Luft 1982, 833) was hardly a description of actual behavior, but a pious wish.

Any reform ideas calling for firms' independence by transferring substantial property rights to the firm level were considered as contrary to the essence of social ownership and, hence, revisionist. "Such independence of firms from central management and planning would be equivalent to conversion of societal people's property into group property of the firms' collective thus making the interests and actions of the firms independent. In consequence there would be competition between firms, economic disproportions, social insecurity, unemployment, and inflationary price movements" (Ibid., 827). Yugoslavia always served as a deterring example. In short, social ownership excludes by definition any forms of socialist market economy and makes central governance and planning a *sine qua non* of socialism. Lenin's principle of democratic centralism is said to be the only possible form of governance of social ownership, thus giving the communist state and the communist party a pivotal role in socialist production relations (*Politische Ökonomie* 1969, 223).

A reform intending to decentralize decision-making, install profit as central success indicator, and enhance the motivation of firms and workers must be stranded on such centralization of property rights. In the preparation and execution of the *New Economic System*, discussion about the distribution of property rights was carefully avoided. The 1969 textbook which was meant to summarize reform economics was quite positive about the reform intentions: "Socialist production units based on the division of labor necessarily exist in the form of economic units planning and producing on their own responsibility, i.e. as economic units. These economic units are the commodity producers of socialist society. […] They bear full responsibility for their reproduction process" (Ibid., 267). How can they without corresponding property rights?

For with respect to the latter, the textbook remained extremely orthodox, "because the fundamental interests of society its classes and each worker [...] concur and find their expression in the central state plans" (Ibid., 227). One has to beware of "the perilousness of revisionist ideas to paralyze the main driving force of harmony of interests by assuming allegedly diverging interests of individual workers and firm collectives" (Ibid., 230).

According to official political economy in the GDR, in the first, socialist, phase of communism social ownership can be implemented in two forms: people's property (*Volkseigentum*), that is, state property (*Staatseigentum*), and cooperative property (*genossenschaftliches Eigentum*). The essence of social ownership consists in appropriating the results of the production process by society as a whole and not by any private owners. But since appropriation of scarce products is necessarily connected with decisions on allocation and distribution, it is the state as agent of society that holds the corresponding property rights of *usus*, *usus fructus*, and *abusus*. It is the state which decides on the establishment, merger, and liquidation of firms, it is the state which nominates their directors, it is the state which determines the production program, it is the state which regulates the supply channels, it is the state which takes the risk of failure, and it is the state which decides about the distribution of net income. Part of these decisions may be delegated to the firm, and the reform discourse and practice of the 1960s were about such delegation, but the state retains the right to define and control the firm's decision-making range and to intervene when deemed necessary. Social ownership and socialist production relations, according to East-German (and Soviet) doctrine, are inherently linked to central state planning and organization.

COOPERATIVE PROPERTY

How can cooperative ownership of the means of production be accepted under such conditions as social ownership? That depends on the property rights that the cooperative commands. They were not well defined. Land ownership was still in the hands of the associate members who had brought the land in when joining the cooperative. It can be considered a dormant right, since no concrete rights or privileges were connected with it.[8] Only after the dissolution of the system were the old owners, respectively their heirs, given back their rights. Ownership of the material means of production lies with the cooperative, but does it have full rights of *usus*, *usus fructus*, and *abusus*? "The products of people's firms [*volkseigene Betriebe*] are property of the whole people, while the products of the cooperatives are property of the members of the respective cooperative" (Luft 1981, 829). In the first case the fictitious character is obvious, in the second case the concrete property rights have to be analyzed.

Full appropriation of the products would comprise the right to dispose of them autonomously. It was Stalin (1952) who claimed commodity production to be characteristic of cooperatives. It implies that individual labor is not automatically social labor, but has to be acknowledged as such by the realization of the products. The question of commodity production and value under socialism would need a separate treatment. Suffice it here to remember that socialist production relations, that is, social ownership and the concomitant identity of owner and producer plus central planning, result in labor being immediate social labor not in need of any process of acknowledgement (*Politische Ökonomie* 1969, 220). Evidently, this was not automatically the case with cooperative production: "Cooperatives, by contrast to people's property, cannot alone, by themselves, adopt socialist character" (Ibid., 224). Only under the leading role of people's property and the workers' class, that is, the party, will cooperatives and their peasant members be included in socialist production relations. This boils down to being subjected to central planning and organization and to a serious attenuation of their property rights.

As long as cooperatives were subject to obligatory deliveries, their limited decision-making scope was evident. But also planned and contractually confirmed deliveries have obligatory character. Prices are centrally planned. Differential land rents which accrue in agriculture due to natural productivity differences are not appropriated by the formal landowners, the peasants, but by the factual land owners, the state. They can be left, however, with the cooperative for accumulation purposes. In any case, there was no market for cooperative products, not even an equivalent to the Soviet *kolkhoz* market. At the input side, cooperatives were totally dependent on state supplies. In the first phase of socialization of agriculture this was guaranteed by the state-owned machine-tractor-stations, the so-called "fulcrum of the workers' class in the countryside" (Ibid., 149). They had not only a material-technical but also a political-economic function. In the 1960s their assets were transferred to the cooperatives, because party and state control of the countryside was fully developed and the substantial subsidies of the machine and tractor stations (MTS) could thus be reduced.

The position of cooperative ownership in the system of socialist production relations was ambivalent. It has developed during the transition from capitalism to socialism as a concession to peasants and craftspeople who were to be organized in larger, allegedly more productive units, but whose petty-bourgeois ideological remnants from capitalism had still to be overcome with the help of the workers' class. Invariably, Lenin's two 1923 articles on cooperatives were quoted in this context, which hardly fit the East-German context. The Russian economy of the early 1920s was far away from socialist production relations: after the revolutionary capture of political power, cooperatives were thought to be the appropriate vehicle for the evolutionary itinerary to socialist production relations. The peasant mass had to be *civilized*, according to Lenin ([1923] 1965), which meant, first of all, to learn to read and write. And most importantly, Lenin's cooperatives had no ownership rights: land and material means of production were state property.

It was repeatedly stressed that cooperative ownership was not a transitory form (Luft 1981, 831). At the same time, people's property was portrayed as a *higher* form of socialist ownership (*Politische Ökonomie* 1969, 224). Due to development and growth, the essential differences between both forms of ownership, and the two classes of workers and peasants, gradually disappear without abolishing, so it was said, the specific character of cooperative ownership. One of the specificities was seen in the impossibility to apply the Leninist principle of democratic centralism to cooperatives because the members' assembly was the highest decision-making body, also electing the chairman. This must not have challenged, however, the authority of the central plan (*Ökonomisches Lexikon* 1978–1980, Vol. A–G, 495).

PRIVATE PROPERTY

Private property was regarded as a defunct institution of the pre-communist world. Under socialism, there existed personal property (*persönliches Eigentum*) that was limited to consumer goods and certain assets with consumptive functions such as homes, gardens, savings, insurance policies, and so on. Intellectual property rights were a remarkable exception since, in principle, they were private.[9] The reasons were twofold: on the one hand, the GDR was member of international agreements on the protection of intellectual property, and on the other hand inventive creativity had to be stimulated internally.

Private property does not conform to socialist production relations, even in the form of simple commodity production where producer and owner of the means of production are not separated people. This did not take away the necessity to accept private property in small industry, artisanry, and trade for an extended transition period. Their immediate nationalization would have disrupted the economy and overstrained the planning authorities. The acceptability of private firms within socialist production relations was justified, as in the case of cooperatives, by the state controlling the *commanding heights* of the economy which, indeed, meant that these firms could operate only within the state system of supply and sales, and hence, planning. In addition, larger private firms had to accept state participation in the form of limited partnership (*Kommanditgesellschaft*) with the private owner as unlimited and the state as limited partner. This form of *cohabitation* functioned quite well for more than 20 years in the GDR, and East Germany was one of those socialist countries that had retained a sizeable share of private property. Only when Erich Honecker (1912–1994) decreed that socialism had reached a fully developed stage did private property seem to be an anachronism. Most private and mixed ownership firms were nationalized or incorporated into cooperatives in 1972.

A final remark about the shadow economy may be apt here. Of course, it existed also in the GDR together with a parallel currency, the Deutsche Mark (DM). It existed even in an official form. There was the so-called commercial coordination unit (*KoKo*), a conglomerate of multiple foreign trade firms under the leadership of a *Stasi* colonel. It operated outside the official planning structure with the aim of earning foreign currency and getting hold of embargoed products and confidential economic information. Its activities were top secret and its budget—amounting to several billion DM—was a shadow budget. Then, there was the *Intershop*, a chain-store where rare imported goods could be bought for DM. Originally, it was meant for foreign travelers and tourists, and the shops were found in hotels, train stations, airports, and on the *Autobahn*. But in the course of time they spread all over the country and GDR citizens gained access to them which made it necessary to lift the legal ban on possession of foreign currency (Wolle 2013, 79–84). This business also took place outside the planning process and was not reflected in official statistics. Finally, there was the normal shadow economy, especially barter between firms and moonlighting called *Pfuschen* (like in Austria). Its currency was also predominantly the DM, the supply of which was provided by West German relatives and friends.

All this had very little to do with the socialist ideal and, hence, was better not discussed. Unlike in Hungary (see Gábor 1979; Galasi and Sziráczki 1985), the shadow economy was not a topic of scientific research in the GDR, but rather a taboo. Only after the fall of Berlin Wall did East-German economists dare to deal with the topic (Manz 1990). Manz puts shadow economy in quotation marks, since apart from exceptions (for example, moonlighting during work hours, theft of material, illegal currency exchange), these activities are said to have been legal in the GDR. The main motive was the shortage of goods and services and not tax avoidance as in market economies. However, the general motivation for participation in shadow activities, avoidance of government regulation, brings the two cases together, since a state plan is the most rigid form of government regulation.

REVISIONISM

No matter what scholars—writers and artists, too—discussed or published, the party checked against conformity with party lines, and each deviation was punished by a reprimand, expulsion from the ranks of the party, demotion, loss of job, or ultimately prison. Constant fear of such measures created self-censorship in the minds of scholars: even if one did not know exactly what was admissible, one knew what was not allowed and stopped short before conducting any risky activities. *Western* science has its own mechanisms to elicit conformity, but the playing field for heterodox views is immensely vaster. It is necessary to remember this when looking for alternative views about basic tenets of communist political economy.

East-German economists learned this lesson during the 1950s when Soviet-type central planning was disputed as a development model throughout Eastern Europe. The main East-German voices of critique were those of Fritz Behrens (1909–1980), Arne Benary (1929–1971), and Gunther Kohlmey (1913–1999). It should be clear that they did not call the socialist system into question. Their primary concern was the role of the state and its administration in governing the economy. Once socialist production relations have been established, the state should retreat to the backstage—Behrens alluded to the Marxian theorem of the withering away of the state under communism—and determine only the main lines of economic development. Production should be guided by the economic laws, in particular, the so-called law of value, which ultimately boils down to supply and demand conditions and gives room to spontaneous actions of firms. Secondly, such a regime presupposes the autonomy and self-determination of the firms. Given social ownership as a fundamental characteristic of socialism, the centralization of property rights within rigid state ownership comes into contradiction with this requirement, and the ideas of economic democracy, workers' codetermination (*Mitbestimmung*) or workers' self-management (*Selbstverwaltung*) commend themselves. The third point of argument concerned the planning mechanism. If administrative command is barred, the planner should use general rules and financial levers (or value forms as they were called) such as prices, interest rates, taxes, exchange rates, and so on. By linking workers' and management's compensation to financial success, that is, profit, efficient corporate governance is stimulated. Kohlmey forcefully advocated monetary and financial relations within the planned economy and called for an independent central bank (Krause 1998, 121–35; Caldwell 2000, 117–18). The East-German economists apparently were in line with the general critical consensus in the region.

A second, much smaller, strand of scientific critique was focused upon forced collectivization. The director of the Institute of Agricultural Economics at the German Academy for Agricultural Sciences, Kurt Vieweg (1911–1976), had launched in 1956 a draft for a new agricultural program (Vieweg [1956] 1997).[10] The draft was inspired by Polish resistance to collectivization and Scandinavian experiences with family farms in a cooperative network. So he pleaded for the coexistence of state and cooperative farms in socialist agriculture with the individual family farm embedded in the traditional cooperative movement.

The reaction to such views was harsh. They were immediately branded as *revisionist*.[11] Vieweg was forced to retire from all functions. He fled to West Germany and returned after a few months to the GDR where he was arrested and finally sentenced as a traitor to 12 years in jail from which he was released only in 1964 (Scholz 1997). Kohlmey lost his chair at Berlin's Humboldt University. Benary was removed from the university and put on probation, in essence meaning that he was relegated to the shop floor. There he engaged himself in implementing the reforms of the 1960s. When, with the advent of Honecker in 1971, it became clear that all such efforts were thwarted, he committed suicide. Behrens was dismissed from his posts as professor at Leipzig University and as director of the Statistical Office and transferred to the Institute of Economics at the Academy of Sciences.

His case is the most interesting, since he used his still prominent position to map the landscape where economic reforms in Central Europe should lead (Behrens 1961, 1966).[12] His book published in 1961 has often been characterized as an attempt to exonerate himself from the accusation of revisionism. Even if the publication was possible only after numerous concessions to his critics, it is one of the few solid theoretical pieces explaining why the socialization of the means of production does not automatically abolish commodities and their realization as values. These derive from the social division of labor disappearing only in the distant future of communism. The theoretical puzzle to be solved boils down to the question of how uniform social ownership, excluding a change of ownership in the process of commodity exchange,[13] can be combined with the relative isolation of state firms, making necessary the realization of the product and its partial appropriation by the firm. This implies limited property rights instead of full ownership:

> Commodity relations between state firms therefore are not relations between owners, but relations between people entitled to dispose. They relate not to already invested, but only to produced means of production. The owner of the invested means of production is society represented by the state. The exchange of labor products between the firms is necessitated by the isolation of the firms as is regulation of production by a plan which still has to be based on commodity relations and has to utilize them as well as the law of value. (Behrens 1961, 40)[14]

According to him, the old Soviet command model must be excused by historical circumstances. The new socialist market and plan model becomes indispensable to fulfill the socialist promise of democracy and welfare. The central problem of the new model is the question: "how can one make compatible the material interests of the working people, the individuals and the firms, with state management of the economy and the execution of central plans?" (Behrens 1966, 10). Behrens is careful not to attack openly state ownership, but claims that social ownership in the market environment of self-responsible individuals must be shaped differently. To do this properly, one needs a new political economy, not the dogmatic defense of socialism against suspected attacks from the outside, but an analysis of concrete human behavior (Ibid., 17).

Later, under the impression of the Honecker period, he elaborated further his critique of really existing socialism, writing a book in the late 1970s which could be published only after the collapse of the GDR and 12 years after his own death (Behrens 1972). He took sides with Rosa Luxemburg, council democracy, and the left-wing socialists of the early 1920s. He was strongly opposed to exclusive party rule, centralization, and state ownership. "Really existing socialism as state-monopolistic socialism is the old class society in a new guise and in addition impregnated with Russian—Asiatic—traditions with bureaucracy and despotism" (Ibid., 78). He is pleading for "the democratic government of a pluralist self-administrated society [...] a society of federal communes" (Ibid., 103). For "Socialization of production and labor leads to centralization and to bureaucratic centralism if it is complemented by state ownership of the means of production; it leads to self-management of the producers and self-government of the whole society if it is complemented by social ownership of the means of production" (Ibid., 56). As with Rosa Luxemburg, the initiative must come from below, and democratic centralism is a caricature of Marx's intentions. Behrens was in doubt whether his ideal was an illusion or a concrete utopia. Obviously, he had to write for the drawer.

Closest to Behrens' critique came Rudolf Bahro (1935–1997), whose book *Die Alternative* (Bahro 1977) was published in the West and which earned him a sentence of eight years in jail.[15] However, Bahro is not inspired by syndicalist or council-democratic ideas. On the contrary, his argument is, on the one hand, historical, seeing in really existing socialism a postcapitalist, that is, progressive even if utterly imperfect, formation, and, on the other, technocratic, seeing in the state and the hierarchical division of labor a necessary complement of the prevalent production technology. He shows little interest in ownership relations and state property in particular. His road to genuine socialism leads via a cultural revolution and education that will enable workers to understand the complexities of the modern world and, hence, to participate in decision-making. Such was the argument of Lenin against the workers' opposition and syndicalists in 1920–21 who Bahro quotes extensively. The most cogent critique of Bahro from the council-democratic point of view was written by Behrens (2010).[16]

THE ENDGAME

There is little wonder that, given the fate of critical voices, East-German economists did not ardently engage in discussions about fundamentals of communist political economy like ownership relations. Attempts at critical discourse were extremely rare.[17] This state of affairs did not change till the end. Only in view of the opening of the economy after the fall of the Berlin Wall did East-German scholars, mostly from the Academy Institute of Economics, take up the reform discourse and the question of ownership.

The diagnosis of the economic problems of the GDR was clear-sighted: "The erroneous identification of socialization and nationalization leads to monopolizing the ownership function by the state" (Ettl, Jünger, and Walter 1990, 166). The endgame considerations on reform reverted to the nationalizations of 1972. Espenhayn (1990) underlined in general the role of medium- and small-scale enterprises in a market economy, which presuppose private property. But on the whole East-German economists remained convinced that socialist ownership relations are indispensable for a socialist country. Ownership forms based on exploitation, that is, private property using wage labor, must be excluded. "Indispensable is [...] the socialization (also in the form of state property, certainly with a different character of the state and an enhanced role of the communes) of the key segments of different industries and public services" (Ettl, Jünger, and Walter 1990, 171; similarly Peche, Ettl, and Walter 1990, 31–32; *Autorenkollektiv* 1990, 321). Any forms of syndicalism or workers' self-management were still out of question: while acknowledging that there were divergent interests within society, scattered property rights would only encourage group egoism (Peche, Ettl, and Walter 1990, 36–37). The planned economy remained "the higher type of economic and social rationality" (Ettl, Jünger, and Walter 1990, 173).

Hans Luft, quoted above, returned in 1990 to the problems of social ownership in the GDR (Luft 1990). In his view, people's property could be preserved by the separation of state and economy, transferring the ownership of combines to the *Treuhandanstalt*, a state trust agency then set up by the GDR government and which only later became a privatization agency. The agency should not execute any management functions. It remained unclear who would nominate firm managers and how social ownership thus could be conducive, as Luft purports, to solving social tasks like an effective structural policy with full employment and securing the ecological equilibrium. In all these admittedly quickly drafted proposals one does not find a single mention of the word *entrepreneur*: Schumpeter stopped at the East-German border. Jena University economist H. Rudolph (1990, 1231) concluded:

> One must get the impression that economic research, in defiance of all realistic insight, once again and totally oriented toward the past, is reanimating Marxist ideals and continues to look for a third-way socialist concept that is not otherwise specified, but in any case superior to the market order.

The period between the fall of the Berlin Wall on November 9, 1989, and the introduction of West German labor law in conjunction with the economic, monetary, and social union of the two German states on July 1, 1990, was a brief interlude that could raise hopes for a new economic democracy. The initiatives at the shop floor, the so-called firm-level turn-around (*Betriebswende*), were very diverse and chaotic. The culture and theoretical background of the traditional labor movement, which for the last time manifested itself during the 1953 uprising, had vanished. "The anti-bureaucratic revolution against the old regime with its general democratic targets, in which this intra-firm revolution is blended in, was a completely different historic task than the creation of new social relations within the firm and beyond in the whole society" (Gehrke 2001, 318). Very soon, private property-based market practices took root. So East-German workers had to realize once more that ideological assertions about their being owners of the means of production did not imply concrete property rights. The state held the exclusive right of *abusus* and thus could legally divest itself of its property by privatizing it.

CONCLUSION

East-German thinking on ownership was a faithful representation of Marxist-Leninist doctrine. As such it deserves a place in the history of communist economic thought. The particular geographic and political situation of the GDR may have caused a specific rigidity. It is rather surprising that the long German tradition of socialist theory and policy has not been taken up as inspiration for new ideas and developments. Just take a look at West Germany where the capitalist crisis of the 1930s and the Nazi experience, both fundamental traumata in the GDR as well, have elicited the novel concept of a social market economy and raised the social commitment of property to constitutional rank, whatever that may have implied concretely. Insisting on Lenin's concept of state-monopoly capitalism, East-German economists were unable to deal adequately with these developments. Comparing East-German thinking with their socialist comrades in arms in Eastern Europe, we notice an astonishing unanimity or inflexibility. There were no conflicting views or schools on ownership theory. The basic tenets were determined politically by the party, and any deviations were sanctioned. Concessions to private property were out of the question. So, unlike the situation in Poland or Hungary, for instance, the economics profession was completely unprepared when transformation of the economic system required a new attitude toward ownership relations. The new system was introduced as a shock and was experienced as such.

NOTES

1. Franz Rudolph, formerly at the Higher School of Economics (*Hochschule für Ökonomie*) and the Central Institute for Socialist Management (*Zentralinstitut für sozialistische Wirtschaftsführung beim ZK der SED*), has contributed the subchapter on socialization in Marxist theory. All translations from German sources are the main author's.

2. Friedrich Wilhelm Raiffeisen adapted Schulze-Delitzsch's ideas to the countryside, in the first instance to create credit opportunities for farmers, since banks were to be found exclusively in the cities.

3. In addition, the trade unions created what were called *Gemeinwirtschaft*. The term is untranslatable. Ludwig von Mises (1881–1973) had used it in the German title of his book of 1922, while the English translation of 1936 put it simply as *socialism* (Mises [1922] 1936). The trade union movement meant it to be a non-profit enterprise in trade union ownership aiming at some undefined general welfare. The model flourished in West Germany in the first post–Second World War decades, with huge companies in banking, insurance, residential construction, retail trade, an so on. Most of these enterprises went belly up in the 1980s and the model was discontinued.

4. In fact, they did not receive full property rights. The right of *abusus* was excluded: the land could not be mortgaged, leased, or sold. It was only possible to return it to the state fund, what quite a lot of the new farmers did. They could not make ends meet because of a lack of physical and human capital.

5. The United States and the West German chancellor Konrad Adenauer were adamant about ignoring any such overtures. It is worth noting that the 1954 Soviet textbook on political economy—it had been prepared over years with strong interference from Stalin, and its German translation of 1955 (Akademie 1955) became the bible in academic education in the GDR—had a chapter (XL) on the economic system of the European socialist people's democracies. It does not mention the GDR with even a single word: it was not yet a member of the camp.

6. In the early 1950s they were partly returned, partly sold to the GDR with one exception, the (uranium producing) *SDAG Wismut* which was incorporated as a Soviet-German joint-stock company.

7. In the GDR the state comprised all levels of public administration. Contrary to German legal tradition, the commune (*Gemeinde*) is not an independent legal entity, but the lowest unit of the state hierarchy. Hence, there is no separate communal property.

8. This is not perfectly true. A small part of net income of the cooperative was distributed according to size and quality of collectivized land, the so-called land shares (*Bodenanteile*), that is, individual ownership of collectivized land was linked to a right of limited usufruct. Its legal status seems to have been unclear, and many cooperatives discontinued payment in the course of time.

9. To be precise, persons who made an invention within state firms or research institutes or with state support were granted a so-called economic patent (*Wirtschaftspatent*). The corresponding property rights were divided: *usus* and *abusus* belonged to the state, *usus fructus* partly to the inventor who was entitled to the *inventor's reward*

(*Erfindervergütung*) (*Ökonomisches Lexikon* 1978–80, Vol. A–G, 561). Copyright for artistic work was regulated more or less in favor of the artist.

10. Vieweg had spent the period 1933–46 in exile in Scandinavia. In the early 1950s he was Central Committee secretary for agriculture. As a *Western* émigré he was automatically suspect, removed from official political positions, and transferred to the Academy for Agricultural Sciences in 1954. Since he was also engaged in secret service activities, his case is difficult to evaluate (Scholz 1997).

11. The term "revisionism" had lost its original meaning in the GDR, namely as an evolutionary alternative to the orthodox revolutionary approach linked to the name of Eduard Bernstein (1850–1932). It was used as an indictment against all deviations from the by no means always straight party line.

12. For a detailed overview of Behrens's economic thinking, see Caldwell 2000 and Kuczynski 2015.

13. Behrens makes clear that the distinction between exchange within the state sector, between the state and the cooperative sector, and between the socialist sector and the consumers—introduced by Stalin 1952—is not decisive.

14. Relations within a joint-stock company are quite similar: there are owners of the capital controlling the firm and there are employees with limited property rights to produce and realize the output. Two features make for the difference: property rights are well defined and the individual firms compete in a market.

15. From which he was released and expelled to West Germany at the end of 1979 after strong international protests.

16. Again written for the drawer and published only in 2010 by his estate.

17. The Humboldt University group "Philosophical and methodological problems of political economy" around philosopher Peter Ruben (*1933) and economist Hans Wagner (1929–2012) became notorious in the late 1970s and early 1980s. In particular, Ruben was fiercely accused of *revisionism*, expelled from the party, and forbidden to teach.

BIBLIOGRAPHY

Akademie der Wissenschaften der UdSSR. Institut für Ökonomie, ed. 1955. *Politische Ökonomie. Lehrbuch*. Berlin: Dietz.

Autorenkollektiv. 1990. "Zum Konzept einer Wirtschafsreform in der DDR." *Wirtschaftswissenschaft* 38, no. 3: 321–41.

Bahro, Rudolf. 1977. *Die Alternative. Zur Kritik des real existierenden Sozialismus*. Köln: Europäische Verlagsanstalt. English translation: *The Alternative in Eastern Europe*. Translated by D. Fernbach. London: New Left Books. 1978.

Behrens, Fritz. 1961. *Ware, Wert und Wertgesetz: Kritische und selbstkritische Betrachtungen zur Werttheorie im Sozialismus*. Berlin: Akademie Verlag.

———. 1966. "Ursachen, Merkmale und Perspektiven des neuen Modells der Leitung der sozialistischen Wirtschaft." In *Sitzungsberichte der Deutschen Akademie der Wissenschaften zu Berlin 1966*, no. 1. Berlin: Akademie Verlag.

———. 1992. *Abschied von der sozialen Utopie*. Berlin: Akademie Verlag.

———. 2010. "Über Alternativen." In *"Man kann nicht Marxist sein, ohne Utopist zu sein ...,"* edited by Günter Krause and Dieter Janke, 147–71. Hamburg: VSA-Verlag.

Bock, Hans. 1973. *Syndikalismus und Linkskommunismus von 1918 bis 1923.* Darmstadt: Wissenschaftliche Buchgesellschaft.

Brus, Włodzimierz. 1986. "Institutional Change within a Planned Economy." In *The Economic History of Eastern Europe, 1919–1975*, edited by Michael Kaser, 40–69. Oxford: Clarendon.

Caldwell, P. C. 2000. "Productivity, Value, and Plan: Fritz Behrens and the Economics of Revisionism in the German Democratic Republic." *History of Political Economy* 32, no. 1: 103–37.

Coase, Ronald. 1988 [1937]. "The Nature of the Firm." In *The Firm the Market and the Law*, edited by R. H. Coase, 33–55. Chicago: University of Chicago Press.

Engels, Friedrich. n.d. [1894]. *Herrn Eugen Dühring's Revolution in Science [Anti-Dühring]*. New York: International Publishers.

Espenhayn, Rolf. 1990. "Die ordnungspolitische Rolle kleiner und mittlerer Unternehmen beim Übergang zur Marktwirtschaft in der DDR." *Wirtschaftswissenschaft* 38, no. 8: 1089–1108.

Ettl, Wilfried, Jürgen Jünger, and Dieter Walter. 1990. "Grundgedanken einer Wirtschaftsreform in der DDR—Thesen zur Diskussion". *Wirtschaftswissenschaft* 38, no. 2. 164–83.

Friedrich, Horst. 1981. *Die Produktionsverhältnisse*. Berlin: Dietz.

Gábor, István. 1979. "The Second (Secondary) Economy: Earning Activity and Regrouping of Income outside Socially Organized Production and Distribution." *Acta Oeconomica* 3, no. 4: 291–311.

Galasi, Péter, and Sziráczki Gábor, eds. 1985. *Labour Market and Second Economy in Hungary*. Frankfurt a.M.: Campus.

Gehrke, Bernd. 2001. "'Der FDGB tagt hinter verschlossenen Türen—Wir reden und handeln offen!' Eine Lesehilfe für die Dokumente der innerbetrieblichen 'Wende.'" In *Der betriebliche Aufbruch im Herbst 1989: Die unbekannte Seite der DDR-Revolution. Diskussion—Analysen—Dokumente,* edited by Bernd Gehrke and Renate Hürtgen, 288–320. Berlin: Bildungswerk Berlin der Heinrich-Böll-Stiftung.

Gündel, Rudi et al. 1967. *Zur Theorie des staatsmonopolistischen Kapitalismus.* Berlin: Akademie-Verlag.

Institut für Gesellschaftswissenschaften, ed. 1976. *Grundlagen des historischen Materialismus.* Berlin: Dietz.

Krause, Günter. 1998. *Wirtschaftstheorie in der DDR*. Marburg: Metropolis.

Kuczynski, Thomas. 2015. "Fritz Behrens und seine rätekommunistische Kritik sozialistischer Reform." In *Reformen und Reformer im Kommunismus*, edited by Wladislav Hedeler and Mario Keßler, 36–52. Hamburg: VSA Verlag.

Lenin, V. I. 1964 [1918]. "The State and Revolution: The Marxist Theory of the State and the Tasks of the Proletariat in the Revolution." In *Collected Works*, Vol. 25, 385–492. Moscow: Progress Publishers.

———. 1964 [1920]. "'Left Wing' Communism: An Infantile Disorder." In *Collected Works*, Vol. 31, 17–118. Moscow: Progress Publishers.

———. 1965 [1923]. "On Cooperation." In *Collected Works*, Vol. 33, 467–75. Moscow: Progress Publishers.

Luft, Hans. 1982. "Sozialistisches Eigentum an den Produktionsmitteln als gesellschaftliches Eigentum, seine Formen und seine Entwicklung." *Wirtschaftswissenschaft* 30, no. 6: 823–37.

———. 1990. "Probleme des gesellschaftlichen Eigentums in der DDR." *Wirtschaftswissenschaft* 38, no. 7: 1027–35.

Manz, Günter. 1990. "'Schattenwirtschaft' in der DDR." *Wirtschaftswissenschaft* 38, no. 2: 219–29.

Marx, Karl. 1972 [1847]. "Das Elend der Philosophie." In *Werke,* Vol. 4, edited by K. Marx and F. Engels, 63–182. Berlin: Dietz.

———. 1872. The Nationalisation of the Land. *The International Herald*, no. 11, June 15. Available online, accessed April 24, 2017: https://www.marxists.org/archive/marx/works/1872/04/nationalisation-land.htm.

———. 1970 [1875]. "Critique of the Gotha Programme." In *Selected Works*, Vol. 3, edited by K. Marx and F. Engels, 13–30, Moscow: Progress Publishers. Available online, accessed April 24, 2017: https://www.marxists.org/archive/marx/works/download/.

———. 1976 [1867]. *Capital: A Critique of Political Economy.* Vol. 1. London: Penguin.

———. 1981 [1894]. *Capital: A Critique of Political Economy.* Vol. 3. London: Penguin.

Mises, Ludwig. 1922. *Die Gemeinwirtschaft: Untersuchungen über den Sozialismus.* Jena: Gustav Fischer. English translation: *Socialism: An Economic and Sociological Analysis.* Translated by J. Kahane. London: Jonathan Cape. 1936.

Naphtali, Fritz, ed. 1928. *Wirtschaftsdemokratie: Ihr Wesen, Weg und Ziel.* Berlin: Verlagsgesellschaft des Allgemeinen Deutschen Gewerkschaftsbundes GmbH.

Ökonomisches Lexikon. 1978–1980. Third edition. Berlin: Die Wirtschaft.

Oppenheimer, Franz. 1896. *Die Siedlungsgenossenschaft: Versuch einer positiven Überwindung des Kommunismus durch Lösung des Genossenschaftsproblems und der Agrarfrage.* Leipzig: Duncker & Humblot.

Peche, Norbert, Wilfried Ettl, and Dieter Walter. 1990. "Konzept einer radikalen Wirtschaftsreform." In *Was heißt radikale Reform?* 7–64. Berlin: Die Wirtschaft.

Pirker, Theo et al. 1995. *Der Plan als Befehl und Fiktion: Wirtschaftsführung in der DDR.* Opladen: Westdeutscher Verlag.

Pokrytan, Anatoly. 1973. *Produktionsverhältnisse und ökonomische Gesetze des Sozialismus.* Berlin: Akademie Verlag.

Politische Ökonomie des Sozialismus und ihre Anwendung in der DDR. 1969. Berlin: Dietz.

Preiser, Erich. 1970 [1964]. "Franz Oppenheimer: Gedenkrede zur 100. Wiederkehr seines Geburtstages." In *Politische Ökonomie im 20. Jahrhundert: Probleme und Gestalten,* 179–93. München: Beck.

Richter, Helmut, ed. 1984. *Politische Ökonomie des Kapitalismus und des Sozialismus.* Berlin: Dietz.

Rudolph, Helmut. 1990. "Aktuelle Probleme des Systemwandels und der Ordnungspolitik im deutsch-deutschen Einigungsprozeß." *Wirtschaftswissenschaft* 38, no. 9: 1231–41.

Scholz, Michael. 1997. *Bauernopfer der deutschen Frage: Der Kommunist Kurt Vieweg im Dschungel der Geheimdienste*. Berlin: Aufbau Verlag.

Steiner, André. 2004. *Von Plan zu Plan: Eine Wirtschaftsgeschichte der DDR*. München: DVA.

Tönnies, Ferdinand. 1979 [1887]. *Gemeinschaft und Gesellschaft: Grundbegriffe der reinen Soziologie*. Darmstadt: Wissenschaftliche Buchgesellschaft.

Vieweg, Kurt. 1997 [1956]. "Entwurf: Neues Agrarprogramm für die Entwicklung der Landwirtschaft beim Aufbau des Sozialismus in der DDR." In *Bauernopfer der deutschen Frage: Der Kommunist Kurt Vieweg im Dschungel der Geheimdienste* , edited by Michael Scholz, 235–42. Berlin: Aufbau Verlag.

Webb, Sidney, and Beatrice Webb. 1897. *Industrial Democracy*. London: Longmans, Green & Co.

Weber, Hermann. 2012. *Die DDR 1945–1990*. Fifth edition. München: Oldenbourg.

Weber, Max. 2009 [1921–1922]. *Wirtschaft und Gesellschaft. Religiöse Gemeinschaften*. Studienausgabe. Tübingen: Mohr-Siebeck.

———. 2014 [1921]. *Wirtschaft und Gesellschaft. Soziologie*. Studienausgabe. Tübingen: Mohr-Siebeck.

Wolle, Stefan. 2013. *Die heile Welt der Diktatur: Alltag und Herrschaft in der DDR 1971–1989*. Fourth Edition. Berlin: Ch. Links.

Chapter 5

From Two to One (And Only)?

Theorizing Ownership in Communist Hungary

János Mátyás Kovács

With the wisdom of hindsight, and under the spell of Whig history, it is tempting to portray the basic pattern of the evolution of Hungarian economic thought under communism as a gradual victory of the concept of private ownership, a lengthy but unmistakable process, in the course of which the notion of private property rights gained legitimacy in Hungary's economic research community. Accordingly, studying ownership would be the most important research program of Hungarian economic theorists, which underwent a four-decade process of both intellectual refinement and ideological radicalization. It started out, goes the argument, in the first half of the 1950s from a soft critique of the powerful concept of *social ownership* (*társadalmi tulajdon*)[1] in the post-Stalinist political economy—that postulated a mild contrast between state property (*állami tulajdon*) and cooperative property (*szövetkezeti tulajdon*) and rejected private ownership (*magántulajdon*)—to end up accepting the basic tenets of *new institutional economics* in the West during the second half of the 1980s. More exactly, economists in Hungary finished their journey in the world of communism by importing or rediscovering standard neoclassical ideas, which they combined with Austrian, Ordo-liberal and/or new-institutionalist theories, particularly public choice and the property rights school. In their eyes, social ownership lost much of its significance over these decades, and ultimately turned into a single imperative of establishing private property rights under the aegis of far-reaching privatization programs.

With the help of an even more Whiggish assumption, one could also describe this evolutionary path as a process of diminishing the simulation of capitalism, resulting in an open recognition of one of its essential constituents, large-scale private ownership. This interpretation would consist of two parts:

1. By and large, Hungarian economists were discussing ownership issues even if they thought to argue about *commodity-money relations*, *economic mechanisms*, *indirect control*, or *small entrepreneurship*, just to mention four of their favorite research themes.
2. During preparations for the New Economic Mechanism in the second half of the 1960s, this—to use an oxymoron—*unintended simulation* of capitalism turned into a deliberate camouflage when a growing number of scholars were forced to accept the deal of *limited marketization without privatization* offered by the party-state but deep down they did not endorse the idea of the superiority of social ownership.

I am afraid that the economic research community in Hungary shares in common the core of the above narrative.[2] The farther we move away from the communist period, the less laborious becomes the birth of the idea of privatization in the memory of the economics profession.[3] Similarly, with time, even moderate reform economists seem to have evolved into liberal thinkers who had to hide their conviction out of a spirit of self-preservation but who, with the weakening of censorship, revealed their hand during the 1980s. Below, I will use the examples of a variety of research programs in ownership theory under communism to challenge (or nuance) this assumption as well as the twin hypotheses of gradual radicalization and improvement of academic quality. This can, in turn, help the historian revalue other major economic research programs in Hungary, such as the ones focusing on investment cycles, shortages, or the shadow economy. It may turn out in the end that in other fields (e.g., optimal planning) the scholarly performance of Hungarian economists deserves similar applause.[4]

Challenging the view of a gradual (unilinear) evolution in ownership theory may not only disturb Whig-style historians in the Hungarian economics community but also the staunchest critics of radical reformism in Hungary and beyond who have been accusing its representatives of hastily borrowing neoliberal ideas of private property from the West, opening up the country for global capitalism, and thereby derailing the process of postcommunist transformation.[5] I hope to be able to ascertain in this chapter that both camps overestimate the liberal leanings of Hungarian economists before 1989.

HYPOTHESES

In the next section, I will tell a concise story of theorizing ownership in communist Hungary. My aim is to collect a few facts and arguments in preparation for testing the following working hypotheses:

1. The evolution of the concept of property rights in Hungarian economic thought under communism seems unnecessarily, even painfully, lengthy given that the concept's major components were available from the very beginning in the works of leading *bourgeois professors* (not to speak of social-democratic and agrarian experts) right after the Second World War. Part of these components came to the fore and challenged the paradigm of social ownership from time to time, only to disappear in the background for longer periods. In a sense, what may appear as scholarly progress during 40 years of communist rule can also be interpreted as an exercise in reinventing the wheel, that is, as a forced detour bringing little scientific innovation in ownership theory. To put it bluntly, in 1989, the Hungarian economists rejoined, in many respects, the German mainstream of legal and economic scholarship of the late 1940s rather than the American (new institutionalist) mainstream of the day.
2. The pattern of evolution seems gradual in the long run but was often interrupted, showing signs of cyclical change if scrutinized from a shorter perspective. The idea of self-management (*önigazgatás*), for example, burst out from time to time. The attraction of social ownership did fade away in Hungary during four decades of communism; nevertheless, the concept provided a strong discursive frame that could not be loosened earlier than a few years before 1989.
3. Private property rights proved to be one of the strongest taboos of economic research under communism (probably equal to *the party's leading role in economic management*, the militarization of the economic system, and the status of the Soviet economy in the *socialist world system*). Because a full acknowledgment of these rights would have demanded not only the reconstruction of the rule of law but also capitalism in general, reformist discourse in Hungary handled the main ingredients of the concept of private ownership, such as the nature and size of the property owned as well as the scope and strength of rights, with special care. In cautiously compartmentalizing property rights, certain entitlements were officially acknowledged while others rejected or informally accepted. Until the last breath was taken by communism, private ownership was

normally linked in economic theory with some kind of collectivist principle (e.g., joint venture of rural households and agricultural cooperatives, intrapreneurship in state-owned firms, cross ownership between private and state companies, etc.); it was not suggested to become a large-scale phenomenon (particularly not in capital goods industries, another taboo of communist political economy); and the rights were regarded as informal/revocable and weak/partial entitlements rather than legally enforceable claims. As time passed, the arguments for private ownership became less shy whereas the legal and sociological reasoning in favor of privatization did not gain much in scholarly quality. In sum, the idea of *pluralization* (hybridization) of ownership dwarfed that of privatization, and the notion of ownership remained pale, that is, devoid of colorful contributions from other social sciences.

4. It is also hard to depict the evolution of ownership concepts in Hungary as a broadening acceptance of liberal principles because, from among the possible collectivist solutions, the idea of workers' self-management (either within the project of cooperative ownership or without) featured as a potential alternative from the very beginning. It flared up as an overarching societal model in 1956; tacitly coexisted in the countryside with that of personal ownership (e.g., links between cooperatives and household plots); was revived as a grand initiative to reform company law in the middle of the 1980s; and remained an important constituent of the program of the social-liberal dissidents and dissenters up until 1989. Perhaps the most (in)famous blend of quasi-Hayekian thoughts and collectivism was to be found in Tibor Liska's socialist and liberal model of *personal ownership of social capital*, which was promulgated by him incessantly from the middle of the 1960s onward.
5. Ownership concepts in Hungary exhibited a whole series of *national specifics*, ranging from the hybridization of property forms, through small entrepreneurship, to informal (creeping) privatization. These specifics were developed and/or studied by local economists with growing interest and expertise but in most cases they fell behind the theoretical/methodological skills and performance of their Western colleagues. The gap between them was perhaps the most spectacular in researching the widely recognized *managerial model* of the Hungarian reform project. This research program connected the pioneering but rudimentary diagnoses of *overcentralization* in the 1950s with the complex governance schemes invented for state-owned large enterprises during the 1980s. Hungarian economic theorists had the rare chance to accumulate empirical knowledge in a large laboratory experimenting with manager-oriented ownership reforms for about three decades following 1956. The outside world expected them to couple local empirical evidence with modern

techniques of institutional analysis, similar to what Yugoslav economists did in modeling self-management, their primary differentia specifica in ownership matters. Hungarian scholars could have profited from a whole series of new research programs (theories of incentives, property rights, public choice, etc.) emerging in the West but they rather insisted on methods of quasi-anthropological description and verbal/qualitative analysis.

THE STORY

Theorizing ownership did not follow one single track and cannot be characterized in retrospect as a nonstop march toward the recognition of private property rights. Its twists and turns have an interesting timeline. In what follows, I will distinguish six phases of evolution. Let me stress upfront that they often overlap, and by evolution I do not necessarily mean scientific progress. True, leaving behind the crude and ideologically overloaded concepts of nationalization and collectivization, and accepting the idea of private property under mixed ownership after four decades was an important achievement in Eastern European comparison. However, this learning process (a) returned in many respects to its origins, namely, to a kind of economic knowledge characteristic of the time before the Sovietization of economic sciences in Hungary in the late 1940s, early 1950s; and (b) proved to be a protracted exercise in *learning by doing* rather than *learning by reading*. In 1989, economic theorists did not know much more about ownership than their predecessors in 1945, with the exception of the fact that they had the *privilege* of observing from close quarters the consecutive flops of their own theories of ownership which were based on the concept of non-private, partly private, artificially private, or other property in the real world of the Hungarian economy.

Life around the Soviet Textbook

By the time the first textbook of socialist political economy was published in the Soviet Union, following a quarter of a century break, in 1954,[6] Hungarian economists began to wake up from the shock of full nationalization supported by no economic theory to which they had originally subscribed.[7] Until 1948, even scholars of Marxist persuasion prepared for the reconstruction of a mixed economy with a sizable private or semi-private sector (especially in agriculture, trade and services), which would probably be less regulated than the war economy had been in the first half of the 1940s. Originally, most of the liberal and social-democratic thinkers as well as the agrarian economists who survived communist *Gleichschaltung* during the late 1940s could not reconcile themselves with blanket nationalization and collectivization. Many of them preferred socialization from below to nationalization (etatization) from above. Interestingly enough, however, they refrained, even during the revolution in 1956, from demanding more than partial decollectivization in agriculture and a limited degree of privatization and self-management in other sectors.

Shying away from Big Capitalism (especially its free-market version) was not only a consequence of the weakness of Austrian traditions in Hungarian economic thought or self-censorship rooted in pragmatic considerations. Regarding the lack of Ordo-liberal influence before the Second World War, what was called in Hungary a *managed economy* (even *managed planned economy* [*sic*]), *bounded economy* (*kötött gazdaság*), or *labor state* (*munkaállam*) lay much farther from the concept of *social market economy* as advocated by the Freiburg School than from the dominant statist-corporatist legacy of the German Historical School. For an overwhelming majority of Hungarian economists, the war economy was an exaggeration in practical terms rather than a failure in principle. To them planning in kind, central distribution of resources, price and wage controls, and so on, did not smell odious. It was the idea of state ownership in large, especially strategic, industries, of cooperative ownership, and small- and medium-sized private ownership in all other industries and agriculture, as well as of some trade union-based co-determination that—in harmony with the *Zeitgeist* influenced by fresh Keynesian thoughts—dominated their minds and souls before the communist takeover in 1948.[8] And almost the same scientific instruments were to be found in their toolbox when they worked out the first reform programs for the government of Imre Nagy between 1953 and 1955 (the "New Course"), and in the economic debates preceding and following the 1956 Revolution. In the first case the agenda of ownership reform was roughly limited to a cautious transition from forced collectivization in agriculture to a system of voluntary cooperation of small (provisionally) private owners whose economic transactions were to be strongly regulated. However, in the period between the economic discussions of the Petőfi Circle in 1956 and the sessions of the Varga Commission for economic reform in 1957, the iconoclastic objective of reestablishing small-scale private ownership also appeared on the horizon of the economics profession.[9]

In ownership theory, decollectivization prior to the 1956 Revolution, however half-hearted it was, meant a return to the notions of small-scale private property and *real* (non-state-led) cooperatives, marking, at the same time, the ideological constraints of such a return. Property rights were compartmentalized: early reformist thought in the 1950s revolved around the *usus* and *usus fructus* of the assets, demanding less state interference and stronger economic incentives, while their *abusus*, particularly, transfer (sale, rent, inheritance, etc.) and transformation, was cautiously put in a sealed compartment. The same precaution led to the ignoring of two crucial requirements: the exclusivist nature of property rights, and the stipulation that the dividing line between rival claims of ownership must not be blurred. Group ownership was preferred to individual ownership, and the protection of private and cooperative property rights were often left without legal sanctions. By and large, this separation (or *unbundling of property rights*, to use modern terminology) determined the basic approach to ownership theory in Hungarian economic thought up until the second half of the 1980s.[10] The ordinary private owner—who does not only operate (use) his/her assets of any size and in any sector, and appropriate their returns but is also entitled to buy, sell, bequeath and inherit, rent out, mortgage, and transform, them, and exclude others from doing the same, while all these transactions are safeguarded by the rule of law in the economy as a whole—did not become a hero, even in the eyes of radical reformers who, by the turn of the 1960s and 1970s, began to touch upon the taboo of capital markets. At best, the private owner was considered an individual, who happened to possess a small (family) firm employing just a few workers, preferably in the service sector, and was tolerated rather than supported and protected by the law. The ironic undertone of the Hungarian neologism *maszek* (combining and abbreviating the words *private* and *sector*) expressed the low esteem of that status adequately.

The 1954 Soviet textbook did not add much to the prevailing consensus in the economic profession. It only strengthened the conviction of what one could already trace from Stalin's (1951) pamphlet *The Economic Problems of Socialism in the Soviet Union*; namely, *socialist commodity production* was thought to be contingent on the existence of two—state and cooperative—forms of social ownership. Although the former was declared to be superior to the latter, *kolkhoz* property gained quite a high degree of legitimacy from the supreme leader, achieving further *scientific* reinforcement in the 1954 textbook. The emphasis on both commodity production and cooperatives, even if it exclusively concerned producers' cooperatives and only in agriculture, opened a window of opportunity for those, like the Hungarian prime minister Imre Nagy and his economic advisors, who wanted to bring back certain traits of private property into the notion of (voluntary) cooperative ownership in the future. The freedom of joining and leaving the cooperative by bringing in or taking out *personal property* (*személyi tulajdon*—see below) was a decisive issue in the rethinking of property rights.

Yet for Hungarian economists the partial re-legitimation of commodity production and the agricultural cooperatives did not sound like an invitation to launch extensive research programs on property rights. The textbook defined the discourse in that field in an unambiguous fashion. Accordingly, social ownership has nothing to do with law; and the abstract taxonomy consisting of two crucial forms of ownership (state and cooperative) and two negligible ones (private and personal) was not required to be filled with meaningful sociological content. I suggest to squeeze these features of ownership theory into the term *paleness*, or to put it more politely, lack of multidisciplinary analysis, and derive them from a strict prohibition implied by the definition of private property in the textbook. Separating, in an artificial manner, the notion of personal property relegated to the sphere of consumption from that of private property that (a) is used in production, (b) can serve as a means of exploitation, and (c) is therefore doomed to wither away, indicated the ideological boundaries of scientific reflection clearly. Small wonder that the early reformist texts of scholarly eminence, such as György Péter's essays on efficiency and profitability (1954, 1956–1957) or Kornai's *Overcentralization* (1957), do not contain any serious reference to private ownership, or more exactly, to any kind of ownership.

With the exception of agricultural cooperatives, in the concept of which the collectivization of formerly private assets could not be camouflaged completely, the issue of ownership was converted into a problem of economic management in the framework of the *plan-and-market discourse* of the early reform economists.[11] Such a discourse offered a comfortable way to study the *economic mechanism* of managing state property without saying anything politically relevant or scholarly rigorous in the fields of economics, law, or sociology about the relative virtues/vices of social ownership itself. As noted, the reformers did not go beyond examining certain aspects of *usus* and *usus fructus*, yet it seemed as if they had focused on the gist of ownership. This way of theorizing ownership by unbundling property rights and ignoring *abusus* with the help of a self-limiting discourse (simply put: advocating marketization without privatization) also became a lasting feature of Hungarian economic thought under communism. Was this a cover discourse for doing at least what was doable/permitted at that time? No, in my opinion. Deliberate simulation practiced by a growing segment of the economics profession began during the *Kádárist consolidation* after 1956 and remained ambiguous until 1989. The term "simulating capitalism" does not adequately describe the mindset of those scholars who disliked or even despised capitalism for one reason or another—a great majority of the research community by the way.

Initially, indulging in the discussion of *commodity-money relationships* and remaining silent about the problem of ownership were not discursive tricks but an expression of a sincere belief in gradually improving planning through the reorganization of some of its techniques and modest market reforms. Nonetheless, accepting the principle of limited marketization provided the opportunity to ask vital questions about capital markets later,[12] that is, after having gone through a series of failed reforms of the product and labor markets, and having realized the need for broadening the scope of the property rights concept to include *abusus* and the rule of law. Until then, the manager, not the owner, remained in the focus of analysis; the manager of a state or cooperative firm who did not have well-defined, irrevocable, and exclusive property rights but amorphous competences in decision-making within the party-state hierarchy. Whether this long detour starting in the early 1950s brought scientific enrichment with it is a question to be answered in the Conclusion.

Small Shocks of the 1956 Revolution: Workers' Councils and Household Plots

The detour was, however, more than obvious. Prestigious members of the old guard among Hungarian economists, Marxists and non-Marxists alike (such as Béla Csikós-Nagy, Farkas Heller, György Péter, and István Varga), must have read or heard about the Mises-Hayek arguments on the impossibility of rational economic calculation under collectivism, which stressed the advantages of private property. Most of them were well versed in legal thought, and some of them, like Péter and Varga, shared their views on certain virtues of private ownership with their younger colleagues (such as András Bródy, János Kornai, and Márton Tardos).[13] However, the fiasco of the 1956 Revolution prevented the research community from revisiting the model of mixed economy prevailing in the profession between 1945 and 1948. In the course of post-1956 *normalization*, there remained nothing else to borrow from the Socialist Calculation Debate than the varieties of the Lange model of market socialism, none of them openly tackling the intricacies of ownership. The same applied to the scientific supply of the Soviet mathematical school of optimal planning.

Nevertheless, at least two promising opportunities remained unexploited to think about the need of reestablishing at least a modicum of private ownership: the discussions of revisionist Marxist economists in the Petőfi Circle prior to the revolution, and the sessions of the economic reform commission led by István Varga in 1957.[14] In the former, the issue of private property was completely ignored, and even the problem of state versus cooperative, communal and self-managing ownership was packaged in the clumsy but neutral term of *separateness* (*elkülönültség*)[15] of companies within unitary social ownership, which had a long career in moderate reform thinking for at least two decades after 1956. The idea of self-management was in the air but eventually boiled down to the sporadic desire to *check what the Yugoslav comrades were doing*. As regards the Varga Commission, its members were a bit more explicit in matters of ownership. Most of them contented themselves with designing an economic mechanism that provides companies with more room to maneuver within the framework of social ownership. However, the question whether or not their growing independence should go *beyond* claiming a greater liberty in using assets and enjoying returns from those assets was left without an affirmative answer.

When it came to the project of profit sharing (a populist measure to appease a traumatized society), there was only one single person in the commission, Sándor Kopátsy, who connected the project with a possible transfer of companies (i.e., state property) to the possession of their employees who thus would become, as he said, *quasi-shareholders*. All others (including former *bourgeois professors*) were clearly, sometimes vehemently, against the extension of group property rights. Their resistance was not only due to self-censorship based on predictions that sooner or later the Kádár regime would smash the workers' councils emerging in the aftermath of the Revolution. The majority were really afraid of following the Yugoslav pattern that would lead, using their words, to *atomization*, *chaos*, *false egalitarianism* (*egyenlősdi*), and a decline in the professional quality of economic decision-making—allegedly demonstrated by the newborn workers' councils. Apparently, these several months of local experience of group ownership, at this time not only in agriculture, reinforced the skepticism among Hungarian economists toward self-management in Yugoslavia. This skepticism resulted, in addition to excluding self-management from institutional options while preparing for the New Economic Mechanism of 1968, in a lackadaisical interest in property rights theory during the communist period as a whole. Yet, Hungarian scholars could have learned a lot from their Yugoslav colleagues in this field from the 1960s onward.

The economics profession in Hungary turned a blind eye to important theoretical aspects of the *in vivo* experiment with the workers' councils. The leading experts were preoccupied with the danger of lay management in firms and lack of macro-coordination. From our perspective, it is more important that the councils' representatives did not call social ownership into question but rather insisted on replacing the hierarchy of the party-state by a horizontal network of self-managing institutions, that is, one kind of social ownership with another. The councils wanted to elect their chambers and employ a planning office, thereby uprooting the then prevailing system of property rights and considerably rearranging their mix. It was no wonder that these—originally Marxian—claims deeply irritated the *nomenklatura* by demonstrating the immense counterweight of horizontal collectivism, particularly in large industries. As a consequence, the ruling elite confined further attempts at conceiving of group property rights to the cooperative sector for almost three decades following the revolution.

Ironically, while fearing uncontrolled collectivism in 1956/57, the Kádár regime allowed for some liberalization of small-scale private property, above all in services. This infringement of social ownership did not incite the fantasy of economic theorists at the time. They became much more interested in a dual component of re-collectivization in 1958–1961, which seemed insignificant in the beginning, namely, the authorization of market production on household plots in combination with the termination of requisitions.[16]

It was not the re-approval of personal property per se (as assumed, without exploitation) that aroused the interest of economic thinkers but its growing symbiosis in the countryside with cooperative ownership as well as the undeniable economic success of such a property mix. This gave an impulse to experimenting with other blends, ranging from sharecropping within the agricultural cooperatives, and renting out state-owned retail shops and restaurants (*gebin*), through the industrial and service units of agricultural cooperatives (*tsz melléküzemág*) in the wake of the New Economic Mechanism, all the way down to the intra-enterprise economic work associations (*vállalati gazdasági munkaközösség—vgmk*)[17] during the 1980s. Because the ownership relations within these hybrid institutions were informal to a large extent, and the property rights were fuzzy, these blends can be characterized in retrospect as stages in a sort of *creeping privatization* that fit in well with the Kádárist social contract widely known as goulash communism. This process gave rise to a broad research program that originated within a solid tradition of agrarian economics and sociology in Hungary, accepted the idea of both (small) private property and cooperative ownership, did not reject ab ovo informality (cf. studies of the so-called second economy from the 1970s onward), and confessed the principle of *small is beautiful*. At a certain point, however, the representatives of this program were ready to stretch beyond studying agriculture and join forces with those economists who focused on the ownership structures of industrial enterprises, both small and large. Actually, this research program came the closest to demanding privatization in the second half of the 1980s (see below). Although the program brought its best results in the 1970s and 1980s, a scholar of great imagination emerged on its edge already in the middle of the 1960s.

The First (and Last) of the Mohicans: Tibor Liska and his *Entrepreneurial Socialism*

A sharp-eyed analyst, a half-educated maverick, a utopian thinker, and an activist who swung between prohibition and toleration, Liska construed a unique Grand Design for individual property of social assets. What he called "personal ownership of social capital" in his *Econostat* (*Ökonosztát*), written in the middle of the 1960s but published only two decades later,[18] became one of the most carefully elaborated and empirically tested reform blueprints as time passed. While most of his colleagues were busy working on the details of the New Economic Mechanism and/or were under the spell of another Grand Design, optimal planning (*computopia*), he came up with an alternative utopia called *entrepreneurial socialism* that was also influenced by cybernetic illusions of the time. Without being aware of the intricacies of the economic and legal literature of property rights, and without reading Hayek, Liska suggested an ownership regime in which the state played no role whatsoever, the entire bundle of rights (not only *usus* and *usus fructus*) was taken into consideration, and sociological arguments were not ignored. In other words, he broke with the consensus in the research community, and instead of putting his faith in marketization and accepting some limited (informal) privatization, he violated the dominant ownership paradigm by propounding a master plan that was radically liberal (anti-statist) and radically socialist at the same time.

Following the dictum of "everybody's property is actually nobody's property," Liska built his model on a distribution of national wealth among citizens (he called this *social heritage*), which they can invest in bidding for assets managed by the Bank of Entrepreneurial Experiments that will replace the state administration. The assets were to become the personal property of citizens. They, or a group of them, may use this kind of property, profit from it as well as transform and/or transfer it under extremely competitive conditions (defending the assets against consecutive bids by rival entrepreneurs, and paying interest to the Bank) in the totally self-regulating system of the *Econostat*. They are shareholders of social capital but cannot bequeath the assets to their heirs; the assets revert to society once the owner terminates business activity or dies. That is why Liska spoke of personal ownership instead of private. In his *Volkskapitalismus* (a term he avoided using) the *capitalists* are not permitted to own the assets for good: their successors should restart business with the help of their own *social heritage*. The question of whether this kind of personal ownership would not breed *exploitation* was carefully ignored.

While in a certain sense Liska may be regarded a forerunner of the inventors of voucher privatization in Eastern Europe and of basic income schemes in the West, his model remained relatively unpopular in the Hungarian research community. Liska could not establish a scientific school (just a small sect of believers). In the eyes of moderate reform economists his liberalism was too pervasive, whereas the radical reformers considered him an unreconstructed socialist dreamer, and both camps called him a faith healer and an illusionist. They bombarded him with counter-arguments revealing the artificial/unfeasible nature of his design (e.g., Why would the party-state withdraw from the planned economy? Why would everybody want to become an entrepreneur?), instead of carrying his concept of property rights a little further by asking why his successful socialist entrepreneurs would accept their ownership to be provisional and non-hereditary, that is, not genuinely private. Unfortunately, even in 1985, when leading Hungarian economists ranging from János Kornai to Márton Tardos or from Rezső Nyers to Iván T. Berend tried to interpret (more exactly, criticize) Liska's thoughts in a volume of essays (Síklaky 1985), the discussion only scratched the surface of property rights theory, public choice, law and economics as already suggested by new institutional economists in the West at the time.[19]

1968: Skipping Ownership Reform

In their own historiography of reform economics, reform-minded analysts used to blame the designers of the New Economic Mechanism (NEM) for failing to crown market liberalization with a major change in the ownership regime. Actually, the NEM considerably relaxed the grip of the state on the companies by abolishing mandatory planning targets and introducing a series of *material incentives* among the new *indirect regulators*. To put it differently, part of the managers' property rights was extended. True, this followed again the logic of compartmentalization. Apart from an aborted attempt at establishing capital markets (under the nickname of *asset transfer* (*eszközátcsoportosítás*) by one of the main architects of the 1968 reform, Tamás Nagy (1970), the economics profession did not pay much attention to reshaping the property rights of the state. For example, any serious thought given to the project of workers' self-management was excluded by a long research trip[20] made by leading Hungarian reformers to Yugoslavia in 1966 who came home frustrated by what they considered as adverse effects of group ownership such as large inter-firm income differentials, wage inflation, and unemployment. Nagy was an integral part of the *marketization without privatization* consensus in reform thinking but did not stop at the frontiers of the product and labor markets. He made a few cautious steps into the forbidden territory of the capital markets instead. In focusing on the problem of transferability of assets between state-owned companies, he helped launch an expanding research program of designing capital markets without flesh-and-blood capitalists. This was later recalled by János Kornai with condescension as an exercise of playing Monopoly on a "Wall Street—all made of plastic" (Kornai 1989–1990, 72).

In its initial form, asset transfer meant horizontal (direct) capital transactions between the companies but the delicate question of whether the government would be entitled to interfere (and if it would, to what degree) with their decisions on buying and selling, renting, and merging assets or supplying credit to each other, was obfuscated. Similarly, it was not clear in Nagy's project whether the companies ought to be permitted to initiate joint ventures, organize associations, or found a new firm freely. While contending that company bonds may be applied, he rejected the idea of shareholding advocated by Sándor Kopátsy again (1969).

Márton Tardos, who proposed to curb the property rights of the state through establishing independent holding companies, became the most influential representative of the research program on introducing capital markets.[21] He called the new institutions *asset owners* or *banks of production and trade*, even though he could have used a softer designation like *asset managers*. He put a great emphasis on the autonomy of these parastatal institutions, which in his view should only be subordinated to parliament. One of their main tasks would be the transfer of assets between their member companies. Part of the profits of the companies within the holding could be reinvested freely, and the companies would be permitted to invest in each other's business ventures as well as to charge interest for the credits they offer to each other. Tardos reflexively ruled out self-management as an alternative, and private property did not even occur in his first holding model. His sympathy lay with the company manager (as a quasi-private owner) who was to be protected from state intervention with the help of the holding/bank. It is predominantly the managers' property rights to transform and transfer assets that would have been increased if his suggestions had been accepted by the party-state. However, even these rights of the managers would have faced severe limitations, not to mention the still indisputable ban on leaving any part of state property to their heirs.

How to Avoid Thinking about Private Property Rights?: Pluralization versus Privatization

Between 1972 and 1989, Tardos devoted a series of studies to develop the idea of regulating the capital markets through state holdings into that of *cross ownership* of public (and, to a lesser extent, private) enterprises (Tardos 1972, 1986, 1992).[22] With time, his governance projects became more and more radical and also a bit more sophisticated but continued to focus on reshaping state ownership instead of urging a transition to any kind of capitalism. For him, like for an overwhelming majority of reform economists, former Marxists, moderates, and radicals alike, a switch from large-scale social ownership under communism to smaller-scale capitalist ownership would have been tantamount to taking a huge step back on the road to modernization. Also, institutional ownership (particularly, in the form of some kind of public-private partnership) appeared to most of them as not only ideologically more desirable but also as more up-to-date than individual ownership, no matter if practised by small private entrepreneurs or capitalist tycoons. A property network of social security and pension funds, banks and insurance companies, investment funds, private and semi-private, for-profit and non-profit companies was the maximum the *crème de la crème* of Hungarian reform economists were willing to demand in terms of the privatization of large assets until 1989. They absorbed patterns of governance from Germany, Italy, and Japan, and combined them enthusiastically. In the course of the 1980s, *holdingology* became a special genre of institutional engineering with the participation of scholars such as László Antal, Tamás Bauer, Lajos Bokros, István Csillag, Sándor Kopátsy, László Lengyel, György Matolcsy, Tamás Sárközy, and Attila Károly Soós.[23] Their projects were invented for large state-owned enterprises with a view of releasing them from the strangulation of the state hierarchy (this was called the separation of management from ownership and ownership from state administration at the time) as well as empowering the enterprises and their managers to survive in the business world. Thus, rather than a huge but unorganized army of sovereign private owners, these conglomerates should have served as a counter-power to the omnipotent state. Remarkably, despite the promising experiences with foreign (private) owners in joint ventures, an institution permitted by law in Hungary since 1972, the idea of using the power of foreign capital to offset state intervention did not occur even in the wildest dreams of reformers until the second half of the 1980s.

Meanwhile, quite a few young researchers of a stronger liberal persuasion who were less constrained by self-censorship entered this research field and wanted to understand the functioning of the existing ownership regime rather than indulging in institution building with a normative fervor. As a consequence, the research program of the reformers was loosened up in at least three fundamental respects. First, the private owner as such (not only the small entrepreneur) emerged on their list of *kosher* legal subjects. At the same time, pluralism of property forms became a catchphrase of ownership discourse. Second, the large state enterprises began to be seen as *perpetrators* rather than *victims*, who, in close cooperation with the party-state, actively contributed to impeding marketization. Many of their top managers belonged to the highest stratum of the *nomenklatura* and successfully lobbied for maintaining the monopoly position of their organizations. Third, the state-company nexus was interpreted in the political context of deep interference in economic policy by the communist party. Accordingly, state ownership was increasingly regarded as party-state (*nomenklatura*) ownership at all levels of the hierarchy. For members of this community of scholars (such as Tamás Bauer, Mária Csanády, Mihály Laki, Erzsébet Szalai, Éva Voszka—supported by Márton Tardos (1980/1983)) it became crystal clear that the fact that certain group-based and private property rights were substantially constrained or unrecognized was due to a complex interplay of interlocking institutions: industrial and agricultural lobbies, the military, the government, the party, the trade unions, and so on. They would only have needed to make a simple logical step to realize that if once this multiple-actor network of ownership were destroyed, it would be very difficult, even pointless, to continue insisting on the idea of some kind of *non-private capitalism* any longer. However, even these scholars came to this subversive conclusion rather reluctantly (if at all).

But how did they begin to accept the comparative advantages of private ownership? In examining their works, one can hardly find references to Ludwig von Mises, Friedrich von Hayek, the Ordo-liberals, or to the various schools of new institutional economics striking roots in the United States at that time (Kornai 1992; Lányi 1996). Yet, for example, the balanced view of "markets *and* hierarchies" prevailing in transaction costs economics could have been to their liking. From among the *old guard* of Hungarian economists, perhaps Márton Tardos was the only one who read authors such as Armen Alchian, James Buchanan, Harold Demsetz, or Oliver Williamson at that time.[24] János Kornai was apparently not too interested in this kind of literature even though it could have improved one of the main concepts of his economics of shortage, paternalism, in terms of institutional precision.

As to other sources, the reform economists got a little help from sociology and law.[25] Thus, by the 1980s, the former paleness of economic theorizing of ownership issues was waning. As early as 1969, András Hegedüs, a prominent Hungarian sociologist, began to experiment with the concept of managerial property under communism, borrowing the logic of James Burnham's managerial capitalism (Hegedüs 1969). He did not apply the term "property rights" but, by making a distinction between formal state ownership of firms and the actual opportunities for company leaders to decide on the use of assets and the distribution of revenues, he started differentiating the various entitlements, too. In contrast to most of reform economists, Hegedüs did not put all his faith in the managers. Rather, loyal to the Lukács School of neo-Marxism, he preferred a combination of technocratic rule and industrial democracy.[26]

As regards legal sciences, a professor of civil law Tamás Sárközy became the most influential interlocutor of the reformers during the 1970s and he did not cease to warn them about the dangers of oversimplifying the notion of ownership. He challenged the inoperational character of high-sounding concepts such as *self-management* or *entrepreneurship*, and called for an accurate specification of the legal subjects and their entitlements (not rights) as well as of their actual legal behavior. Unfortunately, his accuracy was rather old-fashioned and oriented toward German scholarship. Hungarian economists could not really learn formalized new-institutional approaches to property rights analysis from him.[27] Nevertheless, Sárközy called their attention to a peculiar asymmetry between the cautious ownership reforms advocated by the majority of economists and the large opportunities, provided even by the communist legal system, for *smuggling in* a higher degree of managerial autonomy and informal private ownership in the official discourse.[28]

He introduced the term "shared ownership" (*osztott tulajdon*) in order to distinguish between power over the assets, entitlement to their use, and earning income from them. According to him, the state-owned enterprises turned, in many respects, from administrative units that only handle assets into tenants or quasi-owners of state property (Sárközy 1986). On an abstract level, he made the superiority of social ownership questionable, although he did not demand openly the extension of private property rights. At the same time, Sárközy claimed that the distinction between personal and private property should be abandoned, and that both ownership forms be put under the heading of *small entrepreneurship*.

Using this phrase, he expressed a consensus within the research community. Hiding some kind of private property behind the facade of entrepreneurship (an invention by Liska) and stressing the small size of individual (personal and/or private) ownership was, however, more than a pragmatic move to avoid provoking the official ideology. Until the very end of the communist regime, the pluralization of ownership on the basis of a symbiosis of large state enterprises and small cooperative, communal, and private firms was *sincerely* preferred to privatization by most economists in Hungary. Social ownership was planned to be reformed (i.e., restructured) rather than transformed (i.e., abolished) and replaced by private ownership. It was assumed that by the end of the reform process (a) small private properties would not, as a rule, develop into large ones, and (b) the share of social ownership would remain higher than that of private ownership and, equally importantly, than that of public ownership in the West.

Pluralism also meant (formal or informal) partnership between the various regimes of ownership, giving rise to a sort of *anything goes* approach. Quasi-private household plots, industrial and service units in agricultural cooperatives, intra-enterprise economic work associations in large industries, using personal property for business purposes (e.g., hotel or taxi services),[29] renting out part of public assets (shops, restaurants), not to mention a great variety of informal or even illegal economic activities. Many of these were originally designed or discovered by reform-minded economists, legal experts, and sociologists, including researchers of the shadow economy (Sik 1996). Economic experts on agricultural cooperatives,[30] Liska and his followers, rural sociologists and anthropologists, authors of industrial case studies, labor economists and sociologists developed a tightly interwoven empirical research program to study the processes of *creeping privatization*, more exactly *creeping small-scale privatization* ("*embourgeoisement*," to use Iván Szelényi's term), a success story of Kádár's Hungary.[31] A great majority of them applied descriptive rather than analytic methods, preferring verbal explanation to model building. Nevertheless, this was the field in theorizing ownership in which formalized models of neoclassical and new institutional economics were applied in Hungary for the first time (Galasi and Kertesi 1988, 1990, 1991).

Why conceal that the title of this section is slightly misleading? In fact, most of the authors named on its pages did want to avoid thinking about private property rights seriously. However, after a certain point they proved unable to do so. Unfortunately, they seldom proved able to ensure that their research programs could offer cutting-edge results in ownership theory.

Self-Management Forever?

A majority even of those few economists who—after having rid themselves of reformist illusions concerning indirect control, reshaping large-scale state property, entrepreneurship, and the like—suggested to liberalize at least small private ownership simultaneously rediscovered the idea of self-management. Some of the holding projects also contained elements of workers' self-management (cf. Soós's suggestions) or employee shareholding (cf. Matolcsy's and Bokros's schemes). Self-management was also proposed as an adequate form of ownership for the seceding units of large public firms or for the decentralized entities of these firms within the holdings. Even the politically most radical reform programs from 1986/87 (*Turnaround and Reform*, written by radical reformers (dissenters) and *Social Contract* formulated by the Democratic Opposition (dissidents)) emphasized the need of self-management. The authors of *Social Contract*, for instance, contended that "the concentration of power based on private property is not more acceptable than the monopoly of power of state bureaucracy" (Antal et al. 1987; Kis et al. 1987).

The reemergence of the idea of self-management could not be explained by any domestic success story, not even by that of the intra-enterprise economic work associations that functioned as informal semi-private institutions rather than official self-managing units. The fact that in 1984 the government established a system of so-called company councils whose power was immediately overridden by managers and/or the well-known structures of the party-state, did not justify the revival of the idea either.[32] Apart from self-censorship, and a sincere conviction of the advantages of group ownership, be it generated by syndicalist, anarchist, or general democratic beliefs, one cannot explain the cyclical return of self-management principles by anything other than the mounting disappointment with the weakness of market leanings of large enterprises. If we suggest to strengthen their position vis-à-vis the ministries, many reformers argued, we should also check them from below. Accordingly, self-management would serve as a guarantee for proper market behavior. Moreover, the former distrust of trade unions, and of syndicalist/corporatist versions of self-management in general, virtually disappeared in the literature. In this regard, the tradition of social reformism cherished by the German Historical School was reinforced after four decades by a foreign success story, the upcoming triumph of *Solidarność* in Poland.

At the same time, the excessively decentralized model of Yugoslav self-management introduced in the second half of the 1970s did not mobilize the imagination of Hungarian economists. They also failed to study the neoclassical and new-institutionalist models set up to understand self-management in Yugoslavia by scholars such as Saul Estrin, Branko Horvat, Svetozar Pejovich, Jaroslav Vaněk, and Benjamin Ward. Self-management theory in Hungary remained sadly verbal and speculative, ignoring almost all fresh analytical attempts at comprehending communal, municipal, non-profit (Duff Milenkovitch 1992) and other ownership schemes from the *share economy* (Martin Weitzman) to *common-pool resources* (Elinor Ostrom).

Conclusion

Returning to the five working hypotheses formulated at the beginning of this chapter, I have to admit that while working on the manuscript I was crossing my fingers to achieve a reduction, with the help of the historical overview, of the pessimism inherent in my own assumptions. Unfortunately, just the opposite happened: the sorrow felt upon the missed opportunities (including my own)[33] to innovate with scholarly rigor sank deeper and deeper. Nevertheless, the revisiting of the *oeuvre* of the main authors in ownership theory revealed quite a few authentic ideas that might be worthy of development. If that proved to be a dead-end street, the Hungarian story would still provide the analyst with a profound knowledge of a lengthy and complicated process of releasing the concept of private ownership from the prison of the social ownership doctrine—a lesson for those who are ready to experiment with nationalization/socialization lightheartedly. Moreover, some of those semi-liberal concepts such as various forms of entrepreneurship and cross (recombinant) ownership, which seemed like shabby half-way houses on the road leading to private ownership 30 to 40 years ago, may be considered today as useful correctives of property relations, in certain conditions, under modern capitalism.

Browsing through the above six phases of evolution between 1945 and 1989, one sees that during this period the initial canonization of dualism of state and cooperative ownership in communist political economy did not turn into a solemn declaration of the superiority of a single ownership regime: private property. To return to the title of this chapter, *two* did not become *one* and much less *one and only* until the very collapse of communism. The Hungarian reform economists of the late 1980s certainly would have been surprised to see themselves kettled in an extremely mixed crowd of some former professors of Marxist political economy, together with a growing number of neophyte mainstream economists, all celebrating privatization in one way or another in the early 1990s. True, despite sudden and wide recognition, private property came to be regarded as a dominant rather than an exclusive form of ownership even during those revolutionary years.

János Kornai's *passionate pamphlet* from 1989 demonstrates the ambivalence of even the most Westernized, liberal-minded Hungarian reformers when it came to their attitudes to private ownership. Here, he advocated the expansion of small- and medium-sized private ownership, cast doubts upon self-management, mocked the simulation of private property, and insisted on hardening the budget constraints of the large state-owned enterprises instead of suggesting their rapid (non-simulated) privatization (Kornai 1989–1990).[34] Sadly, he did not show interest in (shied away from) integrating the embryonic concepts of *nomenklatura* ownership with the aim of crowning his own transition scenario.

I have to confess in closing that it would cause me a serious headache if I were forced to tell which pattern of scientific evolution would best fit the story described above. True, I have applied the term "research program" in the text a few times. While writing this chapter, I felt justified in using the Lakatosian concept because, undoubtedly, there was a rivalry between the various approaches to theorizing ownership, and from time to time these approaches took the form of detailed research programs (even if these often lacked scientific coherence and were overpoliticized as far as they *hard cores* were concerned). Nevertheless, despite a certain degree of scholarly improvement, most of the programs remained deeply ambiguous and fragmented throughout the entire communist period as far as both the importance of private property rights, and the relationship between social and private ownership were concerned. Also, it would be difficult to explain with the help of the methodology offered by Imre Lakatos why and how the majority of the research community in Hungary switched to a new research program in ownership theory in just a few years.

A general acceptance of the primacy of private property rights in the first half of the 1990s came as a kind of *revelation*, a paradigm shift to cite Thomas Kuhn. This did not simply occur because censorship was abolished, and at a certain point Hungarian economists became free at last to express their love toward private ownership because, as demonstrated above, they rather cherished a love-hate attitude to it—even when they already had a chance to betray their admiration during the greater part of the 1980s. I would be reluctant to call what happened a veritable *scientific revolution*, even if the economic profession definitely *tipped over*. Following 1989, *two* suddenly (and without catharsis) became *one and only*, as if this switch would not have been preceded by a four-decade process of rejection, semi-adoption, and reinterpretation. Non-private ownership did not vanish completely but at a certain point, no plausible argument for the superiority of social property remained in the purview of economic theory.

One faces similar difficulties in assessing the originality and scholarly quality of theorizing ownership in Hungary during the communist era. If we start the narration after the Sovietization of economic sciences, the story will exhibit a learning process of expunging the Stalinist concept of property with more and more refined arguments over time. As Kenneth Boulding would say, the economists took off their blinders. If, however, we depart from the pre-1948 consensus in the economics profession, then the ownership concepts of the reform economists hardly managed to transcend the scientific quality of that consensus by 1989, as if there existed an unbreakable glass ceiling. Moreover, apart from certain ideas suggested by Tibor Liska, Tamás Sárközy, and Márton Tardos, as well as some other adherents of managerial ownership, small entrepreneurship, pluralization and *creeping privatization*, one cannot identify original discoveries, and even theirs seem a bit parochial. In principle, Hungarian economists could have achieved a similar level of scientific analysis and originality as their Yugoslav colleagues in their research programs on workers' self-management (Franičević 2012), provided that they would have developed their thoughts about *Pannonian-type*[35] managerial ownership by combining their empirical knowledge of the evolution of the NEM with new-institutionalist techniques of economic inquiry. While there were promising efforts to build formal models of NEM in the West,[36] in Hungary even János Kornai, who might have been the best-prepared in the research community to suggest a mathematical theory of the Pannonian regime of ownership, contented himself with criticizing the models of Oskar Lange as naïve attempts at comprehending market socialism as such (Kornai 1986).[37] Symptomatically, economic scholarship in Hungary did not even coin an eye-catching term to name the NEM model by referring to the specific property rights of the company managers.

Theorizing ownership in communist Hungary resulted in tens of thousands of pages being published in academic journals and books, not to speak of party brochures, newspapers, textbooks, and *samizdat* publications. In most cases, the theoretical arguments one reads on these pages were rather shallow and inconsistent. Nevertheless, they paved the way to filling only a few hundred pages with two laws from 1986–1988 (the Company Law and the

Transformation Law), which determined a large part of the institutional design of the Hungarian economy until today, by unleashing what was called *spontaneous privatization*. Although these legal documents—pioneering works of Hungarian economists and law experts in Eastern European comparison—did not set the goal of privatizing state assets, they specified, in an instrumental rhetoric, exactly those property rights related to *abusus* that had been disregarded or ignored before.

The question of whether or not this legal breakthrough patterned after German company law helped the economics profession in Hungary reach higher levels of theorizing ownership after 1989 hides a more exciting question: when exactly did the history of economic thought under communism end?

NOTES

1. As social ownership was the exemplary and predominant constituent of "social*ist* ownership," the former often was replaced by the latter in official rhetoric. Within social ownership state property was declared superior to cooperative and communal property, although in terms of hierarchical regulation there was no significant difference between them for a long time.

2. See, for example, Berend (1983), Kornai (1986, 1992, 2008), Lengyel (1989), Mihályi (2005), Sárközy (1986), Szamuely and Csaba (1998).

3. János Kornai's memoirs (2008) are a good example for turning a controversial history of economic thought into a linear *Entwicklungsroman*, a success story leading from Marx to the market and private ownership, disregarding or underestimating the significance of long digressions from this direction. In another paper Kornai (2000, 654) proudly admitted that "I did not use the term 'institution' in every second paragraph as it recently has become fashionable to do, but I think I understood what a system means, and what the difference is between socialism and capitalism."

4. Although the research program of optimal planning was often correctly labeled by the market reformers as utopian, their own program can hardly escape the same designation in retrospect. At the same time, in looking for scientific models of planning, the optimal planners not only made a few original discoveries (e.g., the Kornai-Lipták model of two-level planning) but also laid the foundations for a mathematical culture in Hungarian economic thought, which enabled the economists to rejoin the neoclassical mainstream during the late 1980s.

5. Cf. Bockman (2011), Bockman and Eyal (2002), Éber et al. (2014), and Szalai (2006). Interestingly enough, not only the crux of the arguments they put forward recently but also the wording and the ideological zeal of these remind the observer of the discourse of local anti-reformers in the 1970s and 1980s.

6. The Hungarian translation of the influential Soviet textbook (Osztrovityanov et al. 1955) was published two years after Stalin's death.

7. The communist Constitution of 1949 defines state property as "the wealth of the whole people," and promises to support the right of "working peasants" to the

land and, in general, all "property acquired by work" but adds: "private ownership and private initiative may not infringe public interest" (Constitution 1949).

8. From this perspective, it would be very difficult to make distinctions between scholars of liberal, social-democratic, conservative, or even national-socialist persuasion. In terms of accepting a large dose of government intervention including nationalization, Károly Balás, Béla Csikós-Nagy, Farkas Heller, Mátyás Matolcsy, Ákos Navratil, Jenő Rácz, Tivadar Surányi-Unger, Ede Theiss, Imre Vajda, István Varga, that is, leading economists of the prewar period who were silenced, imprisoned, exiled, or co-opted by the communists, did not differ essentially from those émigrés like Tamás Balog, Vilmos Fellner, Miklós Káldor, Tibor Scitovsky, or the communist Jenő Varga who left Hungary before the war. Cf. Pető and Szakács (1985) and Szamuely (1986).

9. For more details on these fora, see Note 14. Cf. B. Hegedüs and Rainer (1989, 1994) and Szamuely (1986).

10. The first textbook of the political economy of socialism to apply the term "property entitlement" (*tulajdonosi jogosultság*) was published in 1985 (Hámori 1985).

11. See Kovács (1991, 1992, 1994).

12. György Péter began to write about trading with the means of production as early as in 1956 (Péter 1956–57).

13. Cf. Kornai (2008, Ch. 5). If one insisted on the infamous habit in Hungary of dividing the intelligentsia in two conflicting camps, the *populists* and the *urbans*, many young scholars of the same generation as Bródy, Kornai, or Tardos, such as Sándor Kopátsy and Tibor Liska, would represent the first camp. In their minds it was the agrarian traditions that kept the attraction of private (as well as cooperative) initiative and property alive. Cf. Bródy (1994).

14. The *Petőfi Circle* embraced a number of critical intellectuals between March 1955 and October 1956 who organized heated debates on key issues of history, philosophy, economics, education, and the media (B. Hegedüs and Rainer 1989–94). The official name of the *Varga Commission* was Economic Commission. It was established by the government, and worked from February to June 1957. It was headed by the prominent non-communist scholar István Varga (Szamuely 1986).

15. This was a favorite term of Kálmán Szabó (another economist with early agrarian leanings) who became an author of many textbooks of the political economy of socialism during the 1960s and 1970s. See, for example, Szabó (1964). It was imported from Soviet legal theory, more exactly, derived from the fiercely debated views of Anatoly Venediktov who introduced the concept of *operative management* and reconciled the dogma of the legal unity of state ownership with the civil law status of the individual state-owned enterprises as juridical persons in a book published in 1948 (see the Soviet chapter and the *Conclusion*).

16. The household plots could not be sold, were cultivated with the help of means in personal or cooperative property, and the bulk of incomes produced were appropriated by the farmers who were also members of the local cooperative. Another hybrid creature was state-owned housing. The tenants paid rent, did not have the right to sell or inherit the apartments but could profit from it through informal exchange transactions and subletting.

17. These work associations came into being in 1982, and included part of the workforce (a team or a workshop) that used the company equipment to produce similar goods as in the regular working time after it ended but received higher incomes as *intrapreneurs* than they did as workers. During the 1980s, a number of other business institutions (such as *economic work associations* outside the state firms (*gmk*) and *small cooperatives* (*kisszövetkezet*)) emerged along the border of private and public ownership. In the case of small cooperatives, the members had the right to re-appropriate part of the assets if the cooperative stopped functioning. Many of the constitutive ideas of these institutions came from Tibor Liska (see the next section).

18. The book came out in 1988 (Liska 1988) but he had not remained silent as a public intellectual during the years before. He organized regular semi-official discussions at the Karl Marx University of Economics, set up experimental firms to test his entrepreneurial models, published in *samizdat*, and even played the role of the creative but misunderstood reformer in films. Cf. Kovács (1996).

19. The only person who invoked the spirit of Friedrich von Hayek in the debate was Lajos Bokros.

20. See a conversation with Miklós Mandel (Ferber and Rejtő 1988).

21. He had already suggested this idea in a memo written to one of the government commissions evaluating the first experiences of the New Economic Mechanism in 1969 (Tardos 1972, 1983).

22. For similarities between the concepts of cross ownership and *recombinant property*, see Stark (1996).

23. Many of these studies were conducted in the framework of government-sponsored mega-programs such as the "Socialist Entreprise" or "The Organizational System of Our Economy" from the middle of the 1970s onward. For a detailed analysis of the holding proposals (with reprints of some of the original texts), see Mihályi (2005). See also Lengyel (1989) and Sárközy (1986).

24. For the attitude of the *young guard* to new institutionalism, see Kovács (2012).

25. Interestingly enough, the first impulse to rethink the concept of ownership came from the sinologist Ferenc Tőkei (1965) who, when presenting the complicated network of state, private, and communal property prevailing in China prior to capitalism, called for the reintroduction of Marx's notion of the *Asian mode of production* in the official canon of historical materialism.

26. György Lukács and his disciples attracted not only sociologists but also economists such as András Bródy, Ferenc Jánossy, and Márton Tardos, although during the 1970s the radical reformers started distancing themselves from Lukács's disdain for the market and private ownership. Furthermore, members of the school and the so-called Lukács Kindergarten published in *samizdat* a seminal work on Marxian economics in 1972, which, relying on the Mises-Hayek critique of collectivism, rejected the vision of the communist economy but retained the concept of some sort of social ownership (Bence, Kis, and Márkus [1972] 1992). About a decade later, prominent members of the Lukács School published a book in England (Fehér, Heller and Márkus 1983), which also retained the hope of a *true* socialist transformation of Eastern European societies but—in want of a better solution—admitted certain merits of liberal democracies under capitalism and provided a more accurate analysis

of what they called the *corporate property* of the communist ruling elite than any of the Hungarian reform economists. In an attempt to formulate the objective function of the *nomenklatura* as a cohesive group of owners, they described the managers as trustees and specified the distribution of powers among them. Thereby, the three philosophers refused the then popular theory of the Hungarian dissident sociologists György Konrád and Iván Szelényi (1979), contending that the intellectuals as a class seized power in communist regimes.

27. In the middle of the 1980s, a collection of essays (Harmathy and Sajó 1984) was published on *law and economics*, which contained some of the seminal papers of the new discipline. However, this did not attenuate Sárközy's influence on the leading reformers at all.

28. Actually, it was as early as 1967 that the law on cooperatives opened a back door for semi-private business ventures, and thereby prevented cooperative ownership from approaching the allegedly superior form of state ownership as projected by the Stalinist canon. At the same time, the state-owned firms also left, in legal terms, part of the social property paradigm behind. From 1967 on, they were permitted to establish joint companies. In 1977, the new company law defined the state-owned firms as subjects of the *entrepreneurial activity* of the state, banned state intervention in many fields, permitted asset transfer between the companies, and took out the decisions on the legal disputes between the firms from the hands of the ministries. The legal possibilities to organize work associations in- and outside state enterprises were granted in 1981.

29. Here the boundaries between *personal* and *private* were tacitly blurred.

30. While cooperative ownership, particularly in agriculture, was a field of incessant interest among Hungarian economists (in 1968 a special research institute was founded to study the cooperatives), communal property remained a neglected topic throughout the communist period despite the fact that the local councils controlled huge territories of land and a vast number of small and medium-sized industrial firms as well as a whole lot of buildings and apartments. Regional and local communities were not venerated in a collectivist vein, and—with the exception of Gábor Vági (1991)—there were no reform-minded economists who would have tried to combine a radical program of marketization with the idea of local self-government.

31. See Szelényi (1988) and the works of Ferenc Donáth, András Hegedüs, Pál Juhász, István Márkus, and Kálmán Rupp.

32. Ironically, this move toward self-management made it easier to switch to privatization some years later because it required the introduction of the concept of company self-ownership (*öntulajdonlás*), to use Sárközy's term.

33. For my failed attempt to understand a bargaining game between a large state-owned enterprise and a branch ministry in Hungary, see the Conclusion.

34. As a symptom of the inertia of scientific discourse, Kornai (1990) was reluctant to switch to the language of *law and economics* and clung to the term of coordination mechanisms when actually talking about property rights even after the collapse of communism. Yet, he suggested inspiring hypotheses about *strong* and *weak* linkages between them and suggested a number of intermediary—largely collectivist—solutions of what he called *associative coordination* including self-governance,

reciprocity, altruism and the like, solutions, about which he did not elaborate in depth later.

35. The term was invented by Peter Wiles to contrast the Illyrian-type regime of the post-Stalinist communist economy (Wiles 1977).

36. Normally, these models (suggested by, among others, Avner Ben-Ner, John Bonin, David Granick, Michael Keren, John Montias, Egon Neuberger, Richard Portes, Stephen Sacks, and Peter Wiles) were not grounded in new institutional economics, did not necessarily focus on ownership relations, and did not portray the Hungarian economy exclusively. Regrettably, these research programs did not converge into a synthetic doctrine. Cf. Grosfeld (2012).

37. Tardos (1968) began to experiment with such a model following in the footsteps of Robert Dorfman, Paul Samuelson, and Robert Solow but shortly thereafter abandoned this research program for the verbal analysis of the reform process. Turning his back on linear programming was partly due to the strong impact exerted on Hungarian economic thought by Kornai who launched a vigorous attack on general equilibrium theory in his (in)famous book *Anti-equilibrium* in 1970.

BIBLIOGRAPHY

Antal, László et al. 1987. "Fordulat és reform" [Turnaround and reform]. *Közgazdasági Szemle* 34 no. 6: 642–63.

Bence, György, János Kis, and György Márkus. 1992 [1972]. *Hogyan lehetséges kritikai gazdaságtan?* [How is critical political economy possible?]. Budapest: T-Twins.

Berend, Iván T. 1983. *Gazdasági útkeresés (1956–1965)* [In search of reform paths]. Budapest: Magvető.

Bródy, András. 1994. Beszélgetés Kovács János Mátyással [Conversation with János Mátyás Kovács]. In *Miért hagytuk hogy így legyen?* [Why did we let it be so?], edited by Szabó Judit and Madarász Aladár, 271–348, Budapest: Budapest Közgazdasági és Jogi Könyvkiadó.

Constitution of the People's Republic of Hungary—1949. Available online, accessed April 24, 2017: http://lapa.princeton.edu/hosteddocs/hungary/1949%20Hungarian%20constitution.pdf.

Duff Milenkovitch, Deborah. 1992. "An Organizational Theory of the Socialist Economy". In *Reform and Transformation: Eastern European Economics on the Threshold of Change*, edited by János Mátyás Kovács and Márton Tardos, 36–55. London: Routledge.

Éber, Márk et al. 2014. "1989: Szempontok a rendszerváltás globális politikai gazdaságtanához" [1989: On the global political economy of systemic change]. *Fordulat* 21: 11–63.

Fehér, Ferenc, Ágnes Heller and György Márkus. 1983. *Dictatorship over Needs*. Oxford: Basil Blackwell

Ferber, Katalin, and Gábor Rejtő. 1988. *Reform(év)fordulón* [Anniversary and/or turn of reform]. Budapest: Közgazdasági és Jogi Könyvkiadó.

Franičević, Vojmir. 2012. "Soft Institutionalism. The Reception of New Institutional Economics in Croatia." In *Capitalism from Outside? Economic Cultures in Eastern Europe after 1989*, edited by János Mátyás Kovács and Violetta Zentai, 241–62. Budapest—New York: CEU Press.

Galasi, Péter and Gábor Kertesi. 1988. "Patkányverseny a korrupciós piacon" [Rat race in the market of corruption]. *Közgazdasági Szemle* 35 no. 7–8: 900–20.

———. 1990. "Korrupció es tulajdon" [Corruption and ownership]. *Közgazdasági Szemle* 37 no. 4: 389–425.

———. 1991. "A hálapénz ökonómiája" [Economics of gratitude payments]. *Közgazdasági Szemle* 38 no. 3: 260–88.

Grosfeld, Irena. 1992. "Reform Economics and Western Economic Theory: Unexploited Opportunities." In *Reform and Transformation. Eastern European Economics on the Threshold of Change*, edited by János Mátyás Kovács and Márton Tardos, 56–72. London: Routledge.

Hámori, Balázs, ed. 1985. *Politikai gazdaságtan 3. A szocialista gazdaság elmélete* [Political economy 3. Theory of the socialist economy]. Budapest: Közgazdasági és Jogi Könyvkiadó.

Hegedüs, András. 1969. "Adalékok a tulajdonviszonyok szociológiai elméletéhez" [Thoughts about the sociological theory of ownership relations]. *Magyar Filozófiai Szemle* 13 no. 6: 1126–47.

Hegedüs, András B., and János M. Rainer, eds. 1994 [1989]. *A Petőfi Kör vitái* (I–VII) [Discussions of the Petőfi circle]. Budapest: Kelenföld Kiadó—ELTE—Múzsák—1956-os Intézet.

Kis, János, Ferenc Kőszeg, and Ottilia Solt. 1987. *Társadalmi Szerződés* [Social Contract]. *Beszélő* 1 no. 21.

Konrád, György, and Iván Szelényi. 1979. *Intellectuals on the Road to Class Power.* New York: Harcourt, Brave & Jovanovich.

Kopátsy, Sándor. 1969. "A vállalati tevékenység komplex és többéves értékelésének problémája" [The problem of complex assessment of company activities over many years]. *Pénzügyi Szemle* 13 no. 11: 929–36.

Kornai, János. 1957. *Overcentralization in Economic Administration.* London: Oxford University Press.

———. 1986. "The Hungarian Reform Process: Visions, Hopes and Reality." *Journal of Economic Literature* 24 no. 4: 1687–1737.

———. 1989. *Indulatos röpirat a gazdasági átmenet ügyében* [Passionate pamphlet on economic transition]. Budapest: HVG. English translation: 1990. *The Road to a Free Economy: Shifting from a Socialist System—The Example of Hungary.* New York: Norton.

———. 1990. "The Affinity Between Ownership Forms and Coordination Mechanisms: The Common Experience of Reform in Socialist Countries." *Journal of Economic Perspectives* 4 no. 3: 131–47.

———. 1992. "The Principles of Privatization in Eastern Europe." *De Economist* 140 no. 2: 153–176.

———. 2000. "Tíz évvel a Röpirat angol nyelvű megjelenése után: A szerző önértékelése" [Ten years after "The Road to a Free Economy": the author's self-evaluation]. *Közgazdasági Szemle* 47 no. 9: 647–661.

———. 2008. *A gondolat erejével*. Budapest: Osiris. English translation: 2008. *By Force of Thought*. Boston: MIT Press.

Kovács, János Mátyás. 1991. "From Reformation to Transformation: Limits to Liberalism in Hungarian Economic Thought." *East European Politics and Societies* 5 no. 1: 41–72.

———. 1992. "Compassionate Doubts about Reform Economics (Science, Ideology, Politics)." In *Reform and Transformation: Eastern European Economics on the Threshold of Change*, edited by J.M. Kovács and Márton Tardos, 299–333. London: Routledge.

———. 1996. "Liska-torzó" [Liska torso]. *2000* 8 no. 1: 15–16.

———. 2012. "Beyond Basic Instinct? On the Reception of New Institutional Economics in Eastern Europe." In *Capitalism from Outside? Economic Cultures in Eastern Europe after 1989*, edited by J.M. Kovács and Violetta Zentai, 281–310. Budapest: CEU Press.

Lányi, Kamilla. 1996. "Szociális piacgazdaság—nálunk, most? Eszmetörténeti vázlat" [Social market economy—in Hungary, today?]. *2000* 8 no. 4: 4–16.

Lengyel, László. 1989. *Végkifejlet* [Endgame]. Budapest: Közgazdasági és Jogi Könyvkiadó.

Liska, Tibor. 1988. *Ökonosztát* [Econostat]. Budapest: Közgazdasági és Jogi Könyvkiadó.

Mihályi, Péter. 2005. *A privatizáció szellemi előkészítése* [Intellectual preparations for privatization]. Budapest: ÁPVRT.

Nagy, Tamás. 1970. "Az eszközök átcsoportosíthatóságának célszerű formáiról népgazdaságunkban" [On reasonable forms of asset transfer in our national economy]. *Közgazdasági Szemle* 17 no. 6: 675–90.

Osztrovityanov, Konsztantyin et al. 1955. *Politikai gazdaságtan tankönyv* [Textbook of political economy]. Budapest: Szikra.

Pető, Iván, and Sándor Szakács. 1985. *A hazai gazdaság négy évtizedének története. 1945–1985*. [History of four decades of the Hungarian economy. 1945–1985]. Budapest: Közgazdasági és Jogi Könyvkiadó.

Péter, György. 1954. "A gazdaságosság jelentőségéről és szerepéről a népgazdaság tervszerű irányításában" [On the importance and role of efficiency in the planned management of the national economy]. *Közgazdasági Szemle* 1 no. 3: 300–20.

———. 1956–1957. "A gazdaságosság és a jövedelmezőség jelentősége a tervgazdálkodásban" [On the importance of efficiency and profitability in the planned economy]. *Közgazdasági Szemle* 3 no. 6: 695–711; no. 7–8: 851–69.

Sárközy, Tamás. 1986. *Egy gazdasági szervezeti reform sodrában* [In the wake of a reform of economic organization]. Budapest: Magvető.

Sik, Endre. 1996. "Egy ló-öszvér a lovakról és a szamarakról: Adalék a második gazdaság hazai eszmetörténetéhez" [A Mule on horses and donkeys: On the history of ideas of the second economy in Hungary]. *Közgazdasági Szemle* 43 no. 7–8: 704–28.

Síklaki, István, ed. 1985. *Koncepció és kritika* [Concept and criticism]. Budapest: Magvető.

Stalin, Joseph. 1951. *Economic Problems of Socialism in the USSR*. Available online, accessed April 24, 2017: https://www.marxists.org/reference/archive/stalin/

works/1951/economic-problems/index.htm. Hungarian translation: Sztálin, J. V. 1952. *A szocializmus közgazdasági problémái a Szovjetunióban.* Budapest: Szikra.

Stark, David. 1996. "Recombinant Property in East-European Capitalism." *American Journal of Sociology* 101 no. 4: 993–1027.

Szabó, Kálmán. 1964. *A szocialista termelés alapvonásai* [The basic features of socialist production]. Budapest: Kossuth.

Szalai, Erzsébet. 2006. *Socialism: An Analysis of Its Past and Future.* Budapest: CEU Press.

Szamuely, László, and László Csaba. 1988. *Rendszerváltozás a közgazdaságtanban, közgazdaságtan a rendszerváltozásban* [Systemic change in economics, economics in systemic change]. Budapest: Közgazdasági Szemle Alapitvány.

Szamuely, László, ed. 1986. *A magyar közgazdasági gondolat fejlődése (1954–1978)* [Evolution of Hungarian economic thought]. Budapest: Közgazdasági és Jogi Könyvkiadó.

Szelényi, Iván. 1988. *Socialist Entrepreneurs.* Madison: University of Wisconsin Press.

Tardos, Márton. 1968. "Az új gazdasági mechanizmus szabályozó rendszerének modellje" [Model of the regulation system of the New Economic Mechanism]. *Közgazdasági Szemle* 15 no. 10: 1185–95.

———. 1972. "A gazdasági verseny problémái hazánkban" [Problems of economic competition in our country]. *Közgazdasági Szemle* 19 no. 7–8: 911–27.

———. ed. 1980. *Vállalati magatartás, vállalati környezet* [Enterprise behavior, enterprise environment]. Budapest: Közgazdasági és Jogi Könyvkiadó. (1983. Hungarian Enterprise Behavior, *Eastern European Economics* 21, no 3–4.).

———. 1983. "Reform itt és most? Beszélgetés Kovács János Mátyással" [Reform, here and now? Conversation with János Mátyás Kovács]. *Mozgó Világ* 9 no. 2: 8–22.

———. 1986. "The Conditions for Developing a Regulated Market." *Acta Oeconomica* 36 no. 1–2: 67–89.

———. 1992. "Property Rights in Hungary." In *Reform and Transformation: Eastern European Economics on the Threshold of Change*, edited by János Mátyás Kovács and Márton Tardos, 255–67. London: Routledge.

Tőkei, Ferenc. 1965. *Az 'ázsiai termelési mód' kérdéséhez* [On the 'Asian mode of production']. Budapest: Kossuth.

Vági, Gábor. 1991. *Magunk, uraim. Település, tanács, önkormányzat* [Let us do it ourselves, gentlemen. Local settlement, council, self-government]. Budapest: Gondolat.

Wiles, Peter. 1977. *Economic Institutions Compared.* New York: Wiley.

Chapter 6

From Soviet-Type Ownership through Self-Management to Privatization

Debating Ownership in Communist Poland

Maciej Tymiński

Property rights were not a central problem of economic debates in communist Poland. Ownership was disputed particularly in three periods—first, immediately after the war, during the implementation of the Soviet system; then, after the revolt of 1956; and finally, after 1980 when workers' strikes and the foundation of *Solidarność* reopened the debate on communism.

The discussion on property rights pertained to different kinds of ownership. However, most important were the issues connected with social ownership (*własność społeczna*) and its evolution. Therefore, I will focus on the controversies surrounding it, paying less attention to other topics, especially to private ownership (*własność prywatna*) in agriculture and small business in general. Studying the evolution of the concepts of social ownership from 1945 till 1989, the idea of self-management deserves a special emphasis. I will also present the liberal concepts of ownership formulated by anti-systemic opposition circles from the late 1970s onward. They rejected both central planning and market socialism and offered privatization as the solution for the problem of the dominance of state ownership (*własność państwowa*) in the economy.

I want to answer the following research questions:

- What were the main phases of the debate on property rights?
- What were the factors (social, political, economic) that influenced the participants of the debate?
- Is this debate predominantly an academic discussion or rather a social and political phenomenon?

- Were the results of these discussions original scientific discoveries in the field of property rights theory?
- Did the results of the debate have any influence on the political authorities and their decisions regarding ownership?

The following analysis is divided into three main sections. In the first section I give a chronological overview of debates on property rights following the Second World War, including the concept of ownership in the Constitution. The next section is dedicated to the main topics of discussion in communist Poland: social ownership, self-management (*samorząd*), and privatization of state-owned property. In the first part of this section I present the debate around Oskar Lange's concept of ownership as formulated in his book *Ekonomia Polityczna* (*Political Economy*), in the second I focus on the discussion on self-management after 1956 and after 1980, and finally in the third part I analyze the approaches challenging the rationale of the communist system and the first privatization ideas in the 1980s. The third section is dedicated to the analysis of the evolution of scholarly views on property rights during the entire period. I study the factors that influenced the participants and the importance of the results of the debate for economics in Poland and abroad. I also briefly discuss the scientific importance of the discourse on ownership in Poland.

CHRONOLOGICAL OVERVIEW

Prewar Origins and Postwar Controversies

The ideas of ownership presented in the first years after World War II stressed the importance of state in the reconstruction of the economy. They were derived from three different prewar traditions: socialism, the cooperative movement, and statism.

The first tradition had its roots in the early socialist ideas put forward by prominent Polish intellectuals such as Ludwik Krzywicki and Bolesław Limanowski before the First World War. The views of Polish socialists in the interwar period were formed under the strong influence of Marxist economists, especially Rosa Luxemburg. Luxemburg's interpretation of Marxism was significantly different from either the Bolshevik or the reformist theories. On the one hand, she disagreed with Lenin's concept of the vanguard party and its monopoly. She also protested against the bureaucratic character of the Bolshevik regime following the revolution. On the other hand, she supported the idea of the proletarian revolution against the reformists (Bernstein, Kautsky and others) proposing evolutionary change. As regards ownership, she supported the mass socialization of property; however, she stressed that social property should be acquired by workers and it ought to stay under the control of grassroots organizations such as workers' councils. Luxemburg was strongly against managing the economy by the monopolistic revolutionary party. She also criticized the distribution of land among the peasants and implemented by the Bolsheviks right after the revolution (Luxemburg 2005 [1922]). Luxemburg had a great impact on Polish Marxist economists, especially on their views on the structure and character of ownership relations in the future socialist economy.

The group of Polish interwar socialist economists included such important young scholars as Michał Kałecki and Oskar Lange. Ownership was one of the issues discussed by the representatives of this group. Probably the most important were the publications of Oskar Lange who stressed the necessity of the socialization of the means of production. However, he claimed that the transformation of private ownership into social ownership should be limited. The individual property (*własność indywidualna*) of citizens (consumer products, houses) and the property of small entrepreneurs (small firms) and craftsmen (workshops) as well as the peasants' farms should stay private. In his opinion these kinds of properties are not used for exploitation, so they are not barriers to social progress. According to Lange, the centralization of property rights related to the socialization of the means of production should be accompanied by a decentralization of management. In his view enterprises should be grouped in public trusts managed by employees but coordinated by a central planning board. For Lange self-management must dominate in all economic units. In this approach part of the property rights would belong to the employees of the enterprises. The alternative, which is state management, would lead to the domination of irresponsible state bureaucracy in the economy. Lange stressed that bureaucratic central management would result in state capitalism, not socialism (Lange [1938] 1973b, 130–36).

Lange's opinion was strongly related to his famous model of market socialism presented in 1936–1937. Participating in the so-called Socialist Calculation Debate, he proposed the implementation of market tools in central planning. Based on the Walrasian approach, Lange argued that instead of market adjustment the prices should be set by the central planning board using the mechanism of *trial and error*. He was convinced that this kind of socialist economy should be at least as efficient as the capitalist market economy (Lange [1936–1937] 1973a).[1]

The second very important tradition—often closely connected to the socialist tradition—was the idea of cooperation and self-organization. The most influential scholar who developed the idea of cooperatives in Poland was Edward Abramowski. His views were close to Eduard Bernstein's concept of evolutionary change of social and economic systems. He was strongly against the revolution and advocated the idea of a cooperative republic, which was close to the concepts of syndicalists. In his writings Abramowski proposed cooperatives (both of consumers and producers) as a remedy for capitalist inequalities. In the economy the domination of cooperative enterprises should result in the democratization and socialization of ownership (Abramowski 2012). Abramowski's ideas were very influential, primarily among Polish socialists and in the cooperative movement spreading during the interwar period.

The third economic tradition influencing collectivist economics in Poland was agrarianism that developed along with the peasants' political and social movements in the early 20th century. In the interwar period the most important theorists were Adam Doboszyński and Stanisław Miłkowski (Miłkowski 1934; Doboszyński 1934). Agrarianism also had supporters among economists such as Franciszek Bujak, Władysław Grabski, and his brother Stanisław. In Miłkowski's view (1934), it represented a third way between capitalism and socialism, in which family farms played a crucial role. He also proposed to organize cooperatives (in service, finance, and food industries) to support the development of family farms.

The fourth important source of postwar ideas of ownership was the activity and interwar writings of statist theorists such as Eugeniusz Kwiatkowski or Stefan Starzyński. Statism started to develop in the late 1920s. In the 1930s, Kwiatkowski was a deputy prime minister and an author of the program for state-led industrialization. State investment projects and state-owned companies played an important role in this operation. In 1932, Kwiatkowski expressed his ideas on the role of state ownership in the economy (Kwiatkowski 1932). He emphasized that the state should play the role of an entrepreneur in branches (for example, infrastructure or new technologies) where private capital is absent or its activity offers limited benefits to the state and the nation. These ideas were developed during the war by different political parties (not only left-wing) and even by liberal economists such as Ferdynand Zweig (1942).

All the three approaches influenced the discussion during and after the war. The main political parties and economists stressed the importance of state ownership in the reconstruction of the economy after the war. However, the scale of proposed changes differed. In the late 1940s, two main and opposing views were expressed by activists and economists related to two leftist parties—socialist PPS (Polish Socialist Party) and communist PPR (Polish Workers' Party).[2]

For the future discussion of ownership special weight was attached to the ideas of socialist politicians and economists close to PPS. The concept of the so-called Polish way to socialism was based on different views prevalent in socialist circles, including the cooperative movement and on the ideas of economists who were members or supporters of the party (such as Oskar

Lange, Edward Lipiński, Czesław Bobrowski, or Jan Drewnowski). A major role in formulating the ideas was played by the Central Office for Planning (CUP—*Centralny Urząd Planowania*), led by Bobrowski.

In terms of ownership, PPS treated the different forms of property—private, cooperative, and state—as equal. The party called for a hegemony of social ownership, with state ownership limited to the largest infrastructural and industrial enterprises. At the same time, the necessity to keep those enterprises autonomous was pointed out, as well as the need to appoint employee supervisory boards. Private ownership was to be present mainly in agriculture, small manufacturing, and services; nevertheless, private property rights were fully guaranteed and protected. Special importance was placed on the development of cooperatives, in agriculture as well as in industry and services, keeping them independent from the state (Bałtowski 2009, 138). The program of PPS concerning ownership was more or less in line with the interwar propositions of Oscar Lange.

The socialist approach was objected to by PPR, which advocated the adoption of Soviet-type institutions in Poland.[3] The most influential economist in the communist camp was Hilary Minc, minister of industry and (in the first half of 1950s) deputy prime minister, and chairman of the highest planning body, the State Commission of Economic Planning (*Państwowa Komisja Planowania Gospodarczego*). Among the economists who supported the idea of Sovietization were Włodzimierz Brus and Bronisław Minc (Hilary's brother) who returned to Poland from the USSR and had no academic degree in interwar Poland.

Regarding the problems of ownership, PPR called for overall nationalization, including services and trade, and for limiting the importance of cooperatives. It proposed central management of state-owned enterprises and supporting collective and state-owned agriculture at the expense of private farms. Cooperatives (especially in industry and services) were to play an insignificant and not entirely independent role in that system, and were subject to central planning (Kowalik 2006). Nearly all property rights were to be transferred to the state and its apparatus.

The differences between these two programs of left-wing parties were not as pronounced and unequivocal when considered in the context of the views of particular economists associated with either camp, especially regarding Czesław Bobrowski, the head of CUP. Bobrowski, unlike many PPS politicians, was definitely less inclined to support cooperatives and, like Hilary Minc and PPR-associated economists, leaned toward advocating state ownership. As Tadeusz Kowalik wrote, there were no significant differences between Bobrowski and Minc in regard to the range of various types of ownership. "The major concern for both was the expansion of the state sector" (Kowalik 2006, 54). The controversies between them originated mostly in diverging views on the functioning of enterprises and the planning system. While PPR-associated economists (i.e., both Minces and Brus) were supporters of the Soviet model of central planning and strict subordination of the enterprises to the state authorities, Bobrowski thought that enterprises should have a significant level of autonomy and self-management in the form of supervisory boards (Kowalik 2006, 54).

The discussion between the economists close to PPS and PPR culminated during the so-called CUP debate in 1948, resulting in the marginalization of the socialists' program. The controversies did not refer directly to the issue of ownership, but rather to the character of investment projects, the planning system, or the relative importance of different sectors of economy. Nevertheless, the issue of property rights was a very important element of the discussion influencing the emerging reform concepts until the 1980s.

PROPERTY RIGHTS IN THE STALINIST CONSTITUTION

The changes in the system of property rights started right after the Second World War. The nationalization of industry and the banking system was taking shape. Also, the agricultural reforms expropriated landowners' property and enfranchised the peasants. In 1947 the authorities began the so-called battle for trade, leading to the actual fall of the majority of private enterprises in trade and services. As a result, most of the private sector (so-called third sector) was turned into state-owned enterprises or cooperatives controlled by the state. By the late 1940s, the state managed a vast majority of firms. The collectivization (de facto nationalization) of peasants' farms started in the late 1940s. However, this attempt turned out to be unsuccessful, even during the peak of Stalinization in the 1950s. Property of the Catholic Church and other denominations was among the last to be nationalized.

In 1948, following the full seizure of power by PZPR (Polish United Workers' Party),[4] a centrally planned system modeled on the Soviet command economy was introduced. More or less at the same time, property rights were changed to follow the Soviet model. Ownership relations were to be defined in the new Civil Code, but the process lagged because "nobody knew what such a Civil Code would look like" (Skąpski 1992, 66). Finally, the first regulations regarding the new definition of property rights were formally introduced in the Constitution in 1952, although they were practically implemented earlier (Machnikowska 2010, 90).

The Constitution divided ownership—following the Soviet model—into social and individual (previously labeled private). That division was meant "to pronounce the real, socio-economic content of a legal institution"

(Ignatowicz 1972, 361). Social ownership included national ownership (*własność narodowa*), which was de facto state ownership, cooperative ownership (*własność spółdzielcza*), and the ownership of social organizations like trade unions and other associations. Subsequently, individual ownership was divided into capitalist and craftsmen's property.

National (or people's) ownership included natural resources, the means of production, and infrastructure. State authorities also had the right to intervene in the use of Poland's soil as a national resource (even if it was private property). Those regulations led to the rule of unitary state ownership, which was indivisible. Based on those rules, the effort to nationalize was validated and the selling of state-owned assets was forbidden. For example, enterprises had no right to sell part of their assets without permission of the state authorities, they had only rights to use the assets (Machnikowska 2010, 301–02). National property, formally co-owned by citizens, actually was in the hands of the party-state and its administration. As a result "the state did not only receive property rights but was in fact a trustee of social property" (Ibid., 303). The status of the state was confirmed by the way the ownership of cooperatives and social organizations was defined. These rights were not clearly determined. Cooperatives and social organizations had the right only to use the social property, which in reality meant dependence on the state. Social property was also privileged compared to individual (private) property, because it was better protected by law whereby much more oppressive sanctions were implemented for an offense against it than against private property.

Private (individual) property "existed in the Constitution on conditional regulations (the ownership defined as small property [e.g., small shops or workshops—M.T.]) or without any foundation in the Constitution (capitalist property)" (Ibid., 306). As a result, the state had the right to proceed with expropriations or to intervene in the area of individual ownership in the name of social ownership and certain economic goals. A separate category of private ownership was so-called personal property (*własność osobista*), which, unlike the other types of individual property rights, enjoyed full protection.

Two particular forms of private ownership are worth mentioning: a specific form of principal-agent property relation (*ajencja*, whereby the principal and owner was the state, while the agent was an individual entrepreneur), and private ownership in small industry and services. The origins of the first form could be found in the 1950s. It was a kind of long-term property lease necessary for a business activity licensed by the state authorities (as small services or shops). The second form—private property in small industry and services—offered a relatively large protection to property rights. The (reluctant) acceptance of this form of small private enterprise was caused by its important supplementary role. Small industry and services usually eased shortages on the consumer goods market, but also produced some components for state industry. An important source of capital and technology since the late 1970s was the Polish diaspora in the West. New regulations introduced in this period enabled Poles from abroad to invest in small industry and create joint ventures. These solutions were introduced *ad hoc* by authorities to stabilize the supply of goods on the market and later to attract foreign investors. However, none of these forms of ownership was a topic of theoretical academic debate.

The situation—despite many different new legal regulations—remained unchanged until the 1980s when, as a result of workers and farmers' strikes, a number of changes were introduced within individual as well as social property rights. In 1983 Polish peasants received a guarantee of unconditional ownership of their farms (Domińczyk 2008, 161). After the workers' strikes, the authorities adopted a new law on state-owned enterprises, which introduced self-management. It gave enterprises some rights to manage their own property, increasing their autonomy to a limited extent.

AFTER STALIN: FROM RENEWING MARKET SOCIALISM TO THE FIRST IDEAS OF PRIVATIZATION

After Stalin's death, a discussion started among Polish economists about the failures of the centralized economic system (see Brus 1956). The debates concerned the character of the planning system and the position of state-owned firms, which indirectly pertained to the issue of property rights. One of the consequences was changes in the management rules of enterprises introduced in the spring of 1956. The new regulations gave more autonomy to the managers, but were proposed too late, and did not fit the expectations of the managers and employees (Osiatyński 1982, 318–19). At the same time, workers started organizing demonstrations and mass gatherings, which peaked in June 1956 in the riots in Poznań. These were suppressed with bloodshed. The revolt sharpened the debate among economists, especially during the Second Congress of Economists (*II Zjazd Ekonomistów*) in June 1956 (Sadowski 2006). As one participant pointed out years later, at the congress the concept of market socialism emerged as a mainstream idea for reforming the economic system (Madej 2006, 57).

In the largest factories the revolting workers started to set up councils and introduced self-management. They also called for more autonomy for the enterprises. The ideas of self-management were closely related to the problem of property rights and served also as an important topic of discussion among Polish economists. This debate involved the most important Polish economists of the time, among them Oskar Lange, Michał Kałecki, Edward Lipiński, and Włodzimierz Brus.

The Second Congress was followed by the so-called *model debate*. In the first months of the discussion, a number of papers were published pointing to a need for changes in the economy. Some publications were scientific in character but there were also works intended for a wider audience. The majority of the economists advocated self-management and decentralization, that is, they supported the transfer of property rights from state administration to enterprises and their employees.

In regard to ownership two postulates had the utmost importance. The first one concerned the workers' councils conceived as bodies exerting an indirect impact on the management of enterprises. Their status resembled that of supervising boards in capitalist limited liability companies. The second aimed at strengthening the position of managers, and making them responsible for the activity of their firms. Both postulates were included in *Tezy Rady Ekonomicznej w sprawie niektórych zmian modelu ekonomicznego* (Economic Council theses on the issue of certain transformations of the economic model) suggesting a reform of the economic system (*Tezy* 1957, 269). Actually, this reform project was not introduced. Independent self-management in factories was cancelled by the authorities in 1958 and the autonomy of enterprises remained on paper. However, the debates on self-management continued in the following years.

One of the most important changes after 1956 related to the ownership structure was the termination of forced collectivization in agriculture. The majority of cooperatives created in the early 1950s were spontaneously dissolved by their members. In 1957, the agro-economic section of the Polish Economic Society published its theses on agricultural policy (Tezy Sekcji 1957). They supported the idea of socialization of agriculture but also stressed the freedom to choose the ownership form (collective or individual/private), the significance of clear property relations, and the possibility of land trade. The theses underlined the need to strengthen small farms by supplying land to their owners and to counteract the fragmentation of land (Ibid. 122–23). The authors of the theses referred to the tradition of agrarianism promoting family farms and voluntary cooperatives.

In the same year, the communist party declared the coexistence of different forms of agricultural ownership: state farms, cooperatives, and individual (private) property. However, the party did not give up the aim of socialization, but decided to transform ownership in the countryside gradually (Dobieszewski 1977). Gradual transformation was supported by many economists. For example, Michał Kałecki argued that the socialization of agriculture ought to be a long-term process. It should be based on two lines of development: first comes the creation of an *overlay system* based on the state monopoly of contracting and supplying the farms, followed by the second, a natural *crumbling* (disappearance) of peasant farms and a surge in voluntary collectivization (Kałecki 1984 [1961, 1963], 232–33).[5]

In the late 1960s and early 1970s, the discussion on property rights and, more broadly, on the evolution of the economic system in Poland, lost momentum. The debate slowed down not only because of the loss of the two most influential academics (Oskar Lange died in 1966 and Michał Kałecki in 1970), but also as a consequence of the political crisis at that time. It involved conflicts between factions within the party, the students' protest in 1968 and its pacification, followed by an anti-Semitic campaign. As a result of the prosecutions many famous and important professors were dismissed from the universities (e.g., the philosophers Leszek Kołakowski and Bolesław Baczko, the economist Włodzimierz Brus, and the sociologist Maria Hirszowicz). Many others voluntarily resigned from their posts like the economist Czesław Bobrowski. Also younger scholars were dismissed and many of them had to emigrate or suspend their university careers. After 1968, university departments of social sciences often were headed by people who had supported party policy; however, many of them had very few academic achievements.

Probably the most interesting episode related to the property rights issue was the reform plan proposed by the authorities, although it did not include a new theoretical approach. At the end of the 1960s Bolesław Jaszczuk (secretary of the Central Committee of the PZPR) suggested a new form of enterprise, the industrial conglomerate, the so-called socialist holding (*kombinat*). Similar ideas had been proposed in 1957/1958 during the discussion on the changes in the economic system (Kałecki 1982b; Osiatyński 1982, 357–63).

In the early 1970s, after Edward Gierek had become the first secretary of the PZPR, the objective of industrial concentration was developed into the project of WOGs—large economic organizations (*wielkie organizacje gospodarcze*). The WOGs grouped complementary or similar firms under united management. As a result, the managers of these *socialist holdings* had a stronger position than the directors of the individual firms before the reform. They had more freedom to make decisions within the subordinated group of industrial plants. The strengthening of the WOGs' management was the result of transferring certain property rights from the state authorities to the new organizations. The WOGs got part of the right to decide on how to use the enterprises' properties, and were allowed to choose the price and wage levels. All the new prerogatives were divided between the WOGs' managers and the directors of the subordinated plants.

The new rules of organization could be related to the reforms introduced in Hungary in the late 1960s (New Economic Mechanism) and the *Strukturpolitik* implemented in the German Democratic Republic; however, there is no clear evidence of such inspiration. Some scholars (Bałtowski 2009) argued that these rules were similar to Aleksy Wakar and his students' proposition of parametric planning (Wakar 1963), but here, too, there is no proof of such influence. Certainly the WOG reform was in opposition to the former designs of the self-managed enterprise. The introduction of socialist holdings was rather connected with the ideas of managerial reforms in the socialist economy. However, the discussion on WOGs in the context of ownership was rather limited and not as sophisticated as that on self-management. Many of the studies on WOGs focused on describing the new system and the analysis of particular solutions introduced by the reform (see, for example, Cholewicka-Goździk 1977). There were also detailed analyses of the Gierek reforms prepared by Janusz Giedymin Zieliński, AleksyWakar's student and professor at University of Glasgow (Zieliński 1978, 1980). However, Zieliński's studies did not cover the property rights issue.

The WOG reform and Gierek's strategy involving huge investment projects financed by foreign loans were not successful and in the mid-1970s the economy fell into stagnation and then into deep crisis. As a result, workers' strikes and riots broke out in Radom and Ursus in 1976. The pacification of the revolt was an impulse to establish the first organized opposition movements (KOR—Workers' Defense Committee, ROPCiO—Movement for the Defense of Human and Civic Rights). Among the opposition activists a crucial role was played by the supporters of *socialism with a human face* who were associated with the dissidents' movements of the 1960s (Karol Modzelewski, Jacek Kuroń, and Adam Michnik), and one of the initiators of the KOR was the eminent Polish socialist economist Edward Lipiński. In the late 1970s, KOR organized a series of seminars, *Doświadczenie i przyszłość* (Experience and the future). One of the results of the seminar debates was a report on the economic situation prepared by Edward Lipiński (1978). These groups had a great impact on the return of the idea of self-management as one of the main issues in the first phase of *Solidarność* (1980–1981).

Self-management was promoted by many economists in the *Solidarność* movement (e.g., Ryszard Bugaj, Leszek Balcerowicz, Rafał Krawczyk, and Waldemar Kuczyński), although—just like in 1956—they did not directly suggest changes in ownership structure (Bałtowski 2009, 377; Krawczyk 1981). The concept of the self-managed enterprise became an important part of *Solidarność*'s economic program, strongly supported during the negotiations with the government. In effect, at the end of 1981, Parliament passed an act that introduced self-management bodies, however, with certain limitations compared to what had been suggested by *Solidarność*. Economists did research on the functioning of enterprises in the new situation, referring also to earlier discussions on the model of the self-management firm (see, e.g., Dąbrowski 1986).

Self-management was not the only idea related to ownership. Besides the mainstream debate on the character of state-owned enterprises, some experts stressed the importance of private ownership in the socialist economy. As mentioned above, some forms of private business existed in Poland during the entire communist period, mostly in agriculture, but also in small business and services: agency firms, craftsmen' workshops, and—since the 1970s—small businesses created by diaspora members. Another case was the housing cooperatives, which developed from the 1960s. A growing number of flats in the housing cooperatives were, in a sense, owned by members who had paid full price for them. But it was a special case of cooperative property, not full ownership.

For a long time, the problem of private ownership in the socialist economy was a marginal issue for economists and till the second half of the 1980s it did not become a subject of detailed analysis. The first publications to stress the necessity of strengthening private firms were published just after the riots of 1956 (Młynarski 1957). However, such opinions were isolated and did not find at that time supporters in the discussion about reforming the economy. This changed in the 1970s when some economists (and not only economists) indicated the need for reinforcing the status of private ownership. For example, Waldemar Kuczyński emphasized the importance of the development of private ownership in agriculture (Kuczyński 1981). In 1981, the reform project prepared by Stefan Kurowski and Grzegorz Palka for *Solidarność* included support for private business by transferring capital for investment projects from the state to private business or agriculture. But even these economists did not propose the privatization of state-owned enterprises (Luszniewicz 2007, 2009).

This does not mean that the goal of reconstructing the market and private ownership did not exist at all, but it was represented by liberal activists, not by economists. The first ideas of privatization appeared in the late 1970s and the early 1980s in liberal circles in Kraków (Walasek 2005). For instance, Mirosław Dzielski proposed a kind of *nomenklatura* privatization, which would result in a group of new private owners coming from the communist elite (Dzielski 1980).

The idea of mass privatization of the state economy developed in the mid-1980s. In 1985, Rafał Krawczyk argued that self-management would lead to inefficiency. Instead, he proposed to reestablish the capital market and give the shares of the enterprises to the employees (Krawczyk 1985). Lesław Paga, one of the initiators of Warsaw Stock Exchange in the 1990s, together with Michał Zieliński, claimed that "to ensure the growth of effectiveness it is indispensable to break down the general social arrangement where the state is the monopolist and owns all the property but nobody has real responsibility for it, so in effect it becomes nobody's property, and to enfranchise the means of production" (Paga and Zieliński 1987, 106). Such liberal views also spread among young economists in the communist party (e.g., Marek Belka 1986) but the interest in liberal economics was not followed up by further suggestions to change the property rights structure.

Probably, the most important organization of liberal oppositionists was established in Gdańsk. The prominent members of that group were young economists: Janusz Lewandowski, Jan Szomburg, and Jan Krzysztof Bielecki (Luszniewicz 2008). In the second half of the 1980s, they advocated the privatization of state-owned enterprises. The most important and famous project was the first mass privatization program, the so-called voucher privatization, formulated by Lewandowski and Szomburg in 1988 (Lewandowski and Szomburg 1989).

At the end of the same year, the last communist government passed an act on economic entrepreneurship, allowing freedom to establish and operate private business enterprises. Despite the domination of self-management supporters in *Solidarność*, the first non-communist government with Leszek Balcerowicz as deputy prime minister introduced liberal reforms in 1989, including the privatization of state-owned enterprises.

SOCIAL OWNERSHIP—SELF-MANAGEMENT—PRIVATE PROPERTY

What Is Social Ownership? The Lange-Lipiński Discussion

The Sovietization of economic sciences in the first half of the 1950s led to a decrease in any theoretical debate (Kurowski 2006, 41–42; Rychlewski 2006, 12). This also applied to ownership and the categorization of property rights, reflecting the definitions given by the Constitution. True, ownership in economic sense was defined slightly differently as "the actual management of the means of production aimed at reaching the production goals and creating added value" (Minc 1973, 65). In fact, the category of ownership and its division into subcategories survived in academic textbooks at least till the 1980s, and practically till the end of the communist era.[6]

Political changes in Poland after Stalin's death were an impulse for discussions on ownership under communism, though it did not become a central issue. It was not comparable to the debate on the planning system. Nevertheless, a number of important economists, such as Oskar Lange, Edward Lipiński, and Bronisław Minc expressed their views on it. The exchange of opinions started with Lange's book *Political Economy*. According to Lange, the ownership of the means of production is the basic relationship between human beings: "It is not about accidental ownership, but ownership accepted by members of the society, and guarded by accepted rules of coexistence among people and potential sanctions for the violation of the rules, being it a custom or a law. This is the type of property rights that we can call ownership." Furthermore, he pointed out that "the ownership of the means of production is a social relationship which is the foundation of a complex system of human relationships involved in the social production process" (Lange 1963, 31–32). Lange divided ownership into two main categories: social and private. The latter could be individual or group-owned (family, corporate, etc.). What made Lange's approach different from the constitutional categories of ownership was a distinction given to an intermediate category "between social and private, for example, ownership of a cooperative or an association, which pertains to only a certain number of citizens"(Ibid., 32).

Lange's approach met with criticism not only from economists but also lawyers. Bronisław Minc, in a discussion on the book soon after its publication, pointed out that Lange's definition of ownership had a legal dimension and missed on the economic character of property rights. Minc also referred to the categorization of ownership offered by Lange. He criticized the introduction of an intermediate form of ownership and applying that term to cooperative ownership, which, according to Minc, should be treated as a kind of social ownership (*Dyskusja nad książką* 1960, 124; see also Minc 1973, 61–94). Interestingly enough, a criticism similar to Minc's objection regarding the legal character of Lange's definition was expressed by Jan Wasilkowski, a professor of law and a major specialist in the field of property rights. According to Wasilkowski, the problem with Lange's approach, which was overly legal, was that "exposing ownership as a constitutive element of owning in economic sense, does not find enough justification in facts" (Wasilkowski 1972, 15–16).

The most insightful polemic to Lange's approach was provided by Edward Lipiński. In his comments on Lange's work, Lipiński questioned the view of ownership as an organizational rule. In his opinion ownership forms did not fully define all the relations between people involved in the production process and determine the nature of product distribution. Lipiński claimed that

> the type of ownership is not a feature defining the relations within the process of production; property remains social property if the system of goals of all the units cooperating in the production process is in line with the system of goals of the basic production unit, and, therefore, in line with the social system of goals—an effective fulfillment of the growing needs of society. (Lipiński 1969, 43)

The author argued with Lange's concept of intermediate ownership; in his opinion cooperative ownership (and also other forms of intermediate ownership) should be considered as social ownership (Ibid., 41–42).[7] Despite starting with a slightly different set of premises, his conclusions turned out to be similar to those of the previously quoted authors.

An interesting summary of this discussion was made by Michał Kałecki in his paper in honor of Edward Lipiński. Kałecki stressed that Lange's interpretation of Marx was rather traditional, in line with Karl Kautsky's. "For Lange," wrote Kałecki, "ownership of the means of production is the foundation which determines all the relations of production and the entire allocation" (Kałecki 1985, 268–69). As Kałecki pointed out, "Lipiński's view in the understanding of the category of social ownership could be described as extremely maximalist. [... presuming] the compatibility of the social system of goals with the system of goals of the basic production unit and the goals of units cooperating in the process of production" (Kałecki [1969] 1985, 270).

Lange's approach—especially the concept of intermediate ownership—was more or less in line with his prewar writings. The concept had only a limited influence on economic thought during the communist period. Probably, it was the most helpful for scholars studying cooperatives (see, e.g., Boczar 1986).

Workers' Self-Management

The first papers criticizing the centralized economic system were published in 1953. As Jerzy Osiatyński pointed out, the direct cause of rethinking old dogmas was the publication of Stalin's *Economic Problems of Socialism in the USSR* (1952) and his assumption that the law of value was also a basic economic law under socialism (Osiatyński 1982, 315). The first to propose changes in economic theory was a former propagator of Stalinization, Włodzimierz Brus. Starting from 1953, he stressed the need to decentralize economic decisions and to change the methods of central planning (Brus 1956). An important part of the ensuing debate was the scientific conference that took place early in 1956 with the participation of Oskar Lange and Michał Kałecki. The supporters of Brus's view suggested the introduction of profit sharing as a *material incentive* for employees of enterprises. Kałecki was more skeptical and stressed some disadvantages to this idea. He argued that it could lead to undesirable results, for example, uncontrolled reduction of costs, while "in some cases the expansion of production could be more important for the national economy even if it were more costly" (Kałecki 1982a, 90).

This early debate did not relate to problems of ownership directly, but some aspects of the discussion, like profit sharing, concerned the issue of property rights. After the Second Congress of Polish Economists and the riots in 1956, the discussion became more lively (Witczak-Haugstad 2008, 284–87). The most radical opinion was expressed by a group of young economists (Stefan Kurowski, Józef Popkiewicz) called by Kazimierz Kloc *the value group*.[8] As pointed out by Kloc, they "proposed to base the economic mechanism on independent enterprises maximizing profits. The central plan would have a coordinating or corrective function" (Kloc 1997, 127; Kurowski 1957b). As regards property rights, they suggested the reconstruction of the market system, but without the privatization of state property. In their opinion "workers' councils were to take the place of the private owner, thereby guaranteeing the socialist character of the economy" (Ibid.). Those opinions met with the criticism of the majority of the older scholars. Włodzimierz Brus argued that Kurowski's idea was in fact the negation of central planning and the reform should rather be based on coordination between central planning and self-managed enterprises. Brus defended the role of (reformed) central planning as the main institution of the socialist economy, opposing the view of the plan as an instrument of corrections and coordination only (Brus 1957).

The most eminent economists such as Kałecki, Lange, Brus, or Lipiński were far less radical than members of the *value group*. In their view, the main target was to coordinate central planning with decentralization, the autonomy of enterprises and economic incentives. The *model group* (Lange and Brus) pointed out the importance of independent, self-managed enterprises, and the need for a broader use of economic incentives, but also stressed the importance of central planning in setting prices and wages, taking decisions on investment projects, the redistribution of the means of production, and so on. The approach by the group of *realists* (Kałecki and Bobrowski) was similar, the main difference being the smaller scale of autonomy given to enterprises and less resolute changes made in central planning. In Kałecki's opinion expressed as early as 1956, the transfer of some prerogatives to the enterprises could lead, for example, to an increase of unemployment (Kałecki 1956). As pointed out by Osiatyński, the potential increase in unemployment as a result of the behavior of self-managed enterprises was one of the main problems for Kałecki at that time (Osiatyński 1982, 324).

To a certain extent, the discussion on self-management was a return to former ideas expressed by collectivist economists and socialist politicians before and after the war. In a paper published at the end of 1956, Oskar Lange pointed out that "the emancipation of socialist enterprises, with a management based on workers' councils, is the fundamental assumption of the new economic model" (Lange 1956). At the same time, Edward Lipiński stressed that

> a socialist enterprise cannot be divorced from social ownership of the means of production, because the enterprise constitutes a unit of this ownership. However, it should be an autonomous, decentralized unit, which has a broad power of decision making, freedom of adaptation and the right to take a risk. The workers' councils are the link between the society and enterprises as independent centers of production, innovation, sale, adaptation and foresight. (Lipiński 1956, 37)

Michał Kałecki underlined that the two most important elements of the new economic model were workers' councils and central planning: "they seem to be necessary for the quick development of the national economy," he wrote. He stressed that the workers' councils should have three functions: they should (1) stop abuses in the area of working conditions, payments for employees, and so on, (2) limit centralization tendencies and the growth of bureaucracy, and (3) prompt initiatives among employees. However, Kałecki was convinced that the socialist economy also needed central planning, "comprising at least production, wages, larger investments projects, as well as the control of prices and the redistribution of the main resources" (Kałecki 1956).

In his work *Ogólne problem funkcjonowania gospodarki socjalistycznej* (*General Problems of the Functioning of Socialist Economy*) (1961) Włodzimierz Brus allowed enterprises the freedom to define the extent, structure, and methods of production, to select suppliers, and to control the sales process. An enterprise had the autonomy to invest its own means. Decisions on state investments were excluded, and all central plan directives were superior to the plans of a particular enterprise, although Brus renounced a direct hierarchical dependence of enterprises.

This proposal would have meant practically—from the property rights perspective—that part of these rights was to be transferred to the workers' council and to the director of the enterprise. The range of the transfer would depend on the level of autonomy granted to the enterprise itself. This is the point where the opinions of scholars diverged. Kurowski and his colleagues were the most liberal, giving the workers' council a similar position to that of the private owner but without privatization. Lange and Lipiński followed the postwar idea of the socialist party, which proposed the democratization and socialization of ownership. Brus's approach was similar to Lange's, advocating a relatively broad scale for the proposed transfer of rights. Kałecki was more moderate.

In his book published in the West in the middle of the 1970s, Brus stressed the crucial importance of the democratization and socialization of property (Brus 1975). Merging this idea with that of enterprise autonomy led him to a model of the self-managed enterprise. However, his concept of self-management was different from the Yugoslav model that he continued to criticize. In his opinion, "its logic leads to unlimited fragmentation of ownership of the means of production and to fully-fledged group ownership." Brus argued that society as a whole has the right to decide about accumulation, allocation, and investments, and his "attitude toward self-management was that it should operate within the confines of a centrally planned economy with regulated market mechanism, in which the centre is subjected to popular control through a pluralistic political system" (Brus 1989, 207).

The debate on the self-managed enterprise was taken even further during the 1970s, mostly during the initial period of *Solidarność*, when the concept of self-management became one of the main ideas of the independent trade union. A new generation of economists included Leszek Balcerowicz, Ryszard Bugaj, Rafał Krawczyk, and Waldemar Kuczyński. At the end of the 1970s, Balcerowicz, with a team of young economists from the Main School of Planning and Statistics started working on a program of changes in the economic system.

Self-management was an element of the political discourse between *Solidarność* and the authorities rather than a topic of an original academic debate developing the ideas born in the late 1950s. Years later, Leszek Balcerowicz presented the choice of the self-managed enterprise as an element of tactics emerging from the constraints of the political system. According to his account, the goal of that work was

> to conceive a draft of an economic system that would be more efficient than the previously existing one, but, at the same time, would not cross the boundaries of what was considered political reality at the time. [...] Since it excluded privatization as politically unacceptable, the remaining scope for changes included systems that were based on "non-private" property, but that would be, at least to some extent, market-driven. That logic led us to the concept of self-management. (Balcerowicz 1992b, 11, 1992a)

The discussion between *Solidarność* and the government resulted in reforms that introduced self-management in enterprises. As stressed by émigré economists Stanisław Gomułka and Jacek Rostowski, in the principles of the reform "the reader may easily recognize the influence of ideas associated with Oskar Lange and Włodzimierz Brus. If they were implemented in full, in particular the principle of self-management, the Polish reform would be more radical than the Hungarian" (Gomułka and Rostowski 1984, 388). Hence, in the 1980s the importance of the workers' councils and their role in the enterprises were still discussed (Stypułkowski 1986). However, the new studies were rather empirical examinations than theoretical analyses of self-management (Dąbrowski 1986; Błaszczak 1983).

In the late 1980s, the idea of market socialism, including the concept of self-management, weakened. Even the former main representatives of this approach were increasingly skeptical of the idea. Two of them, Włodzimierz Brus and Kazimierz Łaski, published a book that can be seen as a conclusion to the long debate (Brus and Łaski 1992). They dedicated a separate section to the issue of property rights in the reformed socialist economy. The authors argued that the functioning of independent enterprises and, more importantly, entrepreneurship, in the context of the dominance of state ownership was highly unlikely (or entirely impossible). Brus and Łaski pointed out the futility of separating the role of the state as the owner from its role as a regulator. Most of all, they stressed that even if that construct were feasible, it would be impossible to solve the problem of the lack of entrepreneurship "without considering responsibility for loss as personal" (Ibid., 173). The general conclusion was almost unequivocal: "Why stick to state ownership?" (Ibid., 179). If market socialism was to be reasonable, then "it had to sanction income from property and entrepreneurship," but it would have to be followed by rejecting the basic features of socialism, including the dominance of state ownership in the economy (Ibid.,182, 186).

At the end of the 1980s, the idea of self-management clearly was not as popular as in the late 1950s or 1960s, but it was still dominant in the economic program of *Solidarność* during the Roundtable negotiations in the spring of 1989. Market socialism or socially even more sensitive approaches to economic policy also had strong supporters among leftist economists, both those living in Poland (Ryszard Bugaj, Tadeusz Kowalik) and émigrés (Jan Drewnowski). However, social sensitivity had to compete with increasingly popular liberal views that dominated economic discussions in the following years.

The Status of Private Ownership

The subject of private ownership in Marxist economics dominating in Poland from the end of the 1940s did not occupy a major position in economic research. Private property rights became more important as late as the end of the 1970s. In the beginning, though, their discussion was limited mostly to journalistic essays (published in the underground press). True, the problem was identified much earlier. It was right after 1956 that Feliks Młynarski, one of the founders and a vice president of *Bank Polski* (the central bank of Poland in the interwar period) and the president of *Bank Emisyjny* during the war (it was the central bank under German occupation), brought up the issue of private business in the socialist economy. At the same time, young economists like Stefan Kurowski, Józef Popkiewicz, and Jan Mujżel spoke for the strengthening of private property rights.

Młynarski advocated a return to the status quo directly after the war, when the three sectors—state, cooperative, and private—coexisted. He pointed to the fact that the existence of the *third* (private) sector within the socialist economy, in the form of peasant farms, small industrial firms, and service companies, was an important supplement to the dominant state economy (Młynarski 1957). Kurowski's priority was the introduction of the market. Nevertheless, he pointed to the need to strengthen the position of private ownership (Kurowski 1957a). In a later analysis he proved that a nationalized and centrally planned economy was incapable of competing with free market economies (Kurowski 1963). This was the thesis of Kurowski's habilitation, which—as a result—was halted by party authorities, and the author himself experienced problems with the publication of his research until the 1970s (Walasek 2012). Publications regarding the status of private property in the economy in the period after 1956 were scarce and they mostly recommended strengthening the private sector rather than providing a more thorough analysis of the significance of private ownership in socialism (see, for example, Mujżel 1961).

The first voices advocating a deeper transformation of the ownership system came from journalists and opposition activists such as Stefan Kisielewski and Mirosław Dzielski in the 1970s (Luszniewicz 2008, 181). These promoters of liberal ideas exerted only a limited influence on the academic debate. Nearly all of these ideas were published in unofficial or émigré journals and were hardly available to a broader audience. However, they had a significant impact on the younger generation of liberals in the 1980s.

Kisielewski was the first who started representing liberal views; in his memoirs he named Wilhelm Röpke and German Ordo-liberalism as his inspirations (Kisielewski 2001, 114). In articles published in the underground press or abroad he criticized the communist destruction of private entrepreneurship and pointed to the need to desist from the command system and state ownership (Kisielewski 1978, 1979).

Mirosław Dzielski presented the most compelling idea in terms of transforming the structure of property rights. His proposal assumed an evolutionary transformation from state socialism to capitalism. The author suggested a compromise between the opposition and the ruling party. The ruling party would abandon the communist ideology and the command system in favor of the market, and in exchange the opposition would agree to a temporary continuation of the rule of the authoritarian party and to private ownership exercised by the communist *nomenklatura* (for example, by handing over enterprise stocks to leading apparatchiks). According to Dzielski (1980), this would lead to a gradual transition to capitalism.

As mentioned, during the first phase of *Solidarność* (1980–1981), multiple self-management concepts of ownership were discussed. However, even the most elaborate transformation proposals did not go any further than demanding greater autonomy for the enterprises and workers' self-management with large prerogatives in controlling the enterprises. None of these called for a radical change in the ownership structure through privatizing state property.

One of the first scholars examining the ownership structure in a different way was Jadwiga Staniszkis (1984, 1989). In her sociological analysis of the centrally planned economy, Staniszkis brought up a thesis on the ontological particularity of property rights under communism. Using, among others, the categories of new institutional economics, she highlighted the drawbacks of the idea of ownership in standard socialist discourse. First of all, ownership was considered collective, which led to the lack of well-defined economic interests and to the impossibility of using property rights optimally. At the same time, ownership was politicized. In effect, it depended on the rational behavior of the authorities, which was not, and could not be, such. The only efficient reform would have to change the structure of property rights and that would, in turn, have to lead directly to systemic change (Staniszkis 1989).[9]

The evolution of ideas questioning the rationale behind state ownership and promoting private ownership gained momentum in the 1980s. A number of liberal circles emerged, with three of greater significance. The first one was formed around Mirosław Dzielski in Kraków. The second was an ultra-liberal milieu gathered around Janusz Korwin Mikke, the founder of *Ruch Polityki Realnej* (the Realpolitik Movement). The third circle was established in Gdańsk, with the leading roles of young economists like Jan Krzysztof Bielecki, Jan Szomburg, and most importantly, Janusz Lewandowski. That latter group proved to be the most prolific in the analysis of property issues and in building a program of ownership transformation.

The liberals from Gdańsk drew inspiration from the works of Friedrich Hayek and Ludwig Mises as well as from the heritage of German Ordo-liberalism, which was their most important source. In the mid-1980s, mostly thanks to Lewandowski, they started not only to entirely reject the dominance of state ownership in Eastern Europe but also to criticize the statist elements and the overextended social sectors in Western economies (Luszniewicz 2008). Lewandowski also assumed that economic efficiency could be achieved only through rebuilding private ownership. The influence of German Ordo-liberals was apparent in rejecting radical liberalism and accepting a limited welfare state (Lewandowski 1986). The Gdańsk liberals demanded an active role of the state in the democratization of the economy through the promotion of workers' ownership of shares and de-monopolization of economic institutions.

Their views evolved into designing a total overhaul of the ownership structure. It was to happen not only through supporting the private sector, but also through a wide scope of privatization programs rejecting the concept of self-management popular among the *Solidarność* activists. Lewandowski and Szomburg pointed out that property rights distribution among the state, the manager, and the workers' council would create neither effective ownership nor responsibility for decision-making (Lewandowski and Szomburg 1985, 49–50). As a result, in 1988, the two authors proposed a profound privatization program, which was to lead to the total transformation of the ownership structure. This was not the first voice in favor of the privatization of state-owned enterprises (Krawczyk 1985), but compared to the earlier ideas, it was supported by a fully developed proposal of mass privatization (Lewandowski and Szomburg 1989). The authors suggested privatization via personal vouchers handed out to all adult citizens. The vouchers would entitle the owner to acquire stocks of privatized enterprises, on the condition that during the initial period the vouchers would be excluded from free circulation, which would prevent accumulating them. The entire voucher privatization process would have a gradual character and would take three to five years. The result of the implementation of this program should be the reconstruction of the middle class, the *democratization* of ownership and the reduction of excessive concentration of capital. The idea of the Lewandowski-Szomburg project was liberal; however, one could argue that the concept of enfranchisement stood in opposition to liberal principles by excluding the market from the process of privatization.

The publication of the program coincided with the fall of the communist regime in Poland, and due to Lech Wałęsa's presidential victory in 1990, the Gdańsk liberal circle gained a significant influence on government policies. Bielecki became prime minister and Lewandowski minister of privatization in the new cabinet. The latter announced voucher privatization following the earlier plan, but—unlike in Czechoslovakia or Russia—it was never implemented in the form suggested in 1988. The final program put together in 1993 by Lewandowski was based on slightly different assumptions, and its implementation was left to the next government led by the successors of the former communist party (SLD).

EVOLUTION OF THE DEBATES ON OWNERSHIP

The property rights issue was not a leading subject of economic theory in Poland during the communist period. The exception was a discussion provoked by Oskar Lange's book *Political Economy*. The major participants of ownership debates remained faithful to Marxist political economy, and the controversy revolved around the method of defining social ownership in the communist economy.

The disputes on self-management were by far more interesting. Although they did not refer directly to the ownership problem, many of the contributors aimed to transform the nature of property rights. The discussion originated in the 1950s and had a dual character. First, it could be traced back to the traditions of Polish economic thought of the interwar period (market socialism), as well as to the postwar debates on the future economic system. Second, after 1956, the spontaneous formation of workers' councils in enterprises also affected economic thinking on self-management. At that time, the most forward-looking programs to change the economic system were created (Kurowski 1957a, 1957b), including ideas like the restoration of the market and handing over almost all property rights to self-managing state-owned enterprises.

Certainly, an important element of the discussion was the case of Yugoslav self-management. This new model of socialist enterprise was widely discussed in Poland not only among economists and journalists, but also among the rebelling workers. In 1956 reports about the Yugoslav economic system were published in the daily newspaper *Życie Warszawy*. At the same time, the National Bank of Poland issued, for internal use only, Czesław Bobrowski's book *Socjalistyczna Jugosławia (Socialist Yugoslavia)* which propagated the decentralization of the economic system and stressed the advantages of self-management in enterprises (the book was published in 1957; Bobrowski 1957; see Osiatyński 1982, 319–20). In the discussion some economists referred to the experiences of Yugoslav enterprises as an argument supporting the introduction of self-management bodies in Polish firms (Mujżel 1956).

Self-management became one of the main pillars of the economic program of *Solidarność*. Despite supporting the private sector, none of the contemporary economists advising *Solidarność* suggested deeper ownership transformations. The trade union movement grew from workers' protests and focused on social justice, thus, major changes in collectivist forms of ownership were not among its priorities (Luszniewicz 2009).

The discussion surrounding self-management was part of a broader debate on reforming the planned economy. In terms of our subject matter, the debate can be regarded as an attempt to redefine social ownership under communism. In the ideas presented above, one notices a gradual evolution toward handing over more property rights to enterprises and workers' councils.

The majority of the publications had a local appeal. Nevertheless, a few of them were also published outside Poland, exerting a considerable influence among economists in other communist countries irrespective of the fact that their authors often revised their positions. For example, the works of Włodzimierz Brus reflect significant changes in his views. In the 1960s, he supported a concept of limited self-management while at the end of the 1980s, he (together with Łaski) pointed to the limited rationality of not only central planning but also of market socialism. The book by Brus and Łaski, although published abroad, could be considered a symbolic closure of the debate during the communist period. Ironically, these two economists, who in the first half of the 1950s promoted the Soviet version of planned economy, at the end of the 1980s, discovered the superiority of the market and private ownership (Brus and Łaski 1992).

Besides self-management, another very important issue was discussed in the 1980s, which was related to the development of a liberal approach to ownership. A characteristic feature of the discussion was the fact that it was quite removed from the Polish tradition of collectivist economics. Its participants referred mostly to Western liberal economists—Hayek, Friedman, or the Ordo-liberals—though some of them also reached out to prewar mainstream Polish economists, for example, Ferdynand Zweig and Edward Taylor.

The discussion on the restoration of private ownership, mostly conducted in underground and semi-official publications, was of journalistic nature, even though also academic scholars (e.g., Lewandowski) took part in it. The majority of texts were derivative as the authors attempted to adapt Western economics to the particular circumstances of the socialist economy. Nevertheless, a few interesting liberal solutions were devised. The most respected among them was the proposal for voucher privatization that influenced other mass privatization programs in Eastern Europe.

A special case of the liberal approach combining sociology, economics, and political science were the studies of Jadwiga Staniszkis. She provided a particularly interesting and innovative analysis using new institutional economics, including property rights theory.[10]

The economists who took part in the discussion on ownership issues were affiliated with various economic institutions. In the early 1950s, the most important centers of Sovietization were SGPiS (Main School of Planning and Statistics), IKKN (Education of Research Faculty, later transformed into Social Sciences Institute [INS]) subordinated to the Central Committee of the communist party, and the newly created Department of Political Economy at the University of Warsaw (Connely 1996; Czarny 2015). However, the institutional landscape changed after 1956. There is hardly any evidence to tell where the main centers of the reform economists were after 1956 or of liberals in the 1980s. Brus and Bobrowski worked at the University of Warsaw till 1968; Kałecki, during his career in Poland, taught at SGPiS; Lange was connected to all three important Warsaw institutions: the Main School of Planning and Statistics, the University of Warsaw, and the Polish Academy of Sciences. There were also influential economic institutions in other Polish cities like Łódź, Poznań, Wrocław, or Gdańsk. For instance, Popkiewicz, who was one of the most important figures of the *value group*, worked at the Economic Academy in Wrocław. In the 1970s and 1980s, liberal ideas spread not through academic institutions but rather through unofficial, informal opposition circles. However, the main persons developing those ideas were associated with academic institutions, for example, Lewandowski worked at University of Gdańsk, Krawczyk at the University of Warsaw, Balcerowicz at the Main School.

The participation of émigré economists in the debate on ownership was rather limited. Except Brus, Łaski, and, to some extent, Drewnowski, other academics who worked abroad and were interested in economic reforms considered the problem of property rights as marginal. Good examples are Stanisław Gomułka and Jan Giedymin Zieliński, leading representatives of a younger generation who mostly focused on the macroeconomic problems of the Polish economy.

CONCLUSION

The above analysis points to a number of specific features of the ownership discussions among Polish economists. The debates were influenced by the achievements of prewar economists like Oskar Lange in the 1930s, as well as by ideas formed right after the war. As a result, from the mid-1950s till the 1980s, the major trend in thinking about ownership was market socialism, with a particular emphasis on the *democratization* of social ownership. The controversies grew more heated after 1956 and again in 1980 when Polish workers demanded more participation in the management of enterprises. Nevertheless, the frames of the existing political system had a significant impact on the extent of proposed changes in property rights. As a result even the most advanced proposals had to be contained within a radical interpretation of market socialism.

A partial change in perspectives occurred in the 1980s when more and more scholars demanded a complete overhaul of the economic system, but the liberal program remained rather marginal until 1989, at least in the official part of the public space. In addition, due to the dominant role played by *Solidarność* in the opposition, liberal economic ideas did not stand a chance to become the foundation of anti-communist political discourse.

All in all, the accomplishments of Polish economists in developing original concepts of ownership were fairly limited. Probably, the most interesting result of those discussions was the mass privatization program suggested by Lewandowski and Szomburg. In the case of self-management, the proposals mirrored earlier theoretical works (e.g., Lange's publications from the 1930s) rather than introducing any new input in comprehending ownership problems, for example, on the basis of property rights theory unfolding in the West at the time.

Ownership theories had a very limited impact on the economic policies of the authorities. It would be difficult to assume that the policy changes introduced in 1956 and 1981 were the result of a lively debate among economists. For example, the introduction of certain elements of self-management was rather the consequence of social pressure rendered by rebelling workers and the fear of growing social unrest. The best proof of the insignificant influence of economists' opinions is the fate of the Economic Council appointed after 1956, whose proposals were never put in practice.

NOTES

1. An interesting argument against Lange's approach was presented by Jan Drewnowski (1937, 1938). He claimed that equilibrium in a collectivist economy would be different from the one in capitalist economy. Drewnowski showed that

adjustment in different models of economy (he identified five models) would lead to different points of equilibrium.

2. The third important party *Polskie Stronnictwo Ludowe* [Polish Peasant Party], which openly opposed communist rule in Poland, supported the ideas of agrarianism in its program. But following its political marginalization in 1947 and the emigration of its leader Stanisław Mikołajczyk, PSL had no impact on economic decisions.

3. For a summary of the controversies between PPS and PPR, see Kowalik (2006) and Jędruszczak (1983, 58–59); for memories of the participants of the discussion, see also Czesław Bobrowski (1986) and Jan Drewnowski (1979).

4. PZPR was created in December 1948 as a result of the forced unification of PPR and PPS.

5. In the 1960s and especially in the 1970s, the government introduced fiscal instruments leading to the gradual takeover of peasant farms by the state. The most important measure was offering older farmers a pension in exchange for their land (Dobieszewski 1977). The government also introduced some forms of voluntary cooperation (e.g., farmers' working groups [Szambelan 1983]).

6. See the chapter on ownership in Bronisław Minc (1973, 61–69), an approach tightly following Soviet patterns that also could be found in works of less known authors (see, e.g. Dimitrov Kostov et al. 1982).

7. A similar opinion was voiced by Tomasz Piwowarun in his essay on property rights regulations in Poland (Piwowarun 1977, 30).

8. Kloc (1997, 127–29) identified three groups of economists. The most radical economists were called the *value group* (*wartościowcy*) because they stressed the importance of the law of value. A more moderate faction was the "model group" because its members wanted to reform the model of the planned economy. The third group, the so-called realists proposed the deepest changes that were still possible under the existing system.

9. The role of the communist elite (*nomenklatura*) in the economic system was examined in Poland by sociologists of organization from the 1970s. Probably the first scholar who pointed out the *nomenklatura*'s huge impact on the economy was Maria Hirszowicz (1973, 1980) who published her studies in Paris. However, even in communist Poland there were research projects on the importance of cadre recruitment and informal relations on the local levels of the party-state (e.g., Wasilewski 1981, 1990; Najduchowska 1984; Tarkowski 1983, 1990). Moreover, after 1989, those social scientists who studied how the former *nomenklatura* affected the postcommunist transformation also discovered some unknown features of the communist elite (Wasilewski and Wnuk-Lipiński 1995, Wasilewski 2000).

10. Staniszkis was among the first taking a neo-institutionalist approach in Poland. For the reception of new institutional economics, see Kochanowicz (2012).

BIBLIOGRAPHY

Abramowski, Edward. 2012. *Braterstwo, solidarność, współdziałanie* [Brotherhood, solidarity, cooperation]. Łódź: Stowarzyszenie "ObywateleObywatelom."

Balcerowicz, Leszek. 1992a. "The 'Socialist Calculation' Debate and Reform Discussions in Socialist Countries." In *Reform and Transformation: Eastern European Economics on the Threshold of Change*, edited by János Mátyás Kovács and Márton Tardos, 5–17. London: Routledge.

———. 1992b. *800 dni: szok kontrolowany* [800 days: Controlled shock]. Warsaw: BGW.

Bałtowski, Maciej. 2009. *Gospodarka socjalistyczna w Polsce: Geneza—rozwój—upadek* [Socialist economy in Poland: Origins—progress—decline]. Warsaw: PWN.

Belka, Marek. 1986. *Doktryna ekonomiczno-społeczna Miltona Friedmana* [The social-economic doctrine of Milton Friedman]. Warsaw: PWN.

Błaszczak, Barbara. 1983. *Funkcjonowanie samorządu pracowniczego* [The functioning of workers' self-management]. Warsaw: PTE.

Bobrowski, Czesław. 1957. *Socjalistyczna Jugosławia* [Socialist Yugoslavia]. Warsaw: KiW.

———. 1986. *Wspomnienia ze stulecia* [Memories from a century]. Lublin: Wyd. Lubelskie.

Boczar, Kazimierz. 1986. *Spółdzielczość: Problematyka społeczna i ekonomiczna* [Cooperatives: Social and economic problems]. Warsaw: PWE.

Brus, Włodzimierz. 1956. *Prawowartości a problematyka bodźców ekonomicznych* [The law of value and the issues of economic incentives]. Warsaw: PWN.

———. 1957. "Spór o rolę planu centralnego" [Debate on the role of the central plan]. In *Dyskusja o polskim modelu gospodarczym* [*A discussion on the Polish economic model*], 136–48. Warsaw: KiW.

———. 1961. *Ogólne problemy funkcjonowania gospodarki socjalistycznej* [General problems of the functioning of socialist economy]. Warsaw: PWN. English translation: *The Market in the Socialist Economy*. London: Routledge & Kegan Paul. 1972.

———. 1975. *Socialist Ownership and Political Systems*. London: Routledge.

———. 1989. "From Revisionism to Pragmatism: Sketches to a Self-Portrait of a Reform Economist."*Acta Oeconomica* 40, no. 3/4: 204–10.

Brus, Włodzimierz, and Kazimierz Łaski. 1992. *Od Marksa do rynku* [*From Marx to the Market*]. Warsaw: PWN. English edition: *From Marx to the Market: Socialism in Search of an Economic System*. Oxford: Oxford University Press. 1989.

Connelly, John. 1996. "Internal Bolshevisation? Elite Social Science Training in Stalinist Poland." *Minerva* 4, no. 34: 332–46.

Czarny, Bogusław. 2015. "Wpływ aspirantów Katedry Ekonomii Politycznej w Instytucie Kształcenia Kadr Naukowych w Warszawie na polską ekonomię po II wojnie światowej" [The influence of the aspirants from the Political Economy Chair of the Education of Research Faculty in Warsaw on Polish economics after WWII]. *Ekonomia* 15, no. 41: 25–56.

Dąbrowski, Marek. 1986. *Ekonomiczne konsekwencje samorządności pracowniczej* [Economic consequences of workers' self-management]. Wrocław: INE PAN.

Dimitrov Kostov, Ivan et al. 1982. "Rozwój i doskonalenie własności socjalistycznej w PRL" [Development and improvement of socialist ownership in Polish People's Republic]. *SGPS Monografie i Opracowania*, no. 115.

Dobieszewski, Adolf. 1977. "Przemiany własności chłopskiej w Polsce" [Changes in peasant ownership in Poland]. In *Własność: gospodarka a prawo. Studia o marksistowskiej teorii własności* [*Property: economy vs. law. Studies on Marxist theory of ownership*], edited by Stanisław Kozyr-Kowalski, 497–526. Warsaw: PWN.

Doboszyński, Adam. 1934. *Gospodarka narodowa* [National economy]. Warszawa: Tow. Wydawn. "Patria."

Domińczyk, Tadeusz. 2008. "Regulacja prawa własności w Polsce przed i po 1989" [Legal regulations of ownership rights in Poland before and after 1989]. In *Problemy własności w ujęciu historyczno-prawnym* [Property rights problems in the context of history and law], edited by Ewa Kozerska, Piotr Sadowski, and Andrzej Szymański, 154–66. Opole: Wydawnictwa Uniwersytetu Opolskiego.

Drewnowski, Jan. 1937. "Próba ogólnej teorii gospodarki planowej" [Attempt at a general theory of planned economy]. Part I. *Ekonomista* 4: 9–32.

———. 1938. "Próba ogólnej teorii gospodarki planowej" [Attempt at a general theory of planned economy]. Part II. *Ekonomista* 1: 34–56.

———. 1979. "The Central Planning Office on Trial: An Account of the Beginnings of Stalinism in Poland." *Soviet Studies* 31, no. 1: 23–42.

"Dyskusja nad książką *Ekonomia polityczna* tow. Prof. O. Langego" [A discussion on Oskar Lange's book *Political Economy*]. *Nowe Drogi* 14 (1960), no. 3: 116–49.

Dyskusja o polskim modelu gospodarczym [A discussion on the Polish economic model]. Warsaw: KiW. 1957.

Dzielski, Mirosław [Adolf Romański]. 1980. "Jak zachować władzę w PRL: Życzenia noworoczne Adolfa Romańskiego dla por. Jerzego Borewicza" [How to maintain power in communist Poland: New Year wishes from Adolf Romański to lieutenant Borewicz]. *Merkuriusz Krakowski i Światowy* 2, no. 6: 28–43.

Gomułka, Stanisław, and Jan Rostowski. 1984. "The Reformed Polish Economic System 1982–1983." *Soviet Studies* 36, no. 3: 386–405.

Hirszowicz, Maria 1973. *Komunistyczny Lewiatan* [The Communist Leviathan]. Paris: Instytut Literacki.

———. 1980. *Bureaucratic Leviathan: A Study in the Sociology of Communism.* Oxford: Martin Robertson.

Ignatowicz, Jerzy. 1972. *Kodeks cywilny: Komentarz* [Civil Law: Commentary]. Vol. 1. Warsaw: Wydawnictwo Prawnicze.

Jędruszczak, Hanna, ed. 1983. *Wizje gospodarki socjalistycznej w Polsce, 1945–1949* [Visions of socialist economy in Poland, 1945–1949]. Warsaw: PWN.

Kałecki, Michał. 1956. "Rady robotnicze i centralne planowanie" [Workers' councils and central planning]. *Nowe Drogi* 10, no. 11/12: 38–45.

———. 1982a [1956]. "Bodźce zainteresowania materialnego w gospodarce socjalistycznej" [Financial incentives in the socialist economy]. In *Dzieła* [*Collected works*], Vol. 3, 86–91. Warsaw: PWE.

———. 1982b [1957]. "Koncern pionowy jako element nowego modelu gospodarczego" [Vertical concern as an element of the new economic model]. In *Dzieła* [*Collected works*], Vol. 3, 110–12. Warsaw: PWE.

———. 1984 [1961, 1963]. "Głos w dyskusji o perspektywach rozwoju rolnictwa" [Contribution to the discussion about the prospects for agricultural development]. In *Dzieła* [*Collected works*], Vol. 4, 231–35. Warszawa: PWE.

———. 1985 [1969]. "Ekonomia Edwarda Lipińskiego" [Edward Lipiński's economics]. In *Dzieła* [*Collected works*], Vol. 5, 230–73. Warszawa: PWE.

Kisielewski, Stefan [Kisiel]. 1978. "W sprawie reklamy" [On advertisement]. *Kultura* 32, no. 10: 38–43.

———. 1979. "Czy geopolityka straciła znaczenie?" [Has geopolitics lost its meaning?]. *Res Publica* 1, no. 1: 56–76.

———. 2001. *Dzienniki* [Diaries]. Warsaw: Iskry.

Kloc, Kazimierz. 1997. "Rady robotnicze kontra socjalizm rynkowy" [Workers' councils versus market socialism]. *Polska 1944/45–1989: Studia i materiały* 3: 119–36.

Kochanowicz, Jacek. 2012. "Have Polish Economists Noticed New Institutionalism?" In *Capitalism from Outside: Economic Cultures in Eastern Europe after 1989*, edited by János Mátyás Kovács and ViolettaZentai, 203–22. Budapest: Central European University Press.

Kowalik, Tadeusz. 2006. *Spory o ustrój społeczno-gospodarczy w Polsce: Lata 1944–1948* [Debate on the socio-political system in Poland: 1944–1948]. Warsaw: Key Text—INE PAN.

Krawczyk, Rafał, ed. 1981. *Reforma gospodarcza: propozycje, tendencje, kierunki dyskusji* [Economic reform: proposals, trends, and discussion objectives]. Warsaw: PTE.

———. 1985. "Jaki powinien być rynek" [How the market should function]. *Tygodnik Mazowsze* 4, no. 148: 3.

Kuczyński, Waldemar. 1981. *Po wielkim skoku* [After the great leap forward]. Warsaw: PWE.

Kurowski, Stefan. 1957a. "Rynek i plan" [The market and the plan]. In *Dyskusji o prawie wartości ciąg dalszy* [A continuation of the discussion on the law of value], 61–68. Warsaw: KiW.

———. 1957b. "Model a cele gospodarki narodowej" [The model and the goals of national economy]. In *Dyskusja o polskim modelu gospodarczym* [A discussion on the Polish economic model], 76–102. Warsaw: KiW.

———. 1963. *Historyczny proces wzrostu gospodarczego* [The historical process of economic growth]. Warszawa: PWN.

———. 2006. "Obecne spojrzenie na II Zjazd Ekonomistów Polskich w 1956 r." [A current view on the Second Congress of Polish Economists in 1956]. In *Przełomowy rok 1956 a współczesność* [The crucial year of 1956 and the present days], edited by Zdzisław Sadowski, 40–52. Warszawa: PTE.

Kwiatkowski, Eugeniusz. 1932. *Dysproporcje: rzecz o Polsce przeszłej i obecnej* [Disproportion: about the past and present Poland]. Kraków: Towarzystwa Szkoły Ludowej.

Lange, Oskar. 1956. "Budowa nowego modelu gospodarczego musi oprzeć się na dynamice klasy robotniczej i socjalistycznej inteligencji" [The creation of a new model of economy must be based on the dynamic of the working class and the socialist intelligentsia]. *Nowe Drogi* 10, no. 11/12: 25–30.

———. 1963. *Ekonomia polityczna* [Political Economy]. Vol. 1. Third Edition. Warsaw: PWN.

———. 1973a [1938]. "Istota socjalizmu" [The essence of socialism]. In *Dzieła* [*Collected works*], Vol. 2, 130–36. Warsaw: PWE. English edition: "The Economic Structure of a Socialist Society." *Controversy: The Monthly Socialist Forum* 1 (1939), no. 7: 18–20.

———. 1973b [1936–1937]. "O ekonomicznej teorii socjalizmu" [On the economic theory of socialism]. In *Dzieła* [Collected works], Vol. 2, 231–304. Warszawa: PWE. English edition: "On the Economic Theory of Socialism: Part One." *Review of Economic Studies* 4 (1936), no. 1: 53–71; "On the Economic Theory of Socialism: Part Two." *Review of Economic Studies* 4 (1937), no. 2: 123–42.

Lewandowski, Janusz [J. Branecki]. 1986. "Ordoliberałowie i niemiecki cud gospodarczy" [Ordo-liberals and the German economic miracle]. *Przegląd Polityczny* 4, no. 8: 73–107.

Lewandowski, Janusz, and Jan Szomburg. 1985. *Samorząd w dobie"Solidarności": współpraca samorządów pracowniczych Pomorza Gdańskiego na tle sytuacji w kraju w latach 1980/81* [Self-management in the period of Solidarity: Cooperation between the self-management organizations of employees in East Pomerania and the situation in Poland in the years of 1980/1981]. London: Odnowa.

———. 1989. "Uwłaszczenie jako fundament reformy społeczno-gospodarczej: Zarys programu" [Enfranchisement as the foundation of socio-economic reforms: Program draft]. In *Propozycje przekształceń polskiej gospodarki* [Proposals on Polish economic transformation], 61–83. Warsaw: PTE.

Lipiński, Edward. 1956. "'Model' gospodarki socjalistycznej" [The "model" of socialist economy]. *Nowe Drogi* 10, no. 11/12: 31–37.

———. 1969. *Karol Marks i zagadnienia współczesności* [Karl Marx and contemporary issues]. Warsaw: PWN.

———. 1978. *Uwagi o sytuacji gospodarczej kraju* [Notes on the country's economic situation]. Warszawa: Niezależna Oficyna Wydawnicza "Nowa."

Luksemburg, Róża. 2005 [1922]. *Rewolucja rosyjska* [The Russian revolution]. Warsaw: Studenckie Koło Filozofii Marksistowskiej Uniwersytet Warszawski.

Luszniewicz, Jacek. 2007. "Postulaty gospodarcze Sieci Organizacji Zakładowych NSZZ 'Solidarność' wiodących zakładów pracy z 1981 r.: Reformy czy transformacja systemu?" [Economic postulates of the Network of "Solidarity" Organizations in large enterprises in 1981: Reforms or the transformation of the system?]. In *Gospodarkaispołeczeństwo w czasach PRL-u (1944–1989)* [Economy and society in Polish People's Republic (1944–1989)], edited by Elżbieta Kościk and Tomasz Głowiński, 298–325. Wrocław: GAJT.

———. 2008. "Ewolucja koncepcji ekonomicznych liberałów gdańskich na łamach 'Przeglądu Politycznego' w latach 1983–1989" [Evolution of the economic ideas of the liberals from Gdańsk in the "Przegląd Polityczny" in the years 1983–1989]. *Pamięć i Sprawiedliwość* 13, no. 2: 179–209.

———. 2009. "Wizje reformy gospodarczej w koncepcjach pierwszej Solidarności 1980–1981" [Visions of economic reforms in the projects of the first Solidarity 1980–1981]. In *Między zacofaniem a modernizacją: Społeczno-gospodarcze problemy ziem polskich na przestrzeni wieków* [Between backwardness and modernization: *Social-economic problems of Polish territories at the turn of the century]*, edited by Elżbieta Kościk and Tomasz Głowiński, 261–78. Wrocław: GAJT.

Machnikowska, Anna. 2010. *Prawo własności w Polsce w latach 1944–1981: Studium historyczno-prawne* [Property rights in Poland in the years 1944–1981: A historical-legal study]. Gdańsk: Wydawnictwo Uniwersytetu Gdańskiego.

Madej, Zbigniew. 2006. "Głos w sprawie socjalizmu rynkowego" [A voice on market socialism]. In *Przełomowyrok 1956 a współczesność* [The crucial year of 1956 and present days], edited by Zdzisław Sadowski, 57–58. Warsaw: PTE.

Miłkowski, Stanisław. 1934. *Agraryzm jako forma przebudowy ustroju społecznego* [Agrarianism as a form of rebuilding the social system]. Kraków: Związek Młodzieży Wiejskiej Spółdzielni Oświatowej.

Minc, Bronisław. 1973. *Ekonomia polityczna socjalizmu* [Political economy of socialism]. Warszawa: PWN.

Młynarski, Feliks. 1957. "Funkcja trzeciego sektora w gospodarce socjalistycznej" [The function of the third sector in the socialist economy]. In *Dyskusje o polskim modelu gospodarczym* [A discussion on the Polish economic model], 234–246. Warsaw: KiW.

Mujżel, Jan. 1956. "Program doraźny nie wystarczy" [An ad hoc program is not enough]. In *Ekonomiści dyskutują o prawie wartości* [*Economists discuss the law of value*], 105–120. Warsaw: KiW.

———. 1961. *Ekonomia polityczna* [Political economy]. Warsaw: PTE.

Najduchowska, Halina. 1984. *Kwalifikacje i drogi zawodowe dyrektorów przedsiębiorstw przemysłowych: studium socjologiczno-historyczne* [Qualifications and professional paths of the directors of state-owned industrial enterprises: A sociological-historical analysis]. Warsaw: Państwowe Wydawnictwo Naukowe.

Osiatyński, Jerzy. 1982. "Przypisy i dodatki" [Notes and appendices]. In *Dzieła* [*Collected works*], edited by Michał Kałecki, Vol. 3, 299–472. Warszawa: PWE.

Paga, Lesław, and Michał Zieliński. 1987. "Sektor prywatny (wczoraj—dziś—jutro)" [Private sector (yesterday—today—tomorrow)]. *Res Publica* 1, no. 4: 104–07.

Piwowarun, Tomasz. 1977. "Co to jest własność? Spory we współczesnej myśli ekonomicznej" [What is ownership? Discussions in contemporary economic thought]. In *Własność: gospodarka a prawo. Studia o marksistowskiej teorii własności* [*Property: economy vs. law. Studies on Marxist theory of ownership*], edited by Stanisław Kozyr-Kowalski, 19–46. Warsaw: PWN.

Rychlewski, Eugeniusz. 2006. "II Zjazd jako przełom w myśleniu ekonomicznym" [The Second Congress as a breakthrough in economic thinking]. In *Przełomowyrok 1956 a współczesność* [The crucial year of 1956 and the present days], edited by Zdzisław Sadowski, 11–17. Warszawa: PTE.

Sadowski, Zdzisław, ed. 2006. *Przełomowy rok 1956 a współczesność* [The crucial year of 1956 and the present days]. Warsaw: PTE.

Skąpski, Józef. 1992. "Kodeks cywilny z 1964 r.: Blaski i cienie kodyfikacji oraz jej perspektywy" [Civil Law from 1964: Lights and shadows of codification and its perspectives]. *Kwartalnik Prawa Prywatnego* 1, no. 4: 57–90.

Stalin, Józef. 1952. *Ekonomiczne problemy socjalizmu w ZSRR* [Economic problems of socialism in the USSR]. Warsaw: KiW.

Staniszkis, Jadwiga. 1984. "Własność, racjonalność, dynamika, struktura" [Ownership, rationality, dynamic, structure]. *Przegląd Polityczny* 2, no. 4: 21–34.

———. 1989. *Ontologia socjalizmu* [The Ontology of Socialism]. Warsaw: Wydawnictwo In Plus.

Stypułkowski, Cezary. 1986. *Samodzielne i samorządne przedsiębiorstwo* [Independent and self-managed enterprise]. Warsaw: PWE.

Szambelan, Marek. 1982. "Kooperacja pozioma i pionowa w rolnictwie polskim a przemiany stosunków własnościowych" [Horizontal and vertical cooperation in agriculture and the changes of ownership structure]. In *Rozwój i doskonalenie własności socjalistycznej w PRL* [Development and improvement of socialist ownership in Polish People's Republic]. *Monografie i Opracowania,* no. 115: 212–36.

Tarkowski, Jacek. 1983. "Władze terenowe po reformie" [Local authorities after reform]. In *Władza lokalna u progu kryzysu. Studium dwu województw.* [Local authority before the crisis. Study of two voivodships], edited by Jerzy J. Wiatr, 23–76. Warszawa: Uniwersytet Warszawski.

———. 1990. "Endowment of *Nomenklatura*, or Apparatchiks Turned into Entrepreneurchiks, or from Communist Ranks to Capitalist Riches." *Innovation* 3, no. 1: 89–105.

Tezy, Rady. 1957. "Tezy Rady Ekonomicznej w sprawie niektórych zmian modelu ekonomicznego" [Theses of the Economic Council theses on certain transformations of the economic model]. In *Dyskusje o polskim modelu gospodarczym* [A discussion on the Polish economic model], 261–78. Warsaw: KiW.

Tezy, Sekcji. 1957. "Tezy Sekcji Ekonomiki Rolnictwa PTE w sprawie polityki rolnej w Polsce" [Theses of the Agro-Economics Section of PES on agricultural policy in Poland]. *Zagadnienia Ekonomiki Rolnej* 32, no. 5: 22–25.

Wakar, Aleksy. 1963. *Morfologia bodźców ekonomicznych* [*Morphology of economic incentives*]. Warsaw: PWN.

Walasek, Mateusz. 2005. "Etyczne problemy transformacji ustrojowej w myśli Mirosława Dzielskiego" [Ethical problems of political transformation in Mirosław Dzielski's thought]. *Annales: Etyka w życiu gospodarczym* 8, no. 1: 145–56.

———. 2012. "Idee liberalne w polskiej myśli ekonomicznej po II wojnie światowej do lat 70-tych XX wieku" [Liberal ideas in Polish economic thought after WWII till the 1970s]. *Gospodarka w praktyce i teorii* 31, no. 2: 145–65.

Wasilewski, Jacek. 1981. *Kariery społeczno-zawodowe dyrektorów* [The social and professional career of directors]. Wrocław: Zakład Narodowy im. Ossolińskich.

———. 1990. "The Patterns of Bureaucratic Elite Recruitment in Poland in the 1970s and 1980s." *Soviet Studies* 42, no. 4: 743–57.

———. 2000. "Polish Post-Transitional Elite." In *Second Generation of Democratic Elites in Central and Eastern Europe*, edited by Jadwiga Frentzel-Zagórska and

Jacek Wasilewski, 197–215. Warsaw: Institute of Political Studies Polish Academy of Sciences.

Wasilewski, Jacek, and Edmund Wnuk-Lipiński. 1995. "Poland: Winding Road from the Communist to the Post-Solidarity Elite." *Theory and Society* 24, no. 5: 669–96.

Wasilkowski, Jan. 1972. *Pojęcie własności we współczesnym prawie polskim* [Concepts of ownership in contemporary Polish law]. Warszawa: KiW.

Witczak-Haugstad, Aleksandra. 2008. *A Discipline Divided: Polish Economists and the Communist Regime, 1945–1960*. Trondheim: NTNU.

Zieliński, Jan Giedymin. 1978. "On System Remodeling in Poland: A Pragmatic Approach." *Soviet Studies* 30, no. 1: 3–37.

———. 1980. "New Polish Reforms Proposals." *Soviet Studies* 32, no. 1: 5–27.

Zweig, Ferdynand. 1942. *The Planning of Free Societies*. London: Secker & Warburg.

Chapter 7

The Silence of the Herd

Exploring Ownership Concepts in Communist Romania

Radu Ioan Şimandan, Gabriel Claudiu Mursa and Vlad Paşca

> The theory of the Communists may be summed up in the single sentence: abolition of private property.
>
> —Karl Marx and Friedrich Engels[1]

The end of the Second World War brought the instauration of communism in Romania.[2] The ideas of the Russian Revolution, propagated semi-clandestinely in interwar Romania through the writings of a few marginal authors, became manifest, laying the ideological foundation for the new political power.

The transition from the quasi-liberal, individualist perspective on economic matters and especially on property, dominant from the Great Depression until the communist (Soviet) model, was facilitated by a parallel tradition of collectivist and nationalist approaches to ownership. The interwar Romanian state developed its interventionist tendencies into actual policies that matched the authoritarian political regimes of the 1930s and early 1940s. As a result, decision-makers and economic actors were already accustomed to the perpetual presence of the state in society when the communist regime was fully established in 1948. Moreover, besides state *dirigisme* and planning, representatives of the two major democratic parties of the interwar era—the National Liberal Party and the National Peasants' Party (Müller 2013, 223–25)—were contemplating the idea of transforming large land properties into cooperatives through agrarian reform in order to preserve its economic and social potential. Two important authors were the economists

Mitiţă Constantinescu, a liberal politician advocating industrialization, and Virgil Madgearu, a promoter of agrarian doctrines from the standpoint of the National Peasants' Party. Both of them were influential to the nascent macro-policies of the late 1930s designed by the state—they also held ministerial and parliament seats—proposing either a *dirigist* approach (M. Constantinescu 1943) or indicative planning (Madgearu 1930; Malinschi 1975), and were also supporters of the cooperative movement that was incipient among small landowners (M. Constantinescu 1925, 1943; Roberts 1951).

Like in all countries forced to adopt the Soviet model after the war, the communist transformation of Romania included a major shift in ownership. "Expropriation of the expropriators" was a highly publicized slogan at the time in all of Central and Eastern Europe, announcing the debut of a new era in which socialization of private property (also dubbed as nationalization or collectivization) would become state policy. Industrial enterprises, banking and financial institutions, and mining and transportation companies were taken into state ownership in 1948–1949. Collectivization of a large portion of Romania's agrarian property started in 1949 but proved difficult to enforce, officially accomplished only by 1962. Residential properties belonging to industrialists, proprietors, and other *class enemies* were nationalized in 1950. Production and distribution of virtually all goods and services gradually became centralized (Kornai 1992, 27). The outcome of this wave of confiscation is the very goal proclaimed by socialist ideology: a large-scale redistribution of property and income in favor of a privileged social class, namely the working class.

THE CONCEPT OF PROPERTY IN ROMANIAN COMMUNIST CONSTITUTIONS

The institution of property is instrumental in shaping a society where people are free to follow their own plans. The legal recognition and protection of the fundamental right of property is the bulwark of free people. Studying the evolution of constitutional provisions related to property rights is essential for describing the manner in which political power relates to the human freedom to own and dispose of property.

Enforced in 1948, the first communist constitution stated that three forms of property existed in the People's Republic of Romania within the Marxist property triad: state property (*proprietate de stat*), cooperative property[3] (*proprietate cooperatistă*), and private property (*proprietate particulară*, also dubbed as personal property—*proprietate personală*) (Article 5). Article 6 made it clear that all the riches beneath and above Romania soil, whether they be natural resources, mines, water, forests, telephone, telegraph, or radio "belong to the State, as common goods of the people (*bunuri comune ale poporului*)"; it also gave legal grounding to the impending plan of nationalization of the means of production:

> The law shall provide the methods used in order for the State to take possession of the goods from the categories mentioned above that at the time of entry into force of the present law are still in private hands.

The rationale for the primacy of state property (as common goods of the people) was formulated rather vaguely: "The common goods of the people are the material basis of economic betterment and of the national independence of the People's Republic of Romania" (Article 7).

Private property (as well as inheritance) was considered somehow a residual category, recognized and guaranteed by law, even "especially protected" by the state if "gained through work and savings" (Article 8). Article 9 plainly asserts, "The land in the People's Republic of Romania belongs to those that work it." Article 10 provides a surprisingly liberal takings clause: "Expropriations for reason of public utility can be decided upon according to the law and with rightful compensation established by justice."

The Constitution of 1952 brought significant changes to the definition of property rights conferred by the state. It maintained the Marxist triad: "The national economy [...] comprises three socio-economic formations: socialist formation, small craftsmanship production, and private-capitalist formation" (Article 5) and stated more clearly the hierarchy that put socialist ownership (*proprietate socialistă*) over the means of production as the "foundation of the socialist socio-economic formation," in the form of either state property (as common goods of the people) or "cooperative-collectivist property"—such as property within the collective agricultural institutions (*gospodării agricole colective*) or within the cooperative organizations (Article 6).

Article 6 also triumphantly maintains, "In the socialist state of the economy, the exploitation of man by man is abolished," while Article 9 grants members of Agricultural Production Cooperatives (*Cooperative Agricole de Producție*) the "personal right of use" over their yards and "personal property rights" over their houses, outbuildings, and livestock.

The generous takings clause from the Constitution of 1948 can no longer be found in the 1952 Constitution (however, it will make a comeback as Article 12 in the 1965 Constitution, with protection against expropriation explicitly limited to land and buildings), while personal property no longer benefits from special protection: it is no longer *guaranteed* but *protected.*

Moreover, Article 11 states, "The popular-democratic state consistently carries out a policy of restricting and eliminating capitalist elements," while the scope of personal property is overtly identified as follows: "Personal property rights of citizens of the People's Republic of Romania over work-based incomes and savings, over their house and the auxiliary household, over domestic goods and objects of personal use, as well as inheritance rights as to citizens' private property are protected by law" (Article 12).

The Constitution of 1965—the last socialist constitution of Romania—did not make significant changes regarding the concept of ownership. However, as a result of Article 11, the state granted peasants who could not associate in Agricultural Production Cooperatives a guarantee over "the land that they and their family work," as well as over "the tools used, draft animals and farm animals"; it also guaranteed "craftsmen's property rights over their shops."

Like any constitution in the communist world, Romania's constitutions have been used both as a fundamental law that lay down norms for state and society, and as a political statement for what it had been achieved, that is, they had both a legal and a propaganda function (Simons 1980, xv). As a fundamental law, the communist constitutions of Romania were never designed to be the ultimate regulator of state and society. The public did not regard the constitution as a reference point for arguments. It was a commonly shared view that the drafters were the most uncaring violators of the law. Apparently liberal provisions, like the takings clause, were never publicly invoked. Moreover, during the 1980s no proposals for constitutional revision existed as a means to deal with the acute crisis of the communist regime. Regarding property rights provisions, the main function of the constitution was to provide a basis for the socialization of private property. *Socialist property* over all means of production would receive the highest legal grounding. Western scholars largely ignored the propaganda function of communist constitutions. Romanian communist constitutions abound in triumphalist statements proclaiming the definitive end of exploitation of man by man and the victory of the working class. The novel and allegedly superior socialist property was seen as the basis for a more just economy, strictly organized in accordance with an extended master plan.

However, as Boettke and Leeson (2003) argue, the *de facto* institutional organizing principles in socialism were very different from *de jure* proclamations. Failing to appreciate this distinction would later cause major problems for (mostly Western) reform advisors in the postcommunist era. At the heart of this distinction is the impracticability of a fully socialized economic system (or, using the phrase coined by Ludwig von Mises, "the impossibility of socialism"). It is part of human nature for individuals to respond to incentives and to organize their efforts, thus generating markets. It is impossible for any political regime to abolish private property, since stopping the mutually beneficial exchange of goods and services is unattainable. Whenever formal rules are aberrant or absent, informal rules spontaneously emerge to organize private exchanges. Consequently, when analyzing ownership, one must take into account the intricate web of formal and informal rules that governed economic life in communism. Describing some brute facts and their practical consequences as experienced by Romanians, especially in the late stages of communism, may illustrate this idea.

People had to adapt to the grim reality of a general shortage of goods. Formal property rights over the means of production were concentrated in the hands of central authorities. Domestic supply and imports of consumer goods were modest, maintaining generalized shortages. Travelling abroad was virtually impossible. The practical consequences of this state of affairs were diverse, ranging from the development of black markets for a wide range of consumer goods, smuggled from neighboring countries or produced on small plots of land near the housing estates, to in-kind exchange of services, to all-encompassing bribery and immense bureaucratic power conferred to agencies formally in charge of preventing these phenomena.

Therefore, an examination of ownership during socialism must go beyond the classical distinction between private versus state property to analyze the wide array of institutional arrangements related to ownership.

OPINIONS ON COOPERATIVE OWNERSHIP AS INDICATORS OF ECONOMIC THOUGHT

While historians and sociologists focused mainly on the actual evolution of the forms of ownership during communist rule, economists and legal experts rarely endeavored to analyze the conceptual features and theoretical implications of various forms of property during communism. In spite of the dearth of theoretically founded discussions, we estimate that the manner of dealing with particular forms of ownership and with the rights of property regarding specific objects can reveal interesting features of the economic vision of communist Romania.

One form of property well suited to serve as an indicator of economic thought is cooperative property. It was allowed to emerge spontaneously in manufacturing and the service sector but became significant in agriculture as collectivization unfolded. However, the meaning of the concept itself was changed through staged theoretical debates and large-scale propaganda efforts, making it difficult for the nonprofessional to distinguish between state-owned and privately owned means of production. Therefore, in judging the opinions on cooperative property, one must take into account the constant change in the meaning of words, a common feature of dictatorships.[4]

One of the most basic tenets of the communist era was that a huge advance in industrialization and urbanization could be supported only by a totally socialized agricultural production system. Closely following the Marxist-Leninist doctrine that "small property generates capitalism day by day, minute by minute, spontaneously, and in mass proportions"—a phrase often cited by Gheorghe Gheorghiu-Dej (secretary general of the Romanian Workers' Party between 1944 and 1965) in public speeches—Romanian leaders began implementing the so-called socialist agricultural reform pursuing the Soviet model.

As communists feared an uprising, the first steps toward state property in agriculture were timid. During the 1946 electoral campaign, the communists were still depicting themselves as guardians of peasants' property. In a brochure titled "Communists and Individual Property," after criticizing traditional parties for their alleged defense of large landowners, the communists cautioned peasants that "it depends on the results of these elections if the peasants could labor peacefully and gather the fruits of their land" (Şandru 2005, 51). Gheorghiu-Dej clearly stated his party's policy on agricultural land property:

> The ultimate victory of socialism is not possible so long as there continues to be, in the cities and villages, private property of the means of production, including land. But the problem of land nationalization is not topical in the present conditions of our country. (Gheorghiu-Dej 1953, 46)

However, starting in 1947, attacks on private ownership intensified, with even small landowners portrayed as exploitative capitalists, outside of political control. Due to the attachment to their property, the peasantry needed to be re-educated and reinvented as a *socialist community.* Although vaguely defined, the idea of a cooperative form of land property began to be put forward as a solution to improve the living conditions of peasants.

With the introduction of mandatory annual quotas in 1949, peasants were compelled to give large amounts of farm products to the state. Invoking the *duty to the state*, communist leaders engaged in sweeping campaigns to persuade peasants that future contentment will outweigh any current sacrifice. Alongside efficiency reasons, the political motivation behind the quota system was openly admitted: in 1951, Ana Pauker—a prominent political leader at that time—speaking at a meeting with local party leaders in charge of collectivization stated, "the quota system is like a tax we impose on peasants and their households" (cited in Comisia Prezidenţială 2006, 428). This action proved to be a useful implement in the hands of communist leaders, setting the stage for the next step toward a fully socialized agriculture, namely the much-feared collectivization.

Planned at a time when the communist party was fully engaged in the process of consolidating its power, the collectivization of agriculture was the first large-scale political action. Unlike the nationalization of industry that took a relatively short time to conclude (1948–1952), the collectivization of agriculture proved to be far more difficult to put into practice, taking into account the geography, human resources, and the diversity of the sector. Alongside physical violence, this authentic war on peasants needed extensive persuasion and brainwashing. As early as the beginning of the 1950s, the manipulative terminology used by the Soviet policymakers began to be translated and introduced into Romanian. The old Romanian word "*chiabur*" (wealthy peasant)[5] was gradually given a negative meaning borrowed from the Russian term "*kulak*" (rural exploiter), while the Russian "*kolkhoz*" (collective farm) was introduced as "*colhoz*" with a positive connotation. Large-scale manipulation campaigns to portray the *chiaburs* as enemies of the people were put in place. "The *chiabur* is dangerous, tough and combative. The *chiabur* is different from his fellow in the city, as he does not concentrate much on theory. He takes the axe, the hammer and is willing to defend his property with the sacrifice of his own life because he has the sense of property in his blood. We won't attack him the same way we attacked the industrialists," Gheorghiu-Dej stated in a report (1953, 40). The *chiaburs* were depicted as *venomous and greedy* and the need to *contain* them began to be publicized.

Seeking to gain support for collectivized agriculture, political activists were dispatched from the center to persuade reluctant peasants to join. A primary set of techniques employed by the cadres was so-called persuasion work,[6] as communist leaders were claiming that collectivization must be achieved through consensual means. Unlike mass propaganda, the persuasion activities brought the communist envoys in direct and individualized contact with peasants (Kligman and Verdery 2011, 285). The collective farm was praised on its efficiency grounds as an essential ingredient of the *bright future*, but also as a distinctive element of a new communal way of life. However, in spite of high expectations, these methods of influence failed to yield the desired results, as Kligman and Verdery show:

> Perhaps except for the initial round of collectives (formed in 1949 and early 1950), persuasion rarely convinced peasants of the superiority of collective agriculture. [...] Peasants had to sign up, whether they believed in socialized agriculture or not; once they did so, they were considered persuaded. (Ibid., 284)

Despite extensive persuasion and propaganda campaigns, along with staged unmasking and denunciation operations, the peasants maintained their trust in private property in agricultural land. A Soviet-style collectivized agriculture could only be achieved through the vast use of coercion and physical violence.

As the fight against the class enemy moved to the countryside, the eradication of the *chiaburs* as a social class became a major political objective. Speaking at a plenary meeting of the party Central Committee in March 1949, Gheorghiu-Dej made a famous statement about his party's policy over the rural population: "We support the poor peasantry, make an alliance with the mid-level peasants and lead a constant battle against the *chiaburs*" (cited in Comisia Prezidenţială 2006, 429). Moreover, by setting the political agenda for the rural area, the communists aimed for "a complete liquidation of the exploitation of peasants by *chiaburs*, mobilizing in this struggle the entire working peasantry, when conditions allow it" (Ibid., 430).[7] By struggling to eliminate the *chiaburs*, the new communist power in Bucharest intended to send a clear message of obedience to its great Soviet neighbor.

Finally, after many attempts and severe coercion, a majority of peasants were compelled to surrender their plots and become part of agricultural production cooperatives. From the 1960s to the demise of communism, cooperatives controlled more than 60 percent of the agricultural surface of Romania (N. Constantinescu 2000, 190). Although communist rulers did not allow too much self-management and controlled the cooperatives bureaucratically, they nevertheless stressed that cooperative property is different from state property. Nevertheless, Gheorghiu-Dej's successor Nicolae Ceauşescu stated: "We have to eliminate the mentality according to which cooperative property is an inferior form of socialist property" (Institutul Central 1983, 194). He insisted that socialist property belongs not to the state but to the people.

SOCIALIST PROPERTY

In the early 1970s, the academic field of scientific socialism crystallized under close official supervision. As a social science, scientific socialism (as opposed to utopian socialism) aimed at unifying Marxist-Leninist ideas with the concrete experiences of different peoples. A heterogeneous mix of economics, history, sociology, and philosophy, scientific socialism textbooks rendered the official party creed. Related to the central issue of property, a standard scientific socialism textbook argued:

> Socialism puts an end to private-capitalist property of the means of production and to exploitation relations that it generates, abolishes social classes, [...] generates socialist property of the means of production and, on this basis, new, socialist production relations. (Cleja and M. Trăistaru 1975, 290)

Both economic and class-related reasons validated the historic mission of socialism to eradicate private ownership. In terms of economic efficiency, the ensuing economic order was described as *superior*, although a message of caution was unequivocally sent:

> "The instauration of socialist property [...] creates the premises for continual economic, social and cultural progress, but this possibility does not necessarily transform into reality" (*Ibid.*, 293). In order to achieve its full potential, socialism needs that a number of conditions be satisfied, such as "a just political line, a vast organizing activity, [...] competent, scientific administration of all social activities." (Ibid.)

It is also suggested that the economic superiority of a socialist economy is due to the elimination of spontaneity or anarchism specific to capitalism and to the purposeful action achieved through extensive planning. Still, it is surprising that a thorough analysis of the reasons for this claim is lacking, thus remaining an element of the Marxist-Leninist vulgate.

Further, generalized socialist property would eventually lead to a society made up by different social classes with common interests, working together in complete harmony, as there exists an ongoing process of *closing together* and *homogenization* among social classes. Yet "*the leading class* of the entire society is *the working class led by its communist party*" (Ibid., 291, emphasis in the original).

For party leaders and ideologues, socialist property played a very important role in the economic development of the country. Similar to the Stalinist interpretation, it was believed that concentrated socialist property was a prerequisite for optimal resource management and distribution by means of planning, which could lead to industrial development faster than any capitalist model. Furthermore, socialist industrialization was considered the only possible way to strengthen national independence of a country (Moldovan 1965, 8–9), a goal that belonged more to the rhetoric of power than to reality. The term "independence" was not rigorously defined, but the widespread conception referred to the freedom of each party-state's leadership to decide exclusively upon domestic and foreign policies of the country they were ruling over. Consequently, socialist property was deemed an efficient instrument against neo-colonial and hegemonic tendencies of intra- and inter-bloc powers.

NATIONALIZATION AND PERSONAL PROPERTY

Since the exploitation of man by man had to be brought to an end in all spheres of human interaction, housing ownership could not remain private. Once in power, the Romanian communists were especially preoccupied with taking possession of the residences of political opponents, industrialists, bankers, merchants, and proprietors, many of them becoming tenants in their former houses. Workers, public servants, intellectuals, small artisans, and retired persons could retain their housing property. The Nationalization Act of 1950 specified in the preamble that the socialization of privately owned residential properties aimed at

> strengthening and developing the socialist sector of the economy of the People's Republic of Romania; "ensuring a good administration of the housing stock, which is being subjected to degradation because of the sabotage of the large bourgeoisie and the exploiters who own a large number of buildings; and taking away from the hands of exploiters a significant means of exploitation."[8]

Moreover, Article 3 clearly stated the drastic conditions of nationalization: "Nationalized real estate becomes state property as people's goods, without any compensation and free from any encumbrances or real rights."

A matter of legal and political debate after 1989 has been if the Nationalization Decree of 1950 violated the provisions of the Constitution of 1948. Analyzing this aspect, Emanuel Socaciu (2013) identifies two reasons that make the provisions of the decree unlawful. On the one hand, Article 3 of the Nationalization Act was in evident contradiction with Article 10 of the Constitution (the takings clause mentioned above). On the other, local commissions, with the tacit approval of central political authorities, expropriated many residences that did not meet the criteria stipulated in the Nationalization Act. In fact, the 1950 residential property nationalization was nothing more than ideologically covered and politically motivated theft, a forceful act against which constitutional provisions or public opinion about private property could not oppose.

After the nationalization episode of 1950, Romanian communists remained faithful to the Marxist-Leninist doctrine that distinguished neatly between ownership of the means of production and personal property in consumer goods, the latter being regarded as a new economic category that materializes only in socialism as a specific type of socialist property. There has been a political and ideological compromise regarding private property through the conceptualization of personal property. For communists, there was a fundamental difference between private (capitalist) property and personal property. While private property originated from and was an instrument of exploitation, consisting mainly of means of production, personal property of a particular citizen was the result of her/his labor within socialist relations of production, thus exploitation of other people's labor was excluded. As a result, personal property was seen as a derivative of socialist property, because it was the outcome of the socialist principle of distribution and it was based on national income produced by the socialist economy (Cosma 1974; Lupulescu 1975). The capacity of personal property to provide a good incentive was usually admitted: "Personal property sustains and stimulates the material interest of the working class to participate in the social work that results in production of goods" (Lupulescu 1967, 21). As examples of objects of personal property, the early communist legal system explicitly mentioned personal residences, objects of personal comfort, and monetary income and savings *gained through work.*

However, there was a productive side attached to personal property that was acknowledged by the state—although not explicitly and entirely, since the service sector was hardly regarded as part of the GDP—which took such forms as mandatory rental of so-called surplus space in a large household and permission to accommodate tourists into specially built rooms (no more than two) granted to those who owned houses located in resort areas (Cosma 1974, 36). Although the Constitution of 1965 did not limit the quantity of objects of personal comfort, in practice the rule, according to which those objects are to be owned in quantities not exceeding personal use, was enforced (Lupulescu 1967, 99–100).

The constitutional provision regarding personal ownership made it clear that objects of personal comfort did not include productive property. In order to be considered personal property and enjoy legal protection, an object (a typical example in the legal literature of the time being a sewing machine) had to be used to satisfy the needs of its owner and his family, otherwise it would have been considered *production good.*

But party activists and lawmakers did not take into full account the productive potential of personal property in the informal economy, which expanded and became more visible in the shortage economy of Romania. Rooms were sublet to third-party tenants (e.g., students, young workers), cars were used in unauthorized trade, both national and foreign currency were spent on merchandise that was meant to be resold or bartered to peers, and sewing machines and other home devices became vital tools for domestic supply of manufactured goods and services as an alternative to the official, state-owned production sector (Anghelescu, Hodoiu, and Manolache 2003). Another example was the opportunity to either buy imported luxury goods and home appliances in hard currency from special shops located in Romania or acquire them directly on trips abroad. In this case, consumer goods that were not manufactured by socialist industry still counted as personal property even if they were potentially productive, to the frustration of communist officials, in terms of informal trade.

There were at least two advantages to the introduction of personal property rights by communist lawmakers. The first was the propaganda function of obscuring the existence and generation of private property within the

Romanian socialist economy. While small private property was a tolerated diminishing inheritance from the past regime, personal property was in fact newly acquired property under the communist regime. The second advantage was that, under this euphemism, private property could grow unhindered, allowing the socialist state to discharge some of its welfare responsibilities. The most common example was the granting of home building rights to the population, especially in the rural and peri-urban areas. While the state focused on the construction of for-rent housing estates in large urban areas, future owners could build individual homes with the support of the state.

Personal property rights regarding housing during communism did have some notable limitations. First, each nuclear family (wife, husband, and their children) had the right to a single home, a customary rule before 1968, when a law—substituted by a similar one in 1973—regarding the construction and distribution of apartments stated this basic right (Cosma 1974, 6). If it happened that a second house was received through inheritance, donation, exchange, or any other transfer, it had to be sold or donated within one year, otherwise the state or the nearest agricultural cooperative farm would confiscate it, with compensation (Ibid., 13; Chelcea 2004, 104). Since 1967, the right to build and own a second house for leisure purposes in resorts recognized as such by the administration was stated in a decree.[9] The main beneficiaries of this liberalization measure were central and local party and state officials. The interior space of a house and the maximum living area that a single person could occupy were also limited and regulated. Consequently, any space that exceeded the norms of various home categories had to be rented at fixed prices under the supervision of state institutions.

Despite these limitations, it seemed that a shift from an extreme collectivist and revolutionary standpoint (*all goods belong to the people*) to a temperate *personal property* after Stalinism was equivalent to the rehabilitation of some individual rights—but not kin networks (Chelcea 2004, 119)—in home ownership. At the same time, the revolutionary nationalization of private property was not abolished. It was substituted with the vague notion of expropriation for the "public good" (Ibid., 104), which retained nationalization's role as a lever of political control and which was put into practice in an arbitrary and abusive manner during the 1970s and 1980s.

There are countless cases of *comfort goods* that people were simply banned from owning or using, in spite of the official rhetoric. Furthermore, with the state being the only producer of goods and services, the communist authorities could simply cease production of undesirable commodities. For instance, from 1983 individuals owning a typewriter had to register with the police.[10] The process of approval was so arduous that many people simply abandoned the idea. The multiplication of documents could only be accomplished in specialized state-owned units. New, domestic, or imported typewriters were not available. As popular dissatisfaction with the communist regime grew, the ultimately political motivation behind measures of this sort appears obvious.[11]

The attitude of political leaders toward home ownership changed with a large-scale industrialization process and ensuing urbanization that started in the 1970s. The housing capacity of cities expanded as extensive programs of demolition and construction of new apartment buildings were put in practice. As a result, between 1948 and 1989 the proportion of urban population within the total population increased from 23 percent to 53 percent. Romania's urban landscape changed drastically as large neighborhoods of state-owned, multi-story apartment blocks developed. In general, rental accommodation was provided near factories and industrial plants that concentrated a large labor force. Although permitted, very few apartments in newly built blocks were available for sale. At the last stages of communism, private home ownership was severely limited in cities, with the local police in charge of approving migration toward urban areas. Communist leaders' decisions on forced urbanization (called systematization [*sistematizare*]) and the concentration of Romania's population in state-owned dwellings perfectly served their ideological and political ends, making it possible to watch the citizens. In fact, starting with housing nationalization and family relocation in early 1950s and continuing with the industrialization and urbanization in the 1970s, a large-scale social engineering process was put in place with the aim of creating "the new man" (Comisia Prezidenţială 2006, 617).

During the 1970s, legal changes were made in pursuit of the political objective of "restraining and abolishing private property" (stated in Article 11 of the Constitution of 1952), with the ownership and transfer of agricultural and residential land becoming even more restrictive. Communist-forced urban *systematization* brought about a large-scale program of demolition and reconstruction of villages and cities, methodically obliterating the identity of the past. The Law on the Systematization of Territory, Urban, and Rural Localities, as well as the Law on Agricultural Real Estate, both passed in 1974, forbade the alienation of property, practically removing land from general civil circulation, its only lawful method of acquirement being legal inheritance. Furthermore, in case of construction, the land parcel under buildings would become state property, the acquirer of the building obtaining the right to use the land for the entire duration of the building (Diaconu 2011, 200).

Owning precious metals and foreign currencies was severely disapproved from the earliest stages of communism. After a few rounds of mandatory surrender and confiscation of gold and art pieces, especially from ethnic minorities during or immediately after the war, a dedicated law provided the legal framework of owning and trading these items.[12] Accordingly, owning precious metals, jewels, and art pieces was deemed legal; trading these items was also legal provided that the acquisition was not made for future sale.

Owning precious metals in all other forms (such as bullion, wire, etc.) became unlawful, with the legal obligation for owners to sell these items to the state. Owning and circulating foreign currency was strictly prohibited from 1960, foreign currency holders being compelled to surrender it to the state bank in exchange for domestic currency at a predetermined rate.

MIXED PROPERTY/JOINT ENTERPRISES

Socialist Romania established joint international business ventures in trade and industrial production. The rationale of openness toward capitalist-socialist cooperation was not only pragmatic, but also political. Romania would have access to high-end technology and expert knowledge in a less expensive way than directly importing them, while maintaining its sovereignty, as the communist regime was obsessed with the principle of *non-interference with internal affairs of other countries*, targeted at former colonial powers and also at the Soviet Union and the Comecon. In return, foreign capitalist investors were allowed to outsource their material and labor supply in traditionally protectionist communist countries such as Romania.

Control of the joint enterprises established in Romania was achieved through state ownership of at least 51 percent of shares, the compliance with national laws (i.e., with the socialist system), and the correlation of the enterprise plans with the national five-year and annual plans. As a result, it was stressed that joint enterprises, although they were international organizations *sensu stricto*, were not a matter of international law, but subject to the national civil law of the country in which the enterprise was established. For joint enterprises with Romanian share majorities established abroad (in countries of the *Third World*), the downside of this principle was that these had to comply to other jurisdictions, a compromise that was outweighed by the economic gains of the stakeholders and by preferential measures triggered by ample diplomatic actions by the Romanian state (Deteşan 1972; Florescu 1977; Rucăreanu 1976).

The Romanian concept of joint enterprise (*societate mixtă*—mixed company) was defined as the bringing together of national (state) and foreign (private or state) capital, thus excluding the participation of virtually nonexistent Romanian private capital.[13] Moreover, foreign private ownership was not recognized as such, as the resulting joint enterprise was considered a socialist shareholding enterprise. Protectionist tax measures were aiming at keeping profits inside the country, while profits themselves were taxed internally with a reasonable rate (30 percent) in order to encourage the establishment of joint enterprises on Romanian soil. The state maintained its sovereignty over natural resources and land, the latter being leased but not sold to the enterprise.

The communist leadership was particularly sensitive toward the origins of these enterprises because of the precedent of *SovRoms*—Soviet companies with a significant exploitative and colonial characteristic that operated in Romania during the late 1940s and the early 1950s under the guise of joint enterprises.

The legal and institutional framework was provided in March 1971 with a new law on foreign trade, followed by a decree regarding the establishment, organization, and functioning of mixed companies in Romania, issued in November 1972. Prior to this, Czechoslovakia and Yugoslavia had introduced similar joint ventures in 1963 and 1967, respectively. The Romanian initiative was inspired by these models and it also capitalized on the recognition of international joint enterprises by the Comecon in 1971, which helped the Romanian communist leadership ensure against a possible Soviet objection. By 1976, only six industrial joint enterprises were established in Romania, whereas external cooperation—mainly with *third world* countries—amounted to 27 industrial and agricultural enterprises and 33 trade enterprises (Rucăreanu 1976, 17). Hence, Romania—a country challenged by the problems of its heavy industrialization drive such as the shortage of raw materials and hard currency—tried to replicate a Western outsourcing pattern.

Both government and party officials were concerned about the notion of the mixed enterprise and its ideological implications. Although initially Ceauşescu whose nationalist and autarkic agenda was well known was not in favor of joint enterprises in Romania, he finally accepted the principle of reciprocity, admitting that a one-sided approach (i.e., exclusive establishment of joint enterprises with Romanian majority participation abroad) would not be satisfactory for economic partners in the long run. His main concern remained foreign *capital infiltration*; he therefore ordered supplementary control provisions, despite the fact that the Romanian side was the majority shareholder of each joint enterprise. Ceauşescu distanced himself from the Yugoslav model of self-management, which he saw as having negative political implications, whereas the notion of a mixed company did not. The principle of management only could be the *khozraschet* (the customary Soviet method of economic accounting/profitability) and not actual self-management. Entrepreneurial independence was never permitted in Romania during communism.[14] In addition, he distinguished between existing state enterprises and future joint enterprises, mentioning—and again keeping in mind the Yugoslav counterexample—that it was unacceptable that foreign investors would have the right to deal with any of the former (ANIC—Cancelarie 1971, 12, 16). In addition, joint enterprises would become Romanian state property *in integrum* after a few years' time (10 to 15 years).

Some members of the *nomenklatura* were against the recognition of the presence of foreign capitalist private property inside Romania and expressly asked for the obliteration of such ideologically incorrect phrases from the normative texts on Romanian socialist ownership. In one of the few known debates that took place behind closed doors within the party leadership, Aurel Vijoli, a party economist and former minister of finance between 1957 and 1968, argued that in order to avoid putting together socialists and capitalists under the same form of ownership, the Yugoslav legal norms did not use common-property relations and that instead they saw property as solely Yugoslav (Ibid., 11). Leonte Răutu, one of the vice-premiers and a prominent party ideologue, and Emil Bodnăraş, a member of the Politburo, complained that the new provisions of the draft foreign trade law of 1971 were unconstitutional, but their voices were not heard, as Nicolae Ceauşescu explicitly diminished the relevance of the constitutional text and thus acknowledged that the communist regime was not restrained to take arbitrary measures (Ibid., 14–15). As long as the Politburo still included members that were not promoted by Ceauşescu himself, debate—scarce as it had been—was still possible. As soon as the remaining elite members of the former leadership of Gheorghiu-Dej were ousted or retired (during the period 1965–1974), the center of decision-making was subdued by Ceauşescu, and his ideas became the only authority in regard to political economy.

CONCLUSION

The Romanian communist regime remained one of the most repressive and autarkic in the Soviet Bloc. Although the living conditions of all Romanians, workers included, were deteriorating during the 1980s, no reform discussions or actions took place. Run by the Ceauşescu family, the Romanian Communist Party led the country without any real internal opposition. As a result, a researcher on the history of economic thought in Romania during communism is confronted with a classic needle-in-the-haystack puzzle when trying to find debates regarding the forms of ownership that might have taken place within the party leadership.

Official academic discussions never passed beyond dull ideological stereotypes. Romanian intellectuals, cut off from any source of information originating in the free world, could only wish for *perestroika*-like reforms. Political economists, with very few exceptions, were eager to embrace the status quo and propagate the official party line. In academia, the standard economics textbooks were usually divided into two volumes, titled *Economics: The Political Economy of Socialism* and *Economics: Contemporary Capitalism*. The textbook dedicated to capitalism bluntly expressed disagreement with the principles of a free market in such sections like "Capitalist Property—The Base of Capitalist Exploitation" and "The Generalized Crisis of Capitalism" (N. Constantinescu 2000), whereas one of the few economics textbooks for higher education was titled *Political Economy: The Economic Policy of the Romanian Communist Party*. All manuals of instruction in the sphere of social sciences remained structurally unchanged from the early 1970s to the fall of communism, with ever-growing sections covering official speeches and directives.

There were virtually no academic or popular debates concerning the forms of ownership in socialist Romania. Under the guise of a debate, the only discussions that took place lauded all the initiatives of the regime. This lack of critical expression in the Romanian public sphere had at least two main causes. First, most experts and scientists rallied around the communist leadership in order to obtain their share of favors and privileges within the system. Those who dared not to explicitly support the ideology and policies of the regime had a hard time coping with pressures and even oppressive administrative measures from their superiors. Second, from the late 1960s on Ceauşescu was frequently and even exclusively cited in both scholarly and journalistic literature. The Academy of Economic Sciences and the party school, the Ştefan Gheorghiu Academy, endorsed his implausible theoretical skills with academic titles. Inside the academic community, references to Ceauşescu's works were equivalent to declarations of conformity. For example, after he made an ambiguous statement in June 1982, denying the equivalence between state property and public property (*proprietate obştească*—people's property) without giving further details, the conventional socialist theory on property was put back on agenda with great effort and only after several years (Müller 2013, 229).

One modest episode of academic debate questioned the official party line in the economic sphere toward the end of the 1980s (Aligică 2002, 155). In 1985, Daniel Dăianu, a young economist and researcher at the Institute of National Economy, managed to publish in a Romanian academic journal an article entitled "A Model of Immiserising Growth" in which he sought to demonstrate under the lee of an extremely technical language and mathematical modeling the harmful consequences of Ceauşescu's policy of rapid and full repayment of foreign debt. Based on Jagdish Bhagwati's concept of immiserizing growth and drawing from the ideas of János Kornai laid down in his *Economics of Shortage*, the study argued that the Romanian economy acutely needed reforms and that increasing the productive capacity of state-owned enterprises would ease the social consequences of foreign debt repayment. This happened shortly after Dăianu and Vasile Pilat had published a study on the problems of socialist economies in which they criticized the mechanisms of socialist economies, with no specific reference to the Romanian case (Dăianu and Pilat 1984). A handful of other economists joined these "rudiments of public debate," as Dăianu put it, all of whom bore the consequences of their reckless act. The discussion achieved some international notoriety. It is worth noticing that none of these authors openly cast any doubt on the preeminence of the socialist property, nor did they propose any concrete policy measure for ownership reform. The authors made no connections between the acute crisis of the Romanian economy they were witnessing and the regime of ownership. In fact, rather than being an open critique of the fundament of socialism, this chapter of economic debate under communism proves the lack of academic challenge to the far-reaching idea of socialist property.

During the 1980s, in spite of widespread shortages in the context of the systemic crisis of the command economy, private businesses were not permitted to develop—at least in the formal sector of the economy. Reforming state-owned entities and its most radical form—their privatization—became a debate issue only after the Revolution of December 1989. It is no surprise that the Romanian public was not ready to understand the crucial role of private property in a market economy. In fact, the structural transformation of Romania's economy started with entirely different issues like the liberalization of prices (November 1990), restructuring state-owned enterprises, and the introduction of capitalist-like social protection. The implicit assumption followed by early political decision-makers seems to have been the problematic yet common idea that "it is the competition that matters, not ownership." Foreign capital was also met with serious resistance by an unsettled working class proudly shouting, "We are not selling out our country." However, against this background it does come as a surprise that 20 years into capitalist reforms, the private sector accounts for over 70 percent of the economy today.

NOTES

1. *Manifesto of the Communist Party*, Chapter 2: Proletarians and Communists, 22.

2. The authors wish to thank professors Bogdan Murgescu, Paul Dragoş Aligică, and Costea Munteanu for their helpful comments and constant encouragement.

3. The text of the Constitution of 1948 does not explicitly state the existence of cooperative ownership. However, it does assert in Article 5 that the cooperative organizations (*organizaţii cooperatiste*), alongside the state and private individuals (*particulari*), may own the means of production.

4. For instance, a distinctive feature of true cooperation is its voluntary nature, whereas it was the massive use of coercion that set off the formation of cooperative property during the collectivization process.

5. Derived from the Turkish *kibar* (polite, gentle).

6. From the Romanian *muncă de lămurire* (persuasion or enlightening work)—a new phrase coined by the Party in the early stages of communism.

7. It may be instructive to mention here the wording of Decree No. 115/1959 on the liquidation of the last remains of the exploitation of man by man in agriculture, with the aim of continuously raising the material standard of living of working peasantry and developing socialist construction. In the preamble it is stated that "in the process of the socialist transformation of agriculture, a socialist conscience of the working peasantry is formed, its energy and determination to fight for its own good and the common good of the people rise. From its members, a new peasantry is rising [...] representing a huge force for socialist construction, a bright example which attracts the whole peasantry on the way of socialist agriculture." Consequently, the act made it illegal for the *chiaburs* "to lease agricultural land or to exploit external work."

8. Decree No. 92/1950 regarding the nationalization of real estate.

9. See Decree No. 713/1967 concerning the building of personal property houses—for leisure or tourism purposes—by citizens in spas and other tourism settlements.

10. See Decree No. 98/1983 regarding the legal status of copying machines, supplies for copying documents, and typewriters.

11. With the shortage of goods being the most pervasive phenomenon across all socialist economies, it is a matter of historical debate if certain items were lacking for political, economic, or other reasons. However, given the *awakening potential* of some goods (like typewriters, radio receivers, long distance TV antennas, etc.), it is not hazardous to assume that the lack of those goods was the result of politically motivated and purposeful decisions.

12. See Decree No. 210/1960 regarding the status of foreign means of payment, precious metals, and gemstones.

13. Domestic private business consisted mainly of households with adjacent gardens (along with pastures and livestock in the mountain regions), which accounted for approximately 10 percent of Romania's agriculture, and of artisans' workshops.

14. The maximum degree of autonomy was defined in Romanian communist parlance by *autoconducere* (auto-management), which remained on paper due to the widespread practice of top-down decision-making.

BIBLIOGRAPHY

Aligică, Paul Dragoş. 2002. "Economics—Romania." In *Three Social Science Disciplines in Central and Eastern Europe: Handbook on Economics, Political Science and Sociology (1989–2001)*, edited by Max Kaase, Vera Sparschuh, and Agnieszka Wenninger, 152–67. Berlin: GESIS—Leibniz-Institut für Sozialwissenschaften.

Anghelescu, Şerban, Ioana Hodoiu, and Cosmin Manolache, eds. 2003. *Mărturii orale: Anii '80 şi bucureştenii* [Oral testimonies: The 1980s and the Bucharestians]. Bucharest: Paideia.

ANIC—Cancelarie [National Historical Archives—Central Service]. 1971. Fond C.C. al P.C.R.—secţia Cancelarie, file 32. Bucharest.

Boettke, Peter J., and Peter T. Leeson. 2003. "Is the Transition to the Market Too Important to be Left to the Market?" Working Paper 5, Mercatus Center, George Mason University. Available online, accessed April 24, 2017: http://mercatus.org/sites/default/files/publication/Is_the_Transition_to_the_Market_too_Important_to_be_Left_to_the_Market_-_Working_Paper.pdf.

Cazan, Marius-Traian. 2014. *Dinamica habitatului urban în Bucureşti, 1948–1989: Construcţii, dotări, percepţii* [The Dynamics of Urban Habitat in Bucharest, 1948–1989: Buildings, Facilities, Perceptions]. PhD diss., University of Bucharest.

Chelcea, Liviu. 2004. *State, Kinship and Urban Transformations during and after Housing Nationalization (Bucharest, Romania, 1945–2004)*. PhD diss., University of Michigan.

Cleja, A., and M. Trăistaru. 1975. "Dialectica societăţii socialiste: Făurirea societăţii socialiste multilateral dezvoltate" [Dialectics of Socialist Society: Building the Multilaterally Developed Socialist Society]. In *Curs de socialism ştiinţific* [Scientific Socialism Textbook], edited by Institutul Politehnic Bucureşti, Catedra de Socialism Ştiinţific, 289–313. Ediţia a doua. Bucharest: Editura Politică.

Comisia Prezidenţială pentru Analiza Dictaturii Comuniste din România [The Presidential Commission for the Analysis of the Communist Dictatorship in Romania]. 2006. *Raport final* [Final report]. Available online, accessed April 24, 2017: http://www.presidency.ro/static/ordine/RAPORT_FINAL_CPADCR.pdf.

Constantinescu, Mitiţă. 1925. *L'évolution de la propriété rurale et la réforme agraire en Roumanie* [The Evolution of Rural Land and Agrarian Reform in Romania]. Bucharest: Cultura Naţională.

———. 1943. *Politică economică aplicată* [Applied Economic Policy]. Bucharest: Tiparul Românesc.

Constantinescu, Nicolae et al. 1985. *Economie politică: Capitalismul contemporan* [Economics: Contemporary Capitalism]. Bucharest: Editura Didactică şi Pedagogică.

———. 2000. *Istoria economică a României* [The Economic History of Romania]. Vol. 2. Bucharest: Editura Economică.

Constitution of the People's Republic of Romania. 1948. Available online, accessed April 24, 2017: http://legislatie.resurse-pentru-democratie.org/constitutie/constitutia-republicii-populare-romane-1948.php.

Constitution of the People's Republic of Romania. 1952. Available online, accessed April 24, 2017: http://legislatie.resurse-pentru-democratie.org/constitutie/constitutia-republicii-populare-romane-1952.php.

Constitution of the Socialist Republic of Romania. 1965. Available online, accessed April 24, 2017: http://legislatie.resurse-pentru-democratie.org/constitutie/constitutia-republicii-socialiste-romania-1965.php.

Cosma, Doru. 1974. *Regimul juridic al locuinţelor proprietate personală* [The Legal Status of Personal Property Dwellings]. Bucharest: Editura Ştiinţifică.

Dăianu, Daniel. 1985. "Un model de creştere oneroasă" [A Model of Immiserising Growth]. *Revista Economică* 21: 19–20.

Dăianu, Daniel, and Vasile Pilat. 1984. "Probleme ale funcţionării economiilor socialiste" [Problems in the Functioning of Socialist Economies]. *Revue Roumaine d'Etudes Internationales* 3: 34–45.

Deteşan Al. 1972. *Societăţi comerciale—societăţi mixte: formă eficientă de cooperare internaţională* [Trading Companies and Joint Enterprises: Effective Form of International Cooperation]. Supplement of *Viaţa Economică*. Bucharest: Întreprinderea Poligrafică Informaţia.

Diaconu, Ana-Maria. 2011. "Current Aspects Regarding Property Judicial Transfer." *Annals Constantin Brâncuşi U. Târgu Jiu Juridical Sci. Series* 4: 199–206.

Florescu, Grigore. 1977. *Societăţile mixte în România: Nouă formă de cooperare internaţională* [Joint Enterprises in Romania: New Form of International Cooperation]. Bucharest: Litera.

Gheorghiu-Dej, Gheorghe. 1953. *Sarcinile Partidului Muncitoresc Român în lupta pentru întărirea alianţei clasei muncitoare cu ţărănimea muncitoare şi pentru transformarea socialistă a agriculturii: Raport la şedinţa plenară a Comitetului Central al P.M.R. din 3-5 martie 1949* [Tasks of the Romanian Workers' Party in the Struggle for the Strengthening of the Alliance of the Working Class with the Working Peasantry and for the Socialist Transformation of Agriculture: Report to the Plenary Meeting of the Central Committee of the RWP, March 3–5, 1949]. Bucharest: Editura pentru Literatură Politică.

———. 1959. *Articole şi cuvântări—decembrie 1955—iulie 1958* [Articles and Speeches—December 1955—July 1958]. Bucharest: Editura Politică.

Institutul Central de Cercetări Economice. 1983. *Progresul economic al României socialiste în concepţia preşedintelui Nicolae Ceauşescu* [The Economic Progress of Socialist Romania in the View of President Nicolae Ceauşescu]. Bucharest: Editura Politică.

Institutul Politehnic Bucureşti, Catedra de Socialism Ştiinţific. 1975. *Curs de socialism ştiinţific*. Ediţia a doua. [Scientific Socialism Textbook. Second edition]. Bucharest: Editura Politică.

Iordachi, Constantin, and Dorin Dobrincu. 2014. "The Collectivization of Agriculture in Romania, 1949–1962." In *The Collectivization of Agriculture in Communist Eastern Europe: Comparison and Entanglements*, edited by Constantin Iordachi and Arnd Bauerkämper, 251–92. Budapest: Central European University Press.

Kligman, Gail, and Katherine Verdery. 2011. *Peasants under Siege: The Collectivization of Romanian Agriculture, 1949–1962*. New Haven: Princeton University Press.

Kornai, János. 1992. *The Socialist System: The Political Economy of Communism*. London: Oxford University Press.

Lege 1948. Legea nr. 119 pentru naţionalizarea întreprinderilor industriale, bancare, de asigurări, miniere şi de transporturi [Law for the Nationalization of Industrial Enterprises, Banks, Insurance Companies, Mining Companies, and Transportation Companies]. *Monitorul Oficial*. Part I, No. 133, June 11, 1948.

Lege 1950. Decretul nr. 92 pentru naţionalizarea unor imobile [Decree for the Nationalization of Real Estate]. *Buletinul Oficial*, Part I, No. 36, April 20, 1950.

Lege 1959. Decretul nr. 115 pentru lichidarea rămăşiţelor oricăror forme de exploatare a omului de către om în agricultură, în scopul ridicării continue a nivelului de trai material şi cultural al ţărănimii muncitoare şi al dezvoltării construcţiei socialiste [Decree for the Liquidation of the Last Remains of the Exploitation of Man by Man in Agriculture, with the Aim of Continuously Raising the Material Standard of Living of Working Peasantry and Developing Socialist Construction]. *Buletinul Oficial*, Part I, No. 10, March 30, 1959.

Lupulescu, Dumitru. 1967. *Dreptul de proprietate personală* [The Right to Personal Property]. Bucharest: Editura Ştiinţifică.

———. 1975. *Construirea şi cumpărarea de locuinţe proprietate personală cu sprijinul statului* [Construction and Purchase of Private Dwellings with the aid of the State]. Bucharest: Editura Ştiinţifică şi Enciclopedică.

Madgearu, Virgil. 1930. *Rumania's New Economic Policy*. London: P. S. King & Son.

Malinschi, Vasile. 1975. *Profesorul Virgil Madgearu (1887–1940): contribuţii la dezvoltarea gîndirii economice* [Professor Virgil Madgearu (1887–1940): Contributions to the Development of Economic Thinking]. Bucharest: Editura Academiei RSR.

Marx, Karl, and Friedrich Engels. 1848. *Manifesto of the Communist Party*. Available online, accessed April 24, 2017: https://www.marxists.org/archive/marx/works/download/pdf/Manifesto.pdf.

Moldovan, Roman. 1965. "The Scientific Basis of Socialist Economic Construction in the Romanian People's Republic." *Revue Roumaine des Sciences Sociales: Série de Sciences Économiques* 1: 3–15.

Müller, Dietmar. 2013. "The Concept of *Property* in Romania's Economic-Legal History." In *Key Concepts of Romanian History: Alternative Approaches to Socio-Political Languages*, edited by Victor Neumann and Armin Heinen, 183–222. Budapest: CEU Press.

Roberts, Henry L. 1951. *Romania: Political Problems of an Agrarian State*. New Haven: Yale University Press.

Rucăreanu, Ion. 1976. "Noţiunea, fundamentarea şi principiile reglementării societăţilor mixte, cu participare străină, în Republica Socialistă România" [Notion, Basis and Principles of Regulation of Joint Ventures in the Socialist Republic of Romania]. In *Societăţile mixte constituite în Republica Socialistă România: Fundamentare, caractere, constituire* [Joint Enterprises Established in the Socialist Republic of Romania: Basis, Characteristics, Establishment], edited by Institutul de Cercetări Juridice, 9–32. Bucharest: Editura Academiei Republicii Socialiste România.

Simons, William B. 1980. "Introduction." In *The Constitutions of the Communist World*, edited by William B. Simons, xi–xvi. Alphen aan den Rijn, The Netherlands: Sijthoff & Noordhoff.

Socaciu, Emanuel M. 2013. "Applying Taking Clauses Analysis to Communist Nationalization of Houses in Romania." In *Applied Ethics: Perspectives from Romania*, edited by Valentin Mureşan and Majima Shunzo, 176–90. Center for Applied Ethics and Philosophy: Hokkaido University, Sapporo.

Şandru, Dorel. 2005. "Colectivizarea agriculturii şi problema agrară: repere social-politice" [The Collectivization of Agriculture and the Agrarian Problem]. In *Ţărănimea şi puterea: procesul de colectivizare a agriculturii în România 1949–1962* [Peasantry and Power: The Process of Collectivization of Agriculture in Romania 1949–1962], edited by Dorin Dobrincu and Constantin Iordachi, 45–65. Iaşi: Polirom.

Chapter 8

Fighting Dogma, Rescuing Doctrine

Toward a History of Ownership Debates in Soviet Economic Literature

Denis Melnik and Oleg Ananyin

Soviet economic thought typically was (and is) compared with neoclassical economics. Sovietologists usually tried to understand and assess Soviet economic thought as a description of reality. On the contrary, it was aimed at the construction of a new social system since its origins. Before the October Revolution of 1917, in Russia the normative message of socialist thought was conveyed through a critique of capitalist (i.e., really existing) society. Future society was considered to be a result of a long process of development and struggles within the existing capitalist order. The situation changed after the revolution when the real social system was to be understood and managed on the basis of that doctrine. Sooner or later, communist doctrine had to confront reality.

Marxists hailed Marxian political economy as an all-powerful means to change the world. The October Revolution was taken as a proof of their belief. But the remarks on the communist future scattered through the texts of the *classics* did not add up to anything like a comprehensive road map. The lack of such a program made political economy a *political* subject. In fact, theoretical debates echoed the struggle for leadership within the Russian revolutionary movement from its inception. After the revolution the stakes increased: the leaders of just one of several formerly competing and persecuted groups turned into holders of real political power. Around 1922, the stabilization of the new Soviet state allowed for an investigation of its long-term economic prospects. Thus, the project for establishing a brand new field of studies, Political Economy of Socialism (henceforth, PES), was initiated. Lenin's illness and subsequent death in 1924 opened the way for ruthless power games, and the stakes in theory building increased tremendously.

The methodological foundations of the PES project in Russia were laid before the 1917 Revolution. In 1910, Aleksandr Bogdanov and Ivan Skvortsov-Stepanov published the first volume of the *Course of Political Economy* (the second volume would follow in several printings in 1919–1920), where they outlined the so-called broad version of political economy. They elaborated on the line of argumentation advanced by Friedrich Engels in *Anti-Dühring* and proposed a historical notion of political economy as a science relevant not only to the capitalist mode of production but also to preceding and forthcoming modes of production. Their approach acquired important ideological and political significance in the postrevolutionary years, in contrast to the *narrow version of political economy* promoted in the immediate aftermath of the October Revolution by Nikolai Bukharin and other Bolshevik authors. They claimed that the revolution freed the economic ties of the capitalistic order, and the building of communism was the subject of political will and engineer-like management of economy. Thus, the economic analysis of postrevolutionary society was rendered unnecessary. The *narrow version* also was supported by a theoretical reconstruction of Marx's theory of value as proposed by Isaak Rubin (1972) in his *Essays in Marx's Theory of Value*. The clash between the two approaches culminated with Skvortsov-Stepanov's (1925) paper and the subsequent debates, during which the historian Mikhail Pokrovsky sided with Skvortsov-Stepanov but virtually all other leading participants supported the *narrow version*. At the end of the 1920s, under Stalin's supervision, the *narrow version* was condemned and a remake of the *broad version* (purged of many original ideas proposed mainly by Bogdanov) was elevated to the ideological canon (cf. Gloveli 2010, 113–17). This canon legitimized subsequent attempts to develop the analysis of Soviet economy as a distinctive field and made it compulsory from an ideological point of view.

It is important to stress the projective and normative nature of that enterprise. Even if it cannot be compared in scope and nature to some *material* projects of the Soviet state, the endeavor to create a new science for building a new world was ambitious nonetheless. However, Soviet economists had a troublesome task to reconcile (a) the normative prescriptions for building a new society, (b) Marx's legacy assuming that the emergence of a new society should have been the natural outcome of the preceding development of a mature capitalist economy, (c) the dogmas of the official ideology (later to be called *Marxism-Leninism*), and (d) the real state of affairs in the Soviet economy.

PES was (and is) often reproached for its total estrangement from reality. But this was its purpose, not a fault. As long as the task of building a new world was perceived as feasible, precisely the discrepancy between the normative ideals and reality continued to fuel debates among various currents within PES and to inflame zealous efforts of many among the profession to provide solid foundations for society to be, in the world they lived in, by means of analytical instruments they possessed. Construction of a distinctive discourse was part of the PES project, and perhaps the most accomplished one. Accompanying language games were not always lip-service to dogma: while carefully following the established rhetorical canon, Soviet economists were able to convey theoretical messages. But to the extent that PES deserves serious attention, those messages must be deciphered.

The theme of ownership was at the center of the PES enterprise. In line with Marx's view of history, the 1917 Revolution, like all other major political revolutions before, was conceived as a shift in the dominant form of ownership and a matter of class struggle. Soviet political economy presented itself as the direct continuation of *classical teaching*. As such it interpreted the future socialist society as a negation of capitalism, that is, of a system based on private property and composed of antagonistic social classes. Any fact concerning ownership had to be reconciled with this imperative. And any recognition of non-socialist forms of ownership within socialist economy implied a problem: it could mean either a flaw in theory or the absence of the right foundations for building communist society.[1]

CHALLENGES AND RESPONSES IN OWNERSHIP STUDIES: A CHRONOLOGY

Background

In the ideological landscape of pre-revolutionary Russia a romantic trend that referenced communal ownership by Russian peasants (*obshchina*) as a benchmark was influential on both aristocratic and democratic wings of the political spectrum. The latter was initiated in the late 1830s by representatives of two respective strands of thought: the national romantic Slavophil movement and the followers of French utopian socialism (Stein 1948, Ch. 4).[2] The tradition started with the idealization of communal ownership of Russian peasants, which was seen as an antidote to proletarization and leverage to maintain (or to impose) a non-capitalist order. The *obshchina* was conceived as a really existing implementation of the *phalanstère* (hence, the nucleus of communism). Communal ownership within the Russian village constituted its core institution, and despite all major changes, the influence of that institution was still present at the time of the 1917 Revolution. Yet, the successors to this view tended to be more cautious. Many of them did not neglect the backward features of existing communal forms of economic organization; nor did they claim that socialism in Russia was already given in those forms. Instead they considered the existence of the *obshchina* (and the *artel*) as an argument in favor of the non-capitalist path of development of the Russian economy and a precondition for socialist modernization. Such writers as Nikolai Danielson and Vasily Vorontsov insisted that, despite emerging elements of capitalism, a successful capitalist modernization of Russia following the Western pattern was not feasible (Danielson 1899; Vorontsov 2008). They believed that communal ownership could serve as an institutional basis for a viable alternative to capitalist modernization. In the wake of the revolutionary events of 1905, *Narodniks* fiercely criticized agrarian reforms aiming at the dissolution of the *obshchina* and at the implementation of private property in rural Russia—reforms launched by premier Stolypin in 1906. The ideas of agrarian socialism influenced the program of the Socialist Revolutionary Party that would rise in the turbulent months between the February and the October Revolutions of 1917 to become the most popular political party in Russia. Its main proposal was the abolition of the property of the landlords (*pomeshchiki*) and the socialization of Russia's agricultural lands.

In the 1890s the theoretical and political propositions of agrarian socialism were challenged by a group of young Marxist intellectuals who included Peter Struve, Mikhail Tugan-Baranovsky, Vladimir Ulyanov (Lenin), and Sergei Bulgakov among others. They claimed that Russia had already undergone a standard capitalist development and that no path toward socialism existed other than through capitalism, that is, through the development of industry and the dissolution of *obshchina* regarded as a remnant of feudalism. Thus, Lenin's *The Development of Capitalism in Russia* (1899) provided statistical data and theoretical arguments intended to show that the time of the village commune in Russia had expired due to its inclusion in the capitalist market, causing a class differentiation among the rural population and the emergence of a rural proletariat. Thus, it was the latter that was regarded as a potential driving force of revolutionary activity and an ally to urban industrial workers, while the peasantry in general was regarded as a class of small proprietors (inherently alien to the ideal of communism). This was the germ of the Bolshevik approach to rural ownership, which culminated in the drama of collectivization in the 1930s.

However, the group already split into inimical factions at the threshold of the 20th century: Struve's liberalism, Bulgakov's Orthodox Christian socialism, Tugan-Baranovsky's cooperative socialism (resembling that of European social democracy), and a *Bolshevik* radical current headed by Lenin.

The liberal notion of the immunity of property rights as the basis for civil society entered Russia with the spread of the Enlightenment in the 18th century. At the beginning of the 19th century the idea's impact was reinforced in the wake of reform-minded projects that proliferated in the first years of the reign of Alexander I. The government promoted the translation of contemporary economic literature (including the *Wealth of Nations*) and the teaching of political economy, while nascent public opinion was very receptive to some aspects of economic liberalism. However, in Russia the notion of the immunity of property rights was connected mainly with debates on serfdom and the *peasant question*. The connection persisted throughout the 19th century and until the revolutions of 1917. Among the *enlightened* public (of whom the bureaucratic elite was a part), serfdom was increasingly regarded as morally wrong and politically incorrect. Economic liberalism furnished that attitude with a direct link between the immunity of property rights and capital accumulation. Serfdom was seen as a cause of economic backwardness. The plea for an abolition of serfdom was an obvious outcome of the discourse.

A new wave of debates on the *peasant question* started in the late 1850s prior to the abolition of serfdom in 1861. Abolition effectively strengthened the communal form of ownership in the Russian village. The liberal strand of thought, represented by Ivan Vernadsky, Boris Chicherin, and other figures, played a significant part in the debates before and after 1861. It gained considerable prominence among academics and some high-ranking officials (but not the intelligentsia) during the post-abolition period. Yet it did not have a direct impact on policy until 1906, when Stolypin's agrarian reforms attempted a major institutional restructuring of Russia's agricultural sector on the basis of private ownership. During the same period the *Constitutional Democratic Party* emerged to represent a liberal agenda in Russian politics. The liberal tradition was halted with the October Revolution: several articles published in the Petersburg journal *Economist* by Boris Brutskus in defense of *economic freedom* and sharply criticizing the postrevolutionary Soviet economy led the author in 1922 to the famous *Philosophy Steamer* for political exiles (see Chamberlain 2007).

THE FIRST POSTREVOLUTIONARY DECADE

The process of large-scale nationalization of the means of production was launched in January 1918 with nationalization of the banking system and the merchant navy. While a civil war raged in Russia, the process quickened its pace, and a centralized system of direct management of the economy was created by the end of the year. The process brought with it two major challenges, both practical and theoretical: the first was to define the scope of nationalization or the boundaries of state ownership; the second was to design an internal governance structure based on stable rules. These challenges generated heated polemics among various factions of the revolutionary movement. Lenin outlined the initial responses to both challenges, but a real search for viable solutions only started later, when the active phase of the civil war was over and the military regime of so-called War Communism proved to be unworkable and was dismantled.

The response to the first challenge at this early stage of the revolution was predominantly defined by practical considerations: the scope of nationalization was a matter of the political union between winning political forces: the Bolsheviks and the Left Socialist Revolutionaries. One of the very first pieces of legislation, drafted by Lenin on the eve of the October uprising, was the famous *Decree on Land*, which met the demands of Left Socialist Revolutionaries: private ownership of land was abolished and land was *socialized*. This solution did not prevent the civil war but was crucial to the survival of the Soviet regime as it provided the initial support (or neutrality) of the rural population.

Lenin offered a theoretical response in his polemics with ultra-radicals (*Left Opposition*) within his own party, who insisted on the immediate socialization of the economy. Lenin instead advanced the concept of a multi-sectoral economy, implying the coexistence of several forms of ownership or *uklads* (sectors) during the transition period from capitalism to socialism (1918).[3] With the introduction of the New Economic Policy (NEP) in 1921, it was recognized that inter-sectoral relationships were to be based on market exchanges, that is, on commodity-money relations.

The analytical outcome that developed from this view during the industrialization debates of the 1920s was a two-sector economic model. Participants in the debates differed as to the economic (and political) means to ensure the sustainability of the socialist sector vis-à-vis its market counterpart. Bukharin argued in favor of *peaceful coexistence* between agricultural and industrial producers. Yevgeni Preobrazhensky insisted that industrialization could not be conceived as a balanced process and that it required the extensive use of the agricultural sector as a source of industrial investment. But they basically agreed that the only acceptable trend of development was the expanded production of socialist industry and the subsequent socialization of the agricultural sector (Bukharin and Preobrazhensky 1990).

The second challenge was interpreted as largely organizational. Arguing against the same *Left Opposition* demanding an intensification of nationalization, Lenin introduced the distinction between *nationalization* and *socialization* to stress that "we have nationalised, confiscated, beaten down and put down more *than we have had time to count.* The difference between socialisation and simple confiscation is that confiscation can be carried out by 'determination' alone, without the ability to calculate and distribute properly, *whereas socialisation cannot be brought about without this ability" (Lenin 1918). In The ABC of Communism*, a popular prospectus of the Bolshevik

Party's platform adopted in 1919, Bukharin and Preobrazhensky called "proletarian communism (or proletarian socialism)" "a huge cooperative commonwealth," specifying their definition in such a way as to demarcate their idea from the anarchist, Menshevik, and all other "deviations":

> The basis of communist society must be the social ownership of the means of production and exchange [...]. In such a social order, production will be organized. No longer will one enterprise compete with another; the factories, workshops, mines, and other productive institutions will all be subdivisions, as it were, of one vast people's workshop, which will embrace the entire national economy of production. It is obvious that so comprehensive an organization presupposes a general plan of production. [...] All the factories and workshops together with the whole of agricultural production are combined to form an immense cooperative enterprise [...]. Without a general plan, without a general directive system, and without careful calculation and book-keeping, there can be no organization. But in the communist social order, there is such a plan. (Bukharin and Preobrazhensky 1969, §19)

The New Economic Policy revised this view, at least, in relation to the transition period between capitalism and socialism. The slogan of "accounting and control" from 1918 was supplemented with the economic principle of *khozraschet*, according to which enterprises of the nationalized sector were required to be profitable or at least cover their costs. Interpretations of this principle varied from purely calculative to identical with the commercial accounting of capitalist firms (Sibirev 1983). Under the NEP, however, when price formation more or less reflected market conditions, the actual property rights of most state enterprises, at least in relation to their current economic activities, were not that different from those of cooperative and private firms.

This model of governance for the nationalized sector was shaped in polemics with the doctrine of self-management (*samoupravlenie*), a syndicalist project promoted by so-called Workers' Opposition. Its leaders (Aleksandr Shliapnikov, Aleksandra Kollontai, and others) sharply criticized the bureaucratization of the state and party apparatus and insisted on the transfer of the functions of economic management and organization from all levels to the trade unions (Shliapnikov 1921).

Lenin's final contribution to *classical* thought was contained in a series of short articles from 1923, especially in his notes "On Cooperation." By that time Lenin seemed to have become much more preoccupied with the dangers of bureaucratization and came to the conclusion that cooperative enterprises would be able to reconcile the economic imperatives behind the NEP and its political reliance on the working masses without losing sight of the socialist perspective:

> All we actually need under NEP is to organize the population of Russia in cooperative societies on a sufficiently large-scale, for we have now found the degree of combination of private interest, of private commercial interest, with state supervision and control of this interest, that degree of its subordination to the common interests which was formerly the stumbling block for very many socialists. Indeed, the power of the state over all large-scale means of production, political power in the hands of the proletariat, the alliance of this proletariat with the many millions of small and very small peasants, the assured proletarian leadership of the peasantry, etc.—is this not all that is necessary to build a complete socialist society out of co-operatives, out of co-operatives alone [...]. It is still not the building of socialist society, but it is all that is necessary and sufficient for it [...]. Under our present system, co-operative enterprises differ from private capitalist enterprises because they are collective enterprises, but do not differ from socialist enterprises if the land on which they are situated and the means of production belong to the state, i.e., the working class. (Lenin 1965, 468, 473)

A noteworthy novelty in this renewed vision of the future was Lenin's turn to the behavioral prerequisites of the transition to a new society: cooperative ownership could lead to socialism only in combination with a cultural revolution as a means to change peasants' behavior. He was looking for "means that are the simplest, easiest and most acceptable to the peasant," setting the task of "educational work among the peasants," the "economic object" of which was "to organize the [peasants] in cooperative societies" (Ibid.).

Faith in the cooperative idea was shared by the heirs of the *Narodnik* movement. A group of *neo-Narodnik* economists grouped around Aleksandr Chayanov also believed in the peaceful socialist transformation of the Russian peasant economy. But unlike most communist authors who presumed the subordinate position of the cooperative sector, Chayanov saw in the revolution the chance to build cooperative vertical structures uniting agricultural producers with retail and wholesale traders, processing industries, and suppliers, thus enhancing the market power of the peasants' associations vis-à-vis both market and state monopolies. He considered economic incentives generated by the market to be an accelerator of productivity growth in the largest sector of Russian economy, agriculture, creating a material basis for the socialist transformation of the country. Unsurprisingly, Chayanov's school was crushed by the political shift to collectivization, while its leader and some of his colleagues became victims of the purges.

By the end of 1920s a vision of the future society was still far from clear, yet it became tied to the *classical legacy* composed of remarks by Marx, Engels, and Lenin. The final stage, *full-fledged socialism* or communism was still conceived in line with the above-cited picture from *The ABC of*

Communism, that is, as "a vast workshop [...] embracing the entire national economy of production," but the views on the preceding stage(s) varied. Thus the *classical legacy* served as a benchmark for any research into the political economy of socialism, while its ambiguities left space for its various interpretations. These were the rules of the game or the framework within which subsequent discussions among Soviet economists were to develop.

1930s–1950s: THE LONG ROAD TOWARD THE TEXTBOOK

In the economic literature of the 1930s and 1940s several basic stereotypes concerning ownership in the Soviet economy were established. Ownership was considered predominantly in legal terms as a pattern of allocation of property rights. A multi-sectoral structure of ownership was replaced with two forms of ownership—state and cooperative (*gosudarstvennaia i kollektivnaia/ kooperativnaia sobstvennost'*)—of which the latter was treated as less mature and lacking historical perspective. Reference to social (all-national) ownership (*obshchestvennaia/vsenarodnaia sobstvennost'*) became a conventional rhetorical device used to *substantiate* a desired basic feature of the socialist economy.

In the late 1930s, Stalin initiated preparations for the first comprehensive textbook on political economy with an extended section on the political economy of socialism. The economists who were charged with writing the book incorporated the abovementioned stereotypes into their drafts. Given the eclectic nature of the stereotypes and, above all, the reluctance of those few Bolshevik economists who had survived the Great Purges to express anything that could be seen as a challenge to the Supreme Authority, the results were meager. Observing the proposals and drafts during the meeting with a group of economists in 1941 Stalin noted:

> On economic planning many miserable words [have been written]. There is a real mess here: "The direct social character of labor in socialist society"; "Overcoming of the laws of value and disappearance of the anarchy in production"; "Planned economy as a means of realization of conformity of the socialist production relations to the productive forces." It looks like we have a kind of ideal planned economy out there. But you just need to say: under capitalism it is impossible to hold production on a nationwide scale, as there is competition, there is private property which divides. Our enterprises instead are united by socialist ownership. That is why we can and we must hold economy in a planned manner [...]. Just put it plain—they have a divided economy, it is property that divides; instead our socialist ownership unites. [We] are in charge, and power is [ours]. Say it simply." (Stalin 2012)

The beginning of the Second World War prevented Stalin's direct supervision, although the pre-war momentum generated by his interventions was strong enough, the evidence being the editorial, "Some Problems of Teaching the Course of Political Economy," published in the USSR's flagship philosophy journal *Pod Znamenem Marksizma* (1943). Active work was resumed in the late 1940s. It was closely supervised by Stalin, who several times met with the team of authors in 1950 and 1952, initiated in 1951 the decision of the Central Committee to organize a large-scale discussion of the new draft, and summed up its results in *Economic Problems of Socialism in the USSR* (Stalin 1952). The problem of ownership under socialism was upgraded to a fundamental principle within PES. A two-sector model of the Soviet economy was conceived in terms of two forms of *socialist/social* ownership (*sotsialisticheskaia/obshchestvennaia sobstvennost'*) of the means of production, rather than two different economic modes of production—socialist and non-socialist—like in the 1920s debates. The division of socialist ownership between the state and the cooperative (*kolkhoz*) forms;[4] and the corresponding exchange between them, as well as between them and the individual consumers, were posed as the fundamental cause of existence of the commodity-money relations under socialism. The textbook bearing the marks of Stalin's contributions was published after his death in 1954.

BEYOND THE TEXTBOOK: THE *GOLDEN AGE* OF OWNERSHIP DEBATES

The period from the late 1950s to the early 1980s can be regarded as PES's *years of high theory*. It was a time of heated debates aimed at an explanation of Soviet reality, and at providing the theoretical foundations for the reforms needed to restart the economy. The studies followed the line that implicitly depicted the Soviet economy as a peculiar form of reality that corresponded neither to ideal socialism nor to real capitalism. Even if decorated with ideology, this line undoubtedly affected the fermentation of dissenting currents in Soviet social sciences.

Attempts to take an analytical approach to the problem of ownership tried to move beyond the textbook's didactical approach. At the same time, the notion of ownership served as an ideologically accepted *cover* to hide rather heterodox ideas (as compared to textbook orthodoxy). Three main institutional centers attempting to elaborate the theoretical foundations of PES can be distinguished: the Institute of Economics of the Academy of Sciences of the USSR (the IE School), the Economics Faculty of Moscow State University (the MSU School), and the Central Economic and Mathematical Institute of the Academy of Sciences of the USSR (CEMI School). A confrontation among them constituted the main content of the debates.

However, *textbook orthodoxy* was still quite strong during this period and was far from homogeneous. The epigones of the textbook, who reproduced its didactical statements with some minor changes or eclectic additions, arguably constituted the mainstream of Soviet economic science.

1980s: TWILIGHT OF OWNERSHIP DEBATES

As social and economic stagnation was becoming increasingly visible, the perspectives on the development toward communism tended to lose credibility. The core of PES was met with growing skepticism and the debates of the previous period faded in significance. *Perestroika* gave a new impetus to the Soviet economic profession and revitalized the debates. Previous approaches were supplemented and superseded with new topics. The general approach to ownership was a rejection of its governmentalization and unification. A correspondent over-centralization and excessive mandates given to ministries and agencies were considered to be the result of Stalinist and Brezhnevist deviations.

Political changes and the rehabilitation process during *perestroika* found expression in the revival of NEP studies that proliferated and expanded almost into science fiction. NEP experiences were idealized and presented as a lost chance to build a truly efficient socialism *with a human face*. A stylized model of the NEP advanced the ideal of a multi-sectoral economy based on a combination of different (peacefully coexisting) forms of ownership, and structured the late-Soviet version of market socialism. The contemporary illustrations to prove the viability of such a model were borrowed initially, from the experiences of the most advanced countries of the Eastern Bloc, then from so-called Swedish socialism, and the Chinese experience. Finally, following the publication of the provocative article "Whose pies are bigger?" by Larisa Piyasheva (Popkova) in 1987, there appeared in the Soviet public discourse an idea of capitalism as an attractive goal of reforms.

Official rhetoric developed in the same direction but with some delay. In the first years of *perestroika* the ideas of enterprise autonomy and responsibility were supplemented with the notion of workplace democracy and the popular economic slogan of the period called for the *3-S* program (self-management, self-financing, and self-repayment[5]). Some later debates shifted on the ways of *de-statization* (*razgosudarstvlenie*) of state enterprises. Attention was focused on leasing, or rent relations, meaning that enterprise workers should have a right to lease their enterprises from the state, run them independently, and buy them out later with the accumulated profits. Joint stock company was another option that gained in popularity. Until 1989, these discussions were confined to reforms of socialist ownership. However, both leasing and shareholding differed from earlier options in so far as they dealt with capital assets of the enterprises. In fact, vivid discussions under *perestroika* affected real policymaking deeper than corresponding declarations implied: the disintegration of state ownership started as early as 1987 with the Law on Enterprises, and was cemented in place by the Law on Cooperation of 1988 and the Law on Leasing in 1989. These legalized actual private property and wage labor. Moreover, the laws created favorable conditions for cooperative firms in comparison to state enterprises and stimulated the leakage of incomes and assets from the state sector.

The discrepancy between official rhetoric and actual policy reduced considerably after late 1989 when the government's concept of *radical economic reform* was announced. This document introduced a new system that is "neither intended to improve the current economic mechanism, nor to change its individual elements. One internally logical system is to be dismantled and replaced with another, also internally logical and therefore incompatible with the previous [system]." Yet still it was declared that the new system "will comply with the principles of socialism" (Abalkin and Milyukov 1990). This barrier was overcome a year later during the famous struggle between the two programs—Leonid Abalkin's governmental program and Grigory Yavlinsky's *500-day program*, both of which proposed privatization.

AFTER THE IRON CURTAIN

The disintegration of the Soviet political economy was very prompt. The discipline was far too embedded in Soviet ideology and its political system to survive. Even today, nearly 30 years later, the number of economists who were trained before the collapse of the USSR remains large, but the share of those who follow the theoretical line of Soviet ownership studies has dwindled. The followers of the Soviet tradition of political economy, regardless of all possible differences among themselves, usually criticize neoclassical economics, referring to its failure when applied to the transition economy of Russia as evidence. Such a critique is not entirely unfounded, precisely in relation to ownership studies. The neoclassical approach inherited from its classical predecessor an assumption that the property rights required for the effective working of a market mechanism are given and guaranteed. Russian neoclassical economists, who emerged en masse after 1991, indeed believed (initially) that the market economy could have been launched effectively once the corresponding legal framework was established. It could have been one reason why liberal reformers in the Russian government put more emphasis on macroeconomic stabilization rather than careful institution design.

The surprising scale of the transformational shock shifted the focus onto new institutional economics (NIE), increasingly popular in post-Soviet

Russia. The explanation of Russia's transition economy emphasized its path dependence, causing political and cultural checks to the effective implementation of a standard development model. At exactly this point NIE's logic came close to the approach on the opposite side of the political spectrum. This can be defined as *Russian particularism*. Here, both parties (liberals and populists) would agree that private property as an institution tend to fail on Russian soil due to the peculiarity of the Russian soul—that is, due to the lack of supporting moral and cultural foundations.

While rejecting the mainstream approach, Russian particularism does incorporate some mainstream theoretical elements into its reasoning. NIE is the source of choice in this regard. One of the remarkable early attempts was presented by Ryazanov in 1998. He reformulated the old *Narodnik* thesis on the impossibility of capitalism in Russia in terms of transaction costs. In that framework, the vulnerability of the Russian economy due to its unfavorable climate and geographical conditions as well as frequent political upheaval caused a higher transaction cost when compared to an average standard of advanced economies, resulting in less effectiveness for activities based on individual property and more effectiveness for communal forms.

Russian particularism promotes the conservative idealization of preindustrial society and possesses its own inner logic. It is also quite flexible in adopting the elements of approaches from different origins. The most prominent among them is *industrial corporatism* which advocates a substantial revocation of the results of privatization and promotes policies aimed at the amalgamation and vertical integration of dispersed property in the form of state-owned or state-controlled corporations.

IN SEARCH OF A TRUE ECONOMIC SENSE OF OWNERSHIP

To make sense of the ownership discussions among Soviet scholars it is crucial to take into account that socialist economic thought in general, and the Soviet project of PES in particular, diverged from contemporary Western economics at the foundational level. What was rejected is no less than the normative value of a competitive market economy. Neither its regulative function (considered to be wasteful) nor its expected end-state optimum (considered to be unjust due to its dependence on money incomes instead of human needs) were taken for granted. However, the concept of a competitive market plays an integrative role in standard economic theory. It assumes the dominance of private property as a source of motivation for economic agents whose interactions spontaneously create a competitive environment as a necessary condition for the objectivity of criteria in making economic decisions.

The association of capitalism with private property and a market economy suggested a simple solution of replacing private property (*chastnaia sobstvennost'*) with social property (*obshchestvennaia sobstvennost'*) in the form of state ownership. Just as it was expressed in Stalin's comment addressed to economists: "*[We] are in charge, and power is [ours]. Say it simply*" (Stalin 2012). The implicit assumption behind this approach was that the *right persons will be taking the right decisions*. It was a naïve yet attractive solution to many socialist thinkers and to even more of their followers. The history of the debates around socialist ownership can be conceived as a long intellectual journey toward overcoming this naïve view.

It might be objected that the whole enterprise of PES had no chance from the start, just because it failed to recognize the superiority of the market ideal. Yet belief in a perfect market is no less naïve than faith in omnipotent government. Mainstream economics contributed much to reduce its own naivety, introducing concepts ranging from market failure to the Arrow impossibility theorem. Thus, neoclassical economics during the last century became less dependent on market fetishism, while the political economy of socialism has largely emancipated itself from administrative fetishism. They moved along parallel lines toward each other. Over time, having remained different in their scope, method, and rhetorical practice, they gradually shared more in their understanding of reality than their proponents seem to think.

But in the narrow field of ownership theory the trend was rather the opposite. Retrospectively, it is possible to claim that some attempts to disentangle the legal and economic aspects of ownership were at the center of ownership debates among Soviet economists. Unlike Western economics where the *Law and Economics* movement amounted to a new interdisciplinary branch of studies, in the context of PES the nascent imperative was to emancipate economic reasoning from the burden of declarative legal arguments. The differentiation of the two discourses was achieved to a large extent, although not without losses.

Notes documenting Stalin's meetings with leading Soviet economists and philosophers contributing to the textbook project portray their relationship as one of master and pupils (Stalin 2012). However, since the end of the 1950s, the period of the so-called Thaw, the situation changed: former pupils found themselves without a master, and some of them had to assume responsibility for the theoretical elaboration of the path to communism. One group of political economists, especially contributors to the project, took on the task of defending the principles embodied in the textbook. Others, who were not satisfied with these principles, sought out how to renovate a general Marxian theoretical framework by expurgating the received dogma. Such efforts could have different foci: there were attempts to reassess the status quo in the real world with a corresponding adaptation of the theory or, vice versa, to develop the theoretical framework, making it better suited to deal with reality. In both cases the concept of ownership could not be left aside or avoided.

SPECIFYING THE LEGAL STRUCTURE OF STATE OWNERSHIP

One textbook chapter was entitled "Social Ownership of the Means of Production Is the Foundation of Socialist Production Relations" (Ostrovityanov et al. 1954, 391). The real meaning of this statement can be reduced to an assertion that all the power of economic decision-making belongs nominally to the people but actually resides with central authorities. The economic content of such decisions (what and how to produce) was beyond the scope of this theory. Despite all the declarations and numerous references to Marx, ownership was treated legally and separately from economic theory per se. Economic issues were to be dealt with in other sections of PES: the so-called Basic Economic Law of Socialism was to explain goal-setting including output structure; the Law of Balanced, Proportional Development was *responsible* for principles of interaction between agents within the economic system; the Law of Distribution according to Labor—for income distribution and labor motivation; the Laws of Socialist Reproduction were to follow resource constraints. These mostly normative *laws*, loosely connected with each other and disconnected from their alleged foundation, cried out for reassessment. Several strategies responding to this challenge did appear.

The earliest attempt to reconcile the concept of *state ownership* with economic reality can be traced back to the 1940s, that is, to the pre-textbook period. It belonged to a famous legal scholar from Leningrad State University Anatoly Venediktov. His monograph *State Socialist Ownership* (Venediktov 1948)—awarded the next year with the Stalin Prize—was a casuistic exercise that aimed to resolve the collision between the concept of *state ownership*, implying that the state is a single and direct owner of all the property (except personal property [*lichnaia sobstvennost'*]), and the contemporary practice of asset transfers between state enterprises, which de facto recognized the existence of legal boundaries between enterprises.

First, Venediktov distinguished two kinds of enterprise activities: on the one hand, administrative decisions of enterprises as state organs (focusing on the organization of production process), and production activity as such on the other. The latter also implies taking decisions, but of a different kind: such as providing operations with material resources including their inter-enterprise transfers along cooperation ties. To deal with them legally he then introduced the concept of *operative management of state property*[6] to be provided by state enterprises with respective rights and obligations, coexisting in his theory with ownership rights and obligations and including those delegated to enterprises as state organs. By introducing the new legal institution of operative management, Venediktov could create *legal space* for a qualified reintroduction of a classical bundle of rights, such as *jus utendi et abutendi, jus possidendi,* and *jus disponendi* in relation to socialist enterprises.

THE INSTITUTE OF ECONOMICS: REINTERPRETING OWNERSHIP AS A SOCIAL RELATIONSHIP

A predominantly legal view of ownership was widely criticized by economists. Following the general Marxist dictum that law belongs to *superstructure* which is built upon and determined by an objective economic *structure*, they sought to reveal this relationship. In most cases such attempts focused on the relationship between productive forces and production relations, amounting to discussions of technological preconditions for the maturation of cooperative ownership in agriculture and perspectives on the "amalgamation of the two forms of socialist ownership into a single communist ownership" (Trifonov 1964, 272). Another strategy was adopted by Yakov Kronrod, the leading theoretician of the Institute of Economics (IE) of the Academy of Sciences of the USSR.

Kronrod's approach was based not on a legal distinction between the forms (sectors) of socialist ownership (state and cooperative), but on an economic distinction between different enterprises and sectors of economy within socialist ownership (conceived as a legal entity). Although his general framework remained legal, he used it for non-juridical purposes. Following Marx, Kronrod focused on distribution of property (means of production) as a basis of social stratification. To do so he sought to reconcile his analysis with the official thesis that social (state) ownership implies equality among all members of socialist society in their relation to the means of production. The method of Kronrod's reasoning was similar to that of Venediktov. Departing from the same classical bundle of rights within the concept of ownership, he reinterpreted the ownership of the means of production as a combination of two rights: *appropriation-in-disposal* and *appropriation-in-use*,[7] and asserted that the members of socialist society are equal in exercising *appropriation-in-disposal*, but are unequal in regard to *appropriation-in-use* of the social means of production, meaning that the jobs offered to the members of society vary in quality, technical level, environmental conditions, physical and qualification prerequisites, and so on (Kronrod 1966, 300–02).

Labor's social heterogeneity supplied Kronrod with arguments in favor of the necessity for the material stimulation of producers and *indirect* commodity ties between enterprises (alongside primary direct ties imposed and maintained by centralized planning). For him, commodity-money relations were not a result of underdevelopment of the socialist mode of production, but an immanent feature of socialist economy per se. Several years later Kronrod developed his approach into a revision of the officially accepted periodization of post-capitalist development. Instead of taking the position that socialism and *full communism* are two phases of the same communist mode of production, he argued that socialism should be recognized as a separate mode of production, within what he called the *communist era* (Kronrod 1971). The core idea of Kronrod's new periodization was to break the direct continuity between socialism and communism. In fact, his proposal was in line with then official trend to de-emphasize Khrushchev's promise to build the foundation of communism by 1980. It was the time when new clichés of *developed* and *mature* socialism were coined to stress the relative stability of the current model of Soviet society. Yet Kronrod's position appeared to be too radical and caused harsh criticism and administrative sanction, required self-critical declarations (Kronrod 1973), and the opportunity to publish his ideas was restricted.

MOSCOW STATE UNIVERSITY: BEYOND LEGAL BURDENS

A more radical break with the PES textbook was proposed by a team at the Economic Faculty of Moscow State University (MSU) headed by Nikolay Tsagolov. Referring to Marx's distinction between the legal form of ownership relations as volitional relations and their *real form* as production relations, Tsagolov and his colleagues rejected the principle of assuming ownership to be a foundation of PES's theoretical system.

> From the economic point of view, socialist ownership (it holds true for capitalist and feudal ownership, too) lives inside all production relations, and there is no other way to grasp it than through the study of the whole set of production relations. (Tsagolov 1973, 36)

It followed that the transformation of ownership as a result of the October Revolution did not imply a real transformation of economy: rather it allowed for centralized decision-making and directive planning as instruments to impose the new economic order. Socialized ownership was but a hollow shell that did not constitute in itself essential socialist relations. This approach emancipated the authors of the MSU *Course of Political Economy* (Tsagolov 1963) from the necessity to derive economic concepts from *socialist ownership* as a universal *explanatory* device.

The most radical dismissal of ownership as a principal category of PES was offered by a member of the MSU team, Vladimir Shkredov (1967, 1973). Ownership in a strict sense was—in his approach—a legal cover. It was comprised of acts of volition and social relationships based on subjective will. Thus, ownership appeared to be beyond the scope of economic science unlike the study of the objective laws of material production. The latter were associated with the reproduction process, that is, the real working of the economic system determining—among others—real volumes of income and wealth (property) under control of individual enterprises. From this perspective, ownership relations were but a legal reflection of these objective processes.

The MSU approach allowed (although not necessitated) a more realistic interpretation of the economy. It implied, for example, the existence of *antagonistic contradictions*, to use Marxist language, between the planned economy and commodity production, the latter conceived as real, partly spontaneous market relations, as opposed to numerous attempts to reduce commodity-money relations to mere calculative forms and techniques.

> If actual production does not develop in accord with predictions, then there is no true planning, no true conscious control over economic processes. Society and all its members will find themselves under the power of blind spontaneous forces. […] If state ownership is based on a low level of socialization of production, then planning remains largely formal. […] Moreover, under such conditions formal planned regulation of enterprises might reinforce the influence of factors violating balanced development, since a plan as an ideal form of economic activity tends to diverge more and more from actual reproduction process. (Shkredov 1967, 68–69)

The approaches considered above can be regarded today as ideological or normative (due to applying the ideals of the communist society yet to come to *really existing* socialism). They indicated, however, in one way or another, the incomplete character of real socialism, and strived to provide the theoretical foundation for *non-capitalist and, at the same time, not yet socialist society.*[8]

CEMI SCHOOL: REINVENTING BEHAVIORAL IMPERATIVES

The PES project was launched after fierce debates in the 1920s on the possibility for such a science. Its opponents claimed that political economy is a study of spontaneous and, therefore, objective phenomena of market economy, whereas a socialist planned economy overcomes spontaneity, leaving no ground for scientific inquiry. They thought a planned economy required no more than some engineering discipline to deal with economic problems. The idea of PES managed to survive thanks to a reference to another source of economic objectivity, namely to the objectivity of proportions between different kinds of economic activity. Since then, Soviet economists tended to treat production relations in this way. This approach served an implicit assumption underlying different forms of separation between ownership as a legal, or volitional relation, and economic relations as material proportions, or, at best, as in Kronrod's case, *ex post* relative positions of social groups. Economic behavior as a subject of study was left to economic subjectivists and was vehemently criticized. For a long time it was assumed that economic motivation under socialism is secured by distribution according to labor and incentives to fulfill plans. The motivation of the owners of social property mostly was discussed in moral terms.

A theoretical breakthrough came from the field of mathematical economics. The emergence of the Central Economic and Mathematical Institute (CEMI, *TSEMI*) in Moscow and several departments in leading universities stimulated research and applications of economic models under the conditions of the Soviet economy, including attempts to apply and interpret models borrowed from mainstream economics. At an early stage, mathematical economists preferred avoiding confrontations with PES, but later the boundaries among them became increasingly blurred. This trend strengthened in 1971 when a group of political economists from the Institute of Economics sympathetic to the efforts of their CEMI colleagues came into conflict with Yakov Kronrod and his team and moved to CEMI. Headed by Yuri Sukhotin and Oleg Pchelintsev, this group joined the ambitious theoretical CEMI project that intended to construct the System of Optimal Functioning of the Socialist Economy (SOFSE or SOFE) and helped CEMI to enter discussions on ideologically vulnerable fields of PES, including ownership.

Departing from optimization models of economic interactions, Sukhotin started to discuss informational and motivational aspects of such interactions in terms of ownership functions of socialist enterprises. He wrote:

> It is impossible to explain commodity exchange under socialism directly by the immaturity of the technical base leaving aside ownership. [...] Commodity relations are a reality of a socialist economy as the first phase of communism. They are grounded in the structure of social ownership and reproduced through its functioning. They did not arrive in the same form as they had in a capitalist economy in the socialist one. (Sukhotin 1975, 15–16)

The final purpose of Sukhotin's analyses was to show that the informational and motivational aspects of economic interactions are not confined to commodity-money relations, being universal enough to retain their role in a future full-fledged socialist economy.

Sukhotin shared the position that a socialist planned economy should not be conceived as something like a large home or a single factory based on physical (in-kind) accounting and administrative methods of regulation. He predicted that the future planned economy will develop its own system of value accounting that will not throw away but instead absorb general elements of economic evaluations and utility comparisons invented in market economies. And he believed that administrative methods of regulation would be replaced with mechanisms of workers' participation and democratic decision-making in the future value-based economy.

ALLEGORIES IN OWNERSHIP DEBATES

The idea of social ownership was based on the assumption of the existence of benevolent higher authorities. This assumption was contestable in the 1920s: the *Workers' Opposition* of 1921, as well as Leon Trotsky and some later proponents being the examples. But from the 1930s until late *perestroika*, the party-state was taboo in official discourse. Works of such authors as Milovan Djilas (*The New Class,* 1957) or Mikhail Voslensky (*Nomenklatura*, 1970) were not available, except as samizdat.

Yet, critical analysis of the nature of power in a social system with dominant state ownership was not entirely beyond public discussion. In a disguised form this theme was posed within lengthy debates on pre-capitalist modes of production. It relied on some texts of Marx that deviated from the then canonical exposition of historical materialism based on the so-called five-membered formula of historical progress (primitive society—slavery—feudalism—capitalism—communism). Marx repeatedly wrote about the *Asiatic mode of production* to mean a social system in which power and ownership are fused. Outside the Soviet Union, the theoretical comparisons between Stalin's regime and Eastern despotism were initiated by Karl Wittfogel (1963), even if the very idea was not exactly new at that time. Within the Soviet borders around the same period, the description of the "Asiatic mode of production" enabled a narrative implicitly critical of Soviet reality. Such allegoric discussions suggested an alternative assessment of the place of the Soviet system in history—not between capitalism and communism but rather at some pre-capitalist or even pre-feudal stage.

In 1982, historian Leonid Vasilyev coined the notion of *power-ownership* as a characteristic of the *Asiatic mode of production.* Power-ownership in this context signified the effective lack of private property and dependence of an individual's hold on assets and accumulated wealth on his or her place occupied in the hierarchy of power. In late *perestroika* these ideas reappeared in the public domain supporting the argument that "in fact, society built in the USSR and in some other counties differs by its nature from the socialist ideal" (Nureev 1990, 53). The underdeveloped nature of Russian pre-revolutionary economy resulted in the actual substitution of socialization with etatization. Consequently, society was suppressed by the state, while an established planning system based on state ownership pushed enterprises and whole economic sectors to restrain from cooperative links with other productive units, also subjects of social ownership, and led them to conduct their production activities as preferably isolated in-kind economies (Ibid., 50–54).

In retrospect, studies on the nature of Russian feudalism and socialism, and on the *Asiatic mode of production* resulted in a now widespread vision of Russian history as the continuity between Soviet and post-Soviet (and in many cases, also pre-revolutionary) periods perpetuated by reemergence of a clearly non-capitalist social and economic structure: quasi-feudal or *Asiatic*.

FACTORS OF EVOLUTION IN OWNERSHIP STUDIES

Competing Imperatives

Being a *modernist* project, PES was supposed to perform the functions of any *normal science*, that is, to provide the grounds both for research and teaching activity, as well as for scientific legitimization of the existing order. The latter function was mainly externalized in the dominant ideology as expressed by the party leadership, to which PES texts ought to conform. The former function implied the coexistence of different research programs, among which an official (*classical*) paradigm could be selected to portray an unproblematic, textbook-quality, didactic vision of the world. These tasks were to be solved simultaneously, which was precisely the case of the 1954 textbook. In practice it meant that one task was often to be solved at the expense of another. But the fate of the first textbook appeared to be more intricate: a few years after publication it was dethroned in the wake of the Twentieth Party Congress (1956). From then on, a degree of variability—and hence, uncertainty—as to the foundations of PES remained until the end of the Soviet period.

During periods of harsher and stricter control from above, the imperative of didactical integrity dominated over the normative tendency of PES. To the contrary, during relatively *liberal* periods the normative function of theory building (as a project for the future) surpassed and undermined the didactic function of legitimization and glorification of the present and the past.

Discussions around the textbook (held in an apologetic mode before 1956 and in a critical mode thereafter) were an exegesis for a younger generation of Soviet economists whose formative years occurred in that period. The textbook generation deserves close attention to better grasp the social history of Soviet economic science. The 1951 discussion was just a culmination of a rather long process launched around 1939–1940 and aimed at establishing a truly Soviet (*Marxist-Leninist*) economics. The PES project was an integral part of this process, which implied not only the elaboration of theory but also the formation of cadres. After 1945, a rapid expansion of the economic profession started, and economists of the textbook generation were the first in a wave of *expanded reproduction* within the profession. Many of them took advantage of fresh opportunities and during the 1960s occupied influential positions that they held well into the 1990s (Melnik 2014).

No wonder that in his post–Twentieth Party Congress account of the history of Soviet economic thought, Konstantin Ostrovityanov (a member of the textbook team and an influential figure within the Soviet academic establishment) credited Stalin for focusing on the division of ownership between the state and the kolkhoz sectors as an explanation of commodity production under socialism (Ostrovityanov 1959, 11–12). Stalin's (1952) contribution was criticized after 1956, and Ostrovityanov urged not to lapse with the criticism of the personality cult beyond the pre-1952 threshold, that is, not to dismiss the distinction between the two forms of ownership within the socialist economy as a theoretical foundation sufficient to allow for fruitful applied studies.

CONTINUITIES AND DISCONTINUITIES

The two most relatively liberal—and for this reason most formative—periods in the history of Soviet economic thought were the 1920s and late 1950s–1960s. Given all the differences, the theory building of the latter period followed approaches that had already been explored in the former in many ways. In some cases it might be a result of coincidence. But in many others it was the result of the direct impact of debates and explorations in the 1920s. Since the 1930s and well into the 1980s such names as Isaak Rubin or Evgeni Preobrazhensky could not be cited at all, or, if cited, only in a derogatory manner. But in memoirs and oral recollections published in the post-Soviet decades there is enough evidence to prove that the existence of a covert continuity is not a matter of sheer speculation.

Thus, industrialization debates received acclaim during *perestroika*, even if the adoption was of a selective nature: Bukharin's line of argumentation was lauded while Preobrazhensky's was usually condemned as proto-Stalinist. Such a reception was understandable in the political context of *perestroika*. In this case the results of development studies made in the context of one economic structure were used as policy recommendations applicable for another. A heterogeneous economic structure comprised of different modes of ownership and economic organization was regarded by communist economists of the 1920s as a given starting point in reality to be superseded in the course of development. Sixty years later it would appear as a paradise lost due to the political deviation of Stalinism. The acclaim of selective empirical studies from the 1920s (as well as those from the pre-revolutionary period) during *perestroika* was largely of an ideological nature.

Another tradition that survived, despite the purges, was that of agrarian cooperative socialism, exemplarily represented by Vladimir Venzher from the Institute of Economics (Voyeykov et al. 1999). His name became known widely after the publication of Stalin's response to Venzher and his wife's, A. Sanina's, letters (Stalin 1952). Stalin criticized their proposal to sell state-owned agricultural equipment and machinery to the kolkhoz in order to improve economic performance. According to Stalin, such a measure would endanger and expand the sphere of commodity exchange. Throughout his lengthy academic career (he died in 1991), Venzher experienced several waves of criticism, but general uncertainty about the nature of kolkhoz ownership and ideological ambiguities allowed him to express his views, even if in a largely latent form. He represented an approach that regarded collectivization as a Stalinist deviation from socialism. Kolkhoz ownership was considered by him not as an appendix to the state sector, but as a distinct form of ownership within socialist economy. He hoped to see a transformation of this form into a truly cooperative one.

OPPORTUNITIES AND COSTS

Although the political economy canon allowed for some flexibility, still it induced self-censorship. Reasoning in PES was held hostage. The practice of Soviet economists presumed a need to *coordinate* their speeches and texts with the updated formula of the communist *credo*. Only a few could afford any attempt to forecast or affect the possible changes in formulations. Those few individuals generally were connected with the centers of power: either by being part of the communist establishment (as was the case in the 1920s when eminent economists were often leading policymakers) or by being part of the academic establishment involved in the political games of the political elite. Political *guidance* in political economy acquired its most visible and direct form during the production of the textbook when some key doctrines were formulated by Stalin. During the 1930s, the situation was dramatic: economists were used as tools in purging the profession, with many of those who had performed the role of persecutors at early stages becoming victims later. Since the late 1950s a certain degree of freedom was allowed but the stakes remained high.

Close connections between the political establishment and academia involved both opportunities and risks. After Stalin's death the political leadership was never consolidated to the extent achieved in the 1930s after the Great Purge. There were different streams and sub-streams, interest groups, and unsatisfied ambitions. They created demand for ideas and programs, thus providing competing economic schools with opportunities to supply their projects. Departments of the Central Committee, *Gosplan* and influential branch ministries, Moscow and regional authorities, domestic imperatives and international ambitions—all such institutions and policies had their projections and preferences in the area of economic knowledge. Leading economists not only had their sponsors but actively promoted their representatives into the party apparatus and government positions.

Thus, the formation of CEMI and the mathematical school in Soviet economic thought took place despite active resistance by the ideological establishment and hardly could occur without support from influential scientists involved in military programs. An attack by MSU on the Institute of Economics at the very beginning of the 1970s was prepared in the corridors of the party apparatus (Popov 2004). The rivalry between CEMI and Yakov Kronrod in the early 1970s was fueled from *Gosplan* circles (Glagolev 2005). During *perestroika* discussions about *khozraschet* and the self-financing of state enterprises, among others, concealed the vested interests of powerful industrial structures eager to convert their strong administrative status quo into market monopolies (Grebennikov 1986).

As regards the evolution of ownership debates among Soviet economists, several stages can be distinguished. In the 1920s the theme of ownership relations was predominantly political, and academic discourse in this field was not yet established. The 1930s and 1940s was a period when the first, mainly ideological canon emerged, and it was based on the legal concept of ownership. Starting from 1940s, and especially after the Twentieth Party Congress, the economics profession made attempts to get rid of dogmatic explanations of economic phenomena relying on the superiority of state ownership, and to emancipate economic discourse from the legal burden. These developments were rooted in the conception of economic theory borrowed from classical and Marxian traditions of political economy, which emphasized the material nature of economic reality, and an *ex post* view of economic phenomena. The subjective, volitional aspects of economic behavior were relegated to more pragmatic managerial studies. As a result the idea of owner's motivation has returned into theoretical economic discourse: first, marginally through mathematical modeling of economic behavior, and only much later, along with privatization processes of 1990s and reforms in economics education, economics as a behavioral science has found its place in the Russian economic profession.

NOTES

1. Following Marx and Engels, the Bolsheviks distinguished between two stages of building communist society; in the established Soviet tradition the first stage was defined as socialism, the second as communism proper. The policy measures adopted before and after the period of war communism were guided by the idea of an additional stage of transition: from capitalism to socialism. That stage was often referred to as state capitalism, with the introduction of New Economic Policy, and the acronym NEP went on to supersede all alternative definitions for the transition period.

2. According to Stein's reconstruction (Stein 1948, 111–18), it was the Slavophiles' influence that induced August von Haxthausen, a German scholar who travelled across Russia in 1843, to discover the *obshchina*, the form of communal ownership and self-government among Russian peasants, as a peculiar and crucial form of Russian economic and social structure.

3. In May 1918 Lenin enumerated five sectors: "(1) patriarchal, i.e., to a considerable extent 'natural' (in-kind), peasant farming; (2) small commodity production (this includes the majority of those peasants who sell their grain); (3) private capitalism; (4) state capitalism; (5) socialism," concluding that "Russia is so vast and so varied that all these different types of socio-economic structures are intermingled. This is what constitutes the specific features of the situation." (Lenin 1918 [1972])

4. In their relation to the planning system, as well as to the supply and procurement systems through which most of agricultural products were sold to the state agencies and large part of resources was supplied, the position of collective farms (*kolkhoz*) was similar to state agricultural enterprises (*sovkhoz*). The cooperative status of a kolkhoz manifested itself mainly in the election of a chairperson (often nominal), and the possibility to sell its surpluses at so-called *kolkhoz* markets at prices higher than in state shops.

5. In Russian, respectively, *samoupravlenie*, *samofinansirovanie*, and *samookupaemost'*.

6. In Russian: *operativnoye upravlenie gosudarstvennym imushchestvom.*

7. In Russian: *prisvoenie-rasporyazhenie* and *prisvoenie-ispolzovanie*, respectively.

8. The latter implicit point indicated that, contrary to the official dogma declaring Soviet society as already having reached the stage of *mature socialism* in the 1970s, the very first stage of transition, the one from capitalism to socialism, had not yet been completed (cf. note 3).

BIBLIOGRAPHY

Abalkin, Leonid, and Anatoly Milyukov, eds. 1990. *Экономическая реформа: Поиск решений.* Материалы Всесоюзной научно-практической конферен ции по проблемам радикальной экономической реформы. Под. ред. Л.И.

Абалкина и А.И. Милюкова [Economic Reform: Search for Solutions. Materials of All-union Conference on the Problems of Radical Economic Reform]. Moscow: Politizdat.

Bogdanov, Aleksandr, and Ivan Stepanov. 1910. А. Богданов и И. Степанов. *Курс политической экономии* [Course of Political Economy]. Vol. 1. St. Petersburg: Znanie.

———. 1919. А. Богданов и И. Степанов. *Курс политической экономии* [Course of Political Economy]. Vol. 2, Issues 1, 2, 4. Moscow—Petrograd: Communist.

Bukharin, Nikolai, and Evgeny Preobrazhensky. 1969. *The ABC of Communism*. London: Penguin Books. Available online, accessed April 24, 2017: https://www.marxists.org/archive/bukharin/works/1920/abc/.

———. 1990. Н.И. Бухарин и Е.А. Преображенский. *Пути развития: дискуссии 20-х гг.* [Paths of Development: Debates of the 1920s]. Leningrad: Lenizdat.

Chamberlain, Lesley. 2007. *Lenin's Private War: The Voyage of the Philosophy Steamer and the Exile of the Intelligentsia*. New York: Picador, St. Martin's Press.

Chayanov, Aleksandr. 1989. А.В. Чаянов. "Организация крестьянского хозяйства" [Peasant Economy]. In *Крестьянское хозяйство*: *Избранные труды* [Peasant Farm Organization: Selected Works], edited by A.A. Nikonov. Moscow: Ekonomika.

Glagolev Vladimir. 2005. В. Глаголев. "*Афера* с *СОФЭ.*"*Российский Кто есть Кто* ["Affair with SOFE." *Russian Who is Who*] 6(51). Available online, accessed April 24, 2017: http://www.whoiswho.ru/old_site/arhiv.htm.

Gloveli, Georgij. 2010. Г.Гловели. "Политэкономия в широком смысле: элементы институционализма и утопизма." *Вопросы экономики* ["Political Economy in a Broad Sense: Elements of Institutionalism and Utopianism." *Voprosy Ekonomiki*] 10: 113–34.

Grebennikov, Valerii, Oleg Pchelintsev, and Stanislav Shatalin. 1986. В.Г. Гребенников, О.С. Пчелинцев, С.С. Шаталин. "О проблемах развития социалистической собственности в СССР." *Известия Сибирского Отделения АН СССР: Серия экономики и прикладной социологии* ["On the Problems of Development of Socialist Ownership in the USSR." *Proceedings of the Siberian Branch of the Academy of Sciences of the USSR: Economics and Applied Sociology Series*] 7, no. 2: 7–16.

Kronrod, Yakov. 1966. Я.А. Кронрод. *Законы политической экономии социализма: Проблемы методологии и теории* [The Laws of the Political Economy of Socialism]. Moscow: Misl'.

———. 1971. Я.А. Кронрод. "К вопросу о социалистическом способе производства и стадиях его развития." *Известия АН СССР: Серия Экономическая* ["On the Issue of the Socialist Mode of Production and the Stages of its Development." *Proceedings of the Academy of Sciences of the USSR: Economics Series*] 3: 82–99.

———. 1973. Я.А. Кронрод. "Некоторые теоретические вопросы экономики развитого социалистического общества." *Вопросы экономики* ["Some Theoretical Issues Concerning the Economy of the Developed Socialist Society." *Voprosy Ekonomiki*] 2: 99–108.

Lenin, V.I. 1964. "The Development of Capitalism in Russia." In *Collected Works*, 2nd English edition, Vol. 3, 21–607. Moscow: Progress Publishers. Available online, accessed April 24, 2017: https://www.marxists.org/archive/lenin/works/1899/devel/index.htm.

———. 1965. "On Cooperation." In *Collected Works*, 2nd English Edition, Vol. 33, 467–75. Moscow: Progress Publishers. Available online, accessed April 24, 2017: https://www.marxists.org/archive/lenin/works/1923/jan/06.htm.

———. 1972. "'Left-Wing' Childishness." In *Collected Works*, 4th English Edition, Vol. 27, 323–34. Moscow: Progress Publishers. Available online, accessed April 24, 2017: https://www.marxists.org/archive/lenin/works/1918/may/09.htm.

Melnik, Denis. 2014. Д.В. Мельник. *Из истории институциализации экономической науки*: «*Ленинградское дело*». Препринт [From the History of Institutionalization of Economic Science: the "Leningrad Affair." Preprint]. Moscow: Institute of Economics of RAS.

Naishul, V.A. 1985. В.А. Найшуль. *Другая жизнь*. Самиздат [The Other Life. Samizdat]. Available online, accessed April 24, 2017: http://www.libertarium.ru/l_libnaulotfe.

Nikolai-on [Danielson N.F.]. 1899. *Die Volkswirtschaft in Russland nach der Bauern-Emancipation*. Munich: Verlag von H. Lukaschik.

Nureev, Rustem. 1990. Р.М. Нуреев. "Азиатский способ производства и социализм." *Вопросы экономики* ["Asiatic Mode of Production and Socialism." *Voprosy Ekonomiki*] 3: 47–58.

Ostrovityanov, Konstantin et al. 1954. К.В. Островитянов и др. *Политическая экономия* [Political Economy]. Moscow: Politizdat.

Popkova, Larissa. [Piyasheva, L.I.]. 1987. Л.Попкова (Л.И. Пияшева). "Где пышнее пироги?" *Новый Мир* ["Whose Pies are Bigger?" *Novy Mir*] 5: 239–41.

Popov, Gavril. 2004. Г.Х. Попов. "Приближая будущее" [Approaching Future]. In *Судьба политической экономии и её советского классика* [Dzarasov, S, Menshikov, S. and Popov, G.Kh, The Destiny of Political Economy and Its Soviet Classic Scholar], 363–94. Moscow: Alpina Business Books.

Rubin, Isaak. 1972. *Essays on Marx's Theory of Value*. Transl. by M. Samardžija and F. Perlman from the 3d ed. Detroit: Black and Red. Available online, accessed April 24, 2017: http://marxists.org/archive/rubin/value/index.htm.

Ryazanov, Viktor. 1998. В.Т. Рязанов. *Экономическое развитие России*: *Реформы и российское хозяйство в XIX-XX вв.* [Economic Development of Russia: Reforms and Russian economy in 19th and 20th centuries]. St. Petersburg: Nauka.

Shkredov, Vladimir. 1967. В.П. Шкредов. *Экономика и право* [Economy and Law]. Moscow: Ekonomika.

———. 1973. В.П. Шкредов. *Метод исследования собственности в «Капитале» К. Маркса* [The Methodology of Studying Ownership in K. Marx's Capital]. Moscow: MSU Press.

Shliapnikov, Aleksandr. 1921. "Theses of the Workers Opposition." *Pravda*, January 25. Available online, accessed April 24, 2017: https://www.marxists.org/archive/shliapnikov/1921/workers-opposition.htm.

Shukhov, Nikolai. 1991. Н.С. Шухов. *Политическая экономия социализма в 20-е годы* [Political Economy of Socialism in the 1920s]. Moscow: Nauka.

Sibirev, A.I. 1983. А.И. Сибирев. “Хозяйственный расчет” [Economic Accounting]. In *История политической экономии социализма* [History of Political Economy of Socialism], 2nd ed., edited by D.K. Trifonov and L.D. Shirokorad, 391–430. Leningrad: LSU Press.

Skvortsov-Stepanov, Ivan. 1925. И. Скворцов-Степанов. “Что такое политическая экономия?” *Под знаменем марксизма* [“What Is Political Economy?” *Pod Znamenem Marksizma*] 1–2: 156–90.

“Some Problems of Teaching the Course of Political Economy.” *Pod Znamenem Marksizma* 1943 no 7–8: 56–78.

Stalin, I.V. 1952. И.В. Сталин. *Экономические проблемы социализма в СССР* [Economic Problems of Socialism in the USSR]. Moscow: Politizdat.

———. 2012. “Беседы И.В. Сталина с учеными-экономистами: 1941, 1950, 1952 г.” *Исторический архив* [“Talks with Economists: 1941, 1950, 1952.” *Istoricheskiy Arkhiv*] 4: 6–28. Available online, accessed April 24, 2017: http://istmat.info/node/26300.

Stein, Viktor. 1948. В.М. Штейн. *Очерки развития русской социально-экономической мысли XIX–XX веков* [Essays in Development of Russian Socio-Economic Thought in the 19th and 20th centuries]. Leningrad: LSU Press.

Sukhotin, Yurii. 1975. Ю.В. Сухотин. *О хозяйственных формах планомерного управления* [About Economic Forms of Planned Management]. Moscow: CEMI.

Trifonov, Dmitrii. 1964. Д.К. Трифонов. *Общие экономические законы* [General Economic Laws]. Leningrad: LSU Press.

Trifonov, Dmitrii, and Leonid Shirokorad, eds. 1983. *История политической экономии социализма.* Под ред. Д.К. Трифонова и Л.Д. Широкорода. [History of Political Economy of Socialism]. Leningrad: LSU Press.

Tsagolov, Nikolai. 1973. “Актуальные вопросы разработки системы политической экономии” [Actual Problems of Designing the System of Political Economy]. In *О системе категорий и законов политической экономии* [About the System of Categories and Laws of Political Economy], edited by N. Tsagolov, 5–43. Moscow: MSU Press.

———, ed. 1973. *Курс политической экономии.* Под ред. Н.А. Цаголова. [Course of Political Economy]. Vol. 2. Moscow: Ekonomika.

Tugan-Baranovsky, Mikhail. 1916. М.И. Туган-Барановский. *Социальные основы кооперации* [Social Foundations of Cooperation]. Moscow: A. Shanyavsky Moscow City University Press.

Vasilyev, Leonid. 1982. Л.С. Васильев. “Феномен власти-собственности: К проблеме типологии докапиталистических структур” [The Phenomenon of Power-Ownership]. In*Типы общественных отношений на Востоке в средние века* [Types of Social Relations in the Ancient East], edited by L.B. Alaev. Moscow: Nauka.

Venediktov, Anatoly. 1948. А.В. Венедиктов. *Государственная социалистическая собственность* [State Socialist Property]. Moscow—Leningrad: USSR Academy of Sciences Press.

Vorontsov, Vasily. 2008. В.П. Воронцов. *Экономика и капитализм* [Economy and Capitalism]. Moscow: Astrel.

Voyeykov, Mikhail, Tamara Kuznetsova, and Lev Nikiforov. 1999. М.И. Воейков и др. "В.Г. Венжер: теоретик русского кооперативного социализма." *Альтернативы* ["V.G. Venzher: A Scholar of Russian Cooperative Socialism." *Alternativy*] 1: 178–88.

Wittfogel, Karl. 1963. *Oriental Despotism: A Comparative Study of Total Power*. London, New Haven: Yale University Press.

Chapter 9

Social Property and the Market

An Uneasy Symbiosis in Yugoslavia

Jože Mencinger

Two basic criteria are used in comparative economics to distinguish among economic systems: ownership of the means of production (private or state) and management of the economy (decentralized or centralized). Thus, four theoretical outcomes are possible: private property and decentralized management or state property and centralized management are two consistent outcomes, while private property and centralized management or state property and decentralized management are inconsistent and should therefore be unstable. But reality differs from theoretical outcomes: the economy of the United States is considered to belong to the first case, the economy of the former Soviet Union to the second, war economies belong to the third, and the former Yugoslavia fits the fourth model.

The ownership criterion is explicitly or implicitly embodied in the constitutional provisions. Thus, the Declaration of the Rights of Man and of the Citizen, adopted in 1789, and an organic part of the French Constitution of 1946, enumerates the right to property among *natural and inviolable rights of man* together with liberty, security, and resistance to oppression (Article 2 of the Declaration). According to Article 17 of the Declaration: "The right to property being inviolable and sacred, no one shall be deprived of it, except in cases of evident public necessity, legally ascertained, and on condition of a previous just indemnity." The above provisions of the declaration became the yardstick for capitalist economies. Similarly, Article 4 of the Constitution of the Union of Soviet Socialist Republics of December 5, 1936, which voiced the social preference function of a socialist economic system, maintained: "The economic foundation of the USSR is the socialist system of economy and the socialist ownership of the instruments and means of production, firmly established as a result of abolishing the capitalist system of economy, the private ownership of the instruments and means of production, and the exploitation of man by man" (Mencinger 1993). Communism was supposed to do away with the shortcomings of the capitalist economy, above all capitalist exploitation and inefficiency. The foundation of the belief was Marx's theory—derived from Ricardo's labor theory of value—of surplus value and capitalist exploitation. Because exploitation is an inherent attribute of private property, one can do away with it only by doing away with private property. This is why the means of production are to be owned by the state or society. It was believed that a communist economy would also resolve other problems of the capitalist market economy allegedly deriving from *the contradiction between social reproduction and private acquisition*, from the dominance of private gains over social gains, and from market uncertainties, defective coordination, and other shortcomings.

FROM CAPITALISM TO SOCIALISM AND BACK AGAIN

Creation of State Property

The major objective of communist government after the Second World War was to transform an underdeveloped, predominantly agricultural, society into an industrial society. Crucial reasons for this objective were ideological and political; economic and social issues were less important. A rigidly planned economy was at the time, at least officially, believed to be the only viable socialist economy, and the transformation of Yugoslavia into such an economy was to be achieved by nationalizing the means of production, collectivizing the agricultural sector, and establishing a planning apparatus. The principle of control over the private sector was included in the Constitution of 1946, which was a copy of Constitution of the USSR, and stipulated that private property could be expropriated if so required by an extendable *common interest.* The organization of the economy was to be modeled on the Soviet pattern; all basic economic problems such as valuation, organization of production, income distribution, savings, and investments were to be solved by central planning. Enterprises were to be agents of the planners obliged to fulfill their instructions.

The creation of state property included different revolutionary measures and was initiated already before the end of the Second World War by the Directive on Transferring Enemy Property into State Ownership on November 21, 1944, followed by the Law on Confiscation of Property and Implementation of Confiscation on June 9, 1945. The confiscation included the property of the German Reich and German citizens on Yugoslav territory; the property of German settlers residing in Yugoslavia, except if they participated on the Partisan side in the war, or if they were citizens of other countries and were not hostile during the occupation; property of war criminals and collaborators regardless of citizenship, of whom many were proclaimed collaborators to justify confiscation of their property. Confiscation was accompanied by sequestration of property of other foreigners. By the end of 1945, 82 percent of industry and most banking and wholesale trade became state owned. These measures were followed by the Law on Nationalization of Enterprises on December 7, 1946, by which state property was extended to all larger industrial enterprises of *federal and republican significance*. The rest of productive assets, that is, 30 percent of the enterprises of *local significance*, mainly in retail trade, catering, and services, were nationalized by the Law on Amendments and Additions to the Law on Nationalization of Enterprises passed on June 20, 1948. It extended state property to also cover cultural, health, and other activities. In the last wave of nationalization houses with more than three apartments and urban land were nationalized on December 1, 1958.

The postwar period was to be dominated by the First Five-Year Plan (1947–1952), an ambitious program of rapid Soviet-type growth, giving priority to industry over agriculture, to heavy industry over light industry, and to the production of the means of production over the production of consumer goods. The plan was never completed. Namely in 1948, the Yugoslav communist party was accused of revisionism by the Soviet communist party and expelled from the communist movement. The USSR responded by recalling its civilian and military experts, canceled commercial contracts, enforced a full economic blockade, severed diplomatic ties, and threatened with military attacks.

For two years, Yugoslav leaders tried to prove that the Soviet accusations were unfair and therefore strengthened their efforts to rapidly transform the country to Soviet-type socialism; the government rushed to another nationalization campaign, which destroyed smaller entrepreneurs, and launched violent collectivization; real or potential supporters of Stalin and other real and potential opponents were imprisoned or taken to concentration camps. The efforts peaked in the early part of 1950, and were then rapidly abandoned.

The development of ownership patterns in agriculture differs from its development in other economic activities. Yugoslavia before the Second World War was a predominantly peasant country, with approximately three-quarters of the labor force employed in agriculture. Landholding patterns (family farms) were, in the region of the country that was ruled by the Austro-Hungarian Empire, to a great extent established in 1848, and, in the rest of Yugoslavia, by agrarian reforms after the First World War. Nevertheless, one of the first moves of the new state was to undertake a radical new agrarian reform with the slogan "Land to those who till it." Already on August 23, 1945, the Law on Land Reform had been passed; accordingly, arable land in excess of 25 hectares for farmers and 5 hectares for non-farmers was confiscated without or with symbolic compensation. Half of the acquired land of 1.5 million hectares was distributed among poor peasants and landless agricultural workers and the other half was given to state farms. Thus, private family farms remained the ownership pattern in agriculture.

In January 1949, the Central Committee of the party decided to accelerate collectivization. The Law on Farmers Cooperatives passed in June 9, 1949, provided a legal basis for various types of associations: *agricultural cooperatives* and *peasants' work cooperatives*. Farmers were theoretically free to join or not to join and to choose among the two institutions. But political propaganda and various administrative and financial devices (compulsory delivery, administrative controls, and taxes) persuaded them to join the *peasants' work cooperatives*, in which peasants would transfer (without formal alienation) ownership of their land and other productive assets to the cooperative. The attempts at forced collectivization were met with stubborn resistance from farmers; the results were disastrous, bringing the country to the brink of starvation. The government had to give up. When the Law on Reorganization of the Peasants' Work Cooperatives enabled farmers to leave in 1953, most indeed left, and peasants' work cooperatives disappeared. However, these attempts also discredited a long tradition of agricultural cooperation emerging in the 19th century when Janez Evangelist Krek[1] organized several peasants' and workers' cooperatives.

Excepting their specific treatment in agriculture, small-scale businesses and employment therein were gradually allowed in many service industries, although some theorists objected to it as a form of exploitation because the employer attains a profit. Others argued that a worker who chooses employment with a private employer reveals that he prefers such employment to employment in a socially owned company. A theoretical explanation was found in the idea that, as long as the employer himself works in the same manner as his employees, they can be considered associates. By it, privately organized production became a constituent part of the socialist economy. Furthermore, the distinction between private and personal property, the former used for the ownership of the means of production, and the latter for the ownership of the consumer goods, was blurred in legal texts as well. In practice, these enabled the functioning of small-scale private economic activity and family firms. The limits, such as the number of workers employed, differed not only among republics but also among local communities.

THE BIRTH AND DEVELOPMENT OF SOCIALIST MARKET ECONOMY

After two years of experiences with the Soviet model and the catastrophic experiment in agriculture, Yugoslavia had to ask for the assistance and support of the West and began introducing a new model of socialism. The country began to move away from central planning by reducing administrative constraints and making the enterprises more independent. The official birth of the new system can be traced to the Law on Management of Government Business Enterprises and Higher Economic Associations by Workers' Collectives, enacted in June 1950, which proclaimed workers' self-management (*samoupravljanje*) as its foundation. At first, self-management was rather limited, even in the normative setting and much more so in practice. In principle, workers were to take over the managerial function, but in reality both the distribution of enterprise income and the investment decisions remained centralized and self-management as such had little impact on resource allocation. The development strategy remained essentially Soviet, that is, based on a high share of investment in GNP and priority for heavy industry. In short, two of the four basic economic decisions, namely the decisions on income distribution and savings-investments, remained under strict government control, while consumers were to decide what to produce, and enterprises were to decide how to organize production and how to combine productive factors. The basic legal and political features of self-management were explicitly defined in the Constitution Act of 1953 (Ustavni zakon, 1953).

In fact, the entire systemic development during the 1950s and the 1960s was a process of permanent reforms. All imaginable solutions were tried, often in an uncoordinated manner. Numerous and varied economic instruments were used, and each new economic instrument tended to change the given structure and the system as such. Nevertheless, throughout this period, the economy was gradually becoming market based, although neither the labor nor the capital market was officially sanctioned, and both remained rudimentary. There were no problems regarding the product market, which performed as in any other market economy. The labor market, however, showed a profound asymmetry between hiring and firing as workers were reluctant to fire their fellow workers.

The functioning of the capital market, that is, the question of how to bring together self-management and social (state) ownership (*družbena [državna] lastnina*), was the real gridlock of the system. The Law on the Management of Capital Goods by Enterprises enacted in 1951 tried to clarify the dilemma about how to handle a firm's assets, which were formally state owned, by giving the workers a *sui generis* property right over the firm's capital goods. The right of use, which is narrower than the right of ownership, did not include inheritance. Indeed, when a worker retired or left the firm, all his formal and informal property rights disappeared. The firm was allowed to sell its assets to other firms and to change the composition of assets, but had to maintain the book value of the assets periodically revaluated by the rate of inflation. Furthermore, the proceeds from the sale of the assets should be used for buying new assets. There were two ways to overcome the gridlock in practice: *obligatory depreciation allowances* and legal prescriptions on the formation and allocation of *total revenues.* Though the prescriptions were constantly changing, a general pattern could be established. First, from *total revenues* consisting of sales of goods and services and other revenue items, *production expenses and obligatory depreciation* were deducted. The latter was, in a way, a practical solution for the inconsistency discussed above; it affirmed social ownership of the means of production. When production costs and depreciation were subtracted from total revenues one obtained *income,* which to some extent was similar to *value added.* After taxes, insurance premiums, and other legal and contractual obligations such as interest payments, banking fees, other (often obligatory) fees for membership in various associations, contributions, court costs, and so on were paid, one could establish a firm's *earnings* which were allocated to four funds: *the wage fund, the business fund, the collective consumption fund,* and *the reserve fund.* The *wage fund* was distributed among employees (together with the payment of personal taxes and social security contributions) in accordance with the firm's internal bylaws. Allocations to the *business fund* had two purposes; financing investments and repaying loans (only principal). The *collective consumption fund* was to provide specific consumption goods such as childcare centers, recreation halls, and low-cost vacations. The *reserve fund* covered the firm's operational losses or, if the firm could not pay minimum wage, then it was also covered by the fund.

A key institution that cared for the functioning of the system was the Agency for Social Bookkeeping (ASB), which had branches all around the country. The ASB monitored all financial transactions of all business firms and other organizations that had social capital. It audited and approved income statements for them, executed all financial transactions among them (except with foreign entities which was left to banks and controlled by the national bank) and among the population. The ASB could be considered as the public financial infrastructure of the country; it lowered the costs of monitoring the use of socially owned assets, facilitated financial controls through the supervision of the banking system, and was a major source of information on the state of the economy.

Poor economic performance from 1966 to 1970 was accompanied by even less desirable developments in the social and political domains. Social property, defined as property of *each and all,* degenerated into group property (Bajt 1986), and inequality among individuals and regions increased, causing social and political tensions. Furthermore, the concentration of economic power in the hands of the managerial elite not only endangered workers' control but also threatened to deprive the party bureaucracy of political control. This threat, it appears, was the most important reason for the counter-reform of the 1970s.

Like in 1950, the new pattern of socialism, called *contractual socialism*, was shaped by the chief ideologue of the party Edvard Kardelj, and again there were no difficulties finding the roots and explanations in Marx's teaching. The system was legalized by the Constitution of 1974 and by the Associated Labor Act in 1976. In the following years every single part of the economic system was gradually affected, and an entirely new and awkward terminology was introduced. Only the most important institutions directly or indirectly related to ownership will be sketched out here.

The Basic Organization of Associated Labor (BOAL) was introduced as the smallest economic unit. According to the law, workers realized their socioeconomic and self-management rights in the BOALs. The relationships among workers within and among BOALs, within Working Organizations (WOs, firms) and within Composed Organizations of Associated Labor (COALs) were to be specified by the Self-Management Agreements (SMAs). Maximization of income was proclaimed to be the basic objective function of BOALs, WOs, and COALs. This was expected to *resolve* the issue of what the appropriate objective function in a self-managed economy was. However, maximization on all levels contradicted the sole idea of maximization. The idea that social property and self-management promote cooperation rather than competition required new instruments, SMAs, which were to replace contracts in a market economy. Vertical and horizontal *pooling of labor and resources* was seen as one of the cornerstones of the system: first, as a replacement of short-term market relations; second, as instruments for channeling investment resources to their most profitable uses (and thereby substituting for capital markets). It was hoped that the pooling could overcome low mobility of capital and encourage the distribution of investible resources between surplus and deficit firms without the mediation of banking institutions.

DISMAL ATTEMPTS TO PRESERVE SOCIALISM AND SELF-MANAGEMENT

While in the 1970s, the criticism of contractual socialism was vigorously refuted as hostile to self-management and socialism, this changed in the early 1980s when the economic situation deteriorated into a most profound economic, social, political, and moral crisis. Attempts at new reforms began. The Long-Run Stabilization Program (*Savezni društveni savet 1984*) was enacted in 1982 as the first of such attempts. Around 300 economists and other social scientists participated in creating seventeen documents (over 1,000 pages) dealing with all aspects of the economy. The program was eclectic and inconsistent in its approaches to particular economic problems. It drew ideas from all schools of economic thought, from extreme monetarism to orthodox Keynesianism, often cloaked in Marxian terminology. Its main message was nevertheless clear: the reintroduction of market socialism that had existed before contractual socialism. Thus social ownership remained untouchable. The program tried to increase economic efficiency by introducing or restoring the modus operandi of capitalist market economies but in the framework of social ownership and self-management. It remained the single official answer to the crisis in the first half of the 1980s. Enormous conceptual differences between this attempt to revive market socialism and the Associated Labor Act, the cornerstone of contractual socialism, deterred neither politicians nor some social scientists from applauding both at the same time.

The dismantling of contractual socialism was slow, hesitant, and uncertain; ideological obstacles and fears of weakening the party's political monopoly being the most decisive determinants of the actual extent of proposed reforms. The stalemate can be easily illustrated by reference to another official document: Critical Analysis of the Functioning of the Political System of Socialist Self-Management (*Savezni društveni savet 1985*), which differed markedly from its predecessor and can be considered an alternative program. Its basic idea was that the breakdown of the system, with its accompanying catastrophic economic results, was caused by the inappropriate behavior of economic units and not by deficiencies in the blueprints. Therefore, indoctrination and changes of attitude, rather than changes in the system, were called for.

While party ideologists and economists speculated about other types of socialism, the government established a new commission that launched a novel program of economic reform in 1988 (*Savezno izvršno veće 1988*). Contrary to expectations, the reform proposals of this so-called Mikulić Commission were extremely radical, although theoretically confused and inconsistent. In short, they would transform socialist economy into a capitalist one.

The document (Principles of Economic System Reform) containing a general outline of the reform was adopted in October 1988. The constitutional conditions for the reform were created by a set of amendments to the Constitution adopted in November 1988. Systemic laws regulating economy and labor relations adopted in 1988 and 1989 were much more radical and straightforward. The most important among them, the Foreign Investment Act and the Enterprise Act, passed in late December 1988 and January 1989, also formally abrogated the existing economic system based on self-management and social property and the existing social contract based on full employment and fairly equal wages. It reestablished the enterprise as a legal entity engaged in economic activities and fully responsible for its business operations. Four types of ownership—social, cooperative, mixed, and unlimited domestic and foreign private ownership of the means of production—were introduced. So-called self-management relationships were replaced by *capital-management relationships*. A new era should begin by privatization, which became a magic word, changing *bad* to *good*.

Preparations for privatization began before the *freely elected* republican governments were shaped. They could be traced to federal amendments to the Constitution adopted in November 1988, and the laws regulating economic and labor relations in 1988 and 1989. Most important among them, the Enterprise Act abandoned *self-management and social property relations* and replaced them by the *capitalist property relations*. The Law on the Circulation and Disposal of Social Capital gave power to the workers' councils to sell companies to private owners. Finally, the Law on Social Property, adopted in August 1990, enabled gradual transformation of socially owned firms into mixed companies, whereas *internal shares* enabling employee buyouts through the purchase of shares at a discount were to be the main instrument of privatization.

IDEOLOGY AND CONTROVERSIES

The Social Market Economy

Yugoslavia often served as the only example of a socialist market economy that was constantly reforming in its struggle to establish symbiosis between the market and socialism. The percentage of the national capital owned by the state was taken as a measure of the degree of communism. However, the hostility toward private initiative was not rooted in belief in the efficiency of the socialist economy alone; it was fueled by the fears of the authorities that a strong private sector could endanger the political monopoly of the communist party. It was also endangered by the market, as shown by the reforms in Yugoslavia; however, the architects of reforms seem to be less aware of that. The motives for reforms and counter-reforms differed, and the reforms in Yugoslavia also differed from reform attempts in other communist countries. In Yugoslavia, the changes brought by reforms were deeper, their scope was not limited by external powers, and they did not bring about changes in political leadership. However, they remained "half-hearted efforts to implement policies promoting free market exchange of goods and services" (Katz 1985). The reforms in particular failed to diffuse political and economic controls; counter-reforms were enacted when the market became too destructive to the political monopoly of the communist party.

Whether the idea of social market economy can be ascribed to Yugoslav communists before their takeover after the Second World War is hard to say. The communist movement in Yugoslav lands between the two world wars was relatively strong.[2] The leaders of the party were made up of many extremely well-educated intellectuals from different nationalities. They were intrigued by the problems of agriculture, labor, social issues, economic crisis, and the *national question*. Their predecessor was Svetozar Marković

(1846–1875),[3] a social and political thinker who introduced the doctrine of social reform among the Serbs. Although perceived by communists as a utopian socialist, Marković had a deep influence on socialist economic thought in Yugoslavia in the interwar period and on the leaders of the communist party. Let us mention only a few, who were often heretics and faced similar fates, being either persecuted by Yugoslav governments, victims of Stalin's purges, killed during the Second World War, or persecuted by communists thereafter: Božidar Adžija (1890–1941),[4] Sima Marković (1890–1937),[5] Veselin Masleša (1906–1943),[6] and Dragutin Gustinčič (1886–1974).[7]

According to official beliefs, shared by some Western scholars, social market economy was contemplated by Yugoslav political leaders before the break with the Soviet Union. However, the opinion that self-management was "in the air before it was officially introduced by the government" (Gurvitch 1966) can hardly be proven by actual developments before or after the break with the Soviet Union. The organization of the economy, the overwhelming nationalization of practically every economic activity, including non-capitalist forms of production, and the increased pressure for forced collectivization in agriculture, suggest the opposite. Speculation that Edvard Kardelj, considered the inventor of the system, was imitating the ideas of Slovenian economist and Christian socialist politician Andrej Gosar,[8] have not been proved. Furthermore, to Boris Kidrič, who together with Kardelj dominated economic thought and who was one of the architects of the system, state ownership was, up to 1950, "the highest form of the ownership of the means of production, and planning was the fundamental law of socialist development" (Kidrič 1949, 1950a). In less than one year, the standing of state ownership became "only the first and the shortest step of the socialist revolution; the building of socialism requires the transformation of state socialism into a free association of direct producers" (Kidrič 1950b). Very soon, similar statements were repeated by practically all Yugoslav social scientists. The ability of both Yugoslav politicians and social scientists to reread and reinterpret Marx according to their daily needs was established for the first time, but certainly not for the last. Thinking differently at that time was neither recommended nor safe.

One would expect that the introduction of self-management to the economy would lead, after the abolition of forced collectivization, to quick liberalization of the agricultural sector. However, a *primeval fear* about the restoration of capitalist relations in agriculture remained. To prevent it, a new land reform in 1953 reduced the landholding limit to 10 hectares. The reform was not met with much opposition since 90 percent of family farms were smaller. However, the new landholding limits had a long-lasting and damaging effect on efficiency in agriculture (Mencinger 1985).[9] Only after 1967 did the slogan "A farmer with a tractor makes a capitalist" vanish, although landholding limits remained in place until 1990. Indeed, one could say that the positive effects of private ownership in agriculture and in other activities, in which ownership enhances the eagerness to work and manage, were victims of ideological prejudices. However, it would be wrong to presume that all Soviet and Eastern European theorists believed that collective farms would be more efficient than family farms, and socialist enterprises in services more efficient than private firms. Collectivization and nationalization of these non-capitalist forms of production were aimed primarily at eliminating social pluralism and potential political competition.

Bad economic results and the need to adapt to the new environment were certainly important reasons for rejecting the Soviet model, but ideological and political motives were decisive in searching for a new non-Soviet form of socialism. A junction of circumstances, such as the fact that the war for liberation was in a large part an independent effort and that the Soviet model was voluntarily adopted, made rejection of the Soviet model and the consecutive threats of Soviet Union feasible. One should not overlook Tito's experience with the fate of many communist leaders under Stalin, and his ability to survive using Stalinist methods. The opinion that something had to be invented quickly to give the break a symbolic meaning rather than launching a full-fledged systemic reform appears to be close to the truth. It might also have been a way for the regime to build popular support during difficult times.

Bićanić (1957) enumerated the differences between the new and the old systems as follows: social ownership of the means of production as opposed to state ownership; reliance on the market mechanism for the allocation of goods and services as opposed to the administrative mechanism; increased use of financial instruments as opposed to the adoption of simple administrative rules; free distribution of available income by workers' councils as opposed to administratively fixed wages; decentralized and functional budgeting at all administrative levels as opposed to an all-embracing state budget; the rehabilitation of consumer sovereignty as opposed to the treatment of personal consumption as residual; and the acceptance of independent farmers as opposed to compulsory collectivization.

THEORETICAL CONTROVERSIES—FOREIGN AND DOMESTIC

Social ownership as a concept, being *property of everybody and nobody*, is not an easily understood concept. Let us start with probably the most comprehensive ideological statement in the Program of the League of Communists in 1958, which defined socialism as

> the social system based on socialized means of production in which social production is managed by associated direct producers, in which income is distributed according to the principle to each according to his work and in which,

> under the rule of the working class, itself being changed as a class, all social relations are gradually liberated from class antagonisms and all elements of exploitation of man by man. (Program SKJ 1958, 133)

The debates on the ownership issues began soon after the introduction of self-management. Suddenly, state property ceased to be the precondition for socialism: "It might be a useful device to initiate socialist reconstruction but is otherwise as alien to socialism as is private property" (Horvat 1971, 107). "State ownership of means of production creates monopoly of economic and political power and makes possible the unification of economic and political power under the control of a social group personifying the state" (Djordjević 1971, 81).

In looking for the definition of social property one is faced with hardly understandable statements, according to which social property is a complex of socioeconomic, political, and legal relations, in which people are connected in the production processes. The *father* of the idea, Edvard Kardelj, has never made a clear-cut definition of social property. Instead, he used descriptions of its elements and presumed characteristics. For example, he claimed that social property is a "precondition for creation of a society in which there is no exploitation" (Kardelj 1977). Such an approach was followed by other political ideologists, for example, Milentije Popović or Mijalko Todorović.

Lawyers agreed that social property is a new legal concept, which does not imply unlimited rights over things presumably characterizing the classical concept of ownership, and that it includes elements of public and private law. For Steve Pejovich, property rights in case of social ownership are somewhat broader than *usus* and *usus fructus*, because the sale of capital goods is possible but narrower than ownership because the right of disposal is not absolute (Pejovich 1966). Some lawyers were pondering whether social property is a legal, economic, or sociological concept or whether it is non-definable in these terms because it relates to quasi property. Some stressed its public, others its private, component. Most respected Yugoslav law professors had problems defining it. To Jovan Đorđević (1971) social ownership is a form of *depropríetization* of the means of production, to Radomir Lukić (1959) social property is not a legal category, to Leon Geršković (1969) legally, social property as a bundle of property rights (*ius utendi, fruendi et abutendi*) does not exist and property is a category of bourgeois law. According to Alojzij Finžgar (1965) the pillar of social property is the right of labor to acquire income by participation in socially owned assets. Among economists who were trying to explain the economic substance of social property one should mention Miloš Samarđija, Ivan Maksimović, Miladin Korać, and Tihomir Vlaškalić.

Branko Horvat preferred to replace the traditional concept of property by a concept of economic control; for him legal titles were irrelevant; if artisans and peasants possess no monopoly power they practice self-management and they represent no alien element in a socialist society. The two most prominent economists in Yugoslavia at the time, Aleksander Bajt and Branko Horvat, came to the conclusion that individual initiative is compatible with and even an integral part of a socialist system. Bajt distinguished between two types of social ownership: individual and collective. In his view, what was formally called social property was indeed collective property (*kolektivna lastnina*). For example, being employed in a successful company implied fringe benefits in different forms (wage above average levels, kindergartens, loans for housing and apartments, fellowships for children, etc.) that were enjoyed by a group instead of society as a whole.

Even at the constitutional level, the issue remained blurred. According to Article 8 of the 1963 Constitution, "the disposal of means of production in social ownership and other rights shall be determined by law" (Ustava SFRJ). But Article 18 of the same Constitution supported the view that the right of use is not a component of social property: "Since no one has the right of ownership of the social means of production, no one may appropriate on any property-rights ground the product of social labor, or manage and dispose of the social means of production and labor, nor can they determine the conditions of distribution."

The first wave of models of self-managed firms (SMFs) abstracted from issues of ownership and financing by taking charge of the capital presumed to be rented by the firm, with the amount of capital and the charge being fixed quantities. The number of workers was taken to be a variable input and the firm's main decision was to select the level of input. Most foreign studies analyzing performance of the socialist self-managed economy have focused on micro-economic issues devoting their attention to differing micro-implications of a capitalist firm and an SMF. Performance has been judged predominantly by deductive analysis, comparing the SMF's behavior to that of the capitalist firm under different assumptions concerning objective functions, production functions, institutional constraints on labor and capital supply, and environmental conditions. The debate was instigated by Benjamin Ward's article, "The Illyrian Firm" (1958). The most notorious result of it is that a SMF would have backward-bending supply curve because workers would maximize average income per worker consisting of contractual wage plus bonuses. Using standard neoclassical methodology, he demonstrated that the firm with this *rational and natural* optimizing function would react to a price increase by lowering output. Namely, the worker-manager as a stakeholder to a claim on the enterprise's profit will get higher earnings by voting for a higher return on an employee; he will therefore be averse to hiring more employees to expand output because that would reduce average earnings of the insiders. The issue attracted other economists as well; the most known were Evsey Domar (1966), Jaroslav Vaněk (1970), and James Meade (1972) who demonstrated that changing rigid and unrealistic assumptions of Ward's analysis produces the results which makes theoretical functioning of the SMF similar to that of the *normal* capitalist firm. Vaněk (1970) suggested external financing as a remedy that leads SMF to a behavior similar to that of the capitalist firm. Longer-run outcomes are less peculiar, as an abnormally high return would attract new firms into the industry and give the long-run supply curve a more conventional shape. According to Dreeze (1976), assuming that there are more firms and that all factors are variable, the outcomes of an SMF and a capitalist firm would be identical. H. Wachtel (2000) sees two problems with the Ward model. First, it is static and ignores the possibility of reinvestment out of surpluses. Second, Ward's SMF optimizing function suffers from absence of symmetry. If SMF maximizes income per employee why would a capitalist firm not maximize income per shareholder, as an employee in a SMF is not much different from a shareholder in a capitalist firm? Thus, if a result in the SMF is biased toward capital intensity, the result in a capitalist firm would be biased toward labor intensity. Yugoslav economists with the exception of Horvat (1967) and Dubravčić (1970) have not participated in these discussions, which is partly due to the lack of managing proper analytical tools. Horvat argued that SMF "plans to increase per person income by a specified amount in the planning period and maximizes the remainder of net income with respect to the firm as a whole" (Horvat 1967, 28). With this modification the backward-bending curve disappears. Dubravčić (2000) explored the likely future of the Illyrian firm with the ratio maximand and concluded that it could be functional only if several conditions were met, which is unlikely. Alec Nove (1983) found many other weaknesses of the SMF related to social ownership. According to him, labor management is not necessarily desired by the workers and they do not like to participate in decision-making. Workers lack interest in the longer run, as capital assets do not belong to them and when they leave they have no saleable assets to dispose of. Their only interest is therefore in the income they earn which inclines them to increase current income rather than invest in the future. Furthermore, neither the workers nor the managers have responsibility for investment decisions. Though the discussions over Ward's maximizing function continued among Western economists, the outcomes do not stand up very well to empirical facts. Indeed, empirical studies reveal that SMFs hoard labor in the form of hidden unemployment (Mencinger 2000).

Macroeconomics of the self-managed economy has been analyzed much less, though both theoretical and empirical studies of macroeconomic performance do exist (Balassa and Bertrand 1970; Bajt 1986; Burkett 1983; Estrin and Bartlett 1982; Mencinger 1979; Tyson 1980). The two most prominent scholars in the field of self-managed economy, Vaněk and Horvat, stressed its macroeconomic advantages. Vaněk's conclusions about the expected performance of the self-managed economy were extremely favorable.

> Comparatively—leaving aside the Soviet-type model as a basically inefficient one (except perhaps when it comes to income distribution)—there is every reason to believe that the participatory economy is, all other things considered, superior to the Western capitalist economy. In the sphere of how well it allocates resources in production, it has both advantages and disadvantages compared to Western market alternative. It has a definite advantage in generating full employment, long-run price stability, and growth. (Vaněk 1971, 38)

Horvat (1972) arrived at similarly favorable macroeconomic implications. According to him, high rates of growth are assured by a higher propensity to invest due to reduced risk and uncertainty, full employment by the reluctance of workers to dismiss fellow workers, and price stability by the absence of the fundamental employee-employer conflict.

Only one of the three testable macroeconomic implications of Vanek and Horvat, generation of full employment, was empirically confirmed. The other two, promotion of growth and long-run price stability, were not proven (Mencinger 1979). Support for a strong economic performance of the Yugoslav economy was provided by earlier empirical studies (Balassa and Bertrand 1970). The performance was often described as impressive before 1965, and the decline after 1965 was attributed to the changes in external conditions and only partly to social property (World Bank 1979).

The decentralized management and/or social ownership controversy was a field of debate among Yugoslav economists and sociologists for 40 years, thus from the birth of SMF in the 1950s to the death of it in 1989; it even affected privatization patterns.

IDEOLOGICAL CONFUSION IN THE 1970s

Although a divergence between practice and doctrine was the rule rather than the exception, the breakdown of the system introduced by institutional reforms in the 1970s can hardly be questioned. It suffices to compare the legislation and actual functioning of the system. The latter was based on ideological constructions of reality and overloaded with needless institutions; its blueprints were either inoperative or produced undesirable results. Both required corrective government intervention and incessant change in legislation, which created instability and chaos.

The stalemate was apparent on the constitutional and legislative level. While the number of previously unacceptable ideas multiplied after the decision to change the Constitution, ideological and political stalemate permitted only modest changes and social property remained taboo. Inconsistency plagued the new statutes; some reintroduced the rules of the game that would restore market socialism, others strengthened the transition to administrative socialism. The variety of ideas concerning the best way out of the overwhelming crisis became particularly wide in academic debates. A number of solutions were suggested and, in the process, most of the taboo topics were opened (Horvat 1985; Jerovšek et al. 1985). These included recognition of labor and capital markets as indispensable segments of the market economy, calls for changes in the principles of self-management (Goldstein 1985), the questioning of the concept of social property and suggestions to replace it with collective property (Bajt 1986, 1988), and the restoration of a mixed economy (Popović 1984). It was hoped that the adoption of economic reforms, by which Yugoslavia would more or less adopt *capitalized* socialism, would make this more efficient.

Economic reforms enabled Yugoslavia to adapt to global structural changes more rapidly than other communist countries. An optimist could thus argue that the proven ability to change systems, revaluate Marxism, and redefine socialism might again push the trade-off between ideology and economic efficiency in favor of the latter. But the flexibility that the country had shown in the past was no longer there. While continuous economic crisis, dysfunctional institutions, and growing ethnic and social tensions required changes, Yugoslavia found itself unable to move in any direction. The number of commissions, meetings, resolutions, and words devoted first to *open questions and serious difficulties*, then to *economic crisis*, and finally to *overwhelming economic, political and moral crisis* grew rapidly, and the assumed pillars of the society, self-management and socialism, became more and more open to question.

Before the breakup of the system and the country it became clear that ownership of the means of production constituted the essence of Yugoslav economic problems. Abandonment of the so-called non-property philosophy of social property, by which everybody and nobody is the owner, was urged; *the subject* (*titulus*) of social property was to be determined.

Namely, the proposals commenced from the premise that ownership as practiced led to the severe difficulties of the Yugoslav economy in the 1980s. They also demanded that the principle according to which management was related to labor be replaced by the principle according to which those who provide capital are also entitled to management and profit sharing, and an integral market consisting of product, labor, and capital markets be established. However, while recognizing the need for property pluralism, proposals insisted that social property remains the predominant form and suggested compulsory depreciation and minimal rates of accumulation to protect it.

One of the basic ideological and practical problems faced by the reform was to reassign decision-making authority and managing rights, which were previously, at least on the ideological level, exclusively given to labor. By acknowledging private ownership of the means of production, the monopoly of the workers over decision-making became untenable. On the other hand, a control of management by the owners of the capital was contradictory to labor management. A compromise was found by retaining reduced decision-making by workers within socially owned enterprises and recognizing a kind of co-management of workers within mixed and private enterprises. As mentioned, the Law on Social Capital enacted in 1989 gave the power to the workers' councils to sell companies to a private owner. It specified that revenues from sales have to be paid into a special fund called the Development Fund. Agencies were set up in each republic to assist enterprises in this respect. The law was amended in August 1990 in several important ways, the most significant being that it allowed employee buyouts through the purchase of *internal shares*. It permitted enterprises to sell internal shares at a discount and prohibited the resale of these in the securities market. The abrogation of the socialist social contract was explicitly corroborated by the Labor Relations Act passed in September 1989. By it, labor relations were established on a completely new basis to be in accordance with the Enterprise Act and with the constitutional changes. In effect, normative regulation of labor relations in the system based on the principles of self-management was transformed to a system based on the principle of co-management.

The degree of theoretical confusion easily can be revealed by inspecting some of the provisions of the new regulations. First, there was hardly any other concept of social property than the non-property concept. By determining the subject of ownership, social property degenerated into collective or state property. Second, the essential problem of social property was its inefficiency, which resulted from differences in management philosophy when social property is involved compared to management philosophy when private property is involved. It seems unlikely that social property could persist as the predominant form if property pluralism were established. The introduction of compulsory depreciation and compulsory minimal rates of accumulation acknowledges that degeneration of social property to collective and private ownership cannot be prevented except by administrative measures. Third, profit and management for those who provide capital constitute the essence of capitalism. The introduction of equity requires the solution of many theoretical and practical problems that arise from the need to reconcile the principle of *one worker, one vote* with that of *one share, one vote*. Fourth, while capital and labor markets existed in a rudimentary form, they were not accepted on an ideological or theoretical level. The proclaimed premises of the system, social property and self-management, could not coexist with the labor and capital markets. A labor market with self-management can operate well when employment in a firm is increasing but cannot when there is a need to reduce employment. In the first case, workers looking for jobs appear as sellers of labor services and firms as buyers; there are no problems. The labor market breaks down when employment is to be reduced. Workers, who by definition become managers by entering the firm, would be in this case forced to dismiss themselves or to decrease wages voluntarily which is unlikely. If some workers are dismissed by their fellow workers, this will contradict the notion of labor management. The second solution, that is, the voluntary decrease of wages that emerges from the solidarity of workers and that should soften the downward rigidity of wages, is rejected in practice; strikes confirmed that workers did not consider themselves managers. These proposals not only indirectly questioned the pillars of the Yugoslav economic system; they reopened the old dilemma: socialism or efficiency (Mencinger 1989).

In 1988, Yugoslavia reached the point at which any economic reforms unaccompanied by political reforms could only increase the inconsistency between the economic and political system. It could sustain the stalemate indefinitely or transform the economic system back to an administrative system. The ability to reread and to reinterpret Marx, which had characterized the past so profoundly, did not suffice anymore. New changes of the economic system that would remain within the bounds of Marxist ideology were no longer feasible. The situation required that the ideology be abandoned. A rather peculiar economic system came to its end after continuous economic crisis, ideological disintegration, dysfunctional institutions, growing ethnic and social tensions, and political stalemate.

HERETIC ALEKSANDER BAJT AND PRIVATIZATION

The Owner in a Legal and Economic Sense

Aleksander Bajt, who can be considered the central figure in the ownership debate, was drawing attention to the distinction between the owner in the legal and owner in the economic sense as early as 1953. The former holds legal title and can be a legal or physical entity; the latter derives actual benefits and can only be an individual. In this sense, social ownership implies the nonexistence of exploitation, which in turn implies the distribution of income according to work performed (Bajt 1953).

According to Bajt, nationalization of tangible capital was not the only fatal communist intervention into the property-rights structure. For him, nationalization of the intangible factors, which proceeded in many different ways, was even more fatal for economic efficiency than the nationalization of tangible assets (Bajt 1974). Namely, by nationalizing capital the state indirectly and simultaneously nationalized entrepreneurship, management, and innovation; their owners were not deprived of their production factors in physical sense but their functions were eliminated. A more general method of indirect nationalization emerged through state intervention in the price and earnings structure, by which market evaluation was replaced by non-market, predominantly political evaluation. Its general result was a depression of real incomes of the factors of production below their relative marginal products. Bajt argued that

> changing legal ownership from private to state was not really necessary for establishing a socialist economy. What really matters is economic ownership as reflected in the distribution of income, that is, prices and earnings that do or do not allow appropriation of people's own value product. In spite of state ownership of the means of production, ownership in the economic sense might have remained predominantly private if people were allowed to earn their value product. On the other hand, within a system of private ownership which as such fosters efficiency not only could socialist "relations in production" be established (via tax redistribution) but could be established on a higher level of economic well-being. (Bajt 1968)

Based on his distinction, Bajt defined other forms of property rights. Thus, according to him, a socialist firm was an intricate system of property rights, consisting of well-defined and generally growing stakes of the employed. All of these rights secured operation and efficiency. Among those, managers were the most powerful, in both decision-making and income-generating processes. A legal framework enabling firms to operate in an orderly and stable way has to be added to these de facto property rights.

Consistent with his analysis, Bajt was extremely critical of the approaching privatization procedures (Bajt 1992). Namely, as the largest part of socialist property rights were of *de facto* origin, their abolition should also proceed in an informal way. Along with the expectation of privatization, the prospects of state-owned firms and of individuals involved with them became dim, their employment income and social status jeopardized, and their stake with their firms lost. They would be deprived of the non-pecuniary rights, particularly those associated with entrepreneurial decision-making and ownership control. Newly recruited owners were likely to remove them from those functions and relegate them to strictly managerial and labor tasks. The independence of managers, whose subordination to state bodies had become progressively feebler, was likely to be substituted by subordination to the new owners, while workers would be confronted with the demotion of their position to the role of hired workers. Facing layoffs, workers could do little to prevent the downgrade. As for managers, the prevailing tendency would be to try to appropriate as much of the state-owned property as possible, and as soon as possible.

Due to the above scenario, Bajt warned of the adverse effects of privatization in the process of postcommunist transition on the existing property rights. He insisted that the property rights, particularly those of managers, should be strengthened rather than weakened and destroyed, which seemed unavoidable under mass privatization.

PRIVATIZATION DILEMMAS

Privatization has been considered the cornerstone of transition; it has also proved to be its major stumbling block. In a broader sense privatization should include provisions which protect private property, provisions which enable its creation, and a legally sanctioned transfer of property from *the people*—state or other public bodies—to private entities—persons, partnerships, and corporations.

In 1990, five republics of Yugoslavia started to draft their own privatization laws. We will conclude by saying a few words about the initial dilemmas of privatization in Slovenia. One could argue that the advantages that the country had, compared to other East-Central European countries, soon turned to disadvantages.

Two major concepts known as the Korze-Mencinger-Simoneti (KMS) code and the Sachs-Peterle-Umek (SPU) code competed. The former proposed a gradual, decentralized and commercial privatization, the latter insisted on a mass, centralized and distributive privatization. The controversy soon proved to be a political rather than an economic issue, the root cause being a struggle for control of the economy. Decentralized privatization presumably would enable control to remain in the hands of managers, that is, in the hands of the old economic elite, which was considered by many to be a continuation of self-management. Centralized privatization, however, would transfer control to the government, and thus to a newly emerging economic and political elite.

The KMS concept tried to observe the economic and social legacies of the previous system and seemed suited for the transition of a relatively efficient Slovenian economy. It was believed that the insiders (workers and managers) would be the best transitional owners and that "to avoid the adverse effects of privatization in the process of transition, the existing property rights, particularly those of managers, ought to be strengthened rather than weakened and destroyed" (Bajt 1992, 19). The notion "decentralized" implied that the existing self-managed firms initiate the process of transforming themselves into private companies using various privatization techniques.

The government's role consequently was limited to determine the rules and to monitor the process by a special governmental agency. "Gradual" marked the possibility that initial privatization (by sale of existing equity or by acquiring additional equity) might be full or partial while "commercial" implied that there would be no free distribution of shares. Instead, the citizens of Slovenia would be entitled to discounts on the purchase of shares up to a certain value, and the employees would enjoy additional discounts. The proposal should have captured the advantages related to the nature of the Slovenian economy characterized by the dispersion of industry and by the majority of workers who were part-time farmers. But it failed to provide a good solution for large unprofitable enterprises, and was politically unattractive because it did not provide for a general, free distribution of shares to citizens. During the general euphoria about privatization, the KMS concept tried to adhere to Bajt's ideas.

The KMS concept was replaced by the SPU concept in April 1991. According to it, political, social, and economic legacies of the past should be destroyed. The notion of "centralized" related to the role of the government in carrying out privatization procedures. *Mass* privatization meant that enterprises were to be immediately converted into joint stock companies through *free distribution* of ownership vouchers. A two-stage approach of free distribution was chosen. In the first stage, shares of the companies were to be transferred to financial intermediaries, while in the second stage, shares of these institutional owners could be *bought* with vouchers distributed free of charge to all citizens. It was believed that the institutional owners would monitor and restructure the companies, and assure that they are efficient and profitable.

The controversy between the two approaches resulted in a stalemate lasting for a year and a half. During this period, the Slovenian economy suffered a number of severe blows: the loss of traditional markets in former Comecon countries and in the Middle East, and, what was far more important, the complete breakup of the Yugoslav market. As a result, about 800 enterprises found themselves insolvent and on the verge of bankruptcy while banks accumulated a large volume of bad loans. In fact, the enterprises could be divided into three groups: (1) large unprofitable enterprises most affected by the political events and transition, (2) enterprises which were less affected and which were to be privatized under the provisions of the new ownership restructuring act, and (3) enterprises such as public utilities and steel mills which were to remain state owned.

On November 11, 1992, The Law on the Transformation of Social Ownership[10] finally was passed as a compromise between the two concepts of privatization. It encompassed features of both approaches: decentralization and gradualism from the KMS code, and predominantly distributive privatization by vouchers from the SPU code. The law provided for several methods by which social ownership could be transformed into private ownership depending on the decisions of the managing body of the existing enterprises.

NOTES

1. Janez Evangelist Krek (1865–1917), a Slovene Christian Socialist politician, priest, journalist, and author, taught philosophy at the Catholic seminary. Between 1898 and 1907, Krek organized several peasant and worker's cooperatives, and transformed the Slovene People's Party into a mass political movement propagating social changes and proposed several measures for social welfare. In 1909, Krek founded the Yugoslav Labor Association (*Jugoslovanska strokovna zveza*), which became and remained the biggest trade union in Slovenia. Krek was also a supporter of the idea of the unity of the Southern Slavs. In 1917, Krek proposed the so-called May Declaration (*Majniška deklaracija*), which suggested the creation of a state of Southern Slavs under Habsburg rule.

2. The communist party was established in Belgrade in 1919, when the Serbian Social Democratic Party joined the newly established Socialist Workers Party of Yugoslavia. During the elections for the Constitutive Parliament held in 1920, the party won 58 seats from a total of 400 and became the third largest party. It immediately acceded to the Third International. At the second congress, in Vukovar in 1922, the party changed its name to Communist Party of Yugoslavia.

3. Svetozar Marković studied in Saint Petersburg, where he came under the influence of Russian radicals (Chernishevsky, Dobrolyubov, and Pisarev). After having to leave Russia he resumed his studies at ETH Zurich, continued to write on social and political issues and launched Serbia's first socialist newspapers *Radenik* (*The Worker*) and *Oslobođenje* (*Liberation*).

4. Božidar Adžija, an avid social democrat, was member of various left-wing and Marxist parties and wrote about labor and social issues. His views gradually shifted toward communism and in 1934 he joined the Communist Party of Yugoslavia. When Yugoslavia collapsed and the Nazi puppet Independent State of Croatia was established, Adžija was shot together with many other members of the Croatian left-wing intelligentsia.

5. Sima Marković, a mathematician, philosopher, and first secretary of the Communist Party of Yugoslavia, belongs among the most ingenious men of the first half of the 20th century inYugoslavia. Beside science, he was interested in politics. In the early 1920s, he was attracted to the so-called national question, which was a central political issue in just created Kingdom of Serbs, Croats, and Slovenians. He published his views in the book *The National Question in Light of Marxism* (1922) and in the brochure "The Constitutional Question and the Working Class"; they were the basis for heated debates and subsequent factional struggles. He was often jailed, released, internally exiled by Yugoslav authorities, but also expelled from the party as a *renegade, counter-revolutionary, bourgeois' servant.* He was readmitted in the party only in September 1935. During the period of exclusion he published several books:

Einstein's Theory of Relativity, Communism in Yugoslavia, The Village Issue and the Agrarian Crisis, Basic Concepts of Political Economy. Marković was employed in Moscow as a research associate at the Philosophy Institute of the Academy of Sciences. Data in connection with his arrest and death are vague and contradictory.

6. Veselin Masleša, a Bosnian Serb writer and activist, studied law in Zagreb, economics in Frankfurt, and political economy and sociology in Paris. In 1941, he joined the Partisans in Montenegro and died in the summer of 1943.

7. Dragutin Gustinčič, a politician and journalist, one of the founders of the Communist Party of Yugoslavia, a veteran of the Spanish Civil War, professor and the first dean of the Ljubljana Faculty of Economics was author of the manuscript "Das nationale Problem der Slowenen," which would be allegedly transcribed and published by Edvard Kardelj as a book with the title *Development of the Slovenian National Question.*

8. Andrej Gosar (1878–1962) was one of the founders of the Christian social doctrine in Slovenia, advocating *self-governing* Christian society and the autonomy of Slovenia. He published several books, among them: *Christian Socialism* (1923), *Social Economy* (1924), and *Crisis of Modern Democracy* (1927).

9. The theory of production distinguishes between the optimum output level of a given production unit and the optimum size of the unit. By restricting the use of an individual factor (land ceiling), the size of the production unit is determined while within such a unit the optimum output level is not guaranteed and the efficiency diminishes. If the production units are the wrong size (too small or too large) they will not adapt to technological changes.

10. Three laws added considerably to the scope of privatization: the Housing Act enabled privatization of approximately 100,000 apartments; the Denationalization Act introduced the restitution of nationalized property; and the Law on Cooperatives assigned 40 percent of shares in some food processing enterprises to the cooperatives.

BIBLIOGRAPHY

Bajt, Aleksander. 1953. "Ekonomski in pravni pojem lastnine." [Economic and legal concept of property] *Pravnik* 8: 139–58.

———. 1968. "Društvena svojina—kolektivna i individualna" [Social ownership—collective and individual]. *Gledišta* 8: 531–44.

———. 1974. "Property in Capital and in the Means of Production in Socialist Economies." In *The Economics of Property Rights*, edited by Eirik G. Furubotn and Svetozar Pejovich, 253–56. Cambridge, Mass: Ballinger Publishing Company.

———. 1975. "Social Ownership—Collective and Individual." In *Self-governing Socialism*, Vol. 2, edited by Branko Horvat, Mihailo Marković, and Rudi Supek, 151–63. White Plains: International Arts and Sciences Press.

———. 1986. "Economic Growth and Factor Substitution: What Happened to the Yugoslav Miracle?" *The Economic Journal* 96: 1084–90.

———. 1987. "Stvarni i potencijalni društveni proizvod 1980" [Real and potential social product]. *Privredna kretanja* 171: 42–52.

———. 1988. *Samoupravni oblik društvene svojine* [The self-managing form of social property]. Zagreb: Globus, 273.

———. 1992. *A Property Rights Analysis of the Transition Problems in the East.* Ljubljana: EIPF, 26.

Balassa, Bela, and Trent Bertrand. 1970. "Growth Performance of Eastern European Countries." *American Economic Review* (Proceedings) 60: 314–20.

Bićanić, Rudolf. 1957. "Economic Growth under Centralized and Decentralized Planning: Yugoslavia—A Case Study." *Economic Development and Cultural Change* 5: 63–74.

Burkett, John. 1980. "Economic Growth and Factor Substitution: What happened to the Yugoslav Economic Miracle?" *Economic Journal* 90: 294–313.

———. 1983. *The Effects of Economic Reform in Yugoslavia: Investment and Trade Policy, 1959–1976.* University of California: Institute of International Studies.

Djordjević, Jovan. 1971. "A Contribution to the Theory of Social Property." *Socialist Thought and Practice*. Savez komunista Jugoslavije, 73–100.

Domar, Evsey. 1966. "The Soviet Collective Farm." *American Economic Review* 56: 734–57.

Dubravčić, Dinko. 1970. "Labor as Entrepreneurial Input: An Essay in the Theory of the Producers Cooperative Economy." *Economica* 37: 297–310.

———. 2000. "Illyrian Theories of Cooperative Rent-Sharing and Their Application in Real Life." In *Equality, Participation, Transition: Essays in Honour of Branko Horvat*, edited by V. Franičević and M. Uvalić, 133–47. New York: MacMillan Press Ltd.

Dreze, Jacques. 1976. "Some Theory of Labor Management and Participation." *Econometrica* 44: 1125–39.

Estrin, Saul, and William Bartlett. 1982. "The Effects of Enterprise Self-Management in Yugoslavia: An Empirical Survey." In *Participatory and Self-Managed Firms*, edited by Derek Jones, 83–109. New York: Lexington Books.

Finžgar, Alojzij. 1965. *Društvena svojina kao pravna kategorija* [Social property as a legal category]. Belgrade: Serbian Academy of Sciences.

Furobotn, Eirik, and Svetozar Pejovich. 1972. "Property Rights and Economic Theory: A Survey of Recent Literature." *Journal of Economic Literature* 10: 1137–62.

———. 1974 [1970]. "Property Rights and the Behavior of the Firm in a Socialist State: The Example of Yugoslavia." *Zeitschrift für Nationalökonomie* 30: 431–54.

Geršković, Leon. 1969. "Društveno ekonomsko uređenje Jugoslavije" [The social economic order of Yugoslavia]. *Socijalizam* 10: 1301–02.

Goldstein, Slavko. 1985. *Prijedlog 8* [Proposal No 8] *5*. Zagreb: Scientia Yugoslavica.

Gurvitch, Georges. 1966. "Les conseils ouvriers." *Autogestion* 1: 50–57.

Horvat, Branko. 1967. "Prilog zasnivanju teorije jugoslavenskog poduzeća" [A Contribution to the Theory of Yugoslav Enterprise]. *Ekonomska Analiza* 1: 7–28.

———. 1968. "The Rule of Accumulation in a Planned Economy." *Kyklos* 21: 239–68.

———. 1971. "Yugoslav Economic Policy in the Post-War Period: Problems, Ideas, Institutional Developments." *American Economic Review Supplement* 61, no. 3: 71–169.

———. 1972. "Critical Notes on the Theory of the Labor-Managed Firm and Some Macroeconomic Implications." *Economic Analysis* 6: 291–94.
———. 1976. *The Yugoslav Economic System*. White Plains, NY: International Arts and Sciences Press, Inc.
———. 1985. *Jugoslovensko društvo u krizi* [Yugoslav society and the crises]. Zagreb: Globus.
Jerovšek, Janez et al. 1985. *Kriza: Blokade i Perspektive* [Crisis: Blockades and prospects]. Zagreb: Globus.
Kardelj, Edvard. 1977. *Pravci razvoja političkog sistema socijalističkog samoupravljanja* [Development directions of the political system of socialist self-management]. Belgrade: ČZP Komunist.
Katz, Arnold. 1985. "Growth and Regional Variations in Unemployment in Yugoslavia: 1965–1980." University of Pittsburg, *The Carl Beck Papers in Russian and East European Studies* 307: 39.
Kidrič, Boris. 1949. "Kvalitet robnonovčanih odnosa u FNRJ" [Quality of the commodity-money relations in Yugoslavia]. *Komunist* 1/1949: 33–51.
———. 1950a. *Privredni Problemi FNRJ* [Economic Problems of Yugoslavia]. Belgrade: ČZP Komunist.
———. 1950b. "Teze o ekonomici prelaznog razdoblja u našoj zemlji" [Theses on the economic transition period in our country]. *Komunist* 6/1950: 1–20.
Lukić, Radomir. 1959. *Osnovi sociologije* [Foundations of sociology]. Beograd: Savez udruženja pravnika jugoslavije.
Mencinger, Jože. 1979. "Theoretical and Actual Performance of the Worker-Managed Economy." *Economic Analysis* 13: 253–65.
———. 1985. "The Limit of Landholdings". *Eastern European Economics* 23, no 2: 29–42.
———. 1985: "Reforme socializma i paradoks izkoriščanja" [Reforms of socialism and the paradox of exploitation]. *Ekonomska revija* 4: 319–31.
———. 1989. "The Quagmire of Socialism." *Communist Economies* 1: 385–93.
———. 1993. "Property and Constitution." Seminar on *The Transition to a New Model of Economy and Its Constitutional Reflections*, Moscow, February 18–19, 1993.
———. 1996. "Privatization Experiences in Slovenia." *Annals of Public and Cooperative Economics* 67, no. 3: 415–28.
———. 2000. "Restructuring by Firing and Retiring: The Case of Slovenia." In *Unemployment in Europe*, edited by Michael Landesmann and Karl Pichelmann, 374–89. London: MacMillan Press.
Nove, Alec. 1983. *The Economics of Feasible Socialism*. London: Allen & Unwin.
Pejovich, Svetozar. 1975. "The Firm, Monetary Policy and Property Rights in a Planned Economy." *Western Economic Journal* 42: 277–81.
Popović, Strašimir. 1984. *Ogled o jugoslovenskom privrednom sistemu* [Overview of the Yugoslav economic system]. Belgrade: Marksistički centar.
Savez komunista. 1958. *Program Saveza komunista Jugoslavije* [Program of the League of Communists of Yugoslavia]. Belgrade: Komunist, 133.

Savezni društveni savet. 1984. *Dugoročni program ekonomske stabilizacije* [Long-term program of economic stabilization]. Belgrade.

Savezni društveni savet. 1985. *Kritička analiza funkcionisanja političkog sistema socijalističkog samoupravljanja* [Critical analysis of the functioning of the political system of socialist self-management]. Belgrade.

Savezno izvršno veće. 1988. *Osnove reforme privrednog sistema* [Basic reforms of the economic system]. Belgrade.

Simonetti, Marko. 1991. "Comments on 'Accelerating Privatization in Eastern Europe: The Case of Poland' by Jeffrey D. Sachs," Proceedings of the World Bank's Annual Conference on Development Economics, Washington, April 25–26, 1991.

Tyson, Laura. 1980. *The Yugoslav Economic System and Its Performance in the 1970s.* Berkeley: University of California Press.

Ustavni zakon FLRJ. [Constitution of the Federal People's Republic of Yugoslavia] 13. Januar 1953.

Ustava SFRJ [Constitution of the Socialist Federal Republic of Yugoslavia] 7. April 1963.

Vanek, Jaroslav. 1970. *The General Theory of Labor-Managed Economies.* Ithaca: Cornell University Press.

———. 1971. *Participatory Economy: An Evolutionary Hypothesis and a Strategy for Development.* Ithaca: Cornell University Press.

———. 1972. "The Macroeconomic Theory and Policy of an Open Worker Managed Economy." *Economic Analysis* 6: 255–69.

Wachtel, Howard. 2000. "Ideas and Ideals: Horvat's Contributions to Twentieth-Century Economic and Social Theory." In *Equality, Participation, Transition: Essays in Honour of Branko Horvat,* edited by Vojmir Franičević and Milica Uvalić, 53–76. New York: MacMillan Press Ltd.

Ward, Benjamin. 1958. "The Firm in Illyria: Market Syndicalism." *American Economic Review* 48: 566–89.

World Bank. 1979. *Yugoslavia: Self-management, Socialism and the Challenge of Development.* Baltimore: John Hopkins University Press.

Conclusion

Expeditions to No Man's Land. Comparing Economic Concepts of Ownership under Communism: An Evolutionary View

János Mátyás Kovács

> Property is only a foundation of expectation—the expectation of deriving certain advantages from the thing said to be possessed, in consequence of the relations in which one already stands to it. There is no form, or colour, or visible trace, by which it is possible to express the relation which constitutes property. It belongs not to physics, but to metaphysics: it is altogether a creature of the mind.
>
> —Jeremy Bentham (1843, 308)

In the summer of 1988, Márton Tardos and I are taking a break with Leszek Balcerowicz in the library of the Institute for Human Sciences, Vienna. We are here for a conference on the economics of market socialism.[1] The conversation is cordial up until we start discussing the chances for privatization back at home. Balcerowicz then decides to challenge Tardos' concept of *cross-ownership* between public and private firms, while defending workers' self-management, a key component of the program of *Solidarność* at the time, against our reservations based—as he says—on the *typical capitalist leanings* of Hungarian economists. "The Poles prefer collectivist solutions"—this is Balcerowicz's last sentence in the short discussion. I was unsure whether he was happy about this truism or not.

At the same library in Vienna in the autumn of 1989, a few weeks before the Velvet Revolution begins, I face Václav Klaus who has come from Prague to meet Austrian politicians and—by the way—discuss with me his country study on Czechoslovakia written together with Tomáš Ježek for a special issue of *East European Politics and Societies (EEPS)* on the rediscovery of liberalism in Eastern Europe (Klaus and Ježek 1991). With the anxious frown of a guest editor, I ask him why they avoided writing about privatization in the context of liberal economic ideas. Klaus responds with an ironic smile: Czechs (maybe he said *Czechoslovaks*) are not Hungarians, our people are not yet ripe for private ownership. In any event, the first task of our emerging coalition government with the communists (*sic*) will be marketization rather than privatization. We are not social engineers: we will let the market develop, and *it* will have to decide on the size of the future private sector.

Balcerowicz and Klaus became emblematic statesmen, masterminds of the postcommunist transformation, and heroes/villains in most historical narratives on the advent of capitalism in Eastern Europe after 1989. They are still celebrated/discarded as pioneers of neoliberalism in the region despite the fact that both of them called for (or conceded to) semi-collectivist methods of reintroducing private ownership such as voucher privatization in the early 1990s, and neither was keen on attracting foreign investors to their countries in great numbers to abolish the old property regimes as fast as possible. Ježek who was later appointed head of the Czech privatization agency shared a similar attitude. Meanwhile, Tardos, who became the chief economist of the Free Democrats (Liberals) in Hungary, left the concept of cross-ownership behind and supported rapid and competitive privatization with an extensive involvement of foreign investors. To be sure, the Polish and the Czechoslovak economists did not agree with one another. At the 1988 conference and in a workshop preparing the special issue of *EEPS* I was witness to heated debates on workers' self-management, the rights of trade unions in privatization, and on employee stock ownership. Many of the Polish colleagues were representing *ouvrierist* principles while their Czechoslovak opponents insisted on a large variety of doctrines ranging from libertarianism through egalitarian liberalism to the Scandinavian version of *social market economy*.

These discussions left a deep impression on me about the diversity of economic ideas in late communism, and—after a quarter of a century—affected some of the working hypotheses of the research program underlying this volume. Without invoking, as both Balcerowicz and Klaus did, the *Volksgeist* of any of the peoples as a variable of comparing dominant economic ideas across borders, the challenge was to explain why the positions of leading theorists in these three countries of Eastern Europe were so far from one another on crucial issues of communist and postcommunist economic thought such as ownership. I came to a hasty conclusion that if these scholars of very similar socio-cultural background and non-communist identity thought so differently, then a broader comparison involving countries like China, the Soviet Union, or Yugoslavia could reveal an even larger variety of theoretical perspectives.

Following the reform wave of the second half of the 1960s, even analysts who once had believed in the essential similarity of economic thought throughout the Eastern Bloc, began to flirt with methodological nationalism and produce classification schemes based on allegedly well-defined country-specific ideal types of economic ideas including principles of ownership. Until the collapse of communism in Eastern Europe, the comparative works were full of descriptions of the Chinese, Hungarian, Yugoslav, et al. ways of redesigning the *classical Stalinist* model. Such a diversity-centered approach was reinforced by the spectacular divergence of the first scenarios of postcommunist transformation. Later a new research program embraced it as a postcommunist branch of Varieties of Capitalism. Hence, it was no wonder that many in our research group, including myself, who otherwise preferred not to idolize the *national specifics* of the postcommunist regimes (see Kovács 2013), cherished a hope for the heuristic value of comparing ownership concepts under communism in both time and space. It seemed reasonable to presume that the differences in the blueprints for privatization prevailing in the ex-communist countries *after* 1989 must have originated in diverging theories of ownership *before* 1989.

In the Introduction I enumerated the key assumptions guiding our research endeavor, including those which, as it turned out, did not perform impeccably. A conclusion is a moment of self-reflection, so why deny that comparative efforts do not always yield the expected results? While the country studies unearthed a plethora of hitherto unknown details about economic thought on property relations, and the comparison of these in time revealed new *evolutionary* features of the main ownership concepts, we can promise the reader less novelty when comparing these concepts across countries.

The relative shortage of new national types of ownership ideas may be attributed to the fact that Sovietization proved extremely effective in standardizing economic thought[2] in one crucial respect. Despite familiar differences between national interpretations of the notion of social ownership, it remained *the* cornerstone of thinking about property regimes from East Berlin to Beijing almost until the collapse of communism. Economists blindly walked into the trap set by this key notion of Marxist-Leninist-style collectivism.[3] Although they rejected the excessively statist variants of social ownership and combined it with private and personal property later, most of them accepted its logical corollary, the denial of the primacy of private ownership, until 1989 (or even thereafter).

Ironically, authentic hybrid solutions were produced by those who were caught in this *trap of collectivism* and who were willing to perform what later became a habitual gymnastic exercise of reform economists: staying in the trap, making it relatively comfortable, and sticking out their neck to search for alternative visions from time to time. Typically, authenticity was not tantamount to a high level of theoretical sophistication. Most emerging hybrids resulted from forced innovation or rapid *bricolage* under severe political and ideological constraints. The invention of workers' self-management in

Yugoslavia, *entrepreneurial socialism* in Hungary, or the *household responsibility system* in China are good examples for experimenting with mixed property rights without overtly specifying them. To refer to the title of this volume, these experiments aimed at identifying quasi-private owners (legal subjects) in the no man's land of social ownership. Yet, despite all their conceptual imperfections, these trials (and errors) have a remarkable history in the communist world as a whole.

By taking an evolutionary view on theories of ownership under communism, we entered a formerly unexplored territory. The country chapters reveal for the first time how the various designs of property competed or joined forces with one another, and why they were modified, mixed, reversed, or simply dropped during the consecutive stages of communist economic history. Moreover, until today, the roads along which these ideas travelled back and forth in the Soviet world and between the East and the West have not been mapped. Expectations that the identification of some major evolutionary traits will reorganize what we know about ownership concepts under communism have been fulfilled to a considerable extent. Interestingly enough, in this respect more similarities emerged among the countries than expected. It also became clear that the working title of our book project "From Nationalization to Privatization" suggested an unduly homogeneous, linear model of evolution.

In what follows, I first focus on two basic similarities in the national histories of ownership concepts: a continual trust in preeminence of social ownership and a growing commitment to the simulation of private property. Then, the alternative roads of evolution, represented by research communities dominated by *conformists* and *explorers*, are sketched out. Finally, I will ask why even the radical reformers, the ultimate explorers were unable/unwilling to leave the trap of collectivism for so many decades. The course of presentation is interrupted twice to highlight a huge gap in economic thought under communism: the lack of a subtle analysis of *nomenklatura* ownership.

BASIC SIMILARITIES: SOCIAL PROPERTY'S LONG SHADOW

By now, the reader may feel a little confused by the various ownership categories that were applied in the nine countries. Let me begin with a brief digression into the world of ownership discourse in the communist era (see Table C.1).

The meanings of the seven terms included in the table (and in most communist constitutions) do not show a high degree of variability during almost the entire communist timeline. They were used in all countries,[4] no matter

Table C.1 Vocabulary of Ownership Terms

	OWNERSHIP FORMS						
COUNTRIES	*Social*	*State*	*Cooperative*	*Communal*	*Self-managing*	*Personal*	*Private*
Bulgaria	sotzialisticheska sobstvenost	darjavna sobstvenost	kooperativna sobstvenost	obshtinska	samoupravlenie	lichna sobstvenost	chastna sobstvenost
Czechoslovakia[a]	společenské vlastnictví	státní vlastnictví	družstevní vlastnictví	obecní vlastnictví	samospráva	osobní vlastnictví	soukromé vlastnictví
China	shehui suoyouzhi	guojia suoyouzhi	hezuoshe	gongshe	gongren zizhi	geti jingjisuoyou	siren suoyouzhi
GDR	gesellschaftliches Eigentum (Volkseigentum)	staatliches Eigentum	genossenschaftliches Eigentum	kommunales Eigentum	Selbstverwaltung	persönliches Eigentum	Privateigentum
Hungary	társadalmi tulajdon	állami tulajdon	szövetkezeti tulajdon	tanácsi tulajdon	önigazgatás	személyi tulajdon	magántulajdon
Poland	własność społeczna (narodowa)	własność państwowa	własność spółdzielcza	własność komunalna	samorząd	własność osobista	własność prywatna
Romania	proprietate socialistă	proprietate de stat	proprietate cooperatistă	proprietate comunală	autoconducere	Proprietate personală	proprietate privată
Soviet Union	obshchestvennaia (vsenarodnaia) sobstvennost′	gosudarstvennaia sobstvennost′	kollektivnaia/ kooperativnaia sobstvennost′	kommunal′naia sobstvennost′	samoupravlenie	lichnaia sobstvennost′	chastnaia sobstvennost′
Yugoslavia[b]	društvena svojina	državna svojina	zadružna svojina	komunalna svojina	samoupravljanje	lična svojina	privatna svojina

[a]Czech terms. In Slovak ownership means *vlastníctvo.*
[b]Serb terms. In Croatian ownership means *vlasništvo,* in Slovene *lastnina.*

if borrowed from Marxism-Leninism, Roman law, or contemporaneous Yugoslav social theory.[5] Social ownership was considered superior to the individual one, and, within the latter, personal ownership to private. Small differences mattered though. The notion of social ownership did not exclude communal property and self-management in most countries, but these were discussed with incessant interest only by economic theorists in China and Yugoslavia, respectively. In other countries, they were regarded for a long time as unimportant relatives of cooperative ownership, the chief representative of *collective* or *group* ownership. In Russian, for instance, the notion of collective ownership replaced that of *cooperative* ownership. Social ownership was called *socialist ownership* in Bulgaria and Romania to suggest that private ownership was alien even to the transitory, socialist stage between capitalism and communism. In the GDR, Hungary, Poland, Romania, and the Soviet Union *people's ownership* served as their synonym but the terms "common" and "public" ownership were also employed in some of the countries. The East-German notion of "socialist social property" (*sozialistisches gesellschaftliches Eigentum*) is perhaps the clumsiest among the official neologisms. However, all these categories were often absorbed by the concept of state ownership to refer to the capture of these property forms by the state in the real world.[6] Conversely, in Yugoslavia the term "social ownership" helped hide the statist character of workers' self-management.

The omnipresence of the party-state caused many problems during the search for a safe harbor in property theory for the local councils (*soviet*s) that were deeply anchored in official ideology since Marx had written about the Paris Commune. Originally, they were conceived by the classics of communism as institutions of self-government that would manage an overwhelming part of socially owned assets and organize the whole lifeworld of citizens. Even after the Leninist and Stalinist reformulation (castration) of the idea of communal ownership, the councils retained a great number of small- and medium-sized firms and an extremely large share of real estate and infrastructure under their patronage. In most countries in our sample the lion's share of communal property rights and their control from below remained on paper.[7] Economists investigating changes in ownership regarded the councils' property as state property, and—with the exception of China and Yugoslavia—focused rather on the Big Beasts, the large state-owned enterprises up until the 1980s. Thus, communal (municipal) property became a step-child of ownership thought, something to be passed over to public administration experts and urban sociologists for research.[8]

Starting with the teachings of Marx and Lenin was not tacitly expected from authors in this volume. The ownership concepts of the *Founding Fathers* did not fully determine the canon of official political economy in our countries. Nevertheless, they managed to homogenize its basic principles even though in this respect homogeneity was somewhat paradoxical. It reflected the similarity of an underlying ambiguity from the outset; an ambiguity stemming from the difference between the original Marxian idea of ownership change (socialization)[9] and its Leninist revision (nationalization).[10] The former embodied the dream of horizontal collectivism while the latter captured the reality of vertical collectivism (etatism/statism).

Ambiguity may sound a bit surprising after the firmness of Lenin's approach[11] in the Soviet Union and its rapid irradiation to the satellite countries after 1945 were part and parcel of communist economic thought, even extending to its non-totalitarian interpretations. Although the latter included strong references to *national specifics* of ownership, they did not cease to presume the existence of a preliminary stage of *blanket Sovietization.*[12] This was supposed to lead to acknowledging state ownership as superior to all other forms of social property until the state withers away, and the notion of property as such becomes meaningless.[13] However, beneath the lid of Leninist theory there boiled a conflict between the social-democratic (orthodox Marxist) and communist (Leninist) principles of ownership in each country of the Eastern Bloc already prior to communist takeover.

In fact, the rivalry between the two principles never resulted in a complete victory of the notion of state ownership over that of social ownership. Even during the former's heyday, it was seen by official ideology as a subtype of the latter, representing a l*ower level of development*, later losing part of its significance to other subtypes (i.e., communal, self-managed, and cooperative property). Indeed, the notions of nationalization and socialization were not so far off from each other. At the end of the 19th century, social democrats from the Second International shifted away from the original Marxian view of socialization that was supposed to lead to *free associations of direct producers*. Instead of conceiving of communism as a society of self-governing communes, they began to venerate the state economy[14] as a centrally managed mega-enterprise. Yet, even the extremely statist (war communist) interpretation of the Leninist alternative in the Soviet Union did not exclude workers' councils or village communes. Or if it did so in practice, it did not eradicate their concepts but reduced them to empty boxes that might be refilled. Furthermore, when the Leninist identification of social ownership with state ownership—confirmed by the day-to-day drill of central planning, forced industrialization, and collectivization in the Soviet Union from the late 1920s—started invading economic thought in the satellite states, the offensive encountered resistance. It emerged not only from local economists of social-democratic persuasion but soon also from their Soviet colleagues after Stalin's theory of the law of value based on the duality of state and cooperative property had germinated in official political economy in the early 1950s.[15]

As a consequence, economists who had been forced to hide their preference for socialization after the communist takeover could restart thinking about non-statist varieties of social ownership.[16] Yugoslav theorists woke up first. For them the schism with the Soviet Union led to the (re)discovery of workers' self-management. For their colleagues in other countries the ironical coincidence of de-Stalinization after 1953 and the success story of Stalin's dual doctrine of social ownership paved the way to experimenting with other concepts of property, sometimes even touching on the taboo of private ownership. In Poland and Hungary the 1956 revolutions pursuing markedly anti-statist yet (horizontally) collectivist goals accelerated the process of reinterpretation.[17] In China the idea of socialization via people's communes, proclaimed by Mao in 1958, burst out during the Cultural Revolution with unprecedented ferocity (like in the case of Yugoslavia, coinciding with the break with the Soviet Union).

In the literature, Stalin's 1952 booklet on the *economic problems of socialism* is depicted, despite its poor logic and offensive style, as an eye-opener in terms of admitting certain advantages of market exchange. The same applies to his thesis of the duality of social ownership, which unleashed a great many attempts at reinterpreting property relations as a whole. Let me put aside the issue of mixed (social and individual) as well as purely individual (personal and private) ownership for a moment. Even so, there remained three avenues of revising the Leninist dogma of nationalization (etatization): (a) emphasizing, in the spirit of horizontal collectivism, the comparative advantages of cooperative and communal property; (b) designing some sort of workers' participation in ownership (such as self-management) within state enterprises; and (c) rethinking managerial property rights in the state sector vis à vis both the workers and the higher officials of the party-state.

A fourth avenue offered a conservative solution deep inside the Leninist universe. It promised the scientific underpinning of the concept of state ownership by means of the theory of optimal planning. The most ambitious variants of this research program returned to the war-communist idea, fostering an all-embracing central administration of a completely nationalized economy. Although this path of evolution of ownership thought gained the greatest acknowledgment in the West (see, for example, Leonid Kantorovich's Nobel Prize in 1975), was supported by most rigorous scholarly arguments, and resulted in the founding of influential research centers in many countries under scrutiny, our research group decided to discuss it in due detail in our next volume devoted to the history of planning concepts in the communist era. The reasons for this choice are manifold. Normally, the adherents of optimal planning were mathematical economists uninterested in (or fearing) the politics of institutional change. Unlike the market reformers, they believed in the possibility of rationalizing state ownership without probing new property regimes, social or private. They did not take part in ownership debates and influenced these only tangentially. With a view of terminating the Socialist Calculation Debate, they postulated the feasibility of an economy excluding private ownership (what their critics called *computopia*), thereby supporting also those theorists who, instead of planning the whole economy, *only* wanted to optimize the behavior of large state-owned conglomerates with the help of system theory, cybernetics, linear programming, and the like.[18]

Our country chapters show that one does not have to take this fourth avenue in order to remain in the realm of social ownership. The economists could search back and forth for new actors and property regulations along the first three avenues for decades without leaving it. As a rule, these expeditions were loosely defined, interrupted, redesigned, distorted, and entangled with one another. In the end, often even those who had launched them denied authorship. Probably the best example for such a co-evolution (or confusion) of ownership concepts occurred during the Soviet 1920s with broad debates on *khozraschet*, village communes (*obshchina* and *mir*) and the various forms of cooperatives, the role of workers' councils in enterprises, the property rights of *soviets*, and so on, not to speak of partial reprivatization at the beginning of NEP, renationalization and collectivization at its end, and a huge diversity of mixed forms of property (e.g., state capitalism) in between. To exaggerate a little, it is impossible for the historian to discover anything new about ownership thought under communism after having studied this period.

Nevertheless, other countries also experienced turbulence. The chapters in this volume provide detailed reports of the unequal, cyclical, even haphazard development of ownership concepts. For example, in Bulgaria, Hungary, and the Soviet Union the cooperatives appeared time and again as saviors of the idea of social ownership when state property showed signs of severe malfunction. In Yugoslavia and Poland workers' self-management played a similar role during long periods of communist rule but economists in countries like Bulgaria, Czechoslovakia, the GDR, Hungary, and the Soviet Union also embraced this doctrine in times of deep societal crises. In Yugoslavia, Poland, and Hungary the property rights of managers and workers were broadened simultaneously in certain phases of communist history. In China, it was the concept of communal ownership that upheld the tradition of socialization for decades. As mentioned previously, *communalism* was imprinted in the public administration system of the communist countries by the establishment of the first *councils of workers', peasants', and soldiers' deputies* in 1917. From then on, it remained an open question in ownership theory whether the nationalized local firms and real estate belonged to central or local (municipal) administration (let alone to citizens themselves), and whether the communes were voluntary organizations or rather represented the lowest level of the party-state hierarchy.

These property regimes served as supplements of (or rivals to) state ownership. The state sector remained the prime target of ownership change from the cradle of communism to its grave. No matter if the battles for change were fought under the banner of economic accounting, decentralization, workers' self-management, indirect planning, market socialism, contractual socialism, and socialist entrepreneurship—or, conversely, under that of *democratic centralism*, optimal planning, strong ministerial guidance, and huge *kombinats*—they all revolved, in the last analysis, around the width and depth of the property rights of management in state enterprises. Simply put, the question was whether there are viable ownership arrangements between two ideal-typical extremes—(1) the company director as a state employee is fully and directly subordinated to the authorities like in a military hierarchy, and (2) the owner-manager depends only on the market—with the proviso that the boundaries of social ownership remain intact. A large majority of economists in most countries and during almost the entire communist period shared the opinion that, if certain results of nationalization are to be sacrificed for some reason, social property (group ownership) must profit from the change. Individual owners should have limited and/or provisional opportunities to take over the tasks of state property that deserves more robust legal protection than any other type of ownership.

Strangely enough, the story of the stubborn attempt to construct the *perpetuum mobile* of communist economy with predominant social ownership was prolonged by a *little help* from non-social forms of property. Both small individual (personal and private) ownership tolerated by the party-state and informal privatization under the aegis of mixed ownership schemes were instrumental in compensating for inefficiency caused by social property. From private workshops, restaurants, retail shops, and apartments, through personal household plots of members in agricultural cooperatives, and semi-private work associations within state companies, all the way down to joint ventures with Western firms, a great number of property arrangements challenged official dogma. Nevertheless, they helped the doctrine of social ownership survive by camouflaging its intrinsic failures. In some countries the informal evolution of individual ownership was accompanied by its half-hearted formalization, but this—creeping—privatization was downplayed in official discourse by stressing the regulation of these private property regimes by the state.[19]

Thus, economic theorists in the nine countries under scrutiny bent the notion of social ownership from both inside and outside in the hope of finding *perhaps*[20] a cure-all for communism's economic malaise. During the terminal phase of the patient, the taboo of private property constrained their imagination less and less. Nonetheless, the lingering trust in non-capitalist or quasi-capitalist solutions in ownership theory, which they thought would prove equally fair and efficient, explains why the first blueprints of postcommunist transformation still harbored heavily collectivist ideas (illusions) during late communism, even a few minutes before the collapse. The *annus mirabilis* of 1989 is still assumed to have exhibited the typical *neoliberal excesses* of economists leaving communism behind. Allegedly, they were *closet capitalists* desperately waiting to come out. Nevertheless, as our country chapters demonstrated, in Bulgaria during that year even the most fervent market reformers did not go beyond demanding the establishment of public shareholding companies and workers' self-management (Georgi Petrov), and were preoccupied with problems of stabilization (Ventsislav Antonov), while others advocated a sort of *communal capitalism*,[21] based on the local traditions of cooperatives, accepting *citizens' ownership* and/or *workers' shareholding*. In the same months, GDR economists (such as Norbert Peche) did not even start dreaming of fully fledged workers' self-management. Privatization remained unthinkable, and leading experts on theories of ownership such as Hans Luft advocated nothing but a mere transfer of property rights from large state firms to the *Treuhandanstalt*, that is, to another state company responsible for asset management. In China, even radical reform economists like Wu Jinglian and Xue Muqiao were promoting market liberalization and the separation of ownership and management in state-owned enterprises rather than the rehabilitation of private property. Another leading reformer, Li Yining (called *Mr. Stock Market* by the *New York Times* (Kristof 1989)), proposed to transform these enterprises into shareholding companies with a majority position of the state, in which management rights are assigned on a competitive basis (an interesting hybrid of Hungarian suggestions). After the brutal suppression of the Tiananmen Square protests, even such milder ownership reforms became anathema for many years. Romanian economists of critical spirit (such as Daniel Dăianu) were suggesting *small privatization* and employee ownership instead of embarking upon the privatization of large public enterprises with the involvement of foreign investors. Otherwise, in preparing for the postcommunist transformation, they widely accepted the truism "it is the competition that matters, not ownership."

In countries with a richer prehistory of market reforms, the picture was not so different. In 1989 even the most liberal-minded Russian economists of the future, such as Yegor Gaidar and Anatoly Chubais, did not yet leave the model of enterprise self-government, workers' self-management, and autonomous cooperatives behind. They wanted to unburden the companies from administrative tutelage (*razgosudarstvlenie*) rather than convert them into privately owned institutions. Similarly, most of the mainstream reformers like Stanislav Shatalin and Grigory Yavlinsky put their faith in mixed economies represented by left-wing social democracy in the West, and until 1991 they did not envision any massive privatization drive in the short run.

In Yugoslavia, prominent economists, such as Aleksander Bajt, Branko Horvat, and Jože Mencinger, even those among them who strongly criticized the self-management system, had mixed feelings about private property rights and favored a partial preservation of social ownership in the form of *co-management* between the new private owners and the workers. Privatization was primarily conceived of as employee buyout through *internal shares*. In Hungary in 1989, the self-proclaimed Hayekian expert and future finance minister Lajos Bokros flirted with the semi-collectivist idea of voucher privatization while the radical reformer Márton Tardos was, as mentioned earlier, working out a scheme of cross-ownership between public and private firms, banks, and trade unions. Others suggested *nomenklatura buyout* programs, Tibor Liska reinvigorated his model of *entrepreneurial socialism*, and most of the economists accepted *spontaneous privatization* governed by the members of the former elites who exploited a chance to legalize their informal property rights enjoyed under the pretext of social ownership. The programmatic documents of most of the new parties indicated the doctrine of s*ocial market economy* as the main goal.

A similar plurality of nonliberal or half-liberal attitudes to private ownership occurred in Czechoslovakia and Poland during 1989—two countries that were regarded by many as bastions of neoliberal economic thought. In the former, most of the economists envisaged a *third-way* social-democratic welfare state (e.g., Ota Šik and Valtr Komárek) whereas in the latter the overwhelming majority of economic experts in the Solidarity movement (e.g., Tadeusz Kowalik and Ryszard Bugaj) supported the concept of workers' self-management, and even émigré radical reformers such as Włodzimierz Brus and Kazimierz Łaski were reluctant to give up the Langean idea of central allocation of capital goods.

True, Václav Klaus and Leszek Balcerowicz had a number of colleagues (more than in any other countries of the region at that time), such as Tomáš Ježek and Dušan Tříska in Czechoslovakia as well as Jan Szomburg and Janusz Lewandowski in Poland, who—at a certain point—began to speak proudly of their own (neo)liberal views. Nevertheless, as mentioned earlier, both eminent economists and their entourage refrained from the project of competitive privatization.[22] Amid the implosion of communism, censorship or self-censorship could not be a sufficient reason for such a degree of circumspection and self-restraint in most countries.

All in all, the Grand Decision between *social* and *private* was postponed until the early 1990s.[23] The delay can hardly be explained by the endless (albeit declining) attraction of social ownership in economic thought: it was also due to a fragile devotion to the idea of private property. Initially, these had been just two sides of the same coin: simply put, one became an admirer of the *social* out of a deep disapproval of the *private* before 1917 or 1945. After many decades, thinking in the opposite direction was far more complicated. Even those among the economic theorists who were deeply dissatisfied with social ownership were not fully convinced that it was the principal cause of inefficiency in planned economies, and were also unsure whether the emancipation of (large) private property would serve as a remedy. When they were blaming central planning or—more rarely—the party-state for lack of competition, excessive income centralization, or mismanagement in the language of market reforms, most of them did not (want to) realize that they actually criticized the formal and informal property rights of the *nomenklatura*. This short-sightedness was natural in the beginning when the pioneers of market socialism advocated *strengthening commodity-money relations* but it became somewhat bizarre when even the radical reformers of the late 1980s continued to refrain from a resolute property rights approach. It was about two decades earlier that the marketization discourse began to work in some countries as an ersatz language for the extension of managerial powers and/or a modest rehabilitation of small private ownership. However, as years passed, this language grew so dominant that many economists were unable to switch to a new vernacular.

BASIC SIMILARITIES: SIMULATING PRIVATE OWNERSHIP

Managers

Our main working hypothesis, according to which the history of economic theories of ownership under communism did not revolve around the emancipation of private property but rather around the personification of social property in the form of quasi-private owners, was convincingly supported by the country chapters. They demonstrate that economists who at some point were dissatisfied with the facelessness of social ownership wanted to see flesh-and-blood actors (but not ordinary private owners) governing the companies who would have wider *decision-making opportunities* (but not precisely defined, complete, exclusive, and legally protected property rights). In other words, they asked the party-state to grant these actors at least some informal independence with the promise of raising efficiency, balancing economic growth, and so on, or, in the worst case, of bailing out the planned economy from its recurrent crises. These actors were presumed to *simulate* private ownership as entrepreneurial-minded, responsible, and accountable managers of socially owned assets without becoming veritable capitalist owners.

In many countries groups of workers (employees, cooperative members, local citizens) were entitled to become such *persons*, though not always juridical persons, in the framework of self-managed firms, cooperatives, and communes. The architects of these institutions were confronted with the problem of defining the allocation of rights and obligations between the representative bodies of the workers and the leading executive personnel within the firm, as well as between them and the firm's superiors in the party-state hierarchy. In organizational terms, the allocation was less complicated in countries where the workers were excluded from this triad. Let me first focus on this case and examine the managers' property rights in state-owned enterprises vis à vis their higher-ups. Due to the weight of the state sector in the planned economy, and the de facto etatization of other forms of social ownership, this case represented the main target of ownership reform in the eyes of economic theorists from the outset.

The imagined quasi-private owners were euphemistically labeled experts or managers—and later technocrats and even entrepreneurs—embracing, to apply current business terms, the companies' CEOs and their close associates (Hereafter, I will use the word "manager"). Institutional reform initially was said to be tantamount to increasing their level of organizational skills and *interestedness* through decentralization, that is, through relaxing the planning hierarchy. Undoubtedly, the scope and intensity of property rights required by market reformers for the quasi-private owners grew with time, but not constantly and beyond all limits.

Economists slowly changed their discourse after witnessing that, despite successful efforts made to persuade the ruling elite to allow the managers more freedom, social ownership continued to lead to organized irresponsibility and a complicit understanding of *everybody's-thus-nobody's property*. In using these terms, they ceased to talk about the need of raising the level of managerial skills, for example, by introducing the results of *scientific-technical revolution*, or to ask the rulers to observe the principle of subsidiarity in order to *perfect* the day-to-day operation of social property. They recognized deep conflicts of interest between the firms and their superiors within the hierarchy, and started describing what had been thought to be a centrally planned (command) economy as a *bargaining economy*. Reformers no longer trusted the benevolence of officials working at the higher echelons of the party-state. Instead of convincing them to become good technocrats rather than *partocrats*, they asked for tangible institutional guarantees,[24] instead of informal concessions with regard to certain powers (property rights) of the enterprise managers.

Seen from another angle, they called for the formalization of informal bargaining procedures, that is, the legalization of powers that the managers, as agents in ordinary principal-agent relationships, enjoyed in the planning process due to their local knowledge and influence.[25] In the last years of communism, some economists began to flirt with the idea of separating the state and the communist party, releasing the former from the prison of the latter, and hoped that thereby state intervention would dwindle. Ironically, the aims of increasing the *formal* power of managers and depoliticizing the planning hierarchy by reducing the influence of party organizations were met with little enthusiasm by the managers themselves. Most of them were representatives of the *nomenklatura*. For example, those who directed large enterprises, trusts, and so on, especially in strategic industries, may have been members of the Central Committee or even the Politburo of the party. They had ample opportunity to liberate themselves from the petty tutelage of state authorities through privileged access to supreme leaders.

The simulation of private ownership was omnipresent in the countries under scrutiny from the invention of *economic accounting* (*khozraschet*)[26] in state-owned industry during the Soviet 1920s all the way down to advocating *nomenklatura* buyout programs in the late 1980s. The academic fabrication of quasi-private owners proved easier in the field of property rights related to *usus* and *usus fructus*. These rights were compartmentalized and *abusus* was dealt with special care and even suspicion. Some freedom for company directors to operate state assets under their guidance became a reasonable requirement rather early, after war communism had collapsed in Soviet Russia, though state/party intervention could restrict their power at any time. Having the right to profit from these assets accepted was much more difficult due to egalitarian promises repeatedly made by the communists. Those economists, the few who did not find some sort of profit sharing within the companies too iconoclastic a claim, had to hide this suggestion behind the façade of strengthening *material incentives*.[27] At the same time, the liberty of *abusus*—that is, the right to buy and sell, merge or destroy capital, first of all, however, to expropriate (inherit/bequeath) it—was the hardest nut to crack. On the level of ideological declarations, the expropriation of social property by managers remained an absolute taboo almost until the collapse of communism, and other forms of *abusus* also were tolerated very late, if at all, and only in certain countries.

From the very beginning, the principle of *capital goods are not commodities* was almost as firmly observed in the state sector as that of the ban on private appropriation of these goods. During nearly the entire communist period, companies were only entitled to barter (or later buy and sell) a fragment of their fixed assets, and did not have the right to take major investment decisions, bring one of their workshops or plants to the market, or—horribile dictu—to liquidate the whole firm or merge it with another. They were not allowed to mortgage their assets or issue bonds and shares, and their institutional relations with the banks were drastically restricted.[28] Practically, the distribution and pricing of a lion's share of capital goods were privileges of the central planner, that is, a small group of party and state officials even in the most liberal communist regimes. This rule was (gladly or obediently) accepted by a great majority of economists until the second half of the 1980s.[29]

First Excurse to Nomenklatura *Ownership*

This is not the place where I can elaborate on the theoretical origins of the idea of prohibiting capital markets in planned economies. They ranged from Marx's vision of communism, through the demonization of *Finanzkapital* and the idealization of the doctrine of war economy by both social democrats and conservatives at the turn of the 19th century, to the Bolshevik concept of war communism, the Stalinist strategy of industrialization, and later to Oskar Lange's model of market socialism in the 1930s, the latter exerting perhaps the greatest influence on reform-minded economists in our countries. Of course, the surge of state interventionism between the two wars, including the second wave of war economies, made a deep impact on the mindset of economists in the emerging communist states. Suffice it to say that these concepts authorized the *nomenklatura* to occupy the virgin territory of social ownership from the very beginning, contributing to the rise of a rather faceless (anonymous) and *sui generis* informal system of exercising essential property rights—with obscure but strong prerogatives and without genuine responsibility and accountability. For example, there was no written law in any of the countries that sanctioned interventions made by the communist party in economic decisions at any level of the hierarchy. In formal terms of ownership the territory was possessed by all citizens. Informally, however, what seemed to be a no man's land belonging to everybody was invaded by the ruling elite right after the communist takeover,[30] the members of which not only used social property and profited from it but were also given the opportunity to create, destroy, and merge, and even to bequeath parts of it (e.g., state-owned apartments, access to privileged healthcare services) as well as their savings and accumulated network capital to their heirs. Most of the powers of the party-state over the enterprises were sanctioned by executive orders and custom rather than law, and even in the latter case there was almost no legal protection (conflict-settlement mechanism) to resist the caprice of authorities.

Unfortunately, although the core hypothesis had been formulated by Lev Trotsky during the 1920s, reinforced by Milovan Djilas 30 years later (followed by a great number of insider observers from György Konrád and

Iván Szelényi through Rudolph Bahro to Mikhail Voslensky), and supported by powerful political movements such as the Cultural Revolution in China or the New Left all around the globe, the concepts of *state capitalism*, *new class*, *red bourgeoisie*, and so on did not rely on a profound economic and sociological analysis of property relations.[31]

The key question about the difference between *nomenklatura* ownership and private ownership has not been answered until today. Despite the fact that economists in our countries did not or could not describe the economic behavior of the ruling elite with sufficient precision, they were aware of its formal and informal property rights with regard to *usus* and *usus fructus*. Any reformer who called for increasing the independence of enterprises wanted at the very least to curb the formal segment of these rights of the state authorities, for example, in determining production plans or the salaries of managers. However, they did not or could not identify, not even on the level of theoretical assumptions, the informal roles state officials and party apparatchiks played as *trustees* or *co-owners* in such decisions.[32] Were they also quasi-private owners? How stable and exclusive were their property rights? Was their *shadow ownership* similar to that of company managers who did not belong to the highest stratum of the communist elite? What were their basic preferences?[33] How did they blur and transgress the formal boundaries of property rights? What kind of bargaining, rent-seeking, free-riding, or predatory strategies did they pursue? Were these strategies individual and conflicting or harmonized within and between the competing groups/networks of the *nomenklatura*? How did state officials and party cadres differ in terms of exercising ownership? Do the fluidity and interpenetration of these groups allow the analyst to speak about clear-cut rules of proprietary behavior? These are just a few of countless questions that remained without answers (or were not asked at all). In our volume it is the Czechoslovak chapter that discusses this issue in detail. Lubomír Mlčoch was one of the few economists who began to explore the fine structure of co-ownership between managers and their superiors in the party-state. That is how he came to the *reverse pyramid* model reflecting the fact that actual power relations were in favor of company managers—a conclusion sharply contradicting the totalitarian paradigm.[34]

One could presume that Western observers would dig a little deeper and apply more rigorous research methods in order to answer the above questions. Besides the well-known works offered by *revisionist* authors in Soviet Studies—mostly political scientists and historians (such as Ellen Comisso, Merle Fainsod, Archibald Getty, Paul Gregory, Mark Harrison, Jerry Hough, Moshe Lewin, Sheila Fitzpatrick, Gabor Rittersporn, and Gordon Skilling)—from the 1960s on how the communist regimes were ruled, economists in our countries could learn the most from sociologists, anthropologists, and legal experts. As noted in the Introduction, many evidence-based innovative concepts in the former two disciplines came rather late. For instance, notions like David Stark's (1996) *recombinant property*, Katherine Verdery's (2003) *elasticity of ownership* and *administrative estate*, or, quite recently, Suava Zbierski-Salameh's (2013) *conjoint ownership* could have contributed significantly to the understanding by the reformers of the proprietary behavior of the *nomenklatura* if they had been put forward earlier.

Fortunately, the historical analogy of feudalism (patrimony, oligarchical rule, patron-client relationship, etc.), or of clans and mafias were effective enough, even without profound empirical underpinning, to convince the radical reform economists to join the *revisionist* stream in challenging the simplistic, totalitarian interpretation of property relations and turn to a network-, interest group-, and bargaining-based approach to the problem of *nomenklatura* ownership. As noted earlier, this complex approach was also promoted by the local theorists of economic bureaucracy and some of the legal researchers. The latter borrowed surprisingly little from their Western colleagues who could have equipped them with a huge toolbox of sophisticated concepts of property rights to define a regime of ownership, the components of which could not be squeezed into distinct pigeon holes of formal rules, complete rights, well-defined legal actors, or characterized by the principles of unambiguity, irrevocability, and the like. In a similar vein, they might have considered the ruling elite as a "self-legitimating bureaucracy" (Duff Milenkovitch 1992) and—moderating fascination with corporeal ownership—focus on immaterial objects of property (e.g., social capital, institutionalized power, cultural hegemony), too. Finally, they might have paid more attention to exclusion and inclusion as well as privileges in and outside the *nomenklatura*.

Nevertheless, some of these concepts and approaches trickled to Eastern Europe and helped persuade the radical reformers (with the exception of China) that (a) at a certain point they would not be able to decouple any serious change in the property regime from a fundamental shift in the political/cultural regime as a whole; (b) if they sincerely wanted to get rid of the party-state, they should prefer liberal democracy based on *real* private ownership over a hitherto unknown collectivist democracy based on self-management, cooperatives, or communes, which does not suffer from the deficiencies of these observed in the communist era. The implicit assumption behind these conclusions originated, on the one hand, in the sad experience of assimilation and corruption of these collectivist ownership forms by the ruling elite and, on the other hand, in a strong (utopian) hope in the immunity of private ownership to the surviving influence of the same elite, or in the impossibility of an emerging non-communist yet illiberal elite who also might distort privatization.[35]

No matter if it came to the state or the party, *abusus* was the largest black box when thinking of *nomenklatura* ownership. This was not because economists presumed that the elite had no say whatsoever in opening, closing, or merging firms but because, with the exception of political dynasties, the right of inheritance under communism seemed different from what they knew about private property under capitalism. Undoubtedly, a district party secretary was not allowed to bequeath to his/her children any of the companies working in his/her territory, in the operation of which he intervened every day. Nevertheless, what the same person expropriated in the form of rents stemming from informal co-ownership along with the managers as well as other state and party officials—which ranged from money bribes and access to shortage goods through having family members employed by the company in his/her sphere of interest to *comradely help* rendered by its director in building his/her summer house—could become legal components of his/her last will and testament. Despite all differences stemming from the fact that property rights were normally not bought and sold in the market (according to Mlčoch, they were status-based entitlements), and were constrained by oligarchical and mafia-like dependencies and conflicts, not to speak of a whole series of ideological directives, enjoying private property rights in other economies in which private property prevails is not a million miles away from what happened under *nomenklatura* ownership. Modeling the peculiar blend of private and group-based property rights of the communist ruling elite could have been a substantial contribution to a universal theory of ownership and a specific theory of bureaucratic ownership studied by new-institutionalist historians and public choice experts. In this respect, it would have been intriguing to ask, for example, whether one could speak of a sort of collectivism in the case in which certain groups of the ruling elite exercised their property rights jointly. Similarly, it would have been interesting to know how the huge distance between their power over and gains from capital (as compared to the case of owners of large companies in capitalist societies) could be maintained for a long time.

***

The trap of social ownership in economic thought was sealed by formal and informal institutions ranging from transnational organizations of the communist countries, through national planning offices, the military, and the secret police, all the way down to party units in enterprises. Economists could barely break out from this trap because it was hardened not only by ideological and scientific arguments, norms, habits, and symbols but also by vital interests of the ruling elite in maintaining/increasing its own power and wealth. The growing desire of economic thinkers to populate (more exactly, to *re*-populate) the no man's land aimed at weakening or eventually replacing its first occupants by means of simulating private ownership, but without violating the prohibition of formal rights related to *abusus*. It took decades until simulation reached its end by touching on this final taboo of the communist economy. Even economists who came to reject the intellectual raison d'être of social ownership had to think twice before taking the risk of challenging the power structure built around it. This land was not empty even if the property rights of the *nomenklatura* members were not accurately specified.

Small-scale private ownership was an issue around which former liberals, social democrats, agrarian experts, not to mention frustrated communists, could have amalgamated after 1917 and 1945 respectively. However, most economists tenaciously presumed that the planned economy's heart was the state sector (above all, state industry, the supreme symbol of modernization) where, through moderate ownership change, one could attain greater results at a lower political price than in agriculture and services. Their ideal quasi-private owners were the managers (no matter if they had been, to use the post-1917 Bolshevik jargon, *red directors* or *bourgeois experts* earlier), even if these were unable to populate the no man's land as thoroughly as revitalized and new private owners could have been. Releasing the company managers from the over-zealous control exercised by the state bureaucracy was a recurrent theme of economic thought after the collapse of war communism in the Soviet Union, the introduction of self-management in Yugoslavia at the end of the 1940s, the first wave of economic reforms in the Eastern European countries in the mid-1950s, and even after the late 1950s in China.[36] Oskar Lange's market socialism in the late 1930s, Anatoly Venediktov's *operative management of state property* in 1948, or János Kornai's *Overcentralization* in 1956, to refer to some of the early milestones in the scholarly elaboration of that theme, were all important concepts—unintentionally—preparing the ground for a breakthrough in ownership theory; a breakthrough that did not take place until 1989. Undoubtedly, the diverse market reforms of the communist economies between the 1960s and 1980s did extend the property rights of the managers of state enterprises to a considerable degree, but virtually no author of these reforms proposed that the managers should become veritable private owners.

The dogmatic problem they had to solve was the following: given the doctrine of unitary state ownership, how should economic and legal theory explain the existence of individual firms in another way than describing them as the lowest links in a hierarchical chain? Even the tiniest taste of enterprise autonomy would make the unity of state ownership questionable, and open the door for a thesis of divisibility of state-owned capital first within its sacrosanct borders, and later even beyond them. The same applied to social ownership as a whole. Venediktov's muddy notion of operative management[37] set the scene for a series of compromises in ownership thought, ranging from the Hungarian concept of *separateness* and *shared ownership* through the Chinese principle of *unified leadership, divided management* to the pragmatic suggestion recurring in countries like Czechoslovakia and Yugoslavia, which depicted the firms as tenant organizations renting the assets from the state as the ultimate subject of ownership, using these assets and paying taxes after them.[38] Beyond challenging the thesis of indivisibility, economists also had to convince themselves that the emerging units of state ownership should be armed with exclusive property rights, including alienability, and that state ownership should not enjoy privileges vis à vis other regimes of property.

As compared to the *visible fist* of the party-state, the *not-yet-invisible hand* of the socialist market economy above all in Yugoslavia, Hungary, and later in China offered managers new freedoms in deciding on substantial issues related to *usus* and *usus fructus* (such as complying with economic regulations instead of planning targets, choosing their business partners, entering joint ventures, launching investment projects, determining prices and wages, sharing profits, etc.). Today, we would call this a governance-oriented rather than ownership-oriented approach. The radicals among liberal-minded economists were only willing to advocate employee shareholding schemes in the last few years before 1989. These would also include the managers and enable them to possess part of the company's capital and, according to the boldest proposals, to trade and bequeath the shares like any other objects of personal property. In the Soviet Union, for example, Liska's model was revisited during *perestroika*: the employees would lease the firms from the state, manage it independently, and buy it out with the emerging profits step by step.[39] Back in the 1950s when the preconditions for such freedoms were first formulated in larger reform packages these did not focus on the managers themselves. The market reformers rather talked about *increasing the independence of enterprises*. Even in the 1960s and 1970s, they showed precaution in publicly referring to James Burnham and John Galbraith whose respective ideas on *managerial revolution* and *technostructure* (both reflecting the illusion of convergence between the East and the West) influenced their views on ownership to a certain extent. Instead of calling the managers at least surrogate owners, economists kept on designing institutional *mechanisms* or *models* in order to grant the managers some operational freedom (pertaining to standard daily activities of the firm), entitle them to earn some profit, and finally allow them to enter certain areas of the capital market. Managerial decision-making was combined with some kind of employee participation (trade union rights for co-determination, workers' self-management, or even employee stock ownership) with a view of controlling the managers *from below* and preventing them from acting like genuine capitalists. Supervision *from above* was not forgotten either. Even the most subversive ideas aiming to replace dependency on the party-state with asset management to be performed by independent holding enterprises would have limited the freedom of company managers by transferring some of their property rights onto the level of the CEOs of the holdings. For example, in studying Japanese, Italian, German, and Austrian regimes of corporate governance, and suggesting the establishment of state holdings similar to INI or ÖIAG, Hungarian economists could not exclude the possibility that the firm managers might turn out to be almost as exposed to the new mega-organizations as they had been to the various trusts, directorates, industrial associations, and branch ministries previously (particularly because it was likely that the chief executives of the holdings would be appointed by the central organs of the party).

Much of economists' insistence on meticulous social engineering to change ownership relations was due to the prohibition of large private property. Evidently, the economic theorists had to "dance hog-tied" (so goes the Hungarian saying). But it is, I think, more than telling that most of the dissidents and/or émigrés among them also did not call for unleashing the capital markets to carry out competitive privatization on a massive scale. This could be explained partly by the fact that in an open bidding for state, cooperative, or communal assets most of the new owners would have come from among the members of the communist ruling elite and the agents of the grey and black markets, or a combination of the two. Foreign ownership was also unpopular with many economists. However, the inertia of fabricating quasi-private owners for several decades also proved remarkable. Market reformers did not cease envisioning managers in pragmatic/technical terms as unbiased experts who would take entrepreneurial risks as responsibly and who would care for the long-term repercussions of their decisions as prudently as veritable private owners under ideal circumstances. Neither were the moral hazards emerging in the relationships of the managers with their principals in the party-state sufficiently taken into account, nor was the simple fact that property rights would not work effectively only because a higher authority portioned them out in a particular combination.

Being *half pregnant* was no perfect solution. When only certain rights of *abusus* were introduced and, in addition, many other property rights pertaining to *usus* and *usus fructus* remained curtailed, one could not reasonably expect the birth of genuine owners. It was sufficient, for example, to ban one of the property rights related to *abusus*: say, corporate takeover. If the threat of merger and/or acquisition transmitted by capital markets does not discipline the managers, one cannot presume that they will show, in an ideal case, signs of wise, careful, and far-sighted, that is, owner-like behavior. If such a threat comes only from their superiors in the party-state, then opportunist attitudes will be more likely. Or let us suppose that in principle all rights of *abusus* are granted to the managers of state-owned firms but the right (or rather the informal power) to fire and hire them remains in the hands of the ruling elite like in the case of communist Eastern Europe yesterday and China today. Opportunism was/is coded into this kind of dependency as well. Most economists nonetheless hoped for a long time that the company managers would adjust to market signals rather than to the whims of the higher-ups.

Despite such dilemmas, ownership concepts usually did not go so far as to finish simulating private property through growing managerial powers, and let it develop on its own. With very few exceptions such as the group of Polish libertarians, private ownership appeared as a dividable idea, certain components of which can be dispensed with, faked, simulated, or replaced at will, as a technical instrument without intrinsic value and social meaning. The ideal *owner* was portrayed as a manager-businessman who organizes, innovates, calculates, and takes risks by using social assets, but is devoid of the Schumpeterian glory of the capitalist entrepreneur.

Unlike the advocates of managerial ownership, the theorists of employee participation also had to assess the property rights of the company directors from below, from the angle of trade unions and workers' councils in state-owned firms or of those bodies that represented the interests of members and employees in cooperatives and communes. Here, one could not start off from the tacit assumption that the workers were nothing more than passive observers. In fact, even members of the Soviet collective farm and the Chinese people's commune had *some* rights (at least formally) to elect their bosses and discuss or challenge managerial rulings with regard to the disposal of and profiting from social assets. In principle, most communist regimes also allowed them to take out at least part of the fixed capital (land, instruments, etc.) they had put in when joining the association if they decided to leave the realm of social ownership. In some countries like Hungary and China economists proposed the deepening of these rights from the late 1950s and the late 1970s, respectively, which contributed to an erosion of group ownership and the consolidation of some kind of individual property.

Nevertheless, their objectives were dwarfed by the Yugoslav experts' ideas about workers' self-management. In the field of ownership theory, Yugoslav economists provided a great intellectual input in terms of both scholarly sophistication and the sheer quantity of thoughts. Their contribution exceeded the scientific performance of economists in other communist countries in terms of the genuine interest shown by a number of Yugoslav economists from Aleksander Bajt to Svetozar Pejovich in neoclassical analysis and property rights research (see, for example, Franičević 2012; Furubotn and Richter 1998), as well as of their original insights. Obviously, they had to model a more complicated search for quasi-private owners than in Hungary or Poland, since simulation concerned two sometimes competing, sometimes cooperating quasi-owners, the managers, and the workers.

Most chapters of the four-decade story of Yugoslav self-management are well known from the literature. The discussion of conflicts between the managers and the workers' councils over issues related to *usus* and *usus fructus*, and the repeated attempts at reconstituting the mix of property rights to solve them, filled libraries. The same applies to the analysis of varying coalitions between the managers, the workers' councils, the local communes, and other institutions of the party-state, especially following a major reform of self-management that introduced *contractual socialism* between 1974 and 1976. However, the issue of *abusus* earned less attention until the 1980s. Yugoslav scholars invested much effort in redesigning the allocation of property rights among the aforementioned actors to test to what extent it was responsible for the familiar pitfalls of the self-managed economy such as underinvestment/overconsumption, undue income polarization, as well as high rates of unemployment and inflation, which were routinely attributed to the excessive powers either of the workers' councils or the managers, or both.

The communist ruling elite regarded the coalition of workers and managers with suspicion, and issued repeated warnings about the *degeneration* of social ownership into manager-dominated group ownership that was considered a symptom of informal privatization. The *nomenklatura* did its best to maintain the primacy of social property[40] through investment and income policies and constraining the exchange of capital, particularly between the social and private sectors. The rise of *contractual socialism* can also be described as a desperate attempt at breaking the alliance of managers and workers through further confusing property rights by radical decentralization as well as an artificial and overcomplicated system of contracts between the self-management units and between these and the local communes—an excellent chance for the rulers to fish in troubled waters. Although many adherents of self-management saw in the workers and managers ordinary stakeholders, hardly any of them suggested that they be entitled to take along part of the company's capital upon changing jobs or retirement. (Even *internal shares* were introduced as late as 1988.) Similarly, the legal opportunity of transforming self-managing enterprises into private ones was provided by the disintegrating party-state only some months before the collapse of communism.[41] Until then, the belief in further adjustments of the self-management system, that is, the expectation that *perhaps* the next configuration of property rights within the framework of social ownership might be *the* solution, remained deep-seated in the research community.

SMALL OWNERS

A powerful alternative of crafting quasi-private owners from managers could have been the development of *real* small-scale private ownership—an institution with a long prehistory in our countries and which would not have needed artificial creation. Yet, instead of inviting the traditional (and provisionally tolerated) small owners in agriculture but also in industry, domestic trade, and other services to settle in no man's land, most economists from the GDR to Bulgaria gave their names to drastic regulations of private property rights for assets that survived nationalization and collectivization. These regulations not only inhibited or blocked *abusus* (by prohibiting, for example, the alienation, leasing, and mortgaging of land[42]), and sometimes even went so far as to ban inheritance, but also limited the use of capital and earning income from it. In certain countries and periods private ownership was deleted from the Constitution, blamed as *reactionary* or *counter-revolutionary*, and exposed to criminal prosecution.[43]

No chapter in our volume points to a substantial enough segment of the economic research community in any of the countries, which would have demanded that the planned economy include a strong and developing sector based on *purely* private ownership of *freely* expanding small-sized enterprises. With the exception of some liberal and *neo-Narodnik* theorists in the Soviet Union during the 1920s, virtually no leading economist propounded such ideas during the whole communist era, not even the majority of Polish and Yugoslav experts who faced large agricultural sectors in the possession of small owners. The radical suggestions envisaged the easing of prevailing restrictions regarding the size of the private firm, the industry it works in, or the citizenship of the owner, but refrained from endorsing a spontaneous concentration of small capital.[44] Exploiting and tolerating small-sized enterprises, and—in the best case—associating them with various types of social property through joint ventures were the maximum goals formulated by the reformers up until the 1980s.[45] Nonetheless, the fear propagated by the classics of Marxism-Leninism that "small production engenders capitalism and the bourgeoisie continuously, daily, hourly, spontaneously, and on a mass scale" (Lenin [1920] 1952) was so deep-seated in official political economy and everyday politics (cf. the *petty-bourgeois menace*) that economists had better stress that toleration was temporary, and disguise private proprietors as junior partners of social owners. Moreover, those few economists who did not shy away from capitalism also had reservations about small-sized private property. For them, it would have meant backsliding, in terms of modernization theory, to the interwar period if the planned economy had sacrificed the idea of large enterprise to the principle of *small is beautiful*.[46]

A peculiar type of quasi-private small-scale ownership was what official political economy denoted as *personal property*. Communist ideology was unable to interpret it in an unambiguous way, oscillating from the very outset between ascetic/egalitarian and hedonistic/meritocratic attitudes to income, wealth, and consumption, and creeping away from the former. The magic formula borrowed from Marx, according to which the crucial difference between personal and private property is that the former cannot be used to exploit others,[47] proved flexible enough to support both attitudes. This approach enabled the rulers to justify the "expropriation of the expropriators," and, at the same time, the "maximum satisfaction of the constantly rising material and cultural needs of the whole of society," to quote Stalin's "basic law of socialism" (1951). The former explained the abolition of private ownership while the latter defended the expansion of personal property, especially from the 1960s onwards.[48] As an unintended consequence, this *law* also provided the economists who hoped for a gradual proliferation of small business ventures with some room to maneuver. Since a piece of land, a building, a car, or even a telephone could be used in both consumption and production, a number of economists began to consider personal ownership as a legitimate surrogate of private property, and thus an ideologically almost harmless concept. This way, in a tacit consensus with moderates in the *nomenklatura*, small hotels, garage firms, taxi cooperatives, household plots, restaurants, shops, sublets, and so on, grew from personal assets in the grey economy and gained some recognition (sometimes even a de facto private proprietary status).[49]

The reformers did not shout from the rooftops that many *abusus* rights remained in force in the case of personal property. Unlike managers of state, cooperative, or communal enterprises, the holders of personal assets were often not quasi-private owners but real ones. In many of the countries you were entitled to sell your home, pass over the family restaurant to your children, or open a small laundry firm, in which you employed, besides your family members, a few other workers. In this sense, personal ownership might have worked as a time bomb in the post-Stalinist canon of political economy, destroying the dominant position of social ownership after a while. Nonetheless, with the exception of Tibor Liska in Hungary (cf. his concept of *personal ownership of social capital*), no Grand Design idolizing personal property was developed in the communist period. At the same time, when personal ownership was regarded as an informal but generally accepted claim for intangible assets like a secure job, equal pay or free education, it could serve also as an inbuilt stabilizer of the communist regime (cf. Granick 1988).

Apparently, mixing social and individual forms of ownership proved to be a more attractive option complying with the collectivist preferences of economists and also satisfying the censors. Browsing through the chapters of this volume, one sees an incredible variety of *hybrid* property arrangements supported by economic theorists, which range from combining the personal assets of farmers (e.g., a small fruit garden or a horse) with those of agricultural cooperatives and state-owned machine and tractor stations in Bulgaria or the Soviet Union, through the joint ventures of self-managed enterprises and small private firms in Yugoslavia, and the *Kommanditgesellschaften* in the GDR, to the Chinese *household responsibility system* in the countryside, the leasing of state-owned shops and restaurants in Poland (*ajencja*) and Romania (*mandatari*), and intrapreneurship (*vgmk*) in Hungary.[50] State, cooperative, communal, private, and personal ownership, both domestic and foreign, formal and informal, legal and illegal—almost all blends of property forms were invented and/or approved retroactively by economists in almost all countries under scrutiny, and in almost all phases of communism, including the darkest years of Stalinism.[51] If our volume has called the attention of the reader only to this patchwork of ownership regimes, we have not worked in vain. Designing and testing these hybrid forms, that is, contributing to a broad pluralization of ownership, took economists a lot of time, and stole the show from preparations for large-scale, rule-based, competitive privatization by raising hopes that the next hybrid *perhaps* would be more successful than the last one.

To avoid misunderstandings, this kind of experimentation was anything but free and undisturbed: it was confined by overt and tacit rules of containing private ownership, and the designers of hybrid property were risking harassment by communist hardliners each time. Among diverse prohibitions, the party-state was probably the keenest on avoiding that capital goods would cross the borders of the fortress called social ownership and leave it behind forever.[52] They could be rented (not sold) out to individual owners for a certain period, possibly under highly incomplete and revocable contracts.[53] Hence, in addition to maintaining a general feeling of uncertainty and dependency, fuzzy property rights enabled the *gatekeepers* within the *nomenklatura* to draw income from corruption (Shleifer and Vishny 1994). Normally, the social owners retained their majority position in the property deals made with selected groups of society, which could be separated from each other and marginalized if they happened to grow too powerful. The power asymmetry and the dispersion of ownership privileges were carefully observed to avoid any political coalition among the advantaged groups. Here, the memory of the emerging alliance between the well-to-do, still not collectivized farmer and the private trader (*nepman*) in the Soviet Union during the mid-1920s served as a serious warning.[54] Guizot's famous message of *enrich yourself* that was announced by Nikolai Bukharin in 1925, and repeated later by several communist politicians including Deng Xiaoping, did not reflect a typical approach to the private sector. The privileges were portioned out cautiously and kept under control by means of income regulation, size limitation, and the like to prevent private owners from becoming medium-sized capitalist entrepreneurs. The majority of economists agreed to such constraints, and only a few entertained the hope that repeated concessions made by communist regimes to small private owners, tenants, renters, and so on would work as a slow poison destroying the health of the very organism it wanted to heal. When, for some reason, the taboo of large private property was no longer respected, like in China since the end of the 1990s, heavy government regulations and direct intervention by the communist party were designed to control the emerging system of *state capitalism*.

COMPARISON: FROM STATIC TO DYNAMIC

My reading of the basic similarities in economic thinking about ownership under communism, that is, of the long-standing primacy of social ownership as well as its flipside, the simulation *and* containment of private property, implies a broad pattern of evolution characteristic of all countries examined. By and large, this pattern includes the following stages of development:

- Hesitation between the principles of socialization and nationalization
- Accepting the dominance of state ownership
- Rehabilitation of other forms of social ownership (pluralization I)
- Transformation of managers in enterprises under social ownership into quasi-private owners (pluralization II)
- Extension of personal ownership (pluralization III)
- Hybridization of social, private, and personal forms of ownership (pluralization IV)
- Hesitation over a radical extension of private property
- Accepting the dominance of private ownership

In a sense, the evolution of key ownership concepts under communism could be subsumed under the poetic subtitle of *long meditation between two hesitations*. Acceptance of dominant private ownership can only be found on the other side of the 1989 watershed. It embodies the first phase of the post-communist era rather than the last phase of the communist one. The popular joke circulating in the wake of the 1989 revolutions was telling: communism did represent the longest possible road from capitalism to capitalism.

During the transition *to* communism, hesitation ended with a sweeping victory of the doctrine of state ownership, while the transition *from* communism resulted in the triumph of private property. (If that triumph were unambiguous and lasting does not concern us at this stage of our research program.) Despite the initial success of state ownership, it did not manage to oust other forms of social ownership from economic thought during the communist epoch as a whole, and private property needed a very long time to appear without any disguise. The first transition began well before 1917–1945, and the second also stretched beyond 1989–1991. What took place between the two was a convolution of various processes of pluralization of ownership concepts. In retrospect one cannot deny that economic theory covered a huge distance between the arch-collectivist doctrine of social ownership under war communism and the cautious individualism of the first blueprints of privatization at the end of the 1980s. However, it was impossible to predict whether the evolution of ownership thought would not mire in the muddy roads of pluralization until the very collapse of communism.

The eight stages above do not represent a strict chronology. The concept of state ownership did not evaporate: it was complemented and pluralized rather than abolished by workers' self-management, cooperative and communal property, and the transformation of managers into quasi-private owners. Similarly, the extension of individual (personal and private) property appeared on the horizon of economic imagination rather early as a corrective to the dominance of social ownership. Most of the time, simultaneity and pluralism prevailed. With the exception of the stages of accepting the dominance of state and private ownership, respectively, one sees powerful trends that coexisted in varying proportions rather than consecutive stages of evolution, let alone progress.

A closer look at these trends reveals further similarities between the countries in our sample. Common catalysts of scientific discoveries, formative experiences, and turning points as well as mental obstacles and cycles of thought come to light when one observes ownership theories under communism from an evolutionary perspective. Let me focus on the post-1945 developments and refer to the period between 1917 and 1945 in the Soviet Union only if it adds a specific color to the overall picture.

As mentioned, the story started with an ideological ambiguity that left a large door open for experimentation within the framework of social ownership, and a much smaller door for reinterpreting individual ownership. After 1945, the ideal of state property that became unquestionable during the Soviet 1930s and 1940s conquered the minds of economists all over the newly created Eastern Bloc, tempting social democrats skeptical about all-out nationalization[55] and even numerous *bourgeois* experts who had subscribed to corporativist/interventionist theories between the two wars.[56] In a decade or so, however, this ideal was damaged by workers' self-management in Yugoslavia, Stalin's partial rehabilitation of the cooperatives (canonized, after his death, by the long-awaited Soviet textbook of the political economy of socialism), and Mao's preference for communal ownership. These semi-statist (or parastatal) variants of social ownership assumed institutional permanence and also served as intellectual instruments in the toolbox of economists in which they could reach whenever they were preparing for a change in the property regime. At the bottom of the toolbox could be found ideas about the usefulness of small-scale individual ownership but these did not enjoy strong ideological support for a long time: they rather underpinned temporary policies to balance markets and ease political tensions like in the case of agriculture and services in many countries.

The fact that some of these instruments were applied also can be explained in the case of Yugoslavia and China by conflicts with the Soviet Union that led to a strong political push for a national *Sonderweg* that revitalized certain institutional legacies. Constant inefficiency and the recurrent breakdown of the machinery of state property were the principal causes in other countries. The repeated economic failures, crises, and even disasters prompted the economists to initiate institutional innovation in the field of ownership relations time and again whereby they could choose among (a) the country's traditions, and/or (b) emulate other countries' institutions, and/or (c) invent new ones.[57] As a result, social ownership became more colorful and was combined with personal/private property in many ways. National traditions in ownership thought heavily influenced, for example, the introduction of workers' self-management in Yugoslavia, the development of cooperatives in Bulgaria, the combination of personal and cooperative ownership in Hungary or personal and communal ownership in China, as well as the experimentation with managerial ownership in Poland. As regards emulation, the forced (hierarchical) imitation of the Soviet model of state property was replaced gradually by a horizontal exchange of ownership ideas among the communist countries, whereby even the imperial center could learn from the peripheries. This is how concepts of self-management travelled from Yugoslavia, managerial ownership from Hungary, or in the very end, voucher privatization from Poland to many countries under Soviet rule.[58] Engaging in *histoire croisée* could bring more twisted itineraries to light, revealing linkages in terms of property arrangements, for example, between Lenin's food tax, the Hungarian regulation of household plots, the Chinese household responsibility system, and the reform of the *kolkhozy* under Gorbachev.

The Western input in this kind of exchange also grew with time, and ideas passed through both the large door of rethinking social ownership and the smaller door of rehabilitating private property. The former let in, for instance, the concept of managerial ownership, especially pertaining to large state conglomerates in industry and agriculture, and—in the last minutes of communism—the project of employee shareholding, whereas the latter was increasingly open to the idea of small entrepreneurship and various models of mixed (private and public) governance. Exchange is probably too big a word for the diffusion of thought that preferred a one-way street leading from West to East. True, the theories of workers' self-management, cooperative, and communal ownership as well as managerial ownership implied by market socialism have repeatedly enticed Western experts searching for alternatives to private property regimes. These four doctrines embody major inventions suggested by economists in the communist epoch, inventions that were originally rooted in non-communist economies but were never tested as large-scale experiments in social engineering. As odd as it may seem, in this sense, predominant state ownership can also be regarded as a major invention, even though its idea has not yet enchanted eminent Western economists. Unfortunately, both these doctrines and their tests lacked scientific accuracy. Notwithstanding the fact that most of these ownership concepts proved unsuccessful in the long run, one cannot exclude *ab ovo* and with absolute certitude that under different circumstances, and above all in an environment of predominant private ownership and liberal democracy, they might thrive in the future (Bardhan and Roemer 1992).

A sixth invention, Liska's entrepreneurial socialism, was trialed only in minor field experiments but it influenced the Polish-Czech project of voucher privatization—perhaps the seventh original grand project in ownership theory that might fertilize Western economic thought at some point.[59] The eighth, large-scale privatization and the emergence of new (*greenfield*) private property in no man's land under communist dictatorship in China, has little to say to economists in the West unaccustomed to brutal types of authoritarian rule. Nevertheless, they cannot disregard the sad news that private ownership can happily coexist with this kind of polity. As mentioned, a ninth invention, potentially *the* fundamental one, namely, construing a general economic theory of *nomenklatura* ownership, is still up in the air. Yet it might have helped the analysts comprehend what seemed an oxymoron at first sight, the Chinese combination of communism with large-scale private ownership. This theory might have been the only one of purely descriptive-analytical nature among the inventions; all the others also had strong normative implications.

In an evolutionary presentation of economic thinking about ownership, one may commit at least two kinds of mistakes: (a) concentrate exclusively on change and forget about the inertia (or revival) of concepts claiming to preserve the original regimes of property; (b) scrutinize the grand and pure projects, and overlook the smaller and mixed ones. Focusing on pluralization of ownership relations may save us from both. On the one hand, it reflected the survival of a preference for state ownership (particularly, in the form of mammoth organizations) as well as for statist types of cooperative and communal ownership in countries under hardline communist rule. On the other hand, pluralization boiled down to projects advocating a multitude of sometimes microscopic hybrids under softer regimes, the real importance of which only became transparent once large-scale privatization had started. In discussing the main trends of evolution of ownership thought, I alluded to four faces of pluralization which overlap to a certain extent.

Arguably, in the long run, searching for new property regimes resulted not only in pluralization of the ownership concepts but also in their scientific refinement. Undeniably, economic scholarship went far beyond the sterile debates about whether or not "ownership constitutes a distinct or a central component or the very totality of the relations of production."[60] Nevertheless, it is a pity to see how little economists learned from other social sciences (especially from sociology, history, and law)[61] in designing ownership reforms, even in countries in which international communication was not blocked, and how persistently they continued to use empty terms of Marxism-Leninism (even Stalinism). Unfortunately, the opportunity to achieve a quantum leap in quality by joining the incipient turn from old to new institutional economics in the West during the last third of the 20th century was missed.[62] Instead, to put it bluntly, from the late 1960s on, economists' collective imagination in the communist countries was oscillating between John Kenneth Galbraith's vision of ownership (based on terms such as new industrial state, technostructure, military-industrial complex)[63] and Ernst Friedrich Schumacher's institutional maxim of *small is beautiful*. In other words, the local research communities were unimpressed not only by new-institutionalist discoveries but also by the (Austrian) classical liberal and the (German) Ordo-liberal schools of old institutionalism, which proclaimed the preeminence of private property. Only a few economists grew receptive to these schools, albeit too late, in the second half of the 1980s.[64] I am afraid that what I wrote in the Hungarian chapter about the difficulties of situating the ownership concepts in any of the conventional schemes of scientific evolution applies to each country here. In retrospect it is clear that the economic theorists of property relations in the communist era were increasingly involved in a wide-ranging search for the quasi-private owner, yet, it is doubtful whether most of their search attempts can be regarded as *scientific* research programs. Instead of Imre Lakatos, one is reminded of Paul Feyerabend and his *anything goes* principle when reading works that depart from foggy hypotheses, employ inoperational concepts such as social ownership, convey heavily ideological messages with an opaque meaning like *independence of enterprises*, and sacrifice rigorous (legal *and* economic) description and analysis for preexisting normative conclusions.

Decades of communism were not enough for ownership theorists to bring forth a fairly consistent self-image that would contain the major expeditions to no man's land and assess the virtues and vices of the above-listed inventions from the perspective of modern economics. Similarly, they did not respect the pioneers in their own research field. Even today, one does not know much about the scholarly quality of dormant discoveries (e.g., in the works of Bajt, Behrens, Brutzkus, Liska, and Mlčoch) or their reception along with many similar ownership ideas in the West. Therefore, the search for the ideal owner seems to flail helplessly in the trap of collectivism rather than following a sequence of trials and errors leading to a paradigm shift from social to private ownership. As a consequence, the ideas of Thomas Kuhn on how *normal science* is surpassed come to mind as a way for a historian to grasp, instead of the last years of communism, the first years of the postcommunist transformation.

SECOND EXCURSE TO *NOMENKLATURA* OWNERSHIP

So far the *homework* that should have been done best by economists possessing the greatest amount of local knowledge was never finished. More than a quarter of a century later, it waits to be accomplished. What could have been the assignment? As noted earlier, the economics of *nomenklatura* ownership might have become the most significant scientific invention of the local research communities. If a new theory had come into being, it would have probably been equally critical and self-critical, demonstrating not only how the ruling elite actually owned what was called social property but also showing the inbuilt illusions of economists about the interest of the elite in giving up voluntarily part of its ownership privileges. Even the radical market reformers failed to examine the economic behavior of the first inhabitants of no man's land following nationalization. The *nomenklatura* owners remained faceless in most cases because their portraits had not been painted by economists and other social scientists with photographic precision, many of whom knew, at least instinctively, that this land was not a desert.[65]

Clearly, *nomenklatura* ownership was difficult (and dangerous) to study,[66] therefore it was opportune for the majority of experts to put this research topic aside. Yet, this was the most important field where economists might have made indisputably original discoveries in ownership theory because the analysis of each and every regime of property specific to the communist system would have highlighted the ways in which rulers *really* exercise ownership over assets that allegedly belong to everybody. As a result, *nomenklatura* ownership remained a bold hypothesis rather than a key concept of economics under communism. Evidently, this hypothesis has been tested in China during the past three decades by means of thorough empirical research and advanced models of new institutional economics.[67] However, despite important similarities between the economic behavior of the ruling communist elites over time, it seems risky to guess on the basis of the current Chinese example what, for instance, Soviet economists may have thought about ownership change in the 1930s if they had possessed the same knowledge of actual property relations. Moreover, it is also unlikely that economic attitudes of the *nomenklatura* were the same in the two countries and periods of time.

To be sure, an inquiry into the actual ownership relations would not have required, beyond political bravery, too much scholarly effort from the economic theorists. The Marxist roots of the national research communities—that is, the attraction of their members to notions such as property, power, class, interest, organization, and so on, as well as the wide-ranging experience they gathered in bargaining about economic reforms—made them predisposed to institutional research. Many of them were also knowledgeable enough in mathematics to be able to transit from old to new institutionalism, the latter applying techniques of neoclassical economics. The reasons why this turn took place only in the postcommunist period were discussed in a similar volume (Kovács and Zentai 2012) preceding our current research program. Here it suffices to refer to the unexploited opportunities themselves. The theory of property rights and transaction costs, principal-agent models, and concepts such as rent-seeking, incomplete contracts, asymmetric information, adverse selection, moral hazard, opportunism, collusion, and so on, could have helped the economists go beyond intuition and a *thin description* of the real world of ownership under communism.

Let me refer here to my own unsuccessful attempt to disentangle the actual ownership relations in a multilateral bargaining game around a large investment project in the Hungarian chemical industry during the late 1970s (Kovács [1980] 1983). At that time, I would have badly needed many of the analytical concepts above to understand the intricacies of how formal property rights and informal powers, as well as state and party hierarchies, and domestic and Soviet interests, crossed each other at various levels of decision-making. Being unfamiliar with new-institutionalist instruments, I had to reinvent some of them in a semi-anthropological project, in which rigorous logic and measurement were substituted by a qualitative case study based on interviews and documentary sources. By insisting on an exclusively verbal analysis of fuzzy property rights, I faced extreme difficulties in mapping a complex bargaining situation. I saw a company director who, due to his long communist past and strong contacts with the moderate wing of the party leadership, was more powerful than his superiors in the branch ministry who wanted to integrate his company in a large chemical trust. They used Galbraithian arguments to justify the reinforcement of state ownership over the enterprises, and referred to the need to enhance transnational cooperation with Soviet partners. According to them, one has to be large to be able to cooperate with the giant Soviet firms. The director struggled to retain limited freedom of disposal over the company's assets, which he enjoyed under the aegis of the New Economic Mechanism introduced in 1968 (*usus*). He took the risk of being excluded from a lucrative *central development program* launched by the government that promised vast resources (*usus fructus*) and he succeeded in preventing the company from being annexed by the planned trust (*abusus*). After all, who owns this company, I asked myself. What kind of costs and benefits appear in the owners' calculations, and how do they order their preferences?

At the time, the basic concepts of property rights economics were unknown to me. The final deal between the company and its ministry could have been captured by a couple of principal-agent or rent-seeking models with the help of factual information extracted from my case study. Without what was then cutting-edge knowledge, I barely scratched the surface of *nomenklatura* ownership. It was clear to me that this kind of property regime cannot be put simply in the pigeon holes of social or state ownership because the actual property rights were shared within a large network of actors (ranging from middle-level ministerial executives, through party officials in the apparatus of the Central Committee, to military specialists and Comecon experts, many of whom were invisible or unapproachable), affecting key ownership decisions informally or even illegally.

***

The failure to conceptualize ownership under communism within the language of new institutionalism was a striking indication of a general incapacity of theorists to develop what I like to call *borderline-case* economics. This could have examined, by means of neoclassical and heterodox methods, the major types of social and mixed ownership under communism, some of which also appear in capitalist economies but on a much smaller scale, along the borderline between private and public property. This sub-discipline of comparative economics would have been able to study the massive ownership-related government and market failures of the communist economy (such as overregulation, persistent shortages, huge informal sectors, etc.) *in vivo*, which occur in capitalism mostly *in vitro*, thereby bringing the *Eastern* and the *Western* streams of economic sciences closer together.

EVOLUTION OF OWNERSHIP CONCEPTS: NATIONAL TYPES?

The main road of evolution presented in the previous sections seems a comfortable generalization. There were no national research communities that abandoned the primacy of social property, and hardly any which did not begin to diversify this type of ownership and complement it with personal/private property long before 1989. Another similarity was that the national byroads did not follow a linear model of conceptual evolution—either in terms of liberalization, radicalization, and pluralization or of scientific refinement. They differed, however, as far as the direction and length of digressions from the imaginary main road were concerned. If, contrary to the intentions of our research group, I injected a drop of methodological nationalism in this section with a view of identifying ideal types nation by nation, the following evolutionary features of ownership thought would transpire from the country chapters.

Bulgaria: unbroken dominance of the doctrines of state (and statist-style cooperative) ownership while cherishing pre-communist cooperative traditions, moderate managerial and Galbraithian reform projects, brief flirtations with the idea of workers' self-management, acceptance of small private ownership under the pretext of personal property.

China: cherishing the pre-communist tradition of village commune, coexistence of the concepts of state and communal ownership, with an upsurge of the latter during the Cultural Revolution that also curtailed personal property, projects of moderate managerial reforms turning into radical ones, acceptance of small private ownership under the pretext of personal property followed by the idea of large-scale privatization under the communist party-state, brief flirtations with the concept of workers' self-management, large degree of pluralization.

Czechoslovakia: dominance of the doctrines of state (and statist-style cooperative) ownership with first moderate, then radical ideas of managerial reform replaced, following the Prague Spring, by a resolute Galbraithian reform project, brief flirtations with the idea of workers' self-management, acceptance of small private ownership under the pretext of personal property.

GDR: unbroken dominance of the doctrines of state (and statist-style cooperative) ownership accompanied by moderate managerial and resolute Galbraithian reforms, limited acceptance of private ownership in partnership with the state, and under the pretext of personal property, brief flirtations with the idea of workers' self-management.

Hungary: dominance of the doctrine of state ownership and mixed (cooperative and personal) ownership, first moderate, then resolute managerial reforms, a weak Galbraithian reform project, periodic upsurge of the idea of workers' self-management, general acceptance of small private ownership under the pretext of personal property, large degree of pluralization.

Poland: cherishing the tradition of market socialism supported by a neoclassical model, dominance of the doctrine of state ownership with moderate managerial reforms replaced first by a resolute Galbraithian project, then by less moderate managerial reforms, constant interest in the idea of workers' self-management, general acceptance of small private ownership under the pretext of personal property, large degree of pluralization.

Romania: unbroken dominance of the doctrines of state (and statist-style cooperative) ownership with no managerial but resolute Galbraithian reform, no acceptance of workers' self-management and private ownership, limited acceptance of personal property.

Soviet Union: following a decade of intense pluralization of ownership relations during the NEP period, an unbroken dominance of the doctrines of state (and statist-style cooperative) ownership with moderate managerial and resolute Galbraithian reforms, brief flirtations with the idea of workers' self-management, limited acceptance of private ownership under the pretext of personal property.

Yugoslavia: cherishing the pre-communist tradition of cooperative ownership, a brief period of accepting the doctrines of state (and statist-style cooperative) ownership followed by a sustained dominance of the idea of workers' self-management accompanied by managerial and communal ownership, general acceptance of small private ownership under the pretext of personal property, large degree of pluralization, understanding self-management on the level of neoclassical economics.

Do these features add up to define new national ideal types of evolution? Is it possible to stylize the above-listed national real types into ideal types? I would not think so: they lack a sufficient extent of internal cohesion and clear evolutionary logic. Evidently, based on selected features and preoccupied by the *narcissism of small differences*, one can always construct dichotomies such as *pioneers* versus *latecomers*, *intransigents* versus *compromise-friendly*, and spell out interesting chronological asymmetries. One of the most spectacular among them was rapid nationalization in Yugoslavia during the 1940s versus its sluggish pace in China until the late 1950s when Yugoslav economists were already preparing for market socialist reforms. The Hungarian model of managerial ownership in 1968 was introduced exactly when similar attempts were blocked in Czechoslovakia, the GDR, Poland, and the Soviet Union. Or let me refer to the idea of communal ownership, which was revived in Yugoslavia during the first half of the 1970s, exactly when Chinese economists started criticizing the communes prevailing during the Cultural Revolution. The symmetries can be equally interesting: think about the fast diffusion of the concept of state ownership in the late 1940s or of self-management in the 1980s.

Should we therefore build broader types of evolution embracing several countries? For instance, it seems rather easy to arrange the national research communities into two big groups: for the lack of better designations, let me call them the *conformists* and the *explorers*. In the former group, including Bulgaria, Czechoslovakia, the GDR, Romania, and the Soviet Union, a great majority of economists did not indulge in intense experimentation in the field of ownership theory (or gave it up at a certain point for a longer period). In the latter, comprising China, Hungary, Poland, and Yugoslavia, theorists were in a constant, sometimes feverish search for new property arrangements with only short breaks between the experiments. Conformism prevailing in almost the entire communist period was characteristic of Bulgaria and Romania,[68] while reflection upon ownership relations froze for decades in Czechoslovakia following the occupation in 1968, in the GDR after the abolition of the New Economic System, and in the Soviet Union after the collapse of the NEP. Conformism pertained to conserving the predominance of state ownership by resisting a major extension of managerial property rights and establishing large state-run conglomerates (*kombinat*s, trusts, directorates, etc.) as well as by keeping mixed and individual ownership at bay. At the same time, explorers' attitudes led to a substantial pluralization of ownership regimes by introducing other than directly statist forms of social property, including quasi-private managerial rights as well as individual ownership, both personal and private.

To avoid misunderstanding, the changes in ownership proposed by the explorers (such as the switch to workers' self-management in Yugoslavia or to people's communes in China) were not necessarily parts of market-prone reforms. Frequently, they aimed exactly at preventing such reforms. Conversely, market reformers did their best to camouflage modifications their reform programs might cause in property relations. Also, the explorer-dominated research communities were not monolithic. While, for example, by the 1980s most Polish and Hungarian economists committed themselves to increasingly liberal types of market socialism, some others still believed, like their colleagues in countries with conformist communities, in the viability of large conglomerates under state ownership.

Explorers brought many other differences in the evolution of ownership thought. The likelihood of making scientific discoveries, cooperating with other social sciences, importing ideas from the *West*, and influencing colleagues in the *East* was much higher in research communities devoted to experimentation. Evidently, this is near to tautology. Moreover, the development of all these features had an ultimate barrier in Eastern Europe, namely, the solid conviction that what later became known as the *Chinese solution*, that is, wide-ranging privatization in a communist dictatorship, was neither feasible nor desirable.[69] Both kinds of research communities shared this conviction, though for different reasons: simply put, the conformists rejected privatization whereas the explorers accepted its half-collectivist varieties but did not favor dictatorship. For notable exceptions, see a handful of Polish and Hungarian thinkers (e.g., Mirosław Dzielski and Elemér Hankiss) who played briefly with the idea of communist-led privatization in the form of *nomenklatura* buyout programs, as well as some members of the future Gaidar group in the Soviet Union reconciling themselves with the *Pinochet model* (i.e., a sort of *dictatorial liberalization*) at the end of the 1980s.

Apparently, the above reflections on the national roads of evolution do not add much to the ideal types of ownership formulated by experts of Comparative Economic Systems many decades ago. Should we then repeat what everyone could learn from them since the 1950s? I do not think the reader would want to hear from us again that, for instance, Soviet-style state ownership was different from Yugoslav self-management, or that Hungarian managers enjoyed stronger property rights than their East-German colleagues even if we precisely located these differences in time. He/she might regret, however, if we also ignored a number of property regimes that rise up from the history of economic ideas but seemed to the comparatists irrelevant from the point of view of really existing practices.

Communal ownership is one of the key examples: it was portrayed as a *quantité négligeable* in the Yugoslav system and a temporary institution of the Cultural Revolution in China. In both cases the communes were regarded as disguised agents of centralized state ownership. Almost the same applied to cooperative property. As to state ownership, in its analysis comparative experts by and large were contented with a distinction between the *classical* Soviet and the Hungarian *managerial* regimes as well as a series of Czechoslovak, East German, Polish, and other national real types of *kombinat*-based ownership between the two. Normally, private ownership appeared in their works as a marginal feature characteristic of Polish and Yugoslav agriculture (or of the Soviet one prior to collectivization) as well as of small industry and trade in countries ranging from the GDR through Poland to China. With the exception of sporadic references to Hungarian cooperatives and the Chinese household responsibility system, personal ownership and its blends with various types of social property usually remained unnoticed. Evidently, the largest blank spot on the map of property relations was *nomenklatura* ownership.

Including the ideal types of all these property regimes (together with their historically nuanced national real types) in the habitual classification schemes, we could suggest a series of new pigeon holes for both the forms of ownership and the countries. This way, economic historians might be able to make distinctions, for example, between communal ownership in a Chinese village and a Bulgarian town, between property rights in a Soviet *kolkhoz* and a Hungarian industrial cooperative, between self-management in Poland and Yugoslavia, between personal ownership in Czechoslovakia and Romania, or between *nomenklatura* ownership in any selection of countries in our sample at various stages of communism. However, the task of intellectual historians ends here. What we can do is to point to trials and errors in the field of producing new ideas about ownership relations, situate them in time, and formulate a number of evolutionary patterns, both ideal and real. The question of whether these patterns can be linked to relevant national projects is to be answered by economic historians. Hopefully, they will follow up, although we can hardly promise them any spectacular new country types. Just the opposite is to be expected: country types that seemed well defined thus far may become tinged until they become unrecognizable. For example, the ideal type of workers' self-management would be certainly refined by taking into account the Hungarian, Polish, or Soviet real types but it is likely that its *Yugoslavness* would fade. Similarly, the emphasis laid on the social-private mix of ownership would make it difficult to regard the *Hungarian model* simply as a managerial type *par excellence*.

LOCKED IN THE TRAP OF COLLECTIVISM

Why was the road to change ownership concepts so bumpy even in the experiment-friendly research communities? Are we aware of the principal drivers of change? This volume is full of scattered hints on possible answers to these questions. Let me sum them up briefly, ignoring the miracle of human creativity that may explain individual scientific discoveries even under very unfavorable circumstances.

Beginning with the conformist research communities, their members were not born to be obedient but became so out of sincere conviction or under the influence of austere isolation, physical oppression, moral indoctrination, and censorship arising from economic and/or political crises like the ones leading to the eradication of the NEP in the late 1920s or the crushing of the Prague Spring in 1968. By isolation I mean both international segregation and the severing of ties with dissenters/dissidents (including émigrés) of liberal, conservative, or other persuasions. It also may be that the initial stage of blind faith in Marxism-Leninism was not disturbed by major crises for a long time (e.g., Bulgaria and Romania), that economists were unmoved by the first fiascoes of the planned economy in sufficiently large numbers, or that they did not attribute the failures primarily to the malfunctioning of social property. Or they did but their toolboxes were empty, or they could not find (or lost) their allies in the political leadership, and therefore opted for a conformist attitude to ownership change. The destiny of New Economic System (NÖS) in East Germany points to this explanation. Corruption, that is, enjoying a relatively easy time in the trap of collectivism also could be a reason to accept the status quo.

Obviously, in countries with an explorer-dominated research community experimentation could be explained by the lack or weakness of the previous reasons for obedience. For example, the ownership concept of a prominent theorist like Oskar Lange (a Marxist with a strong link to *bourgeois scholarship*) or a powerful piece of pre-communist tradition such as the idea of village commune or cooperative property could be revived with a view of overcoming grave crises. Thus, crises did not necessarily lead to apathy and conformism but could serve as a first push for experimentation in which intellectual legacies were mixed with emulation and invention. The switch to self-management in Yugoslavia after the split with the Soviet Union or the encouragement of a combination of personal and cooperative ownership in Hungarian agriculture after the 1956 Revolution are proper examples for this. As time passed, some of the experiments (self-management is perhaps the best case in point) turned into novel traditions. Explorers may have received support from a faction of the ruling elite sympathetic to the idea of property reform or from ownership theories developed by foreign economists or from domestic and foreign experts in other social sciences.

But why did all this take so much time? What explains the decades of experimentation and the frequent relapses on the way leading to the emancipation of large-scale private ownership even in the most inventive and liberal-minded research communities? After having enumerated so many external reasons ranging from institutional legacies and economic cycles to political alliances and status privileges, in closing let me say a few words about the *inherent* inertia of the emancipation process.

I have already referred to the *perhaps effect* several times to describe the recurring hope of economic theorists that, despite past errors, the next trial in reshaping ownership thought within the realm of social property would be successful. Except for the last few years of communism, they could not even dream of having the chance to reintroduce large-scale private ownership. Actually, as the country chapters revealed, most of them never wanted to give up social property. They believed that, if the party-state allowed them to reform (pluralize, tame, mix, etc.) it, and—simultaneously—strengthen its features grounded in horizontal collectivism, they would be able to demonstrate that the primacy of private ownership had a viable alternative within collectivist thought. Today, student economists ask me with some contempt in their voice: were the members of the *old guard* that narrow-minded or scared to think so?

I would not deny that a degree of myopia caused by ignorance, fear, and self-deception (cf. *sour grapes* syndrome) helped sustain the hope of an alternative, semi-collectivist paradigm of ownership—a hope that, with time, turned into an illusion. Nevertheless, at the end of this volume, let me express my compassion with some of my older colleagues: first of all, with Márton Tardos who shared with me his hopes (and doubts) about his own concepts of ownership rather frequently.[70] Now, after having learned a great deal from my distinguished colleagues about the sluggish and twisted evolution of ownership ideas in another eight countries, I would venture to draw the following conclusion: even well-educated, gifted, and brave scholars like Tardos who had lost their faith in communism long before and combined dissent with dissidence found *reasonable* arguments to justify experimentation and continue their search for the quasi-private settlers of no man's land until the very eve of the 1989 revolutions.

The experimentation never reached its end because the boundaries between success and failure were vague. The following reasons largely determined the structure of this *eternal* reform process in which advancement was often encountered by retreat:

- the property reforms started out from the very *bottom*, that is, from the extreme conditions of nearly full state ownership, and their authors made modest claims in the beginning, leaving much room for further trials and errors;
- these reforms were frequently truncated, interrupted, or even reversed by counter-reforms;

- the pros and cons of the reform initiatives were not quantified rigorously but rather compared intuitively;
- the interruptions of the reform process led to longer breaks in critical thought on ownership, and sometimes the same ideas had to be tried out again;
- the reforms often concerned both social and individual ownership, and the respective effects were not checked separately;
- there was a vast number of potential combinations between the various regimes of social ownership and, within these regimes, between the different property rights, and these combinations could also be associated with further blends of individual ownership;
- the property reforms were parts of larger reform packages, and both the virtues and vices of ownership change also could be attributed to other parts of the same package, or, in a larger context, to changes in the economy, economic policy, or politics.

The failure of a given project of property reform in one country did not prevent economists in other countries from introducing similar projects later; and conversely, its success did not necessarily result in a smooth takeover.[71] One could always find good reasons to keep on searching for a *miraculous mix* of social (or social and individual) property regimes instead of calling for radical approaches to privatization. In other words, due to the lack of testable/comparable experiments, and the great number of potential reform projects, it was almost impossible to determine the real merits of any of the expeditions leading to no man's land. If none of the projects initiated under the auspices of social ownership can be discredited with scientific rigor, then one can always trust in the success of a new expedition and postpone the Grand Decision between social and private property.

Moreover, until the second half of the 1970s, no strong intellectual stimulus justifying private ownership came from the West. Even thereafter the economists of closest reference group in the Soviet empire were not the standard neoclassical or heterodox theorists. The impact of the overlapping communities of comparative experts and Sovietologists in the West on how economists thought about property relations on the other side of the Iron Curtain was incomparably greater. Even in the 1980s, the policy amalgam of Keynesian state intervention, the welfare state, indicative planning, and the ideal of large state holdings gave the tenor to their message sent to the East. As regards ownership regimes, Alec Nove's utopia, *The Economics of Feasible Socialism* published in 1983, which celebrated pluralization instead of privatization, probably reflected the consensus between these communities and the radical market reformers of the time the most clearly. In the second half of the 1980s, the reasons for ongoing experimentation within the realm of collectivist principles lost much of their strength, and at a certain point also citizens like those of the GDR, began to voice the slogan "*keine Experimente mehr!*" Nonetheless, one argument pertaining to the cultural prerequisites of private ownership remained effective and prevented economists from leaving the trap of collectivism rapidly. The opinions of Klaus and Balcerowicz cited on the first page of this conclusion reflect a kind of elitist suspicion that can be paraphrased as follows: we are already out of the trap but unfortunately our peoples are still therein. I would like to leave the task of deciding whether or not that suspicion was well-founded to the reader. And if it was, does this explain the current rise of collectivist ideas in the former communist world?

NOTES

1. The revised conference papers were published in Kovács and Tardos (1992).
2. See Table C.1.
3. As mentioned in the Introduction, the notion of collectivism is exposed to rival interpretations stressing its horizontal or vertical traits. The tension between the two within official communist ideology will be dealt in more detail below. For the grave difficulties economic theorists faced in defining the legal and economic features of social ownership, see the Soviet and the Yugoslav chapters.
4. In most countries the categorization of the property of churches, parties, trade unions, and other associations caused painful ideological choices. They were called *social organizations* but it was impossible to decide whether, for example, the property of the Catholic Church and of the communist trade union should be put in the same rubric, and whether that is to be called social or private ownership.
5. Here I cannot dwell upon the common conceptual roots of communal, cooperative, and self-managed property in collectivist thought and draw the fine dividing lines among them. In comparison with state ownership their main specific was that they—theoretically—included certain individual property rights of the associated members, and institutions of common deliberation in the spirit of horizontal collectivism.
6. What to most authors was simply a realistic description of etatization was filled by Anatoly Venediktov with pride. See the title of his magnum opus "State socialist ownership" (*Gosudarstvennaia sotsialisticheskaia sobstvennost'*).
7. China was a clear exception to the rule. In the *heroic* period of the communes during the 1960s, they devoured agricultural cooperatives and local industries. In addition, military organizations, schools and hospitals, and so on were attached to them, and—despite mobilization from above—many communes became uncontrollable by central authorities.
8. This is a pity because the ownership structure of residential housing was extremely complex in many countries, including, with the exception of large private apartment buildings, a great variety of communal, cooperative, company-owned, and private property, formal and informal apartment-sharing communities and sublets, and so on—all these with very diverse property rights for expropriation, alienation,

and inheritance. Pluralization in this field preceded the differentiation of property regimes in other sectors.

The ownership of human capital had an even more unfortunate destiny in economic research. It is not by chance that the authors of this volume wrote little about this subject. It was considered by most economists as an essentially labor market issue even if it was crystal clear that in communism people had little legal influence on the use and remuneration of their manpower, and sometimes they were absolutely (even violently) prevented from selling it. The same applied to intellectual property. For an interesting exception, see Aleksander Bajt's approach to property rights in the Yugoslav chapter.

9. For a critical review of this concept, see the East-German chapter. The question if Marx had assumed that pure socialization allows planning without establishing a central authority endowed with certain property rights (i.e., without some kind of nationalization) has troubled Marxist thinkers to the present day.

10. This ambiguity manifested itself perhaps the most clearly in the so-called CUP debate in Poland in 1948 (see the Polish chapter).

11. In fact, Lenin suggested multiple approaches almost simultaneously. He was one of the first among Bolshevik thinkers who made a distinction between socialization and nationalization (interpreted as confiscation). He believed in centralizing state ownership while, at the same time, called for the organization of the commune system (*soviet*s). In his last works he appeared as a devotee of cooperatives. Nevertheless, he was unwilling to recognize the merits of private ownership even when he approved moderate denationalization for reasons of *Realpolitik* at the beginning of NEP.

12. A symbolic pinnacle of that stage was the establishment of joint companies with the Soviet Union (e.g., *SovRom*s in Romania and *SAG*s in the GDR) after 1945—a short-lived move that was considered even by many local Marxists a colonial gesture.

13. To be sure, Lenin failed to define the transition from social ownership to *no ownership*, thereby causing much headache for textbook political economists who, as usual, had to seek refuge in the utopian hypothesis of a world of general abundance where property will lose its meaning.

14. As a rule, it relied on state ownership of natural resources and all forms of capital (*means of production*), including infrastructure.

15. To avoid misunderstanding, Stalin did not specify what is to be meant by cooperative ownership in terms of property rights of the members. Were they entitled to appoint the managers, earn profit or opt out and sell their deposited assets freely? Was the cooperative allowed to decide on its production program, business partners, merger and acquisition strategy, and so on without any tutelage by the party-state?

16. Cf. Oskar Lange's term of "intermediate ownership" between social and private in the Polish chapter.

17. Interestingly enough, the *democratization* of social ownership remained a prime goal among Polish economists throughout the communist epoch, whereas their Hungarian colleagues rather focused on the pluralization of the property regime and abandoned the aim of challenging dictatorship basically until it started collapsing on its own. While both research communities feared to import Yugoslav-style self-management that might *degenerate* into *selfish* group ownership, to use the rhetoric

of the time, the Polish experts were keen on creating, in the form of workers' councils or some other kind of co-determination, a counter-power to the growing authority of managers in a market socialist model. During his years of emigration, Włodzimierz Brus (1992), for example, became a supporter of polyarchy (in general sense as defined by Robert Dahl and Charles Lindblom) rather than multiparty democracy.

18. Cf. the notion of *Galbraithian socialism* below. Witnessing the practical difficulties in modeling a fully centralized economy, some of the optimal planners (like Leonid Kantorovich in the Soviet Union or András Bródy in Hungary) did not refrain from advancing decentralized models allowing certain market transactions.

19. This dialectic was invented by the sages of the Second International when promoting the concept of state capitalism prior to all-out nationalization by the Bolsheviks, a concept that reappeared in Eastern Europe during the 1980s and in China during the 1990s.

20. For the rational aspects of this *perhaps effect*, see the final section of this conclusion.

21. For the history of the concept, see Avramov (2007).

22. Initially, even the most liberal-minded Czech economists wanted the state-owned banks to hold the assets of state enterprises until the time was ripe for privatization. A similar precaution was suggested by János Kornai who called for hardening the budget constraints of large state-owned enterprises instead of suggesting their rapid privatization. Balcerowicz was similarly cautious. In his articles written during this period *socialist market economy* appeared as a viable option, and the transition to private ownership was not presented as a necessary choice. Cf. Balcerowicz (1987; 1995: 28–34), and Discussion (1989).

23. Even in China where, in comparison with other communist countries, the most extensive privatization drive has taken place under the leadership of the party-state since the 1990s, the Leninist *commanding heights* (*life lines* in Chinese official jargon), including all strategic industries and land, remained under direct state ownership or under strong government control that go far beyond the average scope of state intervention in capitalist states.

24. In parallel, the reform discourse incorporated elements of legal reasoning to complement the initial language based on the sociology of organization.

25. This is what Furubotn and Richter (1998, 414–15) called the attenuating of the state's ownership of the firm.

26. The popularity of this term in all countries of our sample is explained by both its Soviet origin and amorphous nature. In Romania, for instance, it covered the nonexistent self-government of enterprises (*autogestiune*), while in Hungary it was translated into "*independent* economic accounting" to refer to a basic element of market socialism. In the Soviet Union *khozraschet* was replaced under Gorbachev by the *3-S* program: self-management, self-financing, and self-repayment (*samoupravlenie, samofinansirovanie, samookupaemost'*).

27. The façade proved, however, rather weak when the resulting income differentials went beyond certain limits. In Hungary, for example, the introduction of the so-called *80-50-15 percent rule* in 1968, which stipulated profit sharing among the directors, the middle-level managers, and the workers according to these proportions

(percentages of their respective wages), provoked huge resistance from both communist hardliners and workers.

28. These regulations were eased in the case of joint ventures with Western companies in many countries (see, for example, the Romanian chapter), especially if they concerned business contacts with the diaspora (see the Polish chapter).

29. As mentioned earlier, Brus and Łaski insisted on this idea as late as 1989.

30. This land was not an *open-access property* (*res nullius*), from the use of which one could not exclude others. Following its occupation, however, it became a common-pool resource owned by the members/groups of the *nomenklatura*, which therefore was exposed to overexploitation threatening with a *tragedy of the commons*.

31. Cf. Fritz Behrens's view of *state-monopolistic socialism* and the *Russian-Asiatic traditions*, or Jadwiga Staniszkis's concept of the *ontology of socialism* that relies on a property rights approach but falls short of their economic analysis. Other researchers in Poland such as Maria Hirszowicz, Halina Najduchowska, Jacek Tarkowski, and Jacek Wasilewski also focused on the recruitment patterns and informal authority of the *nomenklatura* without regarding its members as some sort of owners. Like in Hungary, the emergence of a *sovereign bureaucracy* and its *coercive* behavior, to use Hirszowicz's phrases, seemed to be a more important field for most economic sociologists to study than the domination of the property regimes by the party-state. An interesting attempt was made by Leonid Vasilyev in the Soviet Union who coined the term "power-ownership" to describe, by means of the Marxian notion of the *Asian mode of production*, how the communist ruling elite exercises its property rights. As mentioned earlier, it was dissident Marxist philosophers (not economists) in Hungary who developed, with the help of the concept of *corporate property*, the most profound analysis of the economic aspects of exercising ownership by the party-state.

32. Testing the analogy of the legal instrument of trust was just one of the numerous unexploited opportunities of research. The ways in which the roles of other co-owners, that is, the employees/citizens and their organizations (trade unions, workers' councils, communes, etc.), were presented will be discussed below.

33. In an article written in 1989, the Polish economist Jan Winiecki (1990: 67) suggested the then pioneering idea that the *nomenklatura* had learned long before that "their wealth does not depend primarily upon the creation of wealth but upon interference in the wealth-creation process." For decades they kept the share of the private sector low because preying on the state was easier for them than extracting rent from private firms. However, they realized at the end of the 1980s that they probably would be able to profit from large-scale privatization to an even larger extent. Interestingly, his fellow countryman Leszek Balcerowicz did not borrow this approach when tackling ownership problems during the 1990s (cf. Balcerowicz 1995: 84–123) while it was taken over by Shleifer and Vishny (1994).

34. To my knowledge, there were no comparable real-time studies of the internal economic networks of party-states in economic sociology to what Mária Csanádi (1997) launched in Hungary before 1989, and has extended to Romania and China since then. A similar research program was implemented by Maciej Tymiński (2011) in Poland.

35. David Stark (1996) was the first among Western analysts who not only warned about these dangers but also offered the concept of *recombinant property* to reflect on them with empirical clarity.

36. True, in the Chinese case bureaucratic tutelage was for the managers like heaven as compared to the hell of popular control during the Cultural Revolution.

37. Despite the murky formulation, the notion represented a turn in Soviet legal thought because it weakened the doctrine of indivisibility of state ownership cemented in the 1936 Constitution. By recognizing the firms as juridical persons like in the 1920s again, it brought some fresh wind in civil law that had been purged and transformed into administrative law during the 1930s. Thus, Venediktov managed to retain some of the ideas of his predecessors (victims of the purge) Evgeny Pashukanis and Piotr Stuchka while avoiding to challenge the principle of erecting a wall between state and private ownership and crowding out the latter. That principle was introduced by the 1922 Civil Code but lost much of its rigor during the NEP, and the two leading legal theorists endorsed the cooperation between the various ownership regimes (see Reich 1972: 191–249, Ioffe 1988: 91–138).

38. In Hungary the firms had to pay a so-called asset lockup charge (*eszközlekötési járulék*), a kind of capital tax from 1964 onward.

39. See the Soviet chapter.

40. Primacy was meant in the official discourse both as ideological/moral superiority of social property and as the largest share it occupied within the ownership regime as a whole.

41. The symbolic switch was represented by replacing the term "self-management" with that of "capital management" or "co-management" in the official discourse.

42. In most countries land was nationalized and the private ownership of a large part of real estate (immovable property) lost its sense. Even state enterprises had nothing but use rights for those pieces of land on which their factory buildings stood. Poland in the 1980s was a clear exception because the Jaruzelski regime legalized the private property of land in order to appease farmers. Home ownership was controlled in complicated and obscure ways, with a large variation across countries. Normally, movable property was recognized as an object of individual (personal rather than private) ownership.

43. The menace of (re)nationalization of private capital was omnipresent during the entire communist epoch. The party-state might decide any time, like in the GDR in 1972 when the large joint state-and-private companies (*Kommanditgesellschaften*) were abolished, to renounce former concessions made to the private sector. Most of the constitutions contained a rather harsh taking clause, according to which private property could be expropriated, if it hurt whatever declared to be of public interest. Good examples are the Cultural Revolution in China, which abolished private home ownership and led to the confiscation of much of the personal property of *counter-revolutionaries*, and *systematization* (forced urbanization) in Romania from the mid-1970s, which erased even small freedoms that citizens enjoyed in disposing of land. In this country even joint ventures with Western firms were supposed to convert into fully state-owned companies in 10 to 15 years.

44. Among those publicly supporting the expansion of the private sector, Polish economists such as Jan Krzysztof Bielecki, Rafał Krawczyk, Waldemar Kuczyński, Stefan Kurowski, Janusz Lewandowski, Feliks Młynarski, Jan Mujżel, and Jan Szomburg as well as liberal journalists/activists like Mirosław Dzielski, Stefan Kisielewski, and Janusz Korwin-Mikke constituted the largest (and probably the boldest) group in communist Eastern Europe during the communist period.

45. Some of the leading economists in Yugoslavia interpreted small private property as a subtype of self-management (thus, of social ownership) if the employer worked together with the employees. In China a citation from Marx's *Capital*, which said that one cannot speak of a capitalist firm below seven employees, served as proof for recognizing small individual ownership during the early 1980s.

46. The idea of *big is beautiful* remained a basic ingredient of market socialism from Oskar Lange to Márton Tardos. See, for example, Lange (1936–37) and Tardos (1983).

47. In Romanian textbooks of political economy personal ownership was therefore subsumed under social ownership as a result of *socialist distribution*.

48. In the Soviet Civil Code of 1964 each citizen could hold in personal ownership his/her income and savings, house/apartment, objects of personal need and convenience, even instruments of household production activities (cf. Raff and Taitslin 2014). In general, these were the only freely transferable objects of property under communism.

49. The Romanian chapter includes a number of examples about recurring limitations and setbacks in the process of accepting personal ownership of homes, typewriters, or foreign currency—well-known phenomena in other countries at certain stages of communist history.

50. The township and village enterprises emerging from the Chinese communes since the 1980s have exhibited a similar diversity of property embracing local state firms, cooperatives, private companies, and a number of their combinations, mixing the so-called *Wenzhou* and *Sunan* models.

51. These ownership institutions were penetrating each other, resulting in new combinations. In this sense pluralization meant much more than what Lenin asserted when distinguishing between five *uklad*s of property that existed side by side, or what Mao meant by *ownership coexistence* in the 1940s and early 1950s. Also, in contrast to Lenin's view, in reformist discourse plurality of ownership was seen as an asset rather than a liability.

52. Capital transactions were not easy even within the fortress. For example, Stalin was furious when confronted with the suggestion of transferring the machine and tractor stations from the state sector to the cooperative one. In Yugoslavia, where after a while firms were entitled to sell parts of their assets, they had to compensate for the capital loss by buying new assets.

53. In China it took more than three decades for the rural responsibility system to include permanent rights to use land in the contracts.

54. The Yugoslav communist slogan "a farmer with a tractor makes a capitalist" could have been formulated in any of our countries.

55. The Pole Oskar Lange is probably the best example of a social democrat who, collaborating with (and surviving) the Stalinist regime, became an influential proponent of the idea of enterprise autonomy, self-management, and the cooperatives as well as of supporting small private ownership. Many from the younger generation of postwar social democracy (e.g., Rezső Nyers in Hungary) turned into top reformers later.

56. See Assen Christophoroff's scornful term "wartime capitalistic socialism" in the Bulgarian chapter.

57. For more on the intellectual sources of institutional design, see Kovács (1996; 2013).

58. A formidable case is the idea of workers' self-management that made a full circle in the Soviet Union, starting out from the program of Russian anarchists and the Workers' Opposition in the Bolshevik party, borrowing from the experience of many communist countries after 1945, and ending up in the world of *perestroika*.

59. This was probably the first powerful project challenging the doctrine of state ownership whose authors were proudly referring to the original source of the project's core in the West, Milton Friedman's voucher scheme.

It is doubtful whether one should count the turn to private ownership as an invention, even though some of its techniques were new. It did not add much to what economists knew of the virtues of private property anyway after Ludwig von Mises had formulated his thesis on the impossibility of rational calculation under collectivism in 1920, or, more exactly, what the consensus was in non-Marxist circles of Eastern Europe with regard to the coexistence of private and public ownership before 1945. For more on *reinventing the wheel*, see the Hungarian chapter.

60. See the Bulgarian chapter. Textbook political economy was full of such ritual disputes. Since they often had a rational core, and in certain periods exerted an enormous influence on the evolution of ownership doctrines, we could not disregard them. See, for example, the debate about the economic versus legal character of ownership in Czechoslovakia or the differences between the ownership concepts of the IE, MSU, and CEMI schools in the Soviet Union. The East-German and Romanian chapters also provide ample reference to official rhetoric.

61. On the "paleness" of ownership studies, see the Hungarian chapter. While the Czechoslovak, Hungarian, Polish, and Yugoslav chapters refer to academic communication between economists and sociologists, joint research by economists and legal scholars was a rare bird even in these countries. If economic theory had borrowed from social anthropology only part of the knowledge it accumulated about popular norms and habits of, and attitudes to private ownership, pertaining to entitlement, accountability, exclusivity, and responsibility, there would have been less surprise at widespread resistance to privatization after 1989 (see the Introduction).

62. See the country studies on the reception of new institutional economics in Eastern Europe in Kovács and Zentai (2012).

63. In the 1980s, János Kornai coined the term "Galbraithian socialism" to denote what he had already discovered in his book *Overcentralization* in the 1950s, namely, an instinctive urge felt by the planners to overcome economic difficulties through concentrating capital. This came in waves of trustification and establishing *kombinat*s

in many countries simultaneously (e.g., VVBs in the GDR, WOGs in Poland, *centrales* in Romania), or transforming the kolkhozy into sovkhozy in the Soviet Union and agro-industrial complexes (APK) in Bulgaria during the 1960s and 1970s, and severely curtailed the powers of managers in firms that fell victim to organizational change.

64. For the marginal position of Ordo-liberalism, see the Hungarian and Polish papers. See also Kovács (1993). With the exception of Poland and Yugoslavia, when Friedrich Hayek arrived in Eastern European economic thought, he brought change in rhetoric rather than substance. His ideas were embedded in strange hybrid doctrines like that of Liska, which Hayek would have surely regarded as a *constructivist* dream. It is also telling that the first serious review by Kornai on Hayek's concept of private ownership was written after 1989 (1992).

65. Did they know it but hide their results in their desk drawers? Unfortunately, these were almost empty, and after 1989, privatization stole the show from revisiting the previous regimes of ownership. Even scholars like János Kornai who did not want to look into the future without comprehending the past proved unable to offer a deeper analysis of property relations under communism in his magnum opus *The Socialist System* published in 1992.

66. In the 1970s, the Institute of Economics of the Hungarian Academy of Sciences issued an internal instruction, according to which the ordinary members of the Institute like me were not permitted to do field research on the higher echelons of the party-state. It was only the director, István Friss, member of the Central Committee of the communist party, who was entitled to conduct interviews there. I would not have been allowed to join him even if I had been a party member, although I belonged to his research group for years.

67. See, for example, Blanchard and Shleifer (2001), Che and Qian (1998), Csanádi (1997), Dickson (2003), Granick (1990), Landry (2008), Nee and Opper (2007; 2012), Qian et al. (1999), Wedeman (2003), Weitzman and Xu (1994), Xu (1995; 2011; 2015).

68. It is symptomatic that in our volume the authors of the Bulgarian and Romanian chapters use the gloomiest metaphors ("dead languages and extinct species" and "silence of the herd," respectively) regarding the demerits of local ownership concepts.

69. If the reform economists had known more about the intimate relationship between *nomenklatura* ownership and private property rights, this solution would have seemed perhaps more viable in their eyes. Similarly, had it seemed more viable, they might have continued to look for compromises with the party-state. These are, of course, ahistorical conclusions but they reveal the ironic advantages of ignorance.

70. Cf. Tardos (1983; 1999) and Bródy (1994). See also Brus's autobiographical sketch from 1992.

71. For example, the respective study trips by Bulgarian and Hungarian scholars and politicians in Yugoslavia during the 1960s resulted in diametrically opposing conclusions: the Bulgarian experts returned home with the intention (which did not materialize) to copy-paste the system of self-management, whereas the Hungarians left Yugoslavia with the strong conviction of not including workers' participation in the model of the New Economic Mechanism.

BIBLIOGRAPHY

Avramov, Roumen. 2007. *Komunalniat kapitalizam: Iz balgarskoto stopansko minalo* [Communal capitalism: Reflections on the Bulgarian economic past]. Volumes I–III. Sofia: Fondatzia balgarska nauka i kultura, Centre for Liberal Strategies.

Balcerowicz, Leszek. 1987. "Remarks on the Concept of Ownership." *Oeconomica Polona* 14 no. 1: 75–95.

Balcerowicz, Leszek, Aleksander Bajt, Włodzimierz Brus, Karel Dyba, András Hegedüs, Branko Horvat, Gennadii Lisichkin, László Szamuely, and Márton Tardos. 1989. "Discussion on Socialist Market Economy." *Acta Oeconomica* 40: 207–412.

———. 1995. *Socialism, Capitalism, Transformation.* Budapest: CEU Press.

Bardhan, Pranab, and John Roemer. 1992. "Market Socialism: A Case for Rejuvenation." *Journal of Economic Perspectives*, 6 no. 3: 101–16.

Bentham, Jeremy. 1843. "Principles of the Civil Code." In *Works of Jeremy Bentham*, edited by John Bowring, Part II. Edinburgh: William Tait, 308.

Blanchard, Olivier, and Andrei Shleifer. 2001. "Federalism with and without Political Centralization: China versus Russia." *IMF Staff Papers* 48: 171–79.

Bródy, András. 1994. Beszélgetés Kovács János Mátyással [Conversation with János Mátyás Kovács]. In *Miért hagytuk hogy így legyen?* [Why did we let it be so?], edited by Aladár Madarász and Judit Szabó, 271–348. Budapest: Közgazdasági és Jogi Könyvkiadó.

Brus, Włodzimierz. 1992. "From Revisionism to Pragmatism: Sketches to a Self-Portrait of a 'Reform Economist'." In *Reform and Transformation: Eastern European Economics on the Threshold of Change*, edited by János Mátyás Kovács and Márton Tardos, 136–42. London: Routledge.

Che, Jiahua, and Yingyi Qian. 1998. "Insecure Property Rights and Government Ownership of Firms." *Quarterly Journal of Economics* 113 no. 2: 467–96.

Csanádi, Mária. 1997. *Party-States and Their Legacies in Post-Communist Transformation.* Cheltenham, UK: Edward Elgar.

Dickson, Bruce J. 2003. *Red Capitalists in China: The Party, Private Entrepreneurs, and Prospects for Political Change.* Cambridge—New York: Cambridge University Press.

Duff Milenkovitch, Deborah. 1992. "An Organizational Theory of the Socialist Economy." In *Reform and Transformation: Eastern European Economics on the Threshold of Change*, edited by János Mátyás Kovács and Márton Tardos, 40–61. London: Routledge.

Franičević, Vojmir. 2012. "Soft Institutionalism: The Reception of New Institutional Economics in Croatia." In *Capitalism from Outside? Economic Cultures in Eastern Europe after 1989*, edited by János Mátyás Kovács and Violetta Zentai, 241–62. Budapest: CEU Press.

Furubotn, Eirik, and Rudolf Richter, eds. 1998. *Institutions and Economic Theory. The Contribution of the New Institutional Economics.* Ann Arbor: The University of Michigan Press.

Granick, David. 1988. "Property Rights vs. Transaction Costs in Comparative Systems Analysis." *Journal of Institutional and Theoretical Analysis* 144 no. 5: 871–78.

———. 1990. *Chinese State Enterprises: A Regional Property Rights Analysis*. Chicago—London: University of Chicago Press.

Ioffe, Olimpiad. 1988. *Soviet Civil Law*. Dordrecht: Martinus Nijhoff Publishers.

Klaus, Václav, and Tomáš Ježek. 1991. "Social Criticism, False Liberalism and Recent Changes in Czechoslovakia." *East European Politics and Societies* 5 no. 1: 26–40.

Kornai, János. 1992. "The Principles of Privatization in Eastern Europe." *De Economist* 140 no. 2: 153–76.

Kovács, János Mátyás. 1983 [1980]. "Bargaining, Assimilation, Bargaining" [Alku, asszimiláció, alku]. In *Eastern European Economics* 21 no. 3–4: 38–77 [*Vállalati magatartás, vállalati környezet*], edited by Márton Tardos, 393–490. Budapest: Közgazdasági és Jogi Könyvkiadó.

———. 1993. "Which Institutionalism? Searching for Paradigms of Transformation in Eastern European Economic Thought." In *The Political Economy of Transformation*, edited by Hans-Jürgen Wagener, 85–96. Heidelberg: Physica-Verlag.

———. 1996. "Örökség, utánzás, felfedezés. Közgazdasági gondolkodás Magyarországon 1989 után." [Legacy, imitation, invention. Economic thought in Hungary after 1989]. *Közgazdasági Szemle* 43 no. 4: 321–26.

———. 2013. "Tradition, Nachamung, Erfindung. Neue Kapitalismen in Osteuropa." *Transit* 43: 32–52.

Kovács, János Mátyás, and Márton Tardos, eds. 1992. *Reform and Transformation. Eastern European Economics on the Threshold of Change*. London: Routledge.

Kovács, János Mátyás, and Violetta Zentai, eds. 2012. *Capitalism from Outside? Economic Cultures in Eastern Europe after 1989*. Budapest: CEU Press.

Kristof, Nicholas. 1989. "Li Yining. Selling China on a 'Public' Privatization." *The New York Times*, January 8.

Landry, Pierre. 2008. *Decentralized Authoritarianism in China: The Communist Party's Control of Local Elites in the Post-Mao Era*. Cambridge—New York: Cambridge University Press.

Lange, Oskar. 1936–37. "On the Economic Theory of Socialism." *Review of Economic Studies* 4 no. 1: 53–71; no. 2: 123–42.

Lenin, V.I. 1952 [1920]. *Left-Wing Communism, an Infantile Disorder*. In: *V. I. Lenin, Selected Works*, Vol. II, Part 2. Moscow: Foreign Languages Publishing House.

Nee, Victor, and Sonja Opper. 2007. "On Politicized Capitalism." In *On Capitalism*, edited by Victor Nee and Richard Swedberg, 93–127. Stanford: Stanford University Press.

———. 2012. *Capitalism from Below: Markets and Institutional Change in China*. Cambridge, MA: Harvard University Press.

Nove, Alec. 1983. *The Economics of Feasible Socialism*. London: George Allen and Unwin.

Qian, Yingyi, Gérard Roland, and Chenggang Xu. 1999. "Why is China Different from Eastern Europe? Perspectives from Organization Theory." *European Economic Review* 43 no. 4–6, April: 1085–94.

Raff, Murray, and Anna Taitslin. 2014. "Property Rights under Socialist Civil Law." In *East European Faces of Law and Society*, edited by William Simons, 251–306. Leiden: Brill Nijhoff.

Reich, Norbert. 1972. *Sozialismus und Zivilrecht*. Frankfurt/M: Athenäum Verlag.

Shleifer, Andrei, and Robert Vishny. 1994. "The Politics of Market Socialism." *Journal of Economic Perspectives* Spring, 8 no. 2: 165–76.

Stalin, Joseph. 1951. *Economic Problems of Socialism in the USSR*. Available online, accessed April 24, 2017: https://www.marxists.org/reference/archive/stalin/works/1951/economic-problems/index.htm.

Stark, David. 1996. "Recombinant Property in East-European Capitalism." *American Journal of Sociology* 101 no. 4: 993–1027.

Tardos, Márton. 1983. "Reform itt és most? Beszélgetés Kovács János Mátyással" [Reform—here and now? Conversation with János Mátyás Kovács]. *Mozgó Világ* 9 no. 2: 8–22.

———. 1999. "Ma jobban tudom, hogy senki sem tudja: Beszélgetés Kovács János Mátyással" [Today, I know it better that no one knows that: Conversation with János Mátyás Kovács]. *2000* 11 no. 3: 3–11.

Tymiński, Maciej. 2011. *Partyjni agenci: Analiza instytucjonalna działalności lokalnych instancji PZPR w przemyśle (1949–1955)* [Party agents: An analysis of institutional activities of PZPR local organizations in industry]. Warszawa: WUW.

Verdery, Katherine. 2003. *The Vanishing Hectare: Property and Value in Postsocialist Transylvania*. Ithaca: Cornell University Press.

Wedeman, Andrew H. 2003. *From Mao to Market: Rent Seeking, Local Protectionism, and Marketization in China*. Cambridge: Cambridge University Press.

Weitzman, Martin, and Chenggang Xu. 1994. "Chinese Township Village Enterprises as Vaguely Defined Cooperatives." *Journal of Comparative Economics* 18 no. 2: 121–45.

Winiecki, Jan. 1990. "Obstacles to Economic Reform of Socialism: A Property-Rights Approach." *Annals of the American Academy of Political and Social Science* 507 January: 65–71.

Xu, Chenggang. 1995. *A Different Transition Path: Ownership, Performance, and Influence of Chinese Rural Industrial Enterprises*. New York—London: Garland Publishing.

———. 2011. "The Fundamental Institutions of China's Reforms and Development." *The Journal of Economic Literature* 49 no. 4: 1076–1151.

———. 2015. "Political and Economic Institutions of China and Their Influences." *Cato Journal*, Fall 35 no. 3: 525–48.

Zbierski-Salameh, Suava. 2013. *Bitter Harvest: Antecedents and Consequences of Property Reform in Post-Socialist Poland*. Lanham: Lexington Books.

Index

About the Contributors

Oleg Ananyin is Professor of Economics at the Research University "Higher School of Economics" in Moscow. He graduated from the Economics Department of the Moscow Lomonosov State University, and received his PhD from the Institute of Economics of the Soviet Academy of Sciences. His research interests cover fields such as economic methodology, history of economic thought, comparative economics, and economic reforms in communist and postcommunist countries. He authored and coauthored several books and textbooks in Russian, his papers and reviews have appeared in *The European Journal of the History of Economic Thought*, *Revue d'études comparatives Est-Ouest*, *Economics of Planning*, *Problems of Economic Transition*. From 2012 to 2018 he was a member of the Council of *European Society of the History of Economic Thought*.

Roumen Avramov is Permanent Fellow at the Centre for Advanced Studies Sofia (CAS). His academic interests include economic history, monetary economics, the economics of inter-ethnic conflicts, and the history of economic ideas (business cycles, long waves, new institutional economics, economic thought under communism). Among other publications, he is the author (in Bulgarian) of *Communal Capitalism: Reflections on the Bulgarian Economic Past* (vol. 1–3, 2007); *Money and De/Stabilization in Bulgaria, 1948–1989* (2008); *"Salvation" and Abjection: Microeconomy of State Anti-Semitism in Bulgaria, 1940–1944* (2012); *The Economy of the "Revival Process"* (2016) (on the Anti-Turkish Assimilation Campaign, 1984–1989). He edited the series *Bulgarian National Bank: Selected Documents, 1879–1990* (eight volumes, 1999–2009).

Fan Shitao is Associate Professor in the Institute of Economics and Resources Management at Beijing Normal University, and former visiting scholar of Fairbank Center for China Studies, Harvard University in 2016–2017. He does research on the history of the Chinese economy and economics. He was editor or coeditor of several anthologies of Chinese economists, including *The Classical Writings of Modern economics in China* (2 volumes, 2011); *The Collected Writings of Xue Muqiao* (20 volumes, 2011); *The Collected Writings of Wu Jinglian* (3 volumes, 2013); *The Collected Writings of Sun Yefang* (10 volumes, 2018). His book, *The Chronicle of Xue Muqiao* (coauthor Xue Xiaohe, forthcoming) lists as *National Important Book* by Chinese government. His recent papers include "Inclusive Institutions, Extractive Institutions and Sustainability of Prosperity," "China's Economic Reform: Processes, Issues, and Prospects (1978–2012)" (with Wu Jinglian), and "How Was the Cultural Revolution Launched?"

Julius Horvath is a member of Academia Europea and Professor at the Central European University in Budapest. He is former Dean of the Business School and former Head of the Department of Economics at Central European University. His research focuses on the political economy of international money, history of economic thought and postcommunist economic transformation. He has published in a variety of peer-reviewed journals. His publications appeared in publishing houses such as Palgrave MacMillan, Publication Office of the European Union, Central European University Press, Edgar Elgar, Duncker & Humblot, and Springer-Verlag. He was a member of the State Accreditation Committee in both the Slovak and the Czech Republic.

János Mátyás Kovács worked as Permanent Fellow at the Institute for Human Sciences (IWM), Vienna from 1991 to 2018. Since 2008, he has taught history of economic thought at the Eötvös Lorand University, Budapest. Until 2017 he served as an editor of *Transit* (Vienna) and *2000* (Budapest). His fields of research include the history of economic thought in Eastern Europe, history of communist economies and polities, political economy of postcommunist transformation, and economic cultures in Eastern Europe. His recent publications include "Petering Out or Flaming Up? New Institutional Economics in East-Central Europe," *Economic Sociology*, 2011; *Capitalism from Outside? Economic Cultures in Eastern Europe after 1989*, 2012 (coeditor: Violetta Zentai); "Tradition, Nachahmung, Erfindung. Neue Kapitalismen in Osteuropa," *Transit*, 2013; "Shooting Sparrows with a Cannon? On the History of Eastern European Economic Thought," *2000*, May/June 2013 (in Hungarian).

Denis Melnik is Associate Professor at the Department of Theoretical Economics of the National Research University "Higher School of Economics", Moscow. His current research focuses on the history of Russian and Soviet economic thought and on theories of economic development. During recent years, he was visiting scholar at the New School for Social Research in New York, and Kanagawa University in Yokohama. He is the author of "Revolutionary Economic Reasoning in the Context of Revolution: The Origins and Fate of Bolshevik Economics" (*Slavic Review*, 2017); and "The Diffusion of Ricardo's Theory in Russia," in: G. Faccarello, M. Izumo (eds) *The Reception of David Ricardo in Continental Europe and Japan*, 2014.

Jože Mencinger is Emeritus Professor of economics at the University of Ljubljana and member of the Economic Institute of the Law Faculty. His PhD in Economics is from University of Pennsylvania. He served as Director of the Economic Institute between 1993 and 2001, and 2008 and 2013. From 1998 to 2005 he was Rector of the University of Ljubljana. In 1990/91 he joined the government of Slovenia as deputy prime minister and minister for economic affairs. His research interests include econometric analysis, the self-management system, economic policy, postcommunist transformation, privatization, and so on. His recent publications include "The impact of FDI in CEE countries and the outlook for the future of CEE and SEE" (2010); "Economic convergence of new member states: opportunities and risks" (2012); and "From the collapse of socialism to the crisis of capitalism: experiences of Central and Eastern European countries" (2013).

Gabriel Claudiu Mursa is Professor in the Department of Economics and International Relations at the Alexandru Ioan Cuza University of Jassy, Romania. He is also founding president of the Hayek Institute Romania. He received his PhD in economics from the same university in 2003. He published two books, *Liberalism* and *Logic of Market*, and coordinated the publishing of other books. His research focuses on free market, history of economic thought, economic liberalization, and so on. He is currently head of Department of Economics and International Relations at the Alexandru Ioan Cuza University.

Vlad Pașca is independent historian and former fellow of New Europe College in Bucharest. His main research interests concern the economic and social policies of Romania during the 20th century, and transnational and trans-systemic collaboration between economic experts during the Cold War. His works include "Exploring the Failure of Economic Reform in Communist Romania (1967–1974)," *Analele Universității București*, 2014;

"Higher Education and Long-Term Manpower Planning in Socialist Romania (1950–1975). An Empirical Study," *International Review of Social Research*, 2014; and "Détente Solutions for Cold War Dilemmas. The United Nations Economic Commission for Europe and Socialist Experts before Helsinki (1947–1975)," *East Central Europe* (forthcoming).

Franz Rudolph was Professor and Chair of the Institute of Management and Export at the East German Berlin High School of Economics until 1991. Then he worked as entrepreneur, consultant, and lecturer. He wrote or contributed to the following books: *Fabrik 2000*, 1989; *Klassiker des Managements*, 1994; *Die Kombinatsdirektoren: Jetzt reden wir*, 2014.

Radu Ioan Şimandan teaches economics at the University *Politehnica* of Bucharest. He received his PhD from the Bucharest University of Economics with a dissertation on the political economy of bureaucracy. His research interests include public sector economics and the role of economic freedom in promoting growth from the perspective of the Austrian school of economics and the public choice school. His most recent article is entitled "Fiscal Stability in Political Discourse: The Romanian Case." He also translated into Romanian James M. Buchanan's and Richard E. Wagner's book *Democracy in Deficit: The Political Legacy of Lord Keynes* as well as Deirdre N. McCloskey's essay "Measured, Unmeasured, Mismeasured, and Unjustified Pessimism: A Review Essay of Thomas Piketty's Capital in the Twenty-First Century."

Vítězslav Sommer is research fellow at the Institute for Contemporary History of the Academy of Sciences of the Czech Republic in Prague. He received his PhD from Charles University in Prague in 2011. His dissertation, which was published in Czech in 2011, explored the origins of communist party historiography in Czechoslovakia and its development in the Stalinist, post-Stalinist, and reform communist period (1950–1970). His recent research concerns the history of expertise in late socialism and post-socialism and the relationship between knowledge production and state socialist governance. He was a head of "The Road to Technocratic Socialism: Concepts of Governance in Socialist Czechoslovakia (1953–1975)" research project (2015–2017). His most recent publication in English is the article entitled "Are We Still Behaving as Revolutionaries? Radovan Richta, Theory of Revolution and Dilemmas of Reform Communism in Czechoslovakia" *Studies in East European Thought*, 2017.

Maciej Tymiński is head of the Chair of Economic History at the Faculty of Economic Sciences, University of Warsaw, and of the Centre for Economic Research at the Robert B. Zajonc Institute for Social Studies, University of Warsaw. His research interests focus on the economic history of Poland in the communist period, especially on the importance of the party apparatus in economic management, the development of Polish lands in the 19th and 20th century, and on the impact of institutional changes on economic behavior. His works include *Party agents. The analysis of the local committees of the PUWP in industry (1949–1955)* (2011, in Polish) and "Local Nomenklatura in Communist Poland: The Case of the Warsaw Voivodship (1956–1970)," *Europe-Asia Studies* 2017.

Hans-Jürgen Wagener is Emeritus Professor of economics at European University Viadrina Frankfurt (Oder) and Rijksuniversiteit Groningen, the Netherlands. His scientific interests center on economic systems, European integration, and history of economic thought. His publications comprise, among others, *Economic Thought in Communist and Post-Communist Europe*, 1998; *Constitutions, Markets and Law. Recent Experiences in Transformation Economies*, 2002 (coeditor: St. Voigt); *The Handbook of Political, Social, and Economic Transformation*, 2018 (co-editors: W. Merkel and R. Kollmorgen).

www.ingramcontent.com/pod-product-compliance
Ingram Content Group UK Ltd.
Pitfield, Milton Keynes, MK11 3LW, UK
UKHW041634031026
15587UKWH00001B/283